STATE OF THE UNION

STATE OF THE UNION
America in the 1990s
VOLUME TWO: SOCIAL TRENDS

REYNOLDS FARLEY

Editor

RUSSELL SAGE FOUNDATION · NEW YORK

The Russell Sage Foundation

The Russell Sage Foundation, one of the oldest of America's general purpose foundations, was established in 1907 by Mrs. Margaret Olivia Sage for "the improvement of social and living conditions in the United States." The Foundation seeks to fulfill this mandate by fostering the development and dissemination of knowledge about the country's political, social, and economic problems. While the Foundation endeavors to assure the accuracy and objectivity of each book it publishes, the conclusions and interpretations in Russell Sage Foundation publications are those of the authors and not of the Foundation, its Trustees, or its staff. Publication by Russell Sage, therefore, does not imply Foundation endorsement.

Library of Congress Cataloging-in-Publication Data

State of the union : America in the 1990s / Reynolds Farley, editor.
    p. cm.—(The 1990 census research series ; 1–2)
    Includes bibliographical references and index.
    Contents: v. 1. Economic trends—v. 2. Social trends.
    ISBN 0-87154-240-4 (v. 1).—ISBN 0-87154-241-2 (v. 2)
    1. United States—Economic conditions—1981– 2. Economic
Forecasting—United States. 3. United States—Census, 21st, 1990.
I. Farley, Reynolds, 1938– . II. Russell Sage Foundation.
III. Series.
HC106.8.S7352   1995
303.4′0973—dc20
                          94-40284
                             CIP

The paper used in this publication meets the minimum requirements of American National Standard for Information Sciences—Permanence of Paper for Printed Library Materials, ANSI Z39.48-1992.

Text design by John Johnston.

RUSSELL SAGE FOUNDATION
112 East 64th Street, New York, New York 10021

10 9 8 7 6 5 4 3 2 1

Contents

Acknowledgments

M AJOR SUPPORT for the 1990 census research project was provided by the Russell Sage Foundation, the Ford Foundation, the Andrew W. Mellon Foundation, the Spencer Foundation, the National Science Foundation, and the National Institutes of Aging, with special additional assistance from the Social Science Research Council, the Bureau of the Census, and the Population Studies Center of the University of Michigan. The project was under the guidance of a National Advisory Board chaired by Eric Wanner, President of the Russell Sage Foundation.

The following were the members of the Board:

William Butz: U.S. Bureau of the Census
Jorge Chapa: University of Texas
Richard Easterlin: University of Southern California
Reynolds Farley: University of Michigan
David Featherman: Social Science Research Council
James Johnson: University of North Carolina at Chapel Hill
Evelyn Kitagawa: University of Chicago
Karen Mason: East-West Center
Charles Westoff: Princeton University

Contributors

Claudette E. Bennett	U.S. Bureau of the Census
Lynne Casper	U.S. Bureau of the Census
Barry R. Chiswick	Department of Economics University of Illinois at Chicago
William H. Frey	Population Studies Center University of Michigan
Roderick J. Harrison	U.S. Bureau of the Census
Dennis P. Hogan	Population Issues Research Center Pennsylvania State University
Daniel T. Lichter	Population Issues Research Center Pennsylvania State University
Sara McLanahan	Office of Population Research Princeton University
Teresa A. Sullivan	Department of Sociology University of Texas at Austin
Ramon Torrecilha	Department of Sociology University of California-Irvine and Social Science Research Council
Judith Treas	Department of Sociology University of California-Irvine

Introduction

REYNOLDS FARLEY

And the Lord spake unto Moses in the wilderness of Sinai in the tabernacle of the congregation, on the first day of the second month in the second year after they were come out of the land of Egypt, saying, take ye the sum of all the congregation of the children of Israel, after their families, by the house of their fathers, with the number of their names, every male by their polls; from twenty years old and upward, all that are able to go forth to war *(Numbers, Chap. 1:1–3).*

CENSUSES have been taken throughout recorded history, primarily to calculate how many men could be mobilized for battle or how much property could be taxed. The gospel of Luke tells us that Christ was born in Bethlehem because Caesar Augustus decreed that all be enrolled and taxed in their home cities. Just after invading England, the Normans carried out a census, henceforth referred to as the Domesday Book, which told them whom they conquered and where they might find tax revenue. Censuses taken in the United States serve purposes other than those of Moses or the Normans. With great ingenuity, the founders of this country decided that population size would determine democratic representation. Therefore, Article I of our Constitution mandates that Congress carry out an enumeration once every 10 years. Thomas Jefferson, serving as secretary of state, supervised the first count, but his report of 3.9 million Americans in 1790 disappointed President Washington, who had already told European heads of state that the new nation exceeded 4 million.

Fifty years ago issues of census undercount interested a few demographers. But then, in 1962, the Supreme Court declared that the "one person, one vote" rule applied to all offices in our democracy down to the lowest local level. Suddenly, the importance of census-taking increased. Since Latinos and African Americans are typically missed more often than whites, census enumeration became an important civil rights issue. Each census—and even the planning of the enumerations—now triggers controversy about the mechanics of counting and the constitutionality of adjusting for undercount. Inevitably, numerous lawsuits are filed by local governments and advocacy groups claiming that errors and omissions in the census reduce their fair share of representation and benefits.

Censuses serve another vital purpose in our democracy. Since the early 1800s, they have been much more than head counts: they tell us about the state of our union. They are the primary sources of information about ourselves, about our jobs and our earnings, our prosperity or poverty, where we live and with whom, what kinds of homes we own or apartments we rent, our skin color, the languages we speak, and our ethnic origins. The 1990 census reports how people are now adapting—some with great success and others not very well at all—to the massive social and economic trends that make the United States of this decade extremely different from what it had been in generations past. And by informing us about where we are as a nation today and how we got here, censuses provide the crucial information we must have if we are to continue our efforts to reduce poverty; to increase the productivity of our work force; to eradicate crime; and to provide equal opportunities for women, for African Americans, and for those Native Americans whose ancestors lived here long before Christopher Columbus sailed from Spain.

In the late 1950s, just about a generation ago, a young white man with a high school education, a dedication to hard work, and a strong back could likely find a good blue collar job with a prosperous manufacturing firm, a job with comprehensive fringe benefits, including health insurance for his family and provisions for retirement. In view of sustained economic growth and low rates of inflation, he knew that if he came to work regularly and pleased his boss, his wages would rise year after year. He could afford to marry while he was in his early 20s and, with assistance from a federally backed mortgage, he could buy a starter home in the suburbs before his 30th birthday. Although some women in the high school graduating classes of the 1950s attended college, most of them married by the time they were old enough to vote or buy Scotch in a tavern. Divorces occurred but were relatively rare, and women expected that their husbands would remain with them and support them quite adequately while they stayed home taking care of the three or four children they had while still in their 20s. Few couples lived together before marrying, and childbearing by single white women was unusual. A young woman aspiring to be a U. S. Senator, a police officer, a corporate executive, or an advocate of equal rights for lesbians was an oddity in the 1950s. Few blacks went beyond high school, and those with college degrees were pretty much limited to preaching, teaching, or low-level clerical jobs in civil service.

Fast-forward to the late 1980s. A young man graduating from high school with a strong back and a dedication to steady work may find a job, but the odds are not in his favor. And if he is successful, the job will pay a modest wage and may have no fringe benefits. A young woman might marry her high school sweetheart right after graduation but, if she does, she realizes that their chances for middle-class prosperity and a nice home in the suburbs are slim. Their earnings will be meager and their financial state precarious unless both of them work full-time and at least one of them gets advanced training. Divorce is probable, since more than one-half of recent marriages are terminated in that way. Realistically, a young married woman must plan for the possibility that, in her 30s, she will be heading her own family with a child or two.

Young people have adjusted to these pervasive social and economic changes. They now stay in school longer and typically delay marriage until they are much older. In fact, recent trends suggest that a substantial proportion may not marry at all. And compared with the 1950s, young people have adapted by reducing their number of children. But other changes provide young people with possibilities unknown—almost unthought of—four decades ago. We have made much progress in expanding opportunities for women, we have reduced some of the barriers that denied rights to blacks, and, to a large degree, we have changed laws and our values about personal living arrangements and sexuality. Women increasingly stay in school longer than men. As recently as the 1970s, just a handful of women earned advanced degrees in medicine, law, and business administration. Now thousands do every year.

Censuses reveal the social trends and economic shifts that are producing a new and different country. They reflect how we adapted to one array of changes in our values and norms—symbolized by events of the 1960s—and another set of macroeconomic changes dating from the 1970s. In the span of one generation, the social landscape of the country has been drastically rearranged, providing recent birth cohorts with a broader range of decisions and possibilities as they pass through adolescence and become adults. Dr. Martin Luther King, Jr., led an effective movement capped by the March on Washington in August 1963. The next year Congress enacted and President Johnson signed the most effective civil rights legislation since Reconstruction, thereby overturning those centuries-old practices of discrimination that denied blacks citizenship rights and economic opportunities. Importantly, Title VII of the 1964 Civil Rights Act prohibited discrimination in the labor market on the basis of both *gender* and *race*. In 1965, after decades of litigation and then the successful but bloody marches in Selma, Alabama, Congress finally put the Fifteenth Amendment into operation in all 50 states with the encompassing Voting Rights Act. By 1993, 40 African Americans were serving in Congress, and four were selected by President Clinton for his cabinet. While blacks still have extremely high poverty and unemployment rates as compared with whites, opportunities for recent generations are much improved and, in all major metropolises, there are now moderate to large middle-class black populations.

The new immigration law, also enacted in 1965, ended those discriminatory policies that favored the English, Irish, Germans, and Scandinavians. It had the unforeseen and unintended consequence of permitting 7 million Latin Americans and 5 million Asians to legally enter the United States after 1968. Censuses—more than any other sources—tell us how and why this nation's racial and ethnic composition is changing as we move toward the middle of the next century, when non-Hispanic whites will become a minority.

Other changes have given us more options about our personal lives. Until the late 1960s, divorce was possible in New York State only if adultery were proven, and until 1964 states had the right to prevent doctors from providing birth control information even to married couples. In the late 1960s, matters of personal sexuality—that is, sexual activities of almost all types among consenting adults—were pretty much privatized as restrictive laws were declared unconstitutional. And then, in January 1973, the Supreme Court ruled that abortion was primarily a matter for pregnant women to decide. No longer could a state force a woman to bear a child if she did not wish to do so. These developments occurred at a time when technological advances provided women with greater control over their childbearing. As a consequence of these shifts in our values, norms, and laws, as baby boom cohorts approached maturity, they could choose among a variety of socially acceptable alternatives about living their personal lives.

Cohabiting couples are now common, and they are not seriously censured in most circumstances. Persons preferring lesbian or gay relationships have opportunities to live as they wish in some communities. By the late 1980s, there were about four abortions performed for every ten births. The responsibilities of child rearing have gradually shifted away from the two-parent activity it had been in the 1950s to an increasingly female activity done in mother-only families. The marital status of women when they become mothers has also changed such that, by the early 1990s, almost three of every ten births were to single women.

The choices people make are strongly influenced by the economic climate. Declining employment opportunities for semiskilled workers and expanded opportunities for skilled crafts workers or health care professionals result from specific policies and decisions. In 1973, finance ministers of the oil-producing nations greatly increased their prices, a decision that shocked Americans as the cost of their gasoline soared from less than 30 cents a gallon to a dollar and a quarter. This dramatic and totally unexpected jump in energy costs divides an earlier period of sustained economic growth, increasing labor productivity, persistently growing wages, and reduced income inequality from the more recent span. Since 1973, the average weekly wage for all employed workers (in constant dollar amounts) has changed little. It was actually lower in the early 1990s than in 1973, but this masks divergent trends. There have been many winners whose economic status greatly improved, but other losers whose earnings stagnated and then declined. The earnings of women—especially those with an associate's degree or more—rose sharply. The earnings of men with more than a college education also increased, but for men with a high school education or less, earnings have fallen since the 1970s. Three trends—the emphasis on greater productivity in manufacturing; the long-run consumer shift toward purchasing more services and fewer durable goods, that is, more health club memberships or vacations and fewer second or third cars; and the increasingly unfavorable balance of trade for manufactured goods—curtailed employment opportunities and earnings for those millions of men with high school educations or less. By almost all important economic indicators, inequality grew during the 1980s as the gap between the prosperous and the poor widened. But in one area the shift was clearly toward greater equality; for the first time, the earnings of women rose faster than those of men. The 1990 census documents these pervasive shifts in how we earn our living and tells us clearly who is "riding high" and who is "just hanging on."

Since the 1900 census, cogent interpretative books—often given the less-than-felicitous name of census monographs—have interpreted what the enumerations revealed about overarching social and economic trends. As a collection, they portray the evolution of the nation during this century: the movement from farms to cities; the growth of the West; the aging of the population; the disappearance of streetcar conductors from the occupational distribution; and the appearance of systems programs and financial analysts as well as the slow emergence of equal opportunities and equal outcomes for women and blacks. Since 1950, the Russell Sage Foundation has supported these census research volumes. The ambitious *Population of the United States in the 1980s* series produced 17 books derived from the 1980 enumeration, covering topics from children to the elderly, from American Indians to Pacific Islanders. This project, based on the 1990 census, is more modest, offering an authoritative but concise interpretation of recent social trends. This is the second of two edited volumes.

The first chapter, "Growing Diversity and Inequality in the American Family," by Sara McLanahan and Lynne Casper, describes four pervasive demographic trends of the last two decades: the delay of marriage; increased marital instability marked by rising divorce rates; the shift in childbearing away from married mothers and toward unmarried mothers; and the growing tendency for women to work even when they are caring for young children. The outcome of these trends is more diversity in the living arrangements of adults and their children and growing economic inequality. Married-couple families—with a child or children—in which the wife works are doing quite well financially, with average incomes in 1989 of more than $50,000 for whites and about $45,000 for blacks. But women who raise children without husbands are not doing well at all, especially those women who are not employed. The poverty rate for these families was 63 percent for whites and 73 percent for African Americans.

McLanahan and Casper confront the question of why the late baby boom generation delayed or avoided getting married, considering such explanations as the availability of welfare payments, the decline in the earnings of men, and the improved economic prospects of women, especially those women who invested in college educations. While welfare payments and the falling earnings of men play some role in depressing marriage rates, the major factor appears to be the rising earnings of women and their ability to be financially independent.

Judith Treas and Ramon Torrecilha, in "The Older Population," analyze the aging of the population and describe the one large group whose welfare has clearly improved during the 1980s. Compared to the recent past, Americans aged 65 and older have lower poverty rates, are more likely to live on their own, and are increasingly homeowners. Traditionally, mortality rates of older women have declined more rapidly than those of men, but during the 1980s the death rates of older men fell as rapidly as those of older women. At least since the 1940s, labor force participation rates of retirement-aged men declined, but that trend ended in the 1980s. New laws overturning mandatory retirement, growing opportunities for part-time employment, and the arrival at older ages of men who hold white-collar jobs that are psychologically and financially rewarding—all these factors are associated with modest increases in employment among men aged 65 to 74.

Although three-quarters of the older population have incomes sufficient to put them safely above the poverty line, about one-quarter are poor or near poor. Treas and Torrecilha remind us that our Social Security system assumes that retirees will obtain income from three sources: their own savings, their own private pension programs, and Social Security. Low-wage workers—and their surviving spouses—who depend solely upon Social Security are at risk of falling into poverty, and this explains why older people in the United States are more likely to be impoverished than those in other prosperous Western Nations.

Dennis Hogan and Daniel Lichter, in "Children and Youth: Living Arrangements and Welfare," turn our attention toward the other end of the age spectrum. As a result of new marriage and fertility patterns, the share of children living with two parents declined. Yet, in 1990, more than seven out of ten youngsters under age 18 lived with a father and a mother. Because children raised in single-parent families are often disadvantaged with regard to both financial resources and parental input and have a more challenging time making successful transitions from adolescence to adult roles, this is an unfavorable trend. But it has been mitigated by two other secular trends: (1) the educational attainment of parents (even single parents) has risen over time, and (2) family size has declined, which translates into fewer children competing for a family's resources.

The authors describe the ways in which the poverty rates of children are linked to their family status and to their parents' employment. Childhood poverty—at least the poverty indexed by a shortage of money—might be virtually eliminated if all children lived with two parents who worked full-time.

"Racial and Ethnic Diversity," by Roderick J. Harrison and Claudette Bennett, takes on the challenging task of describing the nation's heterogeneous racial and ethnic minorities in 1990. They stress the rapid growth of minority populations vis-à-vis the white population. But they point out that the rapidly growing Asian and Hispanic populations are geographically concentrated, so the shift away from numerical dominance by whites is occurring in some places but not in others. They address the question of whether today's minorities will replicate the highly successful assimilation process of the European immigrants who came to the United States between 1880 and the early 1920s. They conclude that this may happen for some groups, including Asians, but will probably not occur for others, especially for African Americans and for American Indians.

Blacks have been and, at least for one more decade, will continue to be the largest racial/ethnic minority. On some indicators there was progress in the 1980s, yet on others the traditional disadvantages of blacks persisted or even became magnified. Blacks and whites are increasingly marrying each other, although this still occurs rarely. Black–white residential segregation declined in the 1980s, but African Americans remain much more residentially isolated from non-Hispanic whites than do Latinos or Asians. While the poverty rate for white families increased in the 1980s, it went down for black families. And a very careful and thorough analysis of earnings finds that black men continue to earn significantly less than ostensibly similar white men. But black women earn as much as white women, suggesting that patterns of racial discrimination may differ by gender. Much more so than whites or other minorities, blacks in the 1980s moved away from the most economically prosperous type of families, husband-wife families, and into the family type associated with poverty, families headed by a single woman with her child or children.

During the first decade of this century, the flow of immigrants reached a peak when more than 9 million people arrived at Ellis Island, Angel Island, and other ports of entry. This number fell sharply in subsequent decades, and the Great Depression and World War II combined with restrictive laws to all but terminate immigration. A new era of high-volume immigration began with the civil rights revolution, and during the 1980s more than 7 million legal immigrants arrived. Unless there is an unforeseen change, the volume of immigration will be greater in the 1990s than ever before. Indeed, the nation is likely to average more than one million legal immigrants every year. Barry R. Chiswick and Teresa A. Sullivan, in "The New Immigrants," describe this new migration, which is gradually making us a much more Latin and Asian nation. They stress three findings: first, the increasing number of immigrants and the rising proportion of foreign-born; second, the greater diversity among migrants in terms of their national origins, their skills, their educational attainments, and their languages; and finally, the persisting pattern that the social and economic characteristics of immigrants converge to those of the native-born population the longer immigrants remain here.

Evidence from the 1990 census reveals that most immigrants are assimilating rapidly in this country. They become fluent in English, their occupational status improves, and eventually, their earnings approach those of comparable natives. But these patterns of assimilation differ by country of origin, and Chiswick and Sullivan help us understand that process by considering five major groups of recent immigrants: those from Europe and Canada, Mexico, other Latin American nations and colonies, Asia, and Africa.

Three major internal migration trends characterize the United States in the years since World War II: a movement away from the Northeast and Midwest into the South and West; a movement from rural America to metropolises; and a shift within metropolises from central cities to suburban rings and then later to the edge cities now booming at the outer limits of urban settlement. William H. Frey's "The New Geography of Population Shifts" describes developments during the 1980s. His chapter is closely linked to Frank Levy's Chapter 1 in Volume 1, since Frey argues that industrial restructuring is the driving force behind most—but not all—of the new migration patterns of the 1980s. He contrasts the internal migration of the early baby boom cohorts (born 1946 to 1955) to those of the late baby boom cohorts (born 1956 to 1965), reporting that they are different because of the different arrays of employment opportunities they faced as they entered the labor market.

Two new trends emerged clearly for the first time in the 1990 census results. One involves the distinctive geographic locations of Asian and Latino immigrants, a process that is now producing rapid changes in the composition of a few large metropolises making non-Hispanic whites a minority in New York, Los Angeles, and Miami. But many metropolises in the nation's center and those in the South away from the seacoast have welcomed few international immigrants, attributable in part to their slow-growing economies. The other new pattern involves African Americans. There is now a substantial net outmigration of blacks from their traditional urban centers (Chicago, Cleveland, Detroit, and New York) and into the South. Metropolises gaining the largest numbers of internal black migrants in the 1980s included Atlanta, Washington, D. C., Norfolk, and Raleigh-Durham. In addition, a cadre of highly educated and seemingly prosperous blacks are moving to locations that once were home to few blacks: Minneapolis, San Diego, Sacramento, and San Bernardino.

This volume describes social trends, but in doing so the authors frequently refer to economic changes. Volume One focuses on economic trends and contains the following chapters: "Incomes and Income Inequality" (Frank Levy); "Labor Force, Unemployment, and Earnings" (James R. Wetzel); "Changing Economic Roles of Women and Men" (Suzanne M. Bianchi); "Changes in Educational Attainment and School Enrollment" (Robert D. Mare); "Industrial Restructuring and the Changing Location of Jobs" (John D. Kasarda); and "The Polarization of Housing Status" (Dowell Myers and Jennifer R. Wolch).

A subsequent book by Margo J. Anderson and Stephen Fineberg will describe undercount issues in the 1990 census along with the fierce political controversies and protracted legal battles that they generated. A companion book in this series, by Francisco Rivera-Batiz and Carlos Santiago, describes the population of Puerto Rico.

Throughout the 1990s there will be vibrant debates—in Congress, on the editorial pages, and particularly on the ever-expanding networks of talk radio—about the condition of our country; that is, about the state of the nation. Are the themes that helped unify this country in its first two centuries threatened by increasing economic gaps separating the rich from the poor and two-parent families from those headed by one parent? What policies, if any, should be adopted to guarantee that all Americans have adequate incomes and shelter? Do affirmative action programs benefit minorities and help to integrate them fully into the union we know as the United States, or are they divisive? Will the millions of immigrants now arriving from Asia and Latin America lead to a much stronger and more diverse nation, or do they take jobs away from natives? These two volumes, *State of the Union: America in the 1990s,* provide basic information about how new social and economic trends emerged in the last several decades, thereby helping us to understand which programs might succeed or fail as we get closer to the millennium year—when the next census will give us a fresh picture of ourselves.

1

Growing Diversity and Inequality in the American Family

SARA McLANAHAN and LYNNE CASPER

D RAMATIC changes have occurred in the American family over the last four decades, as reflected in popular television shows. In the 1950s the typical family portrayed in most situation comedies consisted of a breadwinner-husband, a homemaker-wife, and two or more children. This "ideal" American family was depicted in such shows as *Father Knows Best, Leave It to Beaver,* and *Ozzie and Harriet*. The Nelson family—Ozzie, Harriet, and their children David and Ricky—has recently received renewed fame in the press and has come to symbolize the typical American family of the 1950s. It now serves as a baseline against which to compare current family arrangements. Although the Nelson family was more of an ideal than a reality for many people, even in the 1950s, Americans did share a common image of what a family should look like and how parents and children should behave, which reinforced the importance of the family and strengthened the institution of marriage. No such common understanding exists today, for better or for worse.

Since the 1950s, families like the Nelsons have become increasingly rare, as young men and women have delayed marriage and childbearing, as wives and mothers have entered the labor force in greater numbers, and as divorce rates have soared. This does not mean that families are becoming extinct, but rather that they are taking on different forms. Along with the decline of families like the Nelsons, new types of families and living arrangements have become more dominant, including childless couples with two careers, one-parent families, and cohabiting couples with children. Nonfamily households—defined as households containing a single individual or people unrelated by either blood or marriage—have also become more prominent. Today, successful television shows, such as *thirtysomething, LA Law,* and *Murphy Brown,* feature divorced and never-

1

married characters, employed mothers, and single mothers (defined as divorced, separated, never-married, or widowed mothers raising children alone), reflecting the diversity of families that is characteristic of the 1990s. These "new families" indicate that Americans have more choices today than they did in the past about how to organize their private lives and intimate relationships (Goldscheider and Waite 1991).

At the same time, greater diversity has meant greater economic inequality across households. Some of the new, nontraditional families, such as dual-earner couples, are doing very well; others, such as single-mother families, are doing poorly. In 1991, the typical dual-earner couple with children had an annual income of $46,629.[1] In contrast, the typical mother-only family had an income of only $13,012. Families like that of Ozzie and Harriet (working-husband, homemaker-wife, children) had an annual income of $33,961. The increase in single-mother families and dual-earner families during the 1970s and 1980s has led to increased inequality across households and to a feminization of poverty, with more and more of the poor being concentrated in families headed by unmarried mothers (Pearce 1978). In 1960, 24 percent of poor families were headed by unmarried mothers; in 1990, the number was 53 percent. The diversity of families has also exacerbated racial and ethnic differences in economic well-being. Whereas the fastest growing white families are dual-earner families, a relatively advantaged group, the fastest growing black families are mother-only families, a relatively disadvantaged group.

Many people are concerned about what these changes mean for children and what government can (and should) do to help families and children adjust to change. Since women are spending more of their time working outside the home, their children are spending less time with them; and mothers are confronted with conflicting demands from the workplace and family. Despite the problems encountered by working mothers, today very few people believe that mothers' employment per se is harmful to children, except perhaps during the first year of life. And yet we used to think so, 40 years ago. Today, the policy debate about mothers' employment is primarily a debate over what constitutes quality childcare, how to make quality care accessible and affordable to families, and how to design parental leave policies to suit the needs of parents as well as employers (Da Vanzo, Rahman, and Wadhwa 1994).

The public is much less sanguine about the future implications of marital disruption and single motherhood. When mothers work outside the home, children may spend less time with their parents, but the family also gains income. In contrast, when parents live in separate households, children experience a loss of parental time (typically the father's time) as well as a loss of income. Because the total loss of resources is substantial for children who live with single mothers, many people fear that this type of arrangement may be harmful to children. And indeed the empirical evidence supports their fears. Children who grow up with only one of their parents are less successful in adulthood, on average, than children who grow up with both parents. They are more likely to drop out of high school, to become teenage and single mothers, and to have trouble finding and keeping a steady job in young adulthood, even after adjusting for differences in parents' socioeconomic background (McLanahan and Sandefur 1994). About half of the disadvantages associated with single parenthood are due to lower incomes. Most of the rest are due to too little parental involvement and supervision and too much residential mobility. Given the public concern about the growth as well as the consequences of single motherhood, the policy debate in this area is not just about how to help children adapt to family change, it is about how to reverse change. We use the word single in this chapter to refer to adults who are not currently married and living with a spouse. Many of these people were married in the past or will be in the future.

The idea that government should try to prevent single-mother families from forming is a hotly contested issue. It raises questions about the causes underlying the decline in marriage and the causes of single motherhood. Those who want government to limit the growth of single-mother families often claim that government is responsible for the growth of such families. They argue that the rise in welfare benefits during the sixties and early seventies sent the message to young men and women that if they had children and did not marry, the government would take care of the mothers and children. Thus, fewer couples married and more young women became single mothers. Charles Murray, a leading proponent of this view, argues that the only way to save families is to eliminate welfare entirely, forcing poor young women either to stop having children or to place their newborns with adoption agencies (Murray 1984, 1993).

At the other end of the political spectrum are those who believe that the decline in marriage is due to the decline in job opportunities for poor young men—jobs that would enable them to support a family (Wilson and Neckerman 1986). They argue that young men with the least education and the fewest skills were the hardest hit during the 1970s and 1980s by the loss of jobs from central cities and the restructuring of the workplaces that occurred. With no visible means of support and with bleak prospects for the future, these young men are not seen as potential marriage partners by the young women they are dating, even when the women become pregnant. Nor are the parents of the girl likely to try to arrange a "shotgun marriage" as they might have done in the 1950s, when the likelihood of finding steady work was much greater for low-skilled men. In short, marriage has declined because the pool of marriageable men has declined.

These two theories tell us something about why marriage might have declined among women from disadvantaged backgrounds during the past few decades, but they do not explain why the trend also occurred among young women from more advantaged backgrounds. To fully understand what has happened to

American families, we must look farther than welfare benefits and the loss of jobs for low-skilled men.

Another theory with considerable merit is that marriage declined because women became more economically independent; increased education, job opportunities, and hourly wages during the past three decades reduced the gains from marriage and gave women an alternative source of income outside marriage (Becker 1981). This allowed them to be more selective in choosing mates and it encouraged them to leave bad marriages. The women's independence theory incorporates the two previous arguments. Welfare benefits, like earnings, provide less-educated women with an alternative source of income outside marriage. Similarly, the decline in good jobs for low-skilled men makes marriage less attractive for these women, especially if the level of welfare benefits remains constant.

Finally, some people blame the decline in marriage and increase in single motherhood on changes in American culture (Bellah et al. 1985; Lestaeghe and Surkyn 1988). The cultural argument has many different facets. Some people see the sexual revolution in the 1960s as the principal engine of change. Changes in attitudes about premarital sex made it easier for young men and women to live together without being married and destigmatized single motherhood. And improved and accessible birth control methods and more widely available abortions facilitated intimate relationships without the responsibilities and commitments they once entailed.

Other analysts focus on the shift in values that has taken place throughout the twentieth century, especially after 1960. The shift in values from those favoring family commitment and self-sacrifice to those favoring individual growth and personal freedom has given rise to the so-called "me generation." Many of the characters in recent television shows, such as *Northern Exposure, Seinfeld,* and *thirtysomething,* show young people struggling with the tension arising from making permanent commitments to others while remaining true to their own ideals and personal growth.

The debate over the causes of family change has important policy implications. If welfare benefits are the major reason for the decline in marriage and the increase in single motherhood, reducing benefits or redesigning welfare incentives to be more marriage-neutral may have merit. If the decline in men's opportunities, the increase in women's employment opportunities, or value changes are the problem, eliminating welfare is not likely to have much effect on marriage, and it will definitely make poor children worse off economically. Ironically, if the increase in women's economic independence is a major cause of single motherhood, then encouraging welfare mothers to enter the labor force, which is a principal thrust of recent efforts to reform welfare, may actually exacerbate the trend in single motherhood, since it will increase the economic independence of women in the long run.

In this chapter we examine the changes that have made the prototypical Ozzie and Harriet family increasingly rare in the latter half of the twentieth century. We begin by focusing on four major demographic trends: the decline in marriage, the rise in marital disruption, the changes in marital and nonmarital childbearing, and the increase in mothers' labor force participation. Certain of these trends, such as the rising divorce rate, are extensions of long-term patterns that have been reshaping family life since the turn of the century. Others, such as the employment of mothers with young children, are more recent and represent a break with the past.

We also examine demographic changes in other Western industrialized countries in order to place the U.S. experience in the broadest possible context. The cross-national comparisons help us think about the causes underlying the changes in the American family, and how we might minimize the cost of change for children. Too often, commentators and political pundits in the United States speak as though the changes affecting the American family were unique to this country. As noted above, the growth of single-mother families is often attributed to the increase in welfare benefits during the 1960s and early 1970s. As we shall see, however, the United States is not unique with respect to divorce, nonmarital childbearing, and women's employment. Nor is there a simple 1:1 relationship between the prevalence of single parenthood and the level of welfare benefits across different countries. Many European countries, such as France, Great Britain, and Sweden, are much more generous toward single mothers, and yet they have less single motherhood than we do.

In the second part of the chapter, we examine family diversity and its implications for the economic well-being of American women. Census data allow us to compare the characteristics of several different types of "new families," including single-mother families, single-father families, and cohabiting couples. They also allow us to examine the prevalence of different work and family roles among American women and the standard of living commensurate with these statuses. As in the previous section, we compare the U.S. case with other industrialized countries. We find that married-couple families in which the wife is employed have the lowest poverty rates in nearly all the countries examined, whereas families headed by nonemployed single mothers have the highest poverty rates. We also find that single mothers are much worse off in the United States, relative to other families with children, than in most other countries.

The final part of the chapter directly addresses the question of why marriage has declined during the past two decades. Here we present new evidence based on our own empirical analysis of marriage market characteristics in different metropolitan areas of the United States. We find that marriage is more common in areas where women's employment opportunities and earnings are low, where welfare benefits are low, and where men's employment opportunities and earnings are high. We also find that increases in women's employment opportunities can account for a good deal of the decline in marriage between 1970 and 1990 among white women but not among blacks. Our results do not support the argument that increases in welfare benefits or declines in men's employment opportunities have led to large declines in marriage.

FOUR DEMOGRAPHIC TRENDS

Four demographic changes have profoundly affected the American family in the past 40 years: the decline in marriage, the increase in marital instability, the change in marital and nonmarital fertility, and the increase in mothers' labor force participation. To understand what has happened to the family, we must understand what has happened in each of these domains (Da Vanzo and Rahman 1994).

The Delay in Marriage

Throughout the 1950s, the typical young woman married when she was about 20 years old and the typical young man when he was about 23. This situation prevailed throughout the 1950s. By 1990, however, the median age at first marriage—the age at which half of the population has married for the first time—was 24 for women and 26 for men. In just three decades, the median age at first marriage increased by 4 years among women and by 3 years among men.

The postponement of marriage that took place after 1960 led to a substantial increase in the percentage of never-married young adults. In 1970, about 6 percent of women and 9 percent of men aged 30–34 had never married. By 1990, the figures were 16 percent and 27 percent, respectively.[2] In one sense, the rise in the age at first marriage was not as unusual as it might at first appear. Marital patterns in the 1950s and early 1960s were unique (Cherlin 1992). Never before in this century had so many people married, and never before had they married so young. Thus, using 1950 or 1960 as a benchmark against which to evaluate recent behavior makes the current situation appear much more unusual than it actually is. Had we used 1900 as our baseline, for example, we would have found a much smaller increase in the median age at first marriage—no change among men and only a 2-year increase among women.

Yet, certain aspects of the relatively high age at first marriage today differ from those at the turn of the century. In 1900 most young adults lived with their parents or other relatives until they married: today they are more likely to leave home and establish independent households. Thus, the increase in the age at first marriage after the 1960s led to a substantial increase in nonfamily households—households containing a single person or several unrelated adults. This further undermined the institution of marriage, since it provided young people

FIGURE 1.1   Median age at first marriage, by sex and year.

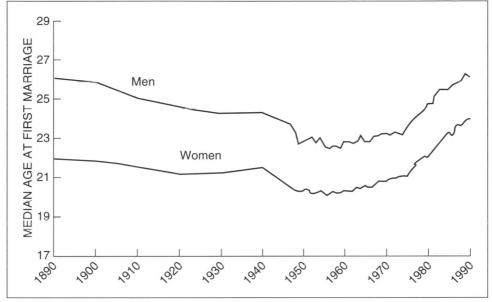

SOURCE: U.S. Bureau of the Census. 1991. *Current Population Reports.* "Marital Status and Living Arrangements: March 1990." Series P 20, No. 450.

NOTE: Data points after 1947 are plotted for single years.

with an alternative way of establishing their independence from their families of origin.

Living away from home prior to marriage was especially pronounced throughout the 1960s and 1970s as the baby boom generation came of age, as contraception techniques improved, and as young men and women became active in the civil rights and women's liberation movements. During the 1980s, the trend reversed as economic conditions worsened for young people, who found it harder to find jobs and become self-supporting. Even so, the proportion of unmarried adults living on their own or with unrelated adults was substantially higher in 1990 than it was in 1970.

The increasing median age at first marriage and the rising percentage of never-married adults has coincided with an increase in cohabitation—two persons of the opposite sex living together in a marriagelike relationship. In 1960 and 1970, the earliest years for which cohabitation data are available, about 2 percent of unmarried adults were cohabiting.[3] After 1970, the percentage increased rapidly. Between 1980 and 1990, it grew from 5.3 percent to 7.9 percent among unmarried men and from 4.3 to 6.6 percent among unmarried women (Table 1.1). The increase in cohabitation occurred among all age groups (except people over 65), but it was greatest among men and women in their late twenties and early thirties.

TABLE 1.1 Percentage of unmarried males and females
cohabiting: 1980 and 1990.[a]

	Males		Females	
	1980	1990	1980	1990
15–24	2.3%	3.4%	4.0%	5.6%
25–34	11.4	13.1	11.9	16.2
35–44	10.9	13.9	5.1	10.1
45–64	7.8	9.7	3.2	4.8
65 and Over	4.6	4.5	1.4	0.8
Total	5.3	7.9	4.3	6.6

SOURCES: U.S. Bureau of the Census. 1991. *Current Population Reports.*
"Marital Status and Living Arrangements: March 1990." Series P-20, No. 450;
U.S. Bureau of the Census, *Current Population Reports.* "Marital Status and
Living Arrangements: March 1980." Series P-20, No. 365, U.S Bureau of the
Census. Unpublished tabulations.

[a]The term cohabiting refers to adults living in unmarried-couple households.

Although some analysts argue that cohabitation reinforces the institution of
marriage by allowing people to "try out" potential marriage partners, thereby
choosing their mates more carefully, there are several reasons for believing otherwise.[4] First, cohabiting unions are less stable than legal marriages and of
much shorter duration (Bumpass, Sweet, and Cherlin 1991). Second, a sizable
proportion of cohabitors (10 percent) intend to continue living together, but
do not intend to marry their current partner (Casper 1992). For these couples,
cohabitation is clearly an alternative rather than a precursor to marriage. There
is another subset of cohabitors (7 percent) who plan to marry eventually but
who do not plan to marry the person they are currently living with (Sweet and
Bumpass 1992). And finally, regardless of how people view their relationship,
the rights and obligations that go with legal marriage are much more difficult to
enforce among cohabiting couples than among married couples. To take just
one example: an unmarried woman who becomes a mother has a much weaker
claim on the resources of the child's father than a women who is married to the
father. Only about 30 percent of children born outside marriage have a legally
designated father (Garfinkel 1992). Although the courts have been moving in
the direction of extending "marital rights and obligations" to cohabiting couples,
there continues to be a large disparity between these two types of partnerships.

The increase in Marital Instability

A second major factor affecting families is the increase in divorce. Whereas
in 1950, most people married once and remained married until they (or their
spouses) died, as Ozzie and Harriet presumably did, today over half of all cou-

FIGURE 1.2   Ratio of divorced persons per 1,000 married persons, by race and year.

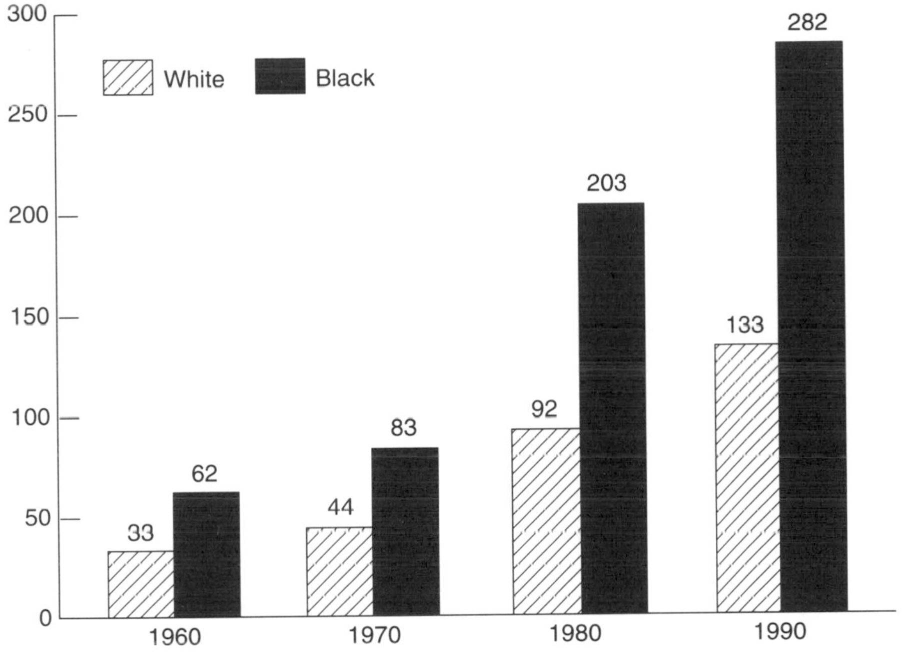

SOURCE: U.S. Bureau of the Census. 1991. *Current Population Reports.* "Marital Status and Living Arrangements: March 1990." Series P-20, No. 450.

ples end their marriages voluntarily. The divorce rate—the number of divorces each year per 1,000 married women—rose steadily during the first half of the twentieth century and increased dramatically after 1960. Over half of all marriages contracted in the mid-1980s were projected to end in divorce (Castro-Martin and Bumpass 1989). The divorce rate leveled off during the 1980s but this was not necessarily a sign of greater marital stability. We would have expected such a leveling off, given the increase in cohabitation (which means that the couples who do marry are likely to be the most committed), given the increase in the average age at first marriage, and given the fact that the large baby boom cohorts have reached middle age and passed through the period of their lives when they were most likely to divorce (Bumpass and Sweet 1989a).

The increase in divorce and the delay/decline in marriage led to a rise in the ratio of divorced to married people (Figure 1.2). In 1960, there were 35 divorced men and women for every 1,000 married adults; by 1990, there were 140. The ratio of divorced to married people is nearly twice as large for blacks as for whites, and this was true throughout the period from 1960 to 1990. In just three decades, the ratio of divorced to married adults grew over fourfold!

Although the ratio was higher for blacks than for whites, the percentage increase over time was the same for both races. The increase in the divorce ratio is likely to have a feedback effect on marriage. By increasing the chance that married and single people will interact with people who have ended their marriages through divorce, a high divorce ratio makes divorce more acceptable and marriage more uncertain. In addition, legal changes since the 1950s have made divorce easier and more accessible. For example, until the 1960s, divorce was permissible in New York State only if one partner proved the other had committed adultery.

The Shift in Marital and Nonmarital Fertility

A third change affecting the American family is the shift in marital and nonmarital fertility rates. Between 1960 and 1990, marital fertility rates—births to married women between the ages of 15 and 44—declined sharply, while nonmarital fertility rates—births to unmarried women of similar ages—increased gradually. Together, these two trends represented a reduction in overall fertility while increasing the proportion of children born outside of marriage.

The rapid rise in the illegitimacy ratio—the proportion of all births each year occurring to unmarried women—has recently attracted considerable attention, as the public has become increasingly concerned about the economic and social costs of nonmarital childbearing for children, mothers, and the country at large.[5] What is often missing from such discussions, however, is the recognition that "marital" fertility has a significant effect on the trend in the illegitimacy ratio. Since married women account for a much larger proportion of all births than do unmarried women, a change in the fertility behavior of married women can have a large impact on this measure. In addition, an increase in the proportion of women who are single can also have a large effect on the proportion of children born outside marriage.[6] To understand why the illegitimacy ratio has gone up so fast in recent years, we must understand what is happening to both the marital and nonmarital birthrates as well as to the changing marital status composition of women, that is, the proportions of women who are married and unmarried.

The 1950s were an unusual decade. Not only did men and women marry at relatively young ages, they also became parents when they were quite young, and they gave birth to more children than in the previous decade. This increase in marital fertility caused what demographers called a baby boom from the mid-1940s to the early 1960s.

However, married women began to change their behavior in the early 1960s. Marital fertility rates declined by more than 40 percent between 1960 and 1975, from 157 births per 1,000 married women to 92 births per 1,000 married women. During this same period, nonmarital fertility hovered around 22–24

FIGURE 1.3   Birthrates for women aged 15–44, by marital status: 1950–1991.

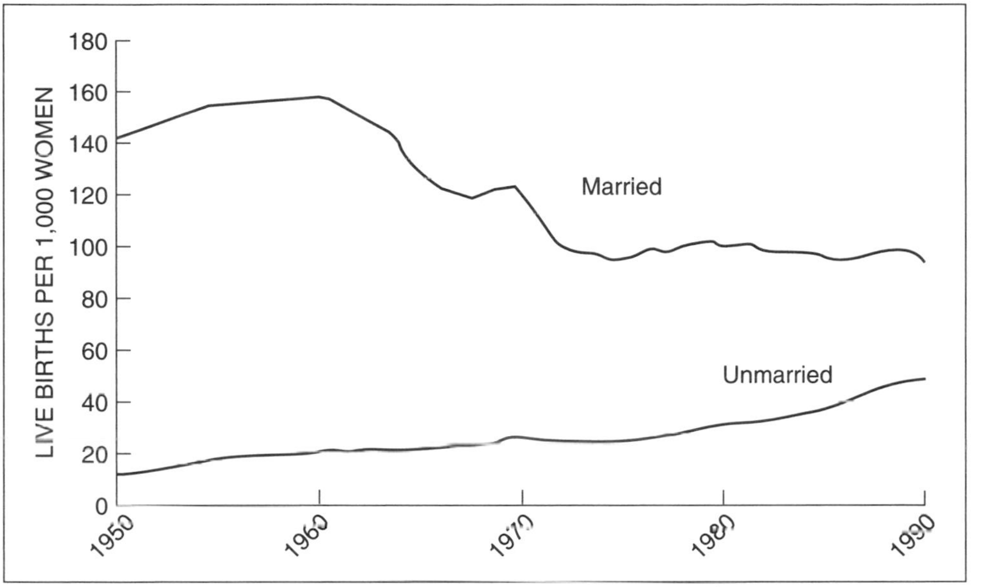

SOURCES: National Center for Health Statistics, *Vital Statistics of the U.S. 1988*, Vol. 1, Natality; National Center for Health Statistics, *Advance Report of Natality Statistics, 1993*, Vol. 41, No. 9.

births per 1,000 unmarried women. The increase in the illegitimacy ratio between 1960 and 1975 was due to two factors: the decline in the fertility of married women and the delaying of marriage. But not to an increasing birthrate of unmarried women.

Beginning in the mid-1970s, marital fertility rates stopped declining, nonmarital fertility rates begin to rise, and the age at first marriage continued to rise. After 1975, the rise in the illegitimacy ratio was due to increases in nonmarital fertility as well as to increases in the number of women at risk of having a nonmarital birth.

The distinctions between the different forces underlying the rises in the illegitimacy ratio are crucial for understanding the recent debate over the causes of out-of-wedlock childbearing. In this debate, policymakers and political pundits often point to the rise in the illegitimacy ratio as evidence that increases in welfare benefits were responsible for the increases in nonmarital childbearing. But their explanations do not fit the data. During the period when welfare benefits were going up—from 1960 to 1975—the rise in the illegitimacy ratio was driven primarily by the *decline* in marital birthrates and *delays* in marriage. Birthrates of unmarried women rose only 13 percent during this period. Not until the late 1970s and 1980s was the rise in the illegitimacy ratio driven by an actual increase in nonmarital fertility, and by that time, welfare benefits had started to decline in value. This does not mean that welfare has no impact on unmarried childbearing, but it does suggest that the relationship is much weaker and more complex than many people think. Clearly, the rise in the percentage of births occurring to unmarried women is not the simple consequence of more welfare benefits. And curtailing welfare benefits now will probably not reduce the illegitimacy ratio.

Changes in marital and nonmarital fertility altered family life in two major ways: they reduced the prevalence of parenthood overall, and they increased the proportion of families headed by single mothers. In 1960, 44 percent of American households contained a married couple with a minor child. Recall that a household includes all the persons who share a dwelling unit, while a family includes two or more persons who share a dwelling unit *and* are related to each other by blood, marriage, or adoption. A person living alone is counted as a household but not a family. An additional 4 percent of households contained a child and either a single parent or neither parent (Wetzel 1990). Thus, nearly half of all households included children, and nearly 90 percent of the households with children contained two parents. But by 1990, only about 35 percent of all households contained children, and an increasing proportion of households with children did not contain two parents. Between 1960 and 1990, the proportion of children living in single-parent families grew from 9 percent to 25 percent.[7] And this number understates the proportion of children that will ever experience single parenthood. Demographers estimate that over half of all children born in the late 1970s will live in a single-parent family at some point before reaching age 18 (Bumpass and Sweet 1989a).

The growth of single-parent families is covered in more detail in the next section. (It is also treated in Chapter 3 in this volume.) For now, we simply note that single-parent families are very different from two-parent families in terms of their economic status, and this difference has important implications for the future well-being of children.

The Increase in Mothers' Employment

The final, and perhaps most fundamental, change affecting the American family is the increase in mothers' employment. Women's labor force participation—the percentage of women who are working or looking for work—has been going up since the beginning of the twentieth century. In the early part of the century the increase occurred primarily among young unmarried women. After 1940, married women began entering the labor force in greater numbers, and after 1960, married mothers with children at home followed suit. (See Bianchi, Chapter 3 in Volume 1 for a more thorough description of these trends.)

In the early 1950s, only about 30 percent of married mothers with school-aged children were working outside the home. By 1990, this number had risen to over 73 percent. In just four short decades, a behavior that once described

FIGURE 1.4 Labor force participation rates for mothers with children under 6.

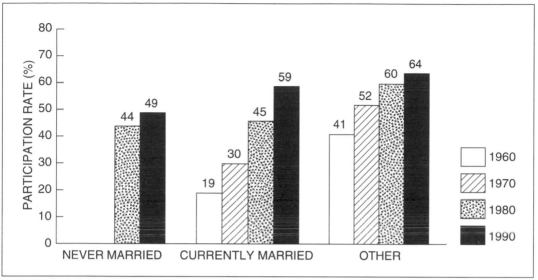

SOURCE: Statistical Abstract of the United States, 1993.

NOTES: *Not available for 1960 and 1970.

"Other" includes widowed, divorced, and separated mothers.

only a minority of mothers now fit a large majority of mothers, and this was true of mothers of all marital statuses. The figures for mothers with preschool children (under age 6) are even more dramatic. In 1960, only 19 percent of married mothers with preschool children were in the labor force, whereas by 1990, 59 percent were employed. By 1990, currently married mothers were nearly as likely to be in the labor force as formerly married single mothers (64 percent), and they were more likely to be employed than never-married mothers (49 percent).[8]

Race Differences

Racial and ethnic groups differed considerably in 1990 with respect to the prevalence of marriage, parenthood, and employment among mothers. The trends, however, were consistent for all of the groups we examined. White women were the most likely to be married in 1990; black women the least likely; and Hispanic women fell in between. All three groups experienced a decline in the prevalence of marriage between 1980 and 1990.

The pattern for single parenthood was just the opposite. Black women were four times as likely as white women to be single mothers—28 percent versus 7 percent—and Hispanic women, again, were in the middle. Single includes women who reported they had never married or were divorced, separated, or

TABLE 1.2   **Percentage of women aged 18–55 who are married, single parents,[a] and employed mothers, by race: 1980 and 1990.**

	Percent Married			Percent Single Mothers			Percent all Mothers Who Are Employed[b]		
	1980	1990	%Δ	1980	1990	%Δ	1980	1990	%Δ
Whites	66%	64%	−2	7%	7%	0	53%	69%	+16
Blacks	38	34	−4	26	28	+2	60	68	+8
Hispanics	60	55	−5	13	14	+1	51	58	+7

SOURCE: Public Use Microdata Sample, 1980 and 1990.
[a] Single; includes divorced, separated, widowed, and never-married mothers.
[b] Usually worked 20 or more hours per week outside of the home last year.

widowed at the time of the census. The prevalence of single motherhood, as a percentage of all women, did not increase among white women during the 1980s, and increased by only 2 and 1 percentage points among blacks and Hispanics, respectively. (Single motherhood grew much more rapidly in the 1960s and 1970s than in the 1980s.) With respect to mothers' employment, all three racial and ethnic groups experienced an increase in mothers' labor force participation (mothers working at least 20 hours per week) between 1980 and 1990. White mothers were the most likely to be working outside the home in 1990, and Hispanic mothers were the least likely.

Cross-National Comparisons

The United States is not the only country to have experienced significant demographic changes during the past three decades. Declines in marriage, increases in divorce, growth in the proportion of children born outside marriage, and increases in the labor force participation of women have affected family life in most European countries as well as in Canada and the United States. The average age at marriage has risen since the beginning of the 1970s in most Western countries as it has in the United States. Europeans who were born in the 1950s and who came of age during the "free-love generation" of the 1960s initiated the retreat from marriage characterized by both later and less frequent marriage (Sorrentino 1990). Indeed, the age at first marriage is actually lower in the United States than in most of the European countries.

Divorce rates have also increased throughout the Western world. While the United States had by far the highest rate of divorce in 1990, the increase over the past several decades was dramatic in nearly all of the Western countries. In Canada and the United Kingdom, the divorce rate grew from about 2 divorces per 1,000 married women in 1960 to 12 per 1,000 in 1990; in France it grew from 3 to 8 per 1,000 married women; and in the Netherlands from 2 to 8 per

TABLE 1.3   International comparisons: divorce rates, illegitimacy ratios, single parents and employed women.

	Divorce Rate[a]		Illegitimacy Ratio[b]		Single Parents[c]		Employed Women[d]	
	1960[e]	1990[f]	1960	1990	1960	1988	1970[g]	1988
United States	9	21	5	28	9	23	45	73
Canada	2	12	4	24	9	15	41	75
Denmark	6	13	8	46	17	20	NA	90
France	3	8	6	30	9	12	52	75
Germany[h]	4	8	6	11	8	14	48	62
Italy	1	2	2	6	NA	NA	44	61
Netherlands	2	8	1	11	9	15	24	55
Sweden	5	12	11	47	9	13	61	89
United Kingdom	2	12	5	28	6	13	43	66

SOURCES: U.S. Bureau of the Census, Statistical Abstract of the United States, 1993, Sorrentino 1990.

NA = Not Available.
[a] Divorce rate per 1,000 married women.
[b] Percentage of all births born to unmarried women.
[c] Percentage of all family households that are single-parent. 1971 and 1986 for Canada. 1976 and 1988 for Denmark. 1968 and 1988 for France. 1972 and 1988 for Germany. 1961 and 1985 for Netherlands. 1960 and 1985 for Sweden. 1961 and 1987 for the United Kingdom. Age restrictions for children differ by country.
[d] Percentage of women aged 25–34 (25–39 in Italy) in the labor force.
[e] 1970 for Italy.
[f] 1989 for France; 1988 for United Kingdom.
[g] 1977 for Italy.
[h] For former West Germany.

1,000. Italy was the only European country that did not experience a sharp rise in divorce between 1960 and the mid-1980s.

The illegitimacy ratio also rose dramatically in nearly all of the Western countries. Sweden and Denmark experienced the largest percentage point increases (from 11 to 47 percent and from 8 to 46 percent for these two countries, respectively). While some countries had much higher illegitimacy ratios than the United States, they did not have a higher percentage of single-mother families. Nearly 23 percent of all families with children in the United States were headed by a single mother in the late 1980s, whereas the percentages were 20 and 13 percent in Denmark and Sweden, respectively. The higher prevalence of single motherhood in the United States is due in part to the fact that divorce is more common in the United States than in other countries and in part because children born outside of marriage are less likely to live with both parents in the United States than in other countries. In the United States about 25 percent of nonmarital births during the 1970s and 1980s were to cohabiting couples, whereas in Denmark and Sweden nearly all nonmarital births were to cohabiting couples (Bumpass and Sweet 1989a; Sorrentino 1990).

Finally, women's labor force participation rates have been going up in nearly all the countries. In the late 1980s, Denmark and Sweden had the highest percentage of employed women, followed by Canada, France, and the United States. The increase in employment was greatest among women in the Netherlands. The labor force participation rates of Dutch women more than doubled, increasing from 24 percent to 55 percent! Canadian women also experienced relatively large increases in employment, from 41 percent in 1970 to 75 percent in 1988.

The labor force participation rate of mothers was lower than the rate of all women in the late 1980s, but a majority of mothers were working outside the home in most countries. Germany and Italy were the only countries in which less than half of mothers were in the labor force in the mid-1980s. Comparable numbers for the Netherlands are not available, but our own estimates indicate that Holland has one of the lowest labor force participation rates for mothers of all the Western European countries (McLanahan, Casper, and Sørensen, forthcoming).

DIVERSITY AND INEQUALITY

The trends described in the previous section have led to dramatic changes in American families and households, most notably to a decline in traditional families and to an increase in nontraditional families, such as dual-earner couples and single-parent families. In 1960, over 50 percent of all families contained a breadwinner-husband and a homemaker-wife, whereas by the end of the 1980s, only 20 percent of all families fit this description. During this same period, dual-earner families grew from under 25 percent to nearly 40 percent of all families, while families headed by single mothers increased from about 9 percent to around 23 percent (Hayghe 1990).

Diversity In Women's Work and Family Status

To illustrate how these demographic forces have altered, and are continuing to alter, the lives of Americans, we examined changes in women's family statuses between 1980 and 1990. We focus on women because the trends described above had their most dramatic effects on women's behavior and family status. Focusing just on men would have obscured the growth of single-parent families, and focusing just on children would have obscured the growth of childless couples and adults in nonfamily statuses.

We identified eight different family statuses, based on women's marital, employment, and parental roles. A woman was coded as employed if she worked 20 hours or more a week. She was classified as a mother if she was living with an "own child" under 19. We restricted our sample to women between the ages of 18 and 55 because this is the age range during which women are most likely to be raising children.

Women who were married and not employed were classified as occupying traditional family statuses. Employed married women and unmarried women raising children were classified as occupying nontraditional family statuses. We recognize that dual-earner couples and single-parent families are nontraditional in very different ways. In the first case, the traditional family form is violated by the wife's working outside the home. In the second, it is violated by the fact that one parent is not living in the household.

Women who were neither married nor raising children were classified as occupying nonfamily statuses, even though some of these women were living with parents or related adults. They occupy nonfamily statuses in the sense that they have not yet started their own families, either by marrying or having a child. Given their high levels of labor force participation, we expect most of these women to move into nontraditional family statuses once they marry or have children.

In 1980, 29 percent of white women of childrearing age were married homemakers (Table 1.4). By 1990, the figure was only 18 percent. (We assumed that most homemakers without children were either anticipating an Ozzie and Harriet family or had experienced such a family in the past.) In just one decade, the percentage of white women in traditional family statuses declined by 11 points.

Along with the decline of women in traditional family statuses came an increase in nontraditional statuses. By 1990, over half of all white women occupied nontraditional family roles, and recent trends suggest that this percentage will continue to grow in the future. For whites, the increase of women in nontraditional statuses was due entirely to increases in working wives.[9] There was no increase in single motherhood among white women during the 1980s.

Some readers may be surprised to find that such a small percentage of white women (of childrearing age) were single mothers in 1990, given the considerable press coverage these women attract. The apparent contradiction between the public perception and the reality can be explained in part by the fact that the numbers in Table 1.4 refer to all women, whereas the numbers most frequently quoted in the press refer to all mothers or all children. The percentage of all white *mothers* who were single (unmarried) in 1990 was 16 percent, whereas the percentage of white *women* who were single mothers was only 7 percent.

The difference between the two figures illustrates a very important point: the prevalence of single-mother families (and the growth of such families) looks much more dramatic when the base is all mothers as opposed to all women. If we are concerned about the conditions under which children are being raised, mothers (or children) are the correct population to focus on. If we are concerned about the condition of women, however, or if we are trying to understand the

TABLE 1.4 Women's employment and family status, by race: 1980 and 1990.

	Percent in 1980	Percent in 1990	Percentage Point Change
Whites			
Traditional family			
Married, child, homemaker	21%	12%	−9
Married, no child, homemaker	8	6	−2
Nontraditional family			
Married, child, employed	21	26	+5
Married, no child, employed	16	20	+4
Single, child, employed	5	5	0
Single, child, homemaker	2	2	0
Nonfamily			
Single, no child, employed	21	24	+3
Single, no child, not employed	6	5	−1
Blacks			
Traditional Family			
Married, child, homemaker	9%	5%	−4
Married, no child, homemaker	4	3	−1
Nontraditional family			
Married, child, employed	17	17	0
Married, no child, employed	8	9	+1
Single, child, employed	14	17	+3
Single, child, homemaker	12	11	−1
Nonfamily			
Single, no child, employed	21	25	+4
Single, no child, not employed	15	13	−2
Hispanics			
Traditional Family			
Married, child, homemaker	22%	16%	−6
Married, no child, homemaker	6	6	0
Nontraditional Family			
Married, child, employed	22	22	0
Married, no child, employed	10	11	+1
Single, child, employed	7	8	+1
Single, child, homemaker	6	6	0
Nonfamily			
Single, no child, employed	17	21	+4
Single, no child, not employed	10	10	0

SOURCE: Public Use Microdata Sample, 1980 and 1990.

NOTES:
1. *Single* defined as never-married, separated, divorced, widowed, or cohabiting.
2. *Child* defined as women living with a natural, adopted, or stepchild under age 18.
3. *Employed* defined as usually worked 20 hours or more a week outside of the home last year.

reasons behind the changes in women's behavior, we should focus on all women rather than mothers.

Focusing only on women with children can be misleading, since it ignores the fact that women are less likely to be mothers today than they were in the past. In 1980, 49 percent of white women were living with a minor child, as compared to 45 percent in 1990. (Add rows 1, 3, 5, and 6 from Table 1.4.) If motherhood declines among married women and remains the same among single women, the proportion of children being raised by single mothers will necessarily increase, even though the proportion of single women who are mothers does not.

Another reason why the percentage of single mothers appears to be low is that the census provides us with only a snapshot of the population in 1990. It does not count women who have been single mothers in the past but are no longer in this status, either because their children moved away or because they married or remarried. Nor does it identify women who will be single mothers at some point in the future. The snapshot tells us only how widespread the phenomenon is at a point in time.

A final indicator of the decline of the traditional Ozzie and Harriet family is the increase in women who were neither married nor raising children—women in nonfamily statuses. Nearly 30 percent of white women between the ages of 18 and 55 occupied this status in 1990. The percentage grew by 2 percentage points (net) between 1980 and 1990. These increases reflect the delays in marriage and increases in employment among recent cohorts of women.

Black women were less likely than white women to occupy traditional family roles in both 1980 and 1990. Like their white counterparts, black women also experienced a decline in traditional statuses and an increase in nontraditional statuses during the 1980s. Black and white women differed primarily in terms of the *type* of nontraditional family roles they occupied: whereas white women were predominantly in dual-earner families, black women were predominantly in single-mother families. This difference increased during the 1980s.

Perhaps the most striking contrast between black and white women was the difference in the prevalence of marriage: nearly two-thirds (64 percent) of white women were married in 1990 as compared to only a third (34 percent) of black women (percentages calculated from Table 1.4). Furthermore, the marriage gap between whites and blacks was just as striking among women without children (47 percent versus 24 percent) as it was among women with children (84 percent versus 43 percent). Regardless of parental status, white women were twice as likely as black women to be married.

The fact that the marriage differential between white and black women was the same for nonmothers as for mothers means that whatever is causing black women to forego marriage is affecting all women, not just mothers. This finding contradicts the argument that welfare benefits are a major cause of the racial difference in marriage. Although welfare might explain why women with children might forego marriage, it does not explain why childless women are behaving in a similar fashion.

Hispanic women were the most traditional of all women—the most likely to be married homemakers and the least likely to occupy nontraditional family statuses in 1990. They experienced the smallest decline (in relative terms) in traditional roles during the 1980s. What is most striking about Hispanic women is their relatively low levels of labor force participation. Regardless of whether they were married or single or were raising children, Hispanic women were more likely to be homemakers than were black or white women. The contrast between Hispanic and white women was especially striking in 1990. Whereas the ratio of employed women to homemakers was 3:1 among whites, it was only 1.6:1 among Hispanic women.

The only area in which Hispanic women were less traditional than white women was in the prevalence of single motherhood. Fourteen percent of Hispanic women were single mothers in 1990, as compared with only 7 percent of white women. While the prevalence of single motherhood among Hispanics did not increase significantly as a percentage of all women between 1980 and 1990, it did increase as a percentage of all mothers. In 1990, over 27 percent of Hispanic mothers were raising a child alone, up from 23 percent in 1980.

Increasing Disparities in Standards of Living

Growing diversity in family roles has given Americans more freedom about how they organize their personal lives and, at the same time, has created greater disparity in standards of living. In 1990, there were large differences in the economic status and poverty rates associated with the different work and family statuses.[10] Women who were married and employed had relatively high household incomes and low poverty rates in 1990. In contrast, single mothers fared poorly, especially mothers who were not employed. Single women without children were doing about the same as women in traditional families. We do not report poverty rates for the last category of women—single, childless, and not working—since we do not believe the family income for these women accurately reflects their standard of living (some were students and others were living with roommates).

Regardless of race or ethnicity, marriage and employment were clearly associated with a higher standard of living for women in 1990, whereas motherhood was associated with a lower standard of living. Holding other factors constant, women who were living with children had higher poverty rates than women who were not living with children, employed women were better off than home-

TABLE 1.5   Total household income and poverty rate of women, by employment and family status: 1990.[a]

	Household Income ($)[b]			Poverty Rate (%)[c]		
	White	Black	Hispanic	White	Black	Hispanic
Married, Child, Homemaker	$45,900	$31,400	$29,600	10%	26%	27%
Married, No Child, Homemaker	50,000	29,900	36,000	8	23	22
Married, Child, Employed	52,100	44,300	42,600	3	6	13
Married, No Child, Employed	57,500	49,000	48,800	2	3	6
Single, Child, Employed	29,100	26,000	26,700	16	27	26
Single, Child, Homemaker	16,500	13,000	15,400	63	73	71
Single, No Child, Employed	43,800	36,000	41,300	8	10	15
Single, No Child, Not Employed	41,000	25,500	30,800	NA	NA	NA

SOURCE: Public Use Microdata Sample, 1990.

[a]Family types defined by the woman's status.
[b]Incomes rounded to nearest hundred dollars. Refers to income received in 1989.
[c]Poverty rate is based on family income adjusted for size.
NA = Not Applicable.

makers, and married women were better off than single women (holding motherhood constant).

A notable difference between white and minority women was the income gap between traditional homemakers (with children) and employed single mothers. Among whites, the former were much better off than the latter, whereas among blacks and Hispanics, the two statuses were very similar. The total household income of married homemakers was slightly higher than the income of employed, single mothers, but the poverty rates were virtually the same. This underscores the fact that black and Hispanic women have much less to gain economically from marriage than do white women.

It is tempting to conclude from these comparisons that if all women were married and employed, poverty rates would be quite low in the United States: 2–3 percent for whites, 3–6 percent for blacks, and 6–13 percent for Hispanics. Such a conclusion would be misleading, however, since people sort themselves into different types of families, depending on what they earn or expect to earn and what their potential partners earn or expect to earn. Women are less likely to marry if their potential partners have low earnings capacity, and they are less likely to be in the labor force if their own earnings capacity is low. Thus, if all single women were married and employed, the average household income of all women would not be as high as the income of the women who are currently married and employed (and the poverty rates would not be as low).

Yet it would be wrong to conclude that marriage and employment have no effect on a person's economic status. Regardless of initial earnings capacity, on-the-job experience usually increases skills and earnings. Therefore, women who are employed are more likely to experience increases in their earnings capacity over time than are women who are not in the labor force. Similarly, pooling resources with another adult usually leads to a higher standard of living simply because of economies of scale.

Consider the case of a two-parent family with two children. If the parents shared a household and pooled resources, the income required for the family to live above the poverty line was approximately $14,000 in 1991, according to the official U.S. poverty thresholds.[11] If the parents lived apart and both children lived with the mother (or father), the same family members needed approximately $18,000 to live above the poverty line, $11,000 for the parent and two children and $7,000 for the parent living alone. Thus, the parents' decision to live together reduces the amount of money required to keep the family above the poverty line.

Without making any assumptions about causality, it is clear that the diversification in women's roles and family statuses that occurred during the 1980s was associated with a growing polarization of women into high- and low-income groups (and children, since they almost always live with their mothers). If we look at the poverty rates associated with each of the work and family statuses, we see that white women in traditional statuses have moderate poverty rates (relative to other white women), white women in dual-earner families have low poverty rates, and white single mothers have high poverty rates. Employed women in nonfamily statuses fall in the middle range.[12]

Assuming that the poverty rates for different statuses were similar in 1980 and 1990, we can see that the changes in the composition of white women's family roles resulted in more women concentrated in high-income statuses and fewer women concentrated in middle-income statuses. The 11 percentage point decline in traditional homemakers—a moderate-income group—was offset by a 9 percentage point increase in employed wives—a high-income group—and a 2 percentage point (net) increase in women not living in families—a moderate-income group (see Table 1.5). Since the proportion of women in the low-income category remained constant, the overall effect of the reconfiguration of white women's roles during the 1980s was toward more polarization.

The story is somewhat different for black and Hispanic women, although here, too, changes in composition resulted in more women in high-income statuses. Among black women, the decline of women in the role of traditional homemaker was offset by an increase in employed single mothers—a group with a moderate economic status—and employed single women with no children—a group with a high economic status. Among Hispanic women, the decline of traditional homemakers was offset primarily by an increase in employed, single women with no children. What is especially noteworthy about the different racial patterns in Tables 1.4 and 1.5 is that white women improved their standard of living by moving into dual-earner families, including families with children, whereas black and Hispanic women improved their position by moving into nonfamily statuses. This means that black and Hispanic children did not benefit from the gains in status experienced by black and Hispanic women, since the latter occurred mostly to women without children.

Not only did the shifts in family roles lead to greater inequality among women of the same race and ethnic backgrounds, they also led to greater disparities in economic status among white, black, and Hispanic women. In 1990, the poverty rate of women (aged 18–55) was 7.3 percent among whites, 19.7 percent among blacks, and 20.3 percent among Hispanics. If black and Hispanic women had occupied the same family statuses as white women (and the poverty rate associated with each status for each group had remained the same), black women's poverty rate would have been about 12.5 percent, and Hispanic women's poverty rate would have been 15.9 percent. The difference in women's family statuses accounts for about 58 percent of the poverty gap between black and white women and for about 34 percent of the gap between Hispanic and white women. The most important family status difference between white and black women is single motherhood, whereas the most important difference between white and Hispanic women is women's employment.

A Closer Look at Three Nontraditional Families

Because of its large sample size, the census allows us to examine relatively uncommon family arrangements in detail, and we took advantage of this opportunity to compare the characteristics of different types of single-parent families in 1980 and 1990 (including families headed by single mothers and single fathers). We also compared cohabiting couples with married couples in 1990.

Single Mothers.   In 1990, single mothers, as a whole, did not appear to be particularly disadvantaged, in terms of their human capital characteristics— education and work experience (Table 1.6). Recall that single mothers include women with a child or children who had never married or were separated, widowed, or divorced at the time of the census. The typical white single mother was in her early thirties, had some college education, and was employed. Only 2 percent of white single mothers were less than 20 years old, only 19 percent had failed to complete high school, and only 23 percent were neither working nor looking for work. The typical black single mother was also in her early thirties, a high school graduate, and in the labor force. Only 4 percent of black single mothers were teenagers, less than a third were high school dropouts, and only 37 percent were not in the labor force. Hispanic single mothers were similar to black and white mothers with respect to age. They were different, however, with respect to education and employment status. Hispanic mothers were

TABLE 1.6 Characteristics of single mothers,[a] by marital status and race: 1980 and 1990.

	All Single Mothers		1990		
	1980	1990	Never Married Mothers	Divorced/ Separated Mothers	Widowed Mothers
Whites					
Education					
Percent high school dropout	25%	19%	25%	17%	25%
Percent high school grad	43	33	39	33	22
Percent at least some college	32	47	36	50	53
Employment					
Percent employed	68	67	52	72	68
Percent looking for job	6	10	16	8	10
Living Arrangements					
Percent related adult	19	11	3	12	29
Percent subfamily	11	18	40	12	13
Percent cohabiting[b]	NA	7	6	7	2
Age					
Percent under 25 years	14	14	35	9	0
Blacks					
Education					
Percent high school dropout	41	32	38	24	43
Percent high school grad	36	33	33	33	33
Percent at least some college	23	35	29	43	24
Employment					
Percent employed	49	52	42	66	44
Percent looking for job	9	12	14	8	13
Living Arrangements					
Percent related adult	26	17	11	23	46
Percent subfamily	14	23	32	12	5
Percent cohabiting	NA	5	6	4	4
Age					
Percent under 25 years	22	21	33	5	1
Hispanics					
Education					
Percent high school dropout	60	51	59	44	69
Percent high school grad	24	25	23	27	20
Percent at least some college	16	24	18	30	11
Employment					
Percent employed	46	48	38	56	34
Percent looking for job	6	10	11	10	6
Living Arrangements					
Percent related adult	22	20	13	23	36

	All Single Mothers		1990		
	1980	1990	Never Married Mothers	Divorced/ Separated Mothers	Widowed Mothers
Percent subfamily	11	24	41	15	14
Percent cohabiting	NA	7	8	7	7
Age					
Percent under 25 years	18	20	41	10	0

SOURCE: Public Use Microdata Sample, 1980 and 1990.

[a] Unmarried mothers living with natural, adopted, or stepchildren under age 18.

[b] The response "unmarried partner" was not added as a relationship code until the 1990 census. Comparisons based on different definitions would be misleading; these estimates are not included in this table.

NA = Not Available.

much less educated—over half had not finished high school—and much less likely to be employed than white or black single mothers.

Despite the rather positive profile of the typical single mother in 1990, there was considerable diversity within this population. Some mothers, divorced or separated, had a considerable amount of education and work experience, whereas others, such as never-married mothers, were much more vulnerable— younger, less educated, and less likely to be employed.

In 1990, only 21 percent of white single mothers were never-married, which means that only a fifth of white mothers were in the "most vulnerable" category. The percentages were much higher among blacks and Hispanics—56 and 37 percent, respectively. The high percentage of black never-married mothers accounted for a good deal of the education and employment differences between black and white single mothers. If we compare black and white single mothers *within* marital status categories, the differences in education and employment are much smaller. In contrast, Hispanic single mothers have much less education and work experience than white and black mothers, regardless of their marital status.

Between 1980 and 1990, the education and employment status of single mothers increased. This occurred for whites, blacks, and Hispanics, and it occurred despite the fact that the proportion of single mothers who were never married also rose between 1980 and 1990. In 1990, 13 percent of white never-married mothers had college degrees and 68 percent were in the labor force, up from 6 percent and 59 percent, respectively, in 1980. The fact that more single mothers had college degrees in 1990 than in 1980 does not necessarily mean that college-educated women were more likely to become single mothers in 1990 than in 1980. The level of education increased among all women during the 1980s, and the increase in education among single mothers reflects this more general trend. (See Chapter 4 in Volume 1.) In fact, the percentage of white women with college degrees who were single mothers actually declined during the 1980s (numbers not reported in Table 1.6). But since education levels increased very rapidly, more single mothers had college degrees in 1990 than in 1980. The picture for blacks was different. Black women with college degrees were *more* likely to be single mothers in 1990 than in 1980, and the increase (in percentage terms) in single motherhood was greater among women with college degrees than among women with less education (numbers not reported in Table 1.6).[13]

Perhaps the most unexpected change affecting single mothers during the 1980s was the shift in living arrangements. After World War II and up until 1980, single mothers had increasingly established their own households as opposed to living as subfamilies, defined as living within the household of another family, such as a mother-child family living with the woman's parents (Wojtkiewicz, McLanahan, and Garfinkel 1990). By 1980, only a small percentage of single mothers were living in subfamilies. After 1980, however, the trend reversed, and by the end of the decade the percentage in subfamilies was almost twice as high as it had been in 1980. Much of the reversal was due to the fact that the proportion of never-married mothers increased, and never-married mothers have always been more likely to live in subfamilies—typically with their own parents or their own mothers—than are other single mothers. Even so, the trend toward subfamilies appears among single mothers who were formerly married as well as those who were never married.

We suspect that this reversal was a response to the worsening economic condition during the 1980s for those at the bottom end of the income distribution and the increase in the cost of housing throughout most of the country. As Bianchi and Levy point out in their chapters in Volume 1, men and women with only a high school education experienced substantial declines in wages and employment opportunities during the 1980s, as jobs for low-skilled workers disappeared or were shipped overseas. Single mothers, like other low-skilled workers, were strongly affected by these economic dislocations. Thus, it is logical that single mothers would have moved in with their parents or other relatives as a way of coping with economic insecurity.

Despite the tendency to double up with relatives during the 1980s, and despite the increase in cohabitation among young adults, single mothers still had relatively low levels of cohabitation in 1990, as compared with single mothers in other countries. In 1990, only 7 percent of white and Hispanic single mothers and only 5 percent of black mothers were cohabiting. As we noted at the beginning of this chapter, a substantial percentage of unmarried mothers in other Western countries, particularly the Scandinavian countries, live with the fathers of their children, even though they are not legally married (Sorrentino 1990).

Single Fathers.   Single fathers (unmarried men living with their own or adopted minor children) are much less common than single mothers. In 1990

TABLE 1.7   Characteristics of single-father[a] families, by race: 1980 and 1990.

	Whites		Blacks		Hispanics	
	1980	1990	1980	1990	1980	1990
Marital Status[b]						
Percent never married	13%	19%	36%	52%	34%	52%
Percent divorced/separated	70	72	50	42	55	43
Percent widowed	17	9	14	6	11	5
Education						
Percent high school dropout	29	28	43	32	53	54
Percent high school grad	39	35	31	37	22	24
Percent at least some college	32	37	26	31	25	22
Employment						
Percent employed	84	84	65	65	72	75
Percent looking for job	9	7	11	12	10	12
Living Arrangements						
Percent related adult	19	11	21	11	21	15
Percent subfamily	7	10	13	40	7	19
Percent cohabiting[c]	NA	30	NA	29	NA	45
Age						
Percent under 25	17	8	15	12	15	18

SOURCE: Public Use Microdata Sample, 1980 and 1990.

[a] Unmarried fathers living with natural, adopted, or stepchildren under 18.
[b] A more detailed table by marital status (see Table 1.6) is not possible due to the small sample size.
[c] The response "unmarried partner" was not added as a relationship code until the 1990 census. Comparisons based on different definitions would be misleading, these estimates are not included in this table.
NA = Not Available.

only about 13 percent of children in single-parent families were living with single fathers.[14] The percentage was somewhat higher among whites (16 percent) and lower among Hispanics (10 percent) and blacks (6 percent). The number of children living in single-father families grew from 748,000 in 1970 to nearly 2 million in 1990, and the proportion of children in one-parent families who were living with their fathers increased from 9 percent to nearly 13 percent over this 20-year period.

In 1990, the typical single father was somewhat older and less educated than the typical single mother. He was also more likely to be in the labor force. The most striking difference between single mothers and single fathers was their living arrangements. A much larger percentage of single fathers than single mothers were cohabiting or living with relatives. Thirty percent of white single fathers were cohabiting, and another 21 percent were living in a subfamily or with a related adult, such as a brother or sister. The numbers for black and Hispanic fathers were even higher—approximately 80 percent. In short, most single fathers were sharing their childrearing responsibilities with another adult.

Cohabiting Couples. In our previous discussion of women's roles and statuses (Table 1.4), cohabiting women were treated as occupying a nonfamily status, unless they were single mothers. Many people argue, however, that cohabitation represents another form of family, to be treated on a equal basis with marriage. Indeed, in producing their family statistics, France, Denmark, Sweden, and Canada sometimes treat cohabiting unions and legal marriages the same (Sorrentino 1990). In the United States there is considerable debate over whether cohabitation is a precursor of marriage, a substitute for marriage, or simply a more serious boyfriend-girlfriend type of relationship.[15] Sweet and Bumpass (1989a) have shown that in the United States, adults who have cohab-

TABLE 1.8   Comparison of married and cohabiting couples aged 30–34, by race[a]: 1990.

	White		Black		Hispanic	
	Married	Cohabiting	Married	Cohabiting	Married	Cohabiting
Percent With Children[b]	80%	35%	85%	67%	88%	70%
Percent Female Head[c]	8	41	14	55	8	37
Education[d]						
Percent male higher	29	28	23	25	23	23
Percent same	47	42	46	42	55	48
Percent female higher	24	30	31	33	22	29
Number of Hours Usually Worked[e]						
Percent male higher	46	23	27	24	45	33
Percent same	51	68	66	64	50	59
Percent female higher	3	9	7	12	5	8
Age[f]						
Percent male higher	37	49	36	49	41	46
Percent same	52	28	50	29	46	31
Percent female higher	11	23	14	22	13	23

SOURCE: Public Use Microdata Sample, 1990.

[a]The race of the couple is defined by the race of the household head.
[b]Children are natural, adopted, or stepchildren under age 18 of the household head.
[c]The census form allows couples to report whom they consider to be the household head. Percent female head is the percentage of couples who reported the woman as the household head.
[d]Educational attainment is divided into five groups: less than high school, high school degree, completed some college, B.A. or B.S. degree, and advanced degree. Couples who have completed the same level of education according to this classification are in the "same" category.
[e]Labor force participation is divided into four groups: not in labor force, low part-time (fewer than 19 hours per week); high part-time (20–34 hours per week), and full-time (35 + hours per week). Couples who worked the same amount of time according to the classification are in the "same" category.
[f]Couples whose ages are both between 30–34 years are categorized as having the same age.

ited in the past are more likely to have egalitarian sex role attitudes than adults who have not cohabited. They are also more likely to approve of mothers of preschool children working full-time.

Given the differences in attitudes, we were not surprised to find that cohabiting couples had less traditional relationships than married couples. Among whites, cohabitors were more likely to report that the woman was the head of the household, suggesting a more egalitarian organization of roles within the household. They were also less likely to mimic the traditional gender roles of breadwinner-husband and homemaker-wife. In cohabiting couples, the woman was more likely to be the primary breadwinner in the family—defined as the partner who works more hours outside the home—and she was more likely to have more education than her partner, as compared with the woman in a married-couple family. Women in cohabiting relationships also were more likely to be older than their partners. These findings indicate that, relative to their partners, women in cohabiting couples have more human capital and are more economically independent than women in married-couple families.

The same pattern exists among black and Hispanic couples. As was true of whites, minority women in cohabiting relationships were more likely than married women to have more education than their partners, and they were more likely to be the primary breadwinners and household heads.

Minority cohabiting couples were more likely to have children than white cohabiting couples. Furthermore, the marital status difference in parenthood was much smaller among minority couples than among white couples. Cohabiting minority couples were about 80 percent as likely as married minority couples to be living with children, whereas cohabiting white couples were less than half as likely as married white couples to be raising children. This is consistent with the high percentage of never-married black and Hispanic single fathers and with the high levels of cohabitation among single fathers of these groups. The fact that parenthood was common among cohabiting minority couples suggests that cohabitation has become more of a substitute for marriage in minority communities than in white communities.

Cross-National Comparisons

The trends affecting American families have touched families in nearly all the Western industrialized countries. And the changes in families and living arrangements have also occurred in nearly all countries. As shown in Table 1.3, divorce rates, illegitimacy ratios, single motherhood, and women's employment increased in nearly all Western industrialized countries between 1960 and 1990, although some countries started from a much smaller base than others, and some countries experienced much faster growth rates than others.

We used information from the Luxembourg Income Study (LIS) to examine the work and family statuses of women in seven different industrialized coun-

TABLE 1.9   International comparisons of women's employment and family status.[a]

	SWE 1987	NET 1987	GER 1984	ITL 1986	CAN 1987	UK 1986	US[b] 1985
Traditional Family							
Percent married, child, homemaker	4%	29%	21%	26%	15%	18%	16%
Percent married, no child, homemaker	3	10	12	30	7	7	7
Nontraditional Family							
Percent married, child, employed	35	13	17	20	25	24	21
Percent married, no child, employed	24	10	16	14	17	20	14
Percent single, child, employed	6	2	3	2	4	4	8
Percent single, child, homemaker	1	5	2	1	3	5	6
Nonfamily							
Percent single, no child, employed	22	18	20	5	21	16	21
Percent single, no child, not employed	5	11	9	4	8	4	7

SOURCE: McLanahan, Casper, and Sørensen (forthcoming).

[a]For women aged 18–57. The family types do not sum to 100% for all countries because of missing labor force data and rounding.
[b]Tabulations are for all races.

tries, including the United States.[16] Sweden had the lowest prevalence of women occupying traditional family roles, which is what we would expect, given the high labor force participation rates of women in that country. In contrast, Italy, the Netherlands, and Germany had the highest percentage of women in traditional statuses—similar to American women in the 1950s. Again, this was not surprising, given that divorce rates, illegitimacy ratios, and labor force participation rates were below average in these countries. Women in Canada and Great Britain were similar to women in the United States.[17]

In the 1980s, women in the United States were more likely to be single mothers than women in the other countries we studied. Even in Sweden, which had a low percentage of women in traditional work and family roles and a high percentage of women in nontraditional roles, women were much less likely to be single mothers than they were in the United States. In Sweden a woman with children was counted as living in a married-couple family if she was cohabiting, whereas in the United States she was classified as a single mother. Since only a small proportion of single women were cohabiting in the United States (see Table 1.6), this practice does not have much effect on the prevalence of single mothers in the United States. In contrast, if we counted cohabiting mothers in Sweden as single mothers, the prevalence of this status would have been much higher in the mid 1980s, about as high as the prevalence in the United States. It would be inappropriate to count cohabiting women in Sweden as single mothers, however, since most of these women were living with the fathers of their children. Except in Italy, between 20 and 30 percent of women in other Western

TABLE 1.10   International comparisons of poverty rates for different family statuses: mid-1980s.

	Poverty Rates (%)[a]			
	Married Couple Family		Single-Mother Family	
	Employed Mother	Nonemployed Mother	Employed Mother	Nonemployed Mother
Netherlands	6%	4%	7%	10%
Germany	2	6	13	44
Sweden	2	8	3	20
Canada	6	19	21	63
Italy	4	17	9	41
United States[b]	10	19	30	69
United Kingdom	8	17	15	21

SOURCE: McLanahan, Casper, and Sørensen (forthcoming).

[a] Predicted poverty rates controlling for age and education. Poverty is defined as having a total family income less than 50% of the median income for each country (adjusted for family size).
[b] Predicted rates for all races.

countries were occupying nonfamily statuses. The low percentage of Italian women in this category underscores once again the continuing importance of traditional family roles in that country.

What are the relationships between family diversity and economic status in other countries? Are single mothers just as disadvantaged elsewhere as they are in the United States? The answer to this question is both "yes" and "no": "yes" in the sense that single-mother families (especially families with a nonemployed mother) have the highest poverty rates of all families in every country; "no" in the sense that the disparity between single-mother families and other families with children is much larger in the United States than in most other countries. (Canada is an exception.) In the Netherlands, for example, the difference in poverty rates between nonemployed single mothers and married homemakers with children was only 6 percentage points in the mid-1980s (Table 1.10). In Sweden, the difference between these two groups was 18 percentage points, and in the United States it was a striking 60 percentage points! Thus, while single-mother families had the highest poverty rates in all countries, they were much worse off, relatively speaking, in the United States than in the European countries.

The cross-national variation in the economic position of single mothers is due partly to differences in women's demographic characteristics and partly to different social welfare policies (and to the economic, political, and cultural differences that gave rise to these policies).[18] Some countries, such as the Netherlands and Sweden, have highly developed welfare states with very generous income-transfer programs (and high tax rates). Poverty rates are relatively low among single mothers in these countries, as they are among all citizens. Other nations, such as the United States and Canada, have a more "free-market" approach to income redistribution, and single mothers receive rather meager benefits that are income-tested. Poverty rates are high in these countries because the government does not provide much of a safety net for families with a nonemployed parent or parents.

The cross-national contrast is instructive for several reasons. Not only does it show that most other countries (except Canada) do a better job than the United States in lowering poverty rates among single-mother families, it also shows that other countries reduce poverty without creating a high prevalence of single mothers and, in some instances, without creating a class of welfare-dependent mothers. In the United States, the debate over how best to help single-mother families is often posed as a dilemma over whether to provide generous benefits, thereby minimizing the poverty of single mothers, or meager benefits, hoping to minimize the prevalence and welfare dependence of single mothers (Garfinkel and McLanahan 1994).

The Swedish and Dutch examples suggest that it is possible to circumvent these apparent trade-offs. Both countries do much more to reduce poverty among single-mother families, and yet the prevalence of single-parent families in these countries is half of what it is in the United States. This alone should tell us that reducing poverty through generous income transfers and social policies does not automatically lead to a high prevalence of single-mother families. Even more intriguing, Sweden has found a way to reduce poverty without encouraging welfare dependence. Single mothers in Sweden are more likely to be employed than single mothers in the United States are, which means that they are not dependent on government for most of their income. Sweden minimizes both poverty and dependence by providing assistance in a way that promotes mothers' employment. The Swedish welfare state provides women with low-cost childcare, flexible work schedules, and well-paying jobs. While these policies are very expensive, they keep poverty rates and welfare dependence low by encouraging mothers to enter the labor force.

The Netherlands' and Great Britain's approaches are different. These countries provide generous benefits, but they do not expect single mothers to work outside the home, just as married mothers are not expected to work. Consequently, single mothers in the Netherlands and Great Britain are not poor, but they are more dependent on government transfers than they are in Sweden.

WHY HAS MARRIAGE DECLINED?

Many explanations have been given for the decline in marriage over the past four decades. One of the major arguments focuses on women's growing economic independence (Becker 1981). According to this view, the rises in women's employment opportunities and earning power have reduced the benefits of marriage and made divorce and single life more attractive. While marriage still offers women the benefits associated with sharing income and household costs with spouses, for some women these benefits do not outweigh other costs, whatever these may be.

There is no doubt that women's earnings have increased since the 1950s. For a while, much of the gain was due to increases in the number of hours women worked. During the 1980s, however, women's wages increased relative to men's (see Chapter 1 in Volume 1). A large body of evidence suggests that women's economic independence—measured as increases in wages as well as increases in labor force participation—is related to declines in marriage and increases in marital disruption.[19]

Another component of women's economic independence is the welfare benefit that is available to poor women raising children. Along with the increase in women's earnings, the value of the welfare benefit (AFDC plus food stamps) rose during the 1960s and early 1970s, which further contributed to the economic independence of women, especially poorly educated women whose earning prospects were limited. Since the mid-1970s, however, the value of welfare benefits has declined. Between 1970 and 1980, the average maximum annual welfare benefit across all states for a family of four went from $9,595 (in 1990 $) to $7,723. Between 1980 and 1990, it dropped to $7,142.[20] In other words, the average maximum welfare benefit for a mother with two children fell by 26 percent in 20 years.

Much has been written about the role of welfare in undermining marriage and encouraging single motherhood in the United States, and many of the proposals for reforming welfare that are currently being proposed at the state and federal levels are aimed at correcting the so-called marriage disincentives in the existing welfare system. Indeed, conservatives such as Murray (1984) often blame welfare for all of the growth of single-mother families during this period. Although welfare makes women at the bottom end of the income distribution more economically independent of the men they might marry, it is less obvious that the growth of welfare benefits can account for very much of the decline in marriage during the past two decades. We say this for several reasons. First, welfare benefits actually declined between 1970 and 1990. Second, the decline in marriage has occurred throughout the population and extends far beyond the group of women potentially eligible for welfare. It is hard to argue that middle-class and upper-middle-class women are influenced by the prospect of receiving welfare. Finally, empirical research indicates that welfare is only weakly related to marriage.[21]

A second set of explanations for the decline in marriage focuses on the availability, or lack of availability, of potential marriage partners for women. Availability is defined both in terms of the quantity and quality of potential mates.[22]

The quantity problem is believed to have originated with the baby boom, which created a surplus of young women (relative to young men 2 or 3 years older) in the late sixties and early seventies. Many more women were born in 1947 than men in 1945, so when these women reached marriageable ages, they found a small pool of appropriately aged men. This phenomenon, which demographers call the "marriage squeeze," may have contributed to the delay in marriage during the late 1960s and early 1970s, but it cannot account for the continuing declines during the 1980s. Indeed, if cohort size were all that mattered, we would have seen a decline in age at first marriage beginning in the late 1970s, when there was a surplus of young men. The quantity of available males is also affected because young men have higher mortality rates than young women, due to homicide and accident rates, and also because young men are much more likely to be incarcerated than young women. Incarceration rates increased during the 1980s, especially among young black men. While not very many men are in jail at any point in time, a jail record may affect a man's chances of marriage by making it harder for him to find a steady job later on.

The quality of potential marriage partners is a function of men's job opportunities. Wilson and Neckerman (1986) define the Marriageable Male Pool Index (MMPI) as the number of employed men per 100 women of the same race and age group. They argue that deindustrialization and economic restructuring, which occurred during the 1970s and 1980s, led to a loss of jobs in the central cities of the Midwest and Northeast which, in turn, reduced the employment prospects for men, especially black men. In addition, economists have recently shown that during the 1980s there was a shift in the demand from unskilled to skilled workers, which further undermined the economic position of low-skilled men. Many of the jobs created during the 1980s were jobs for men with a college education. Men with only a high school degree did not benefit so much from the expansion during the 1980s; hence, the pool of marriageable males did not always improve despite the improvement in the economy overall. (Levy discusses this mismatch between skill and jobs in Chapter 1 in Volume 1.) The major problem with the lack of marriageable males argument is that it does not account for the decline in marriage among men with a college education. Presumably, these men would be seen as attractive marriage partners, and yet they too have experienced a decline in marriage (Lerman 1989).

The hypothesis about the decline in marriageable males is really an extension of the women's economic independence argument, since women's independence is a function of women's earning power *relative* to men's earning power. Women's independence can increase either because women's earning power goes up faster than men's or because it goes down more slowly than men's. Similarly, increases in welfare benefits make women more independent if the earning power of their potential mates does not increase as fast as welfare.

Welfare can also make women more independent if men's earnings are declining faster than welfare benefits (McLanahan 1994).

When we look at the data on men's and women's earning power together, we see that since 1970 women have become more economically independent relative to men. For educated women, this has occurred because women have done better both absolutely and relative to men. For poor women, it has occurred because women have not done as poorly as low-skilled men. Thus, while the source of independence is different for women with different educational backgrounds, the trend in independence is the same for all women. In principal, the independence argument can account for declines in marriage among men and women at all points in the income distribution.

A final set of explanations for why marriage has become less common emphasizes changes in culture, norms, and attitudes.[23] According to this view, a "revolution" in social norms occurred during the 1960s, transforming people's ideas about the importance of marriage and families. The new ideology encouraged people to put personal freedom and self-fulfillment above family commitments. It also encouraged people to expect more from their marriages and to leave "bad" marriages if their expectations were not fulfilled. One example of the change in attitudes about family responsibility is reflected in the response to the statement, "When there are children in the family, parents should stay together even if they don't get along." In the early 1960s, over half of all women agreed with this statement; by the 1980s, only 20 percent agreed (Thornton 1985).

Revolutions in sexual behavior and methods of contraception also occurred during the 1960s, reducing the stigma associated with nonmarital sexual intercourse and childbearing and making cohabitation an attractive option to marriage. The increase in cohabitation that occurred during the 1970s and 1980s, among both never-married and formerly married adults, would not have been possible in a time when sex outside marriage was seen as sinful and deviant.

Although some analysts who have studied these questions conclude that changes in social norms and values followed rather than preceded increases in divorce and delays in marriage, cultural phenomena are likely to have important feedback effects once they get started. Moreover, once women have achieved a certain level of independence—once they can support themselves outside marriage—norms and values may become increasingly important in determining their choices about marriage and childbearing.

To see if differences in women's and men's employment opportunities were related to differences in the prevalence of marriage in the United States in 1990, we selected the 100 largest metropolitan areas and created indices of men's and women's characteristics in each of the areas. We looked at the characteristics of blacks and whites separately, since the two races appear to have separate marriage markets. To measure the level of marriage in a particular area, we used the percentage of women in their late twenties (aged 25–29) who were married. Ideally, we would have liked to have counted only women who had married during the past year—this would be the best indicator of current marriage rates—but the 1990 census does not provide information on date of marriage, and so we used women in their late twenties as a proxy for recent marriages.

We measured women's employment opportunities by the percentage of women in each area with college degrees and the percentage of women who worked full-time, year-round. We also looked at the median earnings of full-time women workers. These three measures were based on women in their late twenties. To measure the quality of potential male marriage partners, we took the percentage of men working full-time, year-round, the percentage unemployed, and the median earnings of all men. We included men with zero earnings in our measure of men's economic status so that we could measure the status of all men, as opposed to only men with jobs. We based our measures on men aged 28–33.

Each metropolitan area was assigned the maximum AFDC-food stamp guarantee for a family of four in that state. In the few cases where a metropolitan area included counties from two states, we used the higher of the two state benefits. We also created measures of the sex ratio—the number of men aged 28–33 over the number of women aged 25–29, population size, and the percentage of the population that was black in each area. We included population size in order to measure urbanization, and we included the percentage of blacks to measure racial concentration. The latter variable also measures regional differences. The marriage market characteristics for the 100 largest metropolitan areas are available from the authors.

In 1990, the Mobile, Alabama, and Tulsa, Oklahoma, metropolitan areas had the highest marriage levels (percentage of women married) among white women. Over 75 percent of young white women living in these areas were married in 1990. The Boston and San Francisco areas had the lowest marriage levels: less than 45 percent of white women aged 25–29 in these areas were married.

The metropolitan areas encompassing San Diego, California, New Brunswick–Perth Amboy, New Jersey, and San Antonio, Texas, had the highest marriage levels for black women. Nearly 50 percent of the young women in these three areas were married. New Haven, Connecticut, had the lowest marriage level—only 9 percent. After New Haven, which is an outlier, Rochester and Buffalo, New York, and Milwaukee, Wisconsin, had the lowest levels of marriage—around 15 percent. Once again we are confronted with the huge disparity in marriage between white and black women.

There was considerable variation across the different metropolitan areas with respect to women's full-time employment and education in 1990. In contrast, the range in the median earnings of full-time women workers was not very

TABLE 1.11   Marriage market characteristics in 100 largest MAs:
1970, 1980, 1990.

	1970	1980	1990
Whites			
Women's characteristics[a]			
Percent married	81%	67%	60%
Percent employed full time	18	37	48
Median earnings[b]	$17,270	$16,557	$19,034
Percent college graduate	16	26	27
Men's characteristics[c]			
Percent employed full time	69	72	72
Median earnings[d]	$26,307	$23,309	$23,907
Percent unemployed	2	4	4
Sex ratio[e]	.87	.96	1.06
AFDC[f]	$9,595	$7,724	$7,143
Percent black	11	12	13
Population size	304,572	365,783	502,264
Blacks			
Women's characteristics[a]			
Percent married	56	42	30
Percent employed full time	22	37	38
Median earnings[b]	$15,766	$15,653	$16,093
Percent college graduate	9	14	14
Men's characteristics[c]			
Percent employed full time	51	53	52
Median earnings[d]	$17,623	$15,676	$13,516
Percent unemployed	6	9	11
Sex ratio[e]	.73	.78	.88
AFDC[f]	$9,308	$7,379	$6,971
Percent black	15	16	15
Population size	459,129	467,602	624,100

SOURCE: Public Use Microdata Sample, 1970, 1980, and 1990.

[a] These characteristics are for women aged 25–29.
[b] Women's earnings are median full-time earnings.
[c] These characteristics are for men aged 28–33.
[d] Men's earnings are for all men.
[e] Sex ratio compares men aged 28–33 to women aged 25–29.
[f] AFDC is the state guarantee.

wide: $14,000–$26,000 among whites and $12,000–$21,522 among blacks. Welfare benefits ranged from a low of $4,621 to a high of $9,513. The availability of quality male marriage partners also differed dramatically across metropolitan areas. Median earnings for all males, including those not in the labor force, ranged from $13,888–$32,000 among whites and from $2,200–$22,000 among black men.

In 1990, the employment picture was much worse for black men than for white men, especially at the low end of the range. In at least one metropolitan area, the median earnings of all black men—$2,200—was lower than the maximum welfare benefit in that state—$4,600. This was not the case for whites. The median income of men in the lowest income area—$13,888—was over $4,000 higher than the maximum welfare benefit.

Accounting for Areawide Differences in Marriage: 1990

To determine which of the marriage market characteristics were important predictors of marriage, we estimated multiple regression equations, using the MAs as our units of analysis.[24] Starting with the 100 largest MAs in 1990, we created variables for each characteristic in each area in 1990, 1980, and 1970. For information on the means and coefficients from these regressions,

TABLE 1.12   Effects of marriage market characteristics on proportion married.

	Whites		Blacks	
	Coef	t	Coef	t
Women's Characteristics[a]				
Proportion employed full-time	−.389	−6.181	−.003	−0.037
Median earnings[b]	−.009	−4.241	−.004	−0.848
Percent college graduate	−.199	−3.948	−.086	−0.801
Men's Characteristics[c]				
Proportion employed full-time	.234	3.929	.135	1.733
Median earnings[b]	.007	4.662	.006	2.907
Percent unemployed	−.468	−2.966	−.146	−1.266
Sex Ratio	.115	3.383	.212	5.715
AFDC[b]	−.007	−3.366	−.015	−3.297
Proportion Black	.094	2.308	.107	1.112
Population Size[d]	−.002	−3.213	−.000	−0.044
Year	−.004	−4.281	−.014	12.606
Constant	.976	12.905	1.417	11.874

SOURCE: Public Use Microdata Sample, 1970, 1980, and 1990.

NOTE: Coefficients are based on pooled data from 1970, 1980, and 1990.

[a]Women's characteristics are based on women aged 25–29.
[b]Median earnings, AFDC (in thousands). Women's earnings are based on full-time earners. Men's earnings are based on all men.
[c]Men's characteristics are based on men aged 28–33.
[d]Population size (in 100,000).

see Tables 1.11 and 1.12. We estimated separate equations for whites and blacks.

We found that all of the indicators of women's earning potential—high education, full-time employment, and high median earnings—were strongly (and negatively) associated with marriage among white women. Marriage was less common in areas where women were well educated and where women's employment opportunities were good. Similarly, all of the indicators of men's earning power—full-time employment, low unemployment, and high median earnings—were positively associated with marriage. A high sex ratio (more men than women) and a low AFDC-food stamp benefit also increased marriage.

The results for blacks were similar to those for whites, with one important exception: none of the indicators of women's earning power were significantly related to marriage, although the signs of the coefficients were in the right direction. The effect of men's unemployment was also much weaker. Otherwise, marriage markets appear to operate the same for blacks and whites.

To get an idea of the relative importance of the different characteristics, we asked: "What if all the metropolitan areas had the same women's characteristics as the area with the most independent women?" "What if all the areas had the same characteristics as the area with the least independent women?" "What if all the areas had the same characteristics as the area with the least and most marriageable men?"

By taking the maximum and minimum values for women's education, full-time employment, and median earnings, and multiplying these values by the coefficients from our multiple regression equation, we came up with predicted marriage levels ranging from 41–76 percent among white women and ranging from 26–32 percent among black women. In short, differences in women's independence had a lot to do with differences in marriage among white women in 1990 and very little to do with differences in marriage among black women. The latter finding is not surprising, given that black women's characteristics were not good predictors of marriage to begin with.

Using the maximum and minimum values for men's earning power, we came up with predicted marriage levels ranging from 45–68 percent among whites and from 15–40 percent among blacks. Differences in men's earning power have a lot to do with differences in marriage for both blacks and whites. Finally, substituting the low and high values of the AFDC-food stamp benefit yielded marriage levels ranging from 57–61 percent among whites and from 26–33 percent among blacks. In general, welfare is less important in determining marriage levels than men's and women's earning power, and it is more important in determining marriage levels among blacks than among whites.[25]

To see how much of the race difference in marriage levels in 1990 could be accounted for by differences in marriage market characteristics, we substituted the means of the black marriage market characteristics into the white equation and calculated predicted percent married among white women 25–29. We performed a similar exercise using the white means and the black equation. This resulted in an 8 percentage point decline in marriage levels for whites and an 11 percentage point increase in marriage levels for blacks. About one-third of the race difference in marriage in 1990 was due to differences in marriage market characteristics, principally differences in men's employment opportunities. But the major share of the race difference in marriage was not due to differences in marriage market characteristics, rather it was a net racial difference.

Accounting for the Trend in Marriage: 1970–1990

In addition to the cross-sectional comparison, we looked at whether changes in marriage market characteristics between 1970 and 1990 could account for the decline in marriage over this period of time. We used the same equation that we used for the cross-sectional model, except that we substituted the means for women's and men's characteristics in 1970, 1980, and 1990 and calculated predicted marriage rates for each of the 3 years. Neither changes in AFDC nor changes in the sex ratio could have accounted for declines in marriage between 1970 and 1990 since these two variables changed in ways that should have increased marriage. AFDC benefits declined during the 1970s and 1980s, and the ratio of men to women increased.

FIGURE 1.5   Effects of changes in marriage market characteristics on proportion of white women married aged 25–29.

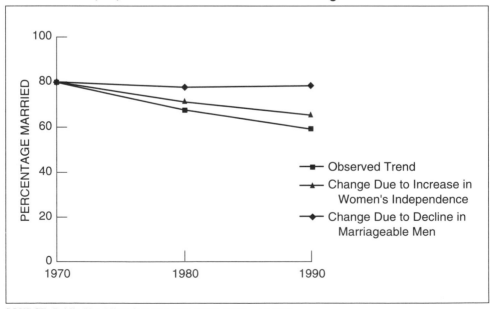

SOURCE: Public Use Microdata Samples, 1970, 1980, and 1990.

FIGURE 1.6   Effects of changes in marriage market characteristics on proportion of black women married aged 25–29.

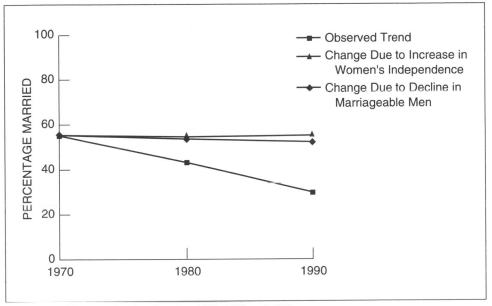

SOURCE: Public Use Microdata Samples, 1970, 1980, and 1990.

Figure 1.5 shows the actual trend in the proportion of women married and the changes that would have occurred had there been trends only in women's independence or in the pool of marriagable men. As shown in this figure, increases in women's earning power can account for over 70 percent of the decline in marriage among white women between 1970 and 1990, whereas decreases in men's earning power can account for only about 8 percent of the decline. Most of the former effect is due to changes in women's employment rather than changes in earnings or education. Since employment may be a *consequence* of the decline in marriage as well as a cause, we must be cautious about how we interpret this relationship. Nevertheless, the fact that women's employment is strongly related to the decline in marriage for whites between 1970 and 1990 is noteworthy and merits further investigation.

For blacks, the story is different. As shown in Figure 1.6, neither changes in women's nor men's earning power account for the substantial drop in marriage rates among blacks during the 1970s and 1980s. The decline in men's employment explains about 12 percent of the decline in marriage, whereas the increase in women's earning power has no effect. This is very different from the cross-sectional results, which showed that differences in men's employment opportunities accounted for a substantial portion of the difference in marriage across MAs. The reason for the disparity is that the decline in men's employment opportunities between 1970 and 1990 was much smaller than the cross-state differences in earnings in 1990. The cross-state variation in black men's earnings was $2,200 to $22,000 in 1990, whereas the decline in men's earnings across all states between 1970 and 1990 was only $4,000.

Our analysis of marriage markets gives the reader an idea of how census data can be used to test some of the different hypotheses about the decline in marriage. Based on preliminary findings, we believe it would be useful to analyze several distinct marriage markets within each metropolitan area: one for men and women with low education, another for men and women with a high school degree, and a third for men and women with some college education. Given the increasing inequality that has occurred during the past two decades, we suspect that a more disaggregated look at marriage opportunities might produce a stronger relationship between men's earning potential and marriage.

CONCLUSIONS

Four demographic trends underlie the changes in the American family during the past four decades: the delay (and decline) in marriage, the increase in marital instability, the change in marital and nonmarital birthrates, and increases in mothers' labor force participation. In the 1950s, the typical family consisted of a breadwinner-husband, homemaker-wife, and two children. Today, there is a much more diverse set of living arrangements, including dual-earner couples, single-parent families, childless couples, cohabiting couples, one person, and nonfamily households.

Family diversity reflects the fact that many people have more freedom and more choice about how to organize their personal lives. Greater diversity also has led to greater income inequality. While dual-earner couples enjoy a high and apparently increasing standard of living, single-mother families are under great economic stress. Diversity has also led to a wider gap in the standard of living between blacks and whites, especially in families with children. Whereas white children are increasingly being raised in dual-earner families, black children are concentrated in single-parent families.

The high poverty rates of single-parent families are not inevitable, as can be seen from the experiences of other Western countries. While marital instability and nonmarital childbearing have risen in all parts of the industrialized world, the economic consequences of single motherhood are much greater in the United States than elsewhere. Other countries are much more generous than the United States in terms of providing income and other kinds of economic support for single mothers (housing, childcare, health care). And surprisingly, their generosity has not led to high levels of single motherhood. Sweden has been especially creative in dealing with the dilemma of how to help single mothers without increasing their prevalence and without encouraging dependence on government. That nation provides generous benefits to single mothers in a way that reduces poverty while promoting self-sufficiency. The United States has much to learn from the Swedish example.

Finally, we found that increases in women's economic independence account for a substantial part of the recent decline in marriage among whites. The independence hypothesis does not account for trends in marriage among black men and women, however. Two other economic explanations for the decline in marriage—lack of marriageable males and welfare benefits—do not account for very much of the recent trends in marriage, not because these factors are unrelated to marriage but because they have not changed in ways that would discourage marriage. White men's employment and earnings in the aggregate have remained fairly constant over the past 20 years, while black men's earnings and employment prospects have deterioated somewhat. The value of welfare benefits has also gone down. What the census data do not tell us is whether changes in attitudes and values are related to declines in marriage. To the extent that such changes are important, they are likely to be more important among blacks than among whites.

ENDNOTES

1. U.S. Bureau of the Census (1992). "Money Income of Households, Families, and Persons in the United States: 1991."

2. U.S. Bureau of the Census (1991). "Marital Status and Living Arrangements: March 1990."

3. Percentages calculated from U.S. Bureau of the Census (1960). "Marital Status and Family Status: March 1970" (1981); "Marital Status and Living Arrangements: March 1980" (1991); and "Marital Status and Living Arrangements: Unpublished Tabulations."

4. Lynne Casper (1992). Also see Ronald R. Rindfuss and Audrey Vandenheuvel (1990).

5. The term illegitimacy is a technical term used by demographers and is not intended to be judgmental.

6. For more information on the decomposition of the illegitimacy ratio see Smith and Cutright (1988).

7. U.S. Bureau of the Census (1991). "Household and Family Characteristics: March 1990 and 1989" (1991); and "Marital Status and Living Arrangements: March 1990."

8. U.S. Bureau of the Census (1991). Statistical Abstract of the United States, 1993.

9. Most of these women were in dual-earner families. In 1980 the percentage of families in which women were the sole earners was 7 percent among whites and 13 percent among blacks. In 1990, the percentages were 8 and 12 for whites and blacks, respectively.

10. The categories in Table 1.5 are based on the same definitions as those in Table 1.4.

After sorting women into different statuses, we computed the mean income and poverty rate for each family/work status.

11. U.S. Bureau of the Census (1992). "Poverty in the United States: 1991."

12. We do not report poverty rates for single childless women who were not employed, since many of these women were students and/or living in multiperson households, which makes it difficult to measure poverty reliably. For the purpose of this discussion, we assume the poverty rate of these women is similar to that of employed single women without children.

13. These numbers are based on our own tabulations from the 1980 and 1990 microdata and are not shown here.

14. U.S. Bureau of the Census (1991). "Marital Status and Living Arrangements: March 1990."

15. Rindfuss and Vandenheuvel (1990); Casper (1992); Sweet and Bumpass (1992).

16. Where possible, we used the same countries as described in Table 1.3. Information on women's employment was not available for France, and Denmark was not included in the LIS data. We used a slightly different age cutoff for the international comparison due to restrictions in the data. For more information see McLanahan, Casper, and Sørensen (forthcoming).

17. The U.S. poverty rates in Table 1.10 are different from those reported in Table 1.7 for several reasons. First, the international comparisons are based on surveys carried out in the mid-1980s. Second, the U.S. numbers in Table 1.10 are for all racial and ethnic groups combined. And third, the poverty rates in the international comparison are based on a different definition of poverty than the rates in Table 1.7. In the international comparison, a woman was defined as poor if she lived in a family with income less than 50 percent of the median family income in that country. In Table 1.10, poverty rates are based on the official poverty thresholds used by the U.S. Bureau of the Census.

18. Wong, Garfinkel, and McLanahan (1993); Casper, McLanahan, and Garfinkel (1994). Also see McLanahan, Casper, and Sørensen (forthcoming).

19. For a review of this literature see Cherlin (1992). For conflicting results, see Mare and Winship (1991).

20. Committee on Ways and Means, U.S. House of Representatives, *Overview of Entitlement Programs,* U.S. Government. 1993.

21. For review of the empirical research on welfare effects, see Garfinkel and McLanahan (1986); Moffitt (1992).

22. For a discussion of the "available male hypothesis," see Lichter, LeClere, and McLaughlin (1991).

23. Bellah et al. (1985); Lestaeghe and Surkyn (1988).

24. After combining three MAs in 1990, we ended up with 97 observations. Information from 1970 and 1980 was not available for all 97 of these areas, since some of them were newly created in 1980 and 1990, and therefore our final count of MAs was 287. In addition, we were forced to drop some areas because our sample of blacks was too small to provide stable estimates of marriage prevalence. For the analysis of white marriage markets, our final sample consisted of 252 MAs, and

for the analysis of black marriage markets, our final sample consisted of 173 observations. Missing information on the independent variables was recoded to the mean or median, and dummy variables were used to indicate that a variable had missing information

25. Our model does not adjust for unobserved cross-state differences, which means that the welfare variable may be picking up some of these unobserved effects.

2

The Older Population

JUDITH TREAS and RAMON TORRECILHA

EVIDENCE of the graying of America surrounds us. Politicians argue over the growth of old-age entitlement programs like Medicare; restaurants woo off-hour diners with senior discounts; TV weathermen beam birthday greetings to centenarians. Daily life offers a host of reminders that the older population is growing and changing. More Americans are old than ever before, and more older Americans are very old. The population aged 65 and over, growing twice as fast as the general population, was 22 percent larger in 1990 than a decade earlier.[1] This remarkable aging of the American population ranks among the most significant, long-run demographic trends in our national history. It invites our fascination with a generation that has lived to see advanced ages once known by only by a few, and it raises pragmatic concerns about the needs and resources of older people today and in the future.

Aging baby boomers give added weight to the demographic processes that are aging our population. By the end of the first decade of the twenty-first century, those babies born between 1946 and 1964 will have grown up and grown older. Some will have begun to trade jobs for free time, to draw pensions, to welcome great-grandchildren, and to live with the chronic illnesses of old age. A generation so long associated with youth will be part of the older population even into the second half of the twenty-first century. The idea of elderly baby boomers calls forth such implausible images as the "Doonesbury" cartoon predicting an *Esquire* article on the hot new funeral homes. The aged of the future will surely add to the present diversity of the older population.

The older population of the United States embraces a wide range of ages and circumstances. The 60-plus married couple playing mixed doubles at the country club belongs to the older population, but so does the indigent, 96-year-old widow too frail to get out of bed. This dizzying diversity poses conceptual problems. Which Americans are older Americans? The gravestone marks the end of old age, but where is its threshold? Age 65, when workers qualify for Medicare and for full retirement benefits under Social Security, has long served

as the convenient chronological border to old age. This convention has its difficulties. Few Americans keep working to age 65 any more: some workers in
their fifties abandon jobs to embrace the retirement lifestyle we take as a hall-
mark of old age. Those who associate old age with the slippery slope to decrepi-
tude and institutionalization will also have a hard time reconciling the continuing
vigor and independence of most 65 year olds with this conventional age boundary.

The age-related diversity among older Americans has demanded a new vo-
cabulary to mark off meaningful age groups *within* the older population. Gerontologist Bernice Neugarten (1974) reluctantly popularized the terms "young-old"
(65–74) and "old-old" (75 and older)—a distinction that roughly corresponds to
the "wellderly" and the "illderly." The growing numbers of Americans aged 85
and older have been termed the "extreme aged" and the "oldest-old" (Rosenwaike and Logue 1985; and Suzman et al. 1992). Even centenarians, a tiny
group commanding our curiosity, are sometimes singled out for special study
(Siegel and Passell 1976). In this chapter, we, too, refer to the "young-old"
(65–74), the "old-old" (75+), and the "oldest-old" (85+). Defining the older
population as those aged 65+, we focus attention largely on this diverse population. Those on the threshold of old age, 60–64, offer some interesting insights
on where the older population is headed.

These new terms for different age groups of the elderly recognize that growing older brings changes. There are biological changes in appearance, health,
and functioning as well as social transitions from work to retirement, from marriage to widowhood, from independence to assisted living. Not everyone ages
at the same pace, however, so there is remarkable diversity even within a narrow band of ages. Passing years amplify differences. As a generation ages,
incomes become less equal as some move ahead financially and others fall behind. The social experiences of a lifetime, coupled with biological diversity,
play out in widening differences in cognitive performance and physical health.
Big disparities emerge in older people's ability to go about the routine business
of daily living—walking to the mailbox, handling money, getting dressed.

Diversity *within* age groups of older people is reinforced by the ethnic, racial,
socioeconomic, regional, and religious variety that characterizes the general
population of the United States. Diversity *between* age groups is reinforced by
differences in historical experience that mark different generations. The oldest
Americans grew up on farms, while the "young-old," who were born soon after
World War I, were raised in America's towns and cities. The different generations encountered different educational opportunities and different economic
prospects; they fought different wars. As a consequence of their unique historical experiences, each generation has approached old age with different needs
and resources than its predecessors did. So it will be with the baby boomers.

This chapter begins with the extraordinary story of an aging America. The story is set against a backdrop of global aging and is played out across fifty states whose older populations differ from one another in significant ways. We describe the long-run growth in the older population of the United States and contemplate a future in which the baby boomers grow old. We point to three significant changes in the composition of the population—shifts toward women, ethnic and racial minorities, and the oldest-old. The chapter describes the trends in life expectancy that contribute to the aging of the population before it considers the disabilities limiting older Americans in pursuit of a good old age. We examine troubling trends in the marital status of older Americans and their remarkable success at maintaining residential independence into their later years. We pinpoint a surprising reversal in late-life labor force participation trends and describe the employment of older Americans still on the job. Sketching trends in the economic status of older people, the chapter offers a portrait of older Americans who live in poverty and those who reside in relative comfort. We conclude by describing a small but fascinating group of "new and old" Americans—recent immigrants to the United States.

A NATION AGES

The aging of America's population dates to the beginnings of the nation. Half of Americans alive in 1800 had not yet seen their sixteenth birthday (see Figure 2.1). Although its median age of 16 made the United States a nation of children, demographic currents were already beginning to age America. The extraordinary fertility of the Colonial era 8 or 9 children per woman could not be sustained. As nineteenth century fertility fell, the median age of Americans rose.

It stood at 23 years in 1900. Although the youthful baby boomers enumerated in 1960 and 1970 temporarily rejuvenated the population, they inevitably moved into adulthood. By 1990, the median age of Americans was 33—twice that of 1800. The United States is now largely a nation of adults who are growing older. More aging lies ahead. Assuming constant levels of net immigration, a slow increase in life expectancy, and only a very slight rise in overall fertility due to population shifts, population forecasts show the median age of Americans rising in coming decades. In 2020 as the early baby boomers pass age 65, the median age is expected to be 38, rising to 39 by 2030.

As the population has grown older, the older population has grown, too. The 1870 Census of Population reported about one million people aged 65+ out of a total population of 39 million. The 1990 Census of Population counted over 31 million older people out of 249 million. So many Americans are old that the membership of the American Association of Retired Persons (AARP) exceeds

FIGURE 2.1   Median age of the U.S. population: 1800–1990, with projections to 2050.

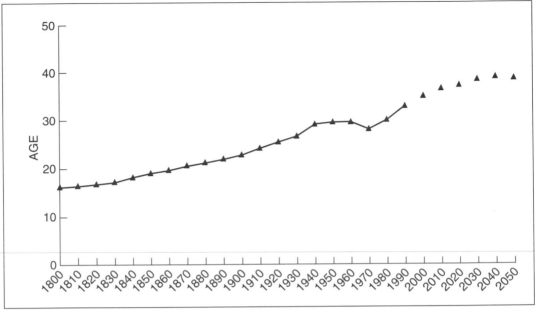

SOURCES: U.S. Bureau of the Census. 1990 Census of Population: *General Population Characteristics, Urbanized Areas.* Table 12: *Current Population Reports*, P-25, No. 1092: *Population Projections of the United States, by Age, Sex, Race and Hispanic Origin: 1992 to 2050.* 1992, Table F: 1980 Census of the Population: *General Population Characteristics, United States Summary.* 1981, Table 43: *Historical Statistics of the United States, Colonial Times to 1970, Bicentennial Edition,* Part I. 1975, Series A, 143–157.

that of all U.S. religious bodies except the Roman Catholic Church.[2] Projections by the U.S. Bureau of the Census place the older population at almost 70 million by 2030; the figure could be even higher if mortality reductions come quicker than the census anticipates or if immigration accelerates (Ahlburg 1993: 159–174).

Although the American population saw a sixfold increase over 120 years, its growth was modest in comparison to the phenomenal growth of the older population. The population aged 65+ was 27 times larger in 1990 than in 1870! As the growth of the older population outpaced that of the U.S. population, the percentage who were elderly climbed. Older people, who constituted only 3 percent of the population in 1870, made up 8 percent of Americans by the middle of the twentieth century. By the 1990 census the percentage of elderly stood at 12.6. One in eight Americans is old.

Sheer numbers are important for, say, estimating the need for hospital beds. Population shares, however, give testimony to our society's capacity to pay for hospital stays, because they consider the aged in relation to the resources of prime-age adults and the competing needs of dependent children. Population pyramids in Figure 2.2 detail the changing age composition of the American population. In 1900, the United States was still a young population with a broad-based age-sex structure. Because of high fertility, each generation was larger than the preceding one. Most Americans were young, and there were relatively few old people. By 1970, the U.S. population pyramid reflected its intriguing demographic history. The middle of the age pyramid was pinched by low fertility of the Depression decade of the 1930s. Children and adolescents swelled the bottom of the pyramid, but the youngest age category, 0–5, demonstrated that the baby boom was now over. The old, particularly older women, had increased their share of total population markedly; large cohorts, born early in the century and benefiting from improvements in mortality, had survived to become older Americans.

What the population structure foretold in 1970 is evident in 1990. The baby boom has worked its way to the middle of the pyramid on its march toward old age. The older age categories have swelled, but the younger age categories have contracted. When we look back from 2020, 1990 may seem a golden era of generational balance. Although there is a sizable older population, its growth has been offset by the decline in children, thus reducing the overall burden of "dependency." Meanwhile, the United States has a bonus of adults in prime working ages, say, 25–44, to support those who are too young or too old to support themselves. By 2020, when today's workers are retirees, they can count on relatively fewer prime-age adults to fund their pensions or look after their daily needs.

A WORLD AGES

In the historical sweep of American demography, the elderly's high share of population is extraordinary. The United States is not, however, exceptional by the contemporary standards of other developed nations: 1 in 8 Americans may be old, but so are 1 in 6 Swedes. Many populations have settled into slow growth or no growth. They have similarly large proportions of older people. Like the United States, these populations face the challenges posed by a sizable older segment.

Figure 2.3 compares the United States with a sampling of other nations in 1990. Japan, our economic competitor, rivals us in the percentage of population aged 65 + . So do European nations. Trepidation sometimes greets forecasts of the accelerated aging ahead for America. However, some countries already manage successfully with the very high percentage of elderly that awaits the United States in the twenty-first century when the huge baby boom generation turns 65. While the aged amount to 12.6 percent of the U.S. population, they make up about 16 percent of the United Kingdom and Norway.

Not all nations have a large elderly segment. Less developed countries like

FIGURE 2.2   Population pyramids: 1900, 1970, 1990, and 2020.

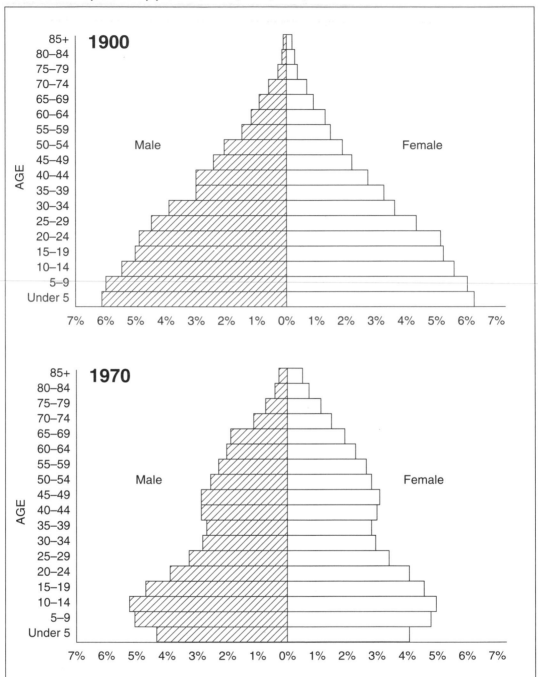

SOURCES: U.S. Bureau of the Census. Fifteenth Census of the United States: 1930, *Population, Vol. II: General Report, Statistics by Subjects*. 1933, Table 7; 1970 Census of the Population, Vol. I: *Characteristics of the Population, United States Summary*. 1973, Tables 49, 50; 1990 Census of the Population: *General Population Characteristics, Urbanized Areas*. 1992, Table 12; *Current Population Reports*, Series P-25, No. 1092: *Population Projections of the United States, by Age, Sex, Race, and Hispanic Origin: 1992–2050*. 1992, Table 44.

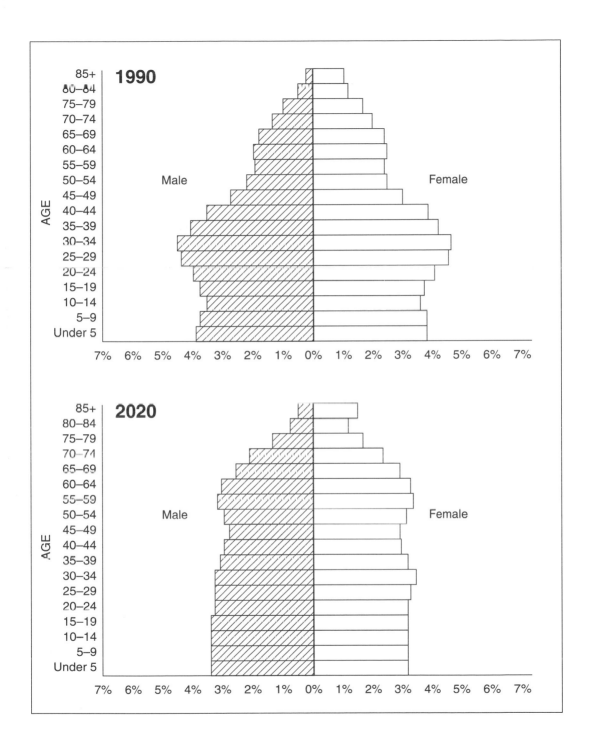

FIGURE 2.3   Persons aged 65+ as a percentage of population, selected countries: 1990.

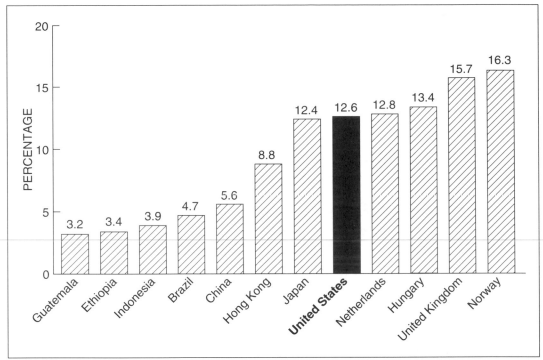

SOURCE: U.N. Department of Economic and Social Development, Statistical Division. *1991 Demographic Yearbook.* 1992, Table 7.

Ethiopia and Guatemala have aged populations that total to little more than 3 percent. What these countries have in common is high fertility; for generations, Guatemalan and Ethiopian women have borne many children, thus reducing the elderly's share in the total population by swelling the ranks of the young. These countries have young and rapidly growing populations: the high mortality thinning their populations is swamped by even higher fertility. But some less developed countries have seen family size fall and their aged's share of population inch up (Treas and Logue 1986). China, the "demographic billionaire" with more old people than any other nation, has nearly 6 percent aged 65+, about what the United States had in 1900. Population aging has become a global phenomenon.[3]

THE U.S. AGE

The aging of the nation's population is reflected in the record of our fifty states. The growth of the elderly population outpaced the growth of the total population in all fifty states and the District of Columbia between 1980 and 1990. As Figure 2.4 shows, even states that were losing total population finished the decade with more old people than they started with. States gained older people largely because long-time residents grew old, not because elderly newcomers moved in. (Nearly 3 in 5 native-born elderly were living in their state of birth.) Retiree migration, however, continued to factor in older population growth, particularly in Sunbelt states.

The lure of retirement communities—and retirees better able to bankroll a move—make the older population more mobile today, but older Americans are not as footloose as younger people are. In fact, 4 out of 5 Americans aged 65 + in 1990 were living in the same home as they had occupied in 1985. Of those who did move between 1985 and 1990, only 1 in 5 relocated to a different state. Their moves were typically short distance moves in response to changing life circumstances. For example, a recent widow might trade a big house for an apartment near her children.

Of course, the aged are not spread evenly across the United States, as Table 2.1 shows. With a remarkable 18 percent aged 65 + , Florida, a favorite retirement destination for prosperous East Coast elderly, leads the states in its proportion of elderly. Some Midwestern states like Iowa also have high percentages of elderly, in part because older people have been left behind as the young have moved away in search of better economic opportunities. Alaska, its population ballooned by several decades of young inmigrants, has only 4 percent old in its population.

Where older people live is of more than passing interest. The older populations of the various states differ so substantially that residence is strongly associated with many of the problems of old age. For example, the percentage institutionalized in the aged 65 + population ranges from less than 3 in Nevada to almost 9 in North Dakota. Institutionalization rates reflect state differences in elderly population shares, availability of kin (resulting from the outmigration of younger residents who might otherwise care for aging parents), and whether public policies encourage nursing home usage. Florida has the largest percentage of ages 65 + , but a very low rate of institutionalization, because the state has not encouraged long-term care facilities.

States also differ in the economic standing of their older residents—differences that reflect regional differences in prices, incomes, and living standards. While about 13 percent of the older population nationwide lives in poverty, the percentage ranges from a low of 7 in Connecticut to a high of 29 in Mississippi. Higher poverty rates are characteristic of southern states, which have high percentages of elderly who report disabilities, particularly health-related mobility limitations that keep them house-bound. The elderly in these states reside disproportionately in rural areas where health and social services are less accessible.

FIGURE 2.4   Percent change in age 65+ and total population, by state: 1980–1990.

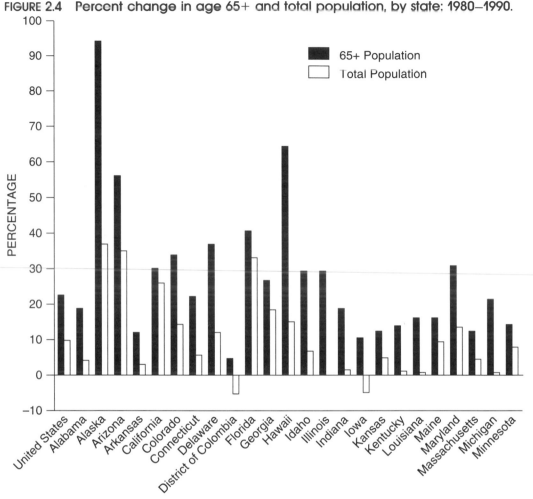

SOURCES: U.S. Bureau of the Census. 1980 Census of Population: *Characteristics of the Population, General Popula-tion Characteristics, United States Summary.* 1981, Table 67; 1990 Census of Population and Housing: *Summary Popu-lation and Housing Characteristics, United States.* 1992, Table 1.

THE COMPOSITION OF THE OLDER POPULATION OF THE UNITED STATES

Three developments stand out in the composition of our older population. First, this population remains predominantly female, but the tilt toward women is slowing. Second, the growth of racial and ethnic minorities is outpacing that of the white majority. Third, the older population itself is aging.

Women Outnumber Men

Most older Americans are women. This was not always the case. As recently as 1930, there were about as many older men as older women. Today, there are

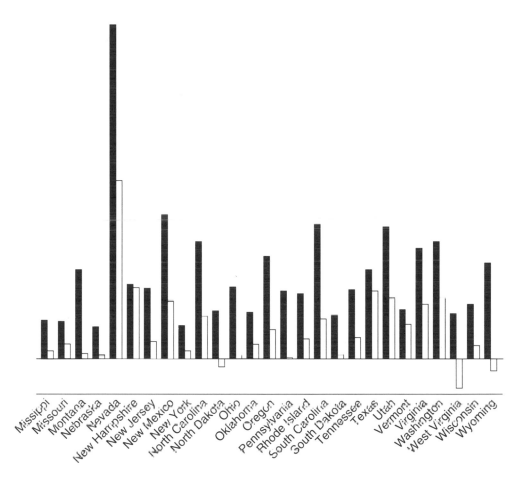

three women for every two men in the population aged 65 +. There are five women for every two men in the population aged 85 +. The feminization of aging has created social worlds of aging couples and elderly widows, of women who have outlived their husbands and men who have outlived their friends. Although this feminization reflects the realization of longer lives for many women, it places them at special risk for the problems associated with advanced old age—poverty, frailty, and institutionalization. This imbalance of the sexes is not unique to the United States; older women outnumber older men in almost all parts of the globe.[4]

We can trace the preponderance of older women to a cumulative female mortality advantage that affects all ages. Women in 1989 could expect to live 6.8 more years than men.[5] Big immigration waves before World War I once blunted the impact of differential mortality on the sex composition of the population (Siegel 1993: 58). Because these largely male immigration cohorts had virtually

TABLE 2.1 Characteristics of the older population, by state: 1990.

	Number 65+ (in thousands)	Percent Aged 65+	Percent Institutionalized	Percent in Poverty	Percent with Mobility Limitation	Percent Rural
United States	31242	13%	5%	13%	16%	25%
Alabama	523	13	5	24	21	38
Alaska	22	4	5	8	13	32
Arizona	479	13	3	11	13	11
Arkansas	350	15	6	23	19	45
California	3136	11	5	8	15	8
Colorado	329	10	5	11	14	18
Connecticut	446	14	7	7	14	17
Delaware	81	12	6	10	15	30
District of Columbia	78	13	8	17	17	0
Florida	2369	18	3	11	13	14
Georgia	654	10	5	20	20	38
Hawaii	125	11	3	8	13	12
Idaho	121	12	5	12	12	42
Illinois	1437	13	6	11	16	16
Indiana	696	13	7	11	15	32
Iowa	426	15	8	11	13	42
Kansas	343	14	7	12	13	35
Kentucky	467	13	6	21	21	45
Louisiana	469	11	6	24	20	30
Maine	163	13	6	14	15	50
Maryland	517	11	5	11	16	19
Massachusetts	819	14	7	9	15	13
Michigan	1108	12	5	11	16	28
Minnesota	547	13	8	12	13	34
Mississippi	321	13	5	29	22	51
Missouri	718	14	7	15	16	32
Montana	106	13	7	13	12	44
Nebraska	223	14	8	12	12	41
Nevada	128	11	3	10	13	11
New Hampshire	125	11	6	10	13	45
New Jersey	1032	13	5	9	15	9
New Mexico	163	11	4	17	15	24
New York	2364	13	5	12	16	14
North Carolina	804	12	5	20	19	50
North Dakota	91	14	9	15	10	57
Ohio	1407	13	6	11	16	23
Oklahoma	424	14	6	18	17	33
Oregon	391	14	4	10	13	30
Pennsylvania	1829	15	6	11	15	27
Rhode Island	151	15	7	12	14	11
South Carolina	397	11	4	21	19	44
South Dakota	102	15	8	16	11	54
Tennessee	619	13	5	21	20	38
Texas	1717	10	6	18	17	25

58

	Number 65+ (In thousands)	Percent Aged 65+	Percent Institutionalized	Percent In Poverty	Percent with Mobility Limitation	Percent Rural
Utah	150	9	4	9	14	14
Vermont	66	12	7	12	13	64
Virginia	664	11	5	14	17	36
Washington	575	12	5	9	13	24
West Virginia	269	15	4	17	21	56
Wisconsin	651	13	7	9	13	34
Wyoming	47	10	6	11	12	33

SOURCES: U.S. Bureau of the Census. 1990 Census of Population: *General Population Characteristics, United States,* Tables 16, 37; 1990 Census of Population: *General Population Characteristics, Urbanized Areas.* 1992, Table 19; 1990 Census of Population: *General Population Characteristics* (by state), CP1-2 to CP1-52. 1992, Table 40; 1990 Census of Population and Housing: *Summary Social, Economic and Housing Characteristics, United States,* 1992, Tables 4, 5; 1990 Census of Population and Housing: *Summary Tape File 1A;* 1990 Census of Population and Housing: *Summary Population and Housing Characteristics, United States.* 1992, Table 1.

died out by 1990, the toll of male–female differences in death rates is all the more apparent.

Although women still enjoy a considerable mortality advantage over men, the feminization of the older population slowed in the 1980s, because the sex gap in life expectancy narrowed. Women's age-adjusted mortality rate from the leading cause of death, heart disease, saw little change between 1982 and 1988, although men's rate continued to decline.[6] The older population remains one where women predominate, but the 59.8 percent female in the population aged 65+ in 1990 was virtually the same as in 1980.

A White Majority Shrinks

The older population is slowly coming to reflect the growing ethnic and racial diversity of contemporary America (see Table 2.2). In 1990, the white majority made up less than 87 percent of older Americans compared to 88 percent 10 years earlier; other older Americans were blacks (8 percent), Hispanics (4 percent), American Indians (.3 percent), and Asians and Pacific Islanders (1 percent). Both blacks and whites lost population shares to Hispanics and Asian and Pacific Islanders over the 1980s.

The decade's trends foretell the population changes ahead if current racial/ethnic fertility differentials persist and if immigration remains unchanged. The white population aged 65+ would fall to 84 percent by 2000, 77 percent in 2020, and 65 percent by 2050, when Hispanic elderly would outnumber their African American counterparts, and when Asians would account for almost 8 percent of older Americans.

These demographic changes in the older population's color and culture mix give new weight to minorities and new immigrant groups who have fared less well economically and have pursued different strategies of old age support than

TABLE 2.2   Estimates and projections of the racial and ethnic composition of the aged 65+ population: 1980–2050.

Year	White	Black	Hispanic	American Indian	Asian and Pacific Islander	Total
1980	88%	8%	3%	<1%	<1%	100.0%
1990	87	8	4	<1	1	100.0
2000	83	8	5	<1	3	100.0
2020	77	9	9	<1	5	100.0
2050	65	11	15	<1	8	100.0

SOURCE: U.S. Bureau of the Census. *Current Population Reports*, Series P-25, No. 1092; *Population Projections of the United States, by Age, Sex, Race, and Hispanic Origin: 1992 to 2050.* 1992, Table 2 (middle series).

the white majority have. These groups have been less likely than whites to rely on institutional care for the aged. As their population shares grow, the United States might see relatively more home care and less nursing home care for impaired older people. Alternatively, assimilation and acculturation might increase the demand for nursing homes and senior services catering to ethnic tastes. We might look for more rice and fewer potatoes on the menus of senior centers and for more skilled nursing facilities that emphasize an ethnic cultural heritage.

The Old Grow Older

The older population itself is aging. Thanks to increases in life expectancy, both the "old-old" and the "oldest-old" have become more prominent, and the United States now has one of the oldest elderly populations in the world (Myers et al. 1992). In 1880, only one American in 100 was aged 75 +. Today, one in 100 is aged 85 +, and one in twenty has lived to see a 75th birthday. Ages that were once extraordinary have come within the reach of a substantial minority of Americans.

The oldest Americans are the fastest growing segment of our population. The 1990 census counted just over three million persons aged 85 +. This segment of the population grew by 38 percent over the 1980–1990 decade and has more than doubled since 1970. With even slow declines in mortality, the U.S. Bureau of the Census projects 17 million persons aged 85 + by 2050, when surviving baby boomers will be very old. Although estimates for 1990 show only 36,000 centenarians, this is twice as many as for 1980. The U.S. Bureau of the Census forecasts a remarkable one million Americans 100 or older by the middle of the twenty-first century![7]

LONGER LIVES

The surer survival of big cohorts born in the early years of this century has translated into a larger population of older Americans. These survivors have been the beneficiaries of remarkable improvements in death rates. Figure 2.5

FIGURE 2.5   Additional years of life expected at selected ages, by sex: 1900–1988.

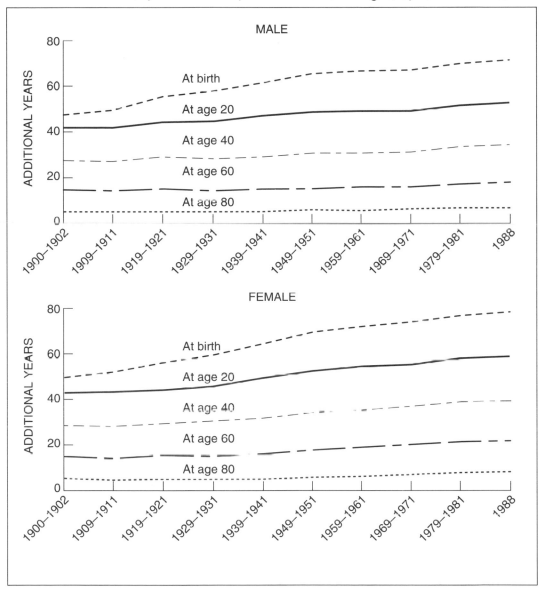

SOURCE: National Center for Health Statistics. *Vital Statistics of the United States*, 1988, Vol. II, *Mortality, Part A*, Table 6-4.

tracks the gains in life expectancy through the decades of the twentieth century. Because early estimates are based on reports from the Death Registration Area, not the whole United States, they overstate 1900–1940 gains, but the trends clearly show that all age groups have benefited from improvements in mortality.

Life expectancy at birth is the most familiar indicator of mortality levels. The age-specific death rates in 1988 for women translated, on average, into 78.3

years of life at birth. What a contrast with the grim mortality prospects confronting baby girls born at the turn of the century, when female life expectancy stood at less than 51 years! At 71.5 years in 1988, male life expectancy at birth also posted big gains over the 48 years calculated for 1900. Each generation has surpassed the average years of life predicted at birth because each has experienced actual mortality conditions that were better than those of its birth year.

Old age may seem virtually unattainable in the face of the low life expectancies at birth prevailing in 1900. However, mortality in earlier eras often claimed infants and children, who were particularly vulnerable to the diarrheas, measles, and other infectious diseases so common and lethal in the past. Those who survived the gauntlet of childhood illness could reasonably hope to reach old age. An American woman reaching 20 at the turn of the century could expect to live another 44 years. At 40, she could expect 29 years. Of course, young and middle-aged women in 1988 could look to many more years ahead—59 years at age 20 and 40 years at age 40.

The old also benefited from improvements in mortality. In recent decades, the percentage gain in life expectancy at age 60 exceeded the gains for younger people, whose already low death rates left less room for improvement. A 60-year-old woman in 1900 had, on average, 15 remaining years of life. Her counterpart in 1988 had almost 23 years ahead of her—an increase of over 7 years. Even octogenarians' life expectancies climbed, especially for women in recent decades. At age 80, an American woman in 1988 could look forward to almost nine additional years of life.

Improvements in mortality, especially in old age, first favored women, thus contributing to a widening sex difference in life expectancy. In the 1980s, gains for men outpaced those for women. Women aged 60 +, who could expect to outlive their male counterparts by 4.8 years at the start of the decade, saw their advantage trimmed to 4.3 years by 1988. What some have seen as an excess of older women looks more and more like a temporary shortage of older men.

Given remarkable progress against mortality, the 1980s saw speculation that Americans' life expectancies were bumping up against a biologically ordained life span for the human species (Fries 1980). The experience of longer-lived nations suggests otherwise: A 65-year-old woman in Japan can look forward to living 2 years more than her American counterpart.[8] Because our fifty states differ in mortality experience, U.S. life expectancy would rise if states with lagging life expectancy were to do no more than emulate the leaders (Siegel 1993:219). Racial gaps in death rates certainly depress life expectancy. At 64.9 years, the life expectancy at birth for black men in 1988 was 7 years shorter than for white men; black women's life expectancy—73.4 years—translated into almost 6 fewer years of life than for white women.[9]

The timing of recent improvements in mortality offers clues as to their causes. U.S. life expectancy plateaued between 1954 and 1968. Most gains in life expectancy since midcentury occurred in the 1970s and 1980s. Since 1968, remarkably rapid declines in mortality from heart disease—the leading cause of death—added years to later life (Crimmins 1981). It is probably not coincidental that the increases in life expectancy followed the 1966 implementation of Medicare. Older Americans' greater use of preventative health care services, for example, led to widespread detection and treatment of high blood pressure, a condition increasing the risk of cardiovascular disease. Undoubtedly, federal support for medical research led to better ways to prevent, diagnose, and treat chronic illnesses. Americans' lifestyle changes (e.g., quitting smoking) also contributed to longer lives.

Ironically, longer lives do not translate automatically into healthier ones (Crimmins et al. 1989). Because of insulin, more diabetics live on with this chronic disease, one that can lead to blindness and amputations. Although improved medical care and healthier lifestyles delay the onset and progress of debilitating disease, large numbers of older people, leading longer lives, may live on ill and impaired.

A GOOD OLD AGE

Most Americans will know old age. This is a virtual inevitability wrought of mortality declines. Less certain is the sort of old age we will live. Americans seem to agree that old age should include good health and adequate income. Most would add opportunities for leisure and freedom from the demands of a full-time job. Like Benjamin Franklin, who aspired to face death "immersed in a cask of Madeira wine, with a few friends" (Gruman 1966), contemporary Americans hope for the support and company of intimates. At the same time, they cherish the goal of maintaining their independence in their later years. The 1990 census tells us that older Americans are advantaged vis-à-vis earlier generations of elderly on most counts. It also points out that successful aging eludes many older people in our diverse older population.

HEALTH AND CAPACITIES

Bob Alexander, 70, loved bicycling since the 1940s, when he raced competitively.[10] Dolores, also 70, never owned a bike. The two widowed retirees met at a Senior Center and married after a courtship passed pedaling his two-seat tricycle along the beach. When Bob gave Dolores a bike for Christmas, she took up riding. In June, the Alexanders flew to the Netherlands for an 11-day, 240-mile bicycle tour organized just for people aged 60+.

People like the Alexanders counter impressions that later life means the oppression of chronic illness and disability. It is true that old age, particularly advanced old age, *is* associated with physical and mental impairments—some of which make it difficult for people to enjoy a good old age. Most policy concerns with the graying of the American population focus not on the still vigorous young-old, but rather on the growing numbers of the oldest-old individuals who are frail, sick, and incapacitated. This oldest-old group depends on the resources of the state, the health care system, and their closest kin. Growth of this highly dependent population subjects more Americans to the stressful caregiver burden associated with providing for the basic personal needs of an impaired parent or spouse. It places greater demands on Medicare (which funds hospitalization and doctor's care) and on Medicaid (which pays for nursing home care for impoverished elderly).

Work Disabilities and Activity Limitations

The 1990 census asked Americans about health conditions that interfered with carrying out activities in the home, community, and workplace. The focus was on the chronic, long-lasting health problems that beset older people, specifically "a physical, mental, or other health condition that has lasted 6 or more months." Although specialized health surveys provide a more complete portrait of the health of older Americans, the broad brush of the 1990 census demonstrates that there are noteworthy differences in functional capacity depending on age, sex, and race/ethnicity.

Consider age differences in Americans reporting a disability that prevents working at a job. Although 21 percent of 65–69 year olds say that they are prevented from working altogether, this figure increases to 31 percent for men aged 75–79. Few older Americans have a big stake in working, but health problems do prevent many older people from going about their day-to-day lives. Of civilian, noninstitutionalized Americans aged 65 +, 1 in 5 reports a mobility limitation that prevents going outside the home and/or a self-care limitation creating difficulties in activities "such as bathing, dressing, or getting around inside the house."[11] In contrast, fewer than 1 in 20 of their counterparts aged 16–64 report such a limitation.

Among older people, almost 16 percent admit to trouble getting around outside the home, while 12 percent report difficulties in taking personal care of themselves at home. Both limitations become more common at the older ages. For example, at the threshold of old age, fewer than 7 percent of men and women aged 60–64 admit to a personal care limitation, but 32 percent of men aged 85 + and 44 percent of their female counterparts indicate that they have trouble caring for themselves.

At each age, a substantially higher percentage of women than men report limitations. Although men are particularly vulnerable to life-threatening conditions like heart disease, women are prone to disabling ailments like arthritis. Also, racial and ethnic minorities report higher levels of late-life limitations than do the white majority. Regarding mobility limitations among men aged 65+: 13 percent of whites report difficulty going outside, 21 percent among blacks, and 15 percent among Hispanics.

The older population's changing composition has tilted toward those very groups beset by greater functional limitations. The continued aging of the older population means more of the oldest-old, those most vulnerable to illness and incapacity. The feminization of the older population—only recently slowed—has meant that women and their higher rates of impairment dominate. The disproportionate growth of ethnic and racial minorities gives new weight to groups who are more likely to say that poor health limits their activities in home, community, and workplace.

If the impairment rates of specific age-sex-race groups persist, demographic forces will deliver a more disabled population, but will impairment rates stay the same? Health care reform proposals, for example, promise improved access to medical prevention and treatment throughout the life course—a development that would particularly benefit ethnic and racial minorities. General rates of disability for the very old might also decline if safer workplaces, medical advances, or healthier lifestyles result in a later onset of chronic disease.

OLD FOLKS AT HOME: THE FAMILY LIVES OF OLDER AMERICANS

For Americans at the threshold of old age, kin are even more important than for younger people. By late middle age, adults are more likely to socialize with relatives, to single out family members as people who can be counted on, and to prefer friends met through kin (Rossi and Rossi 1990). Although school, jobs, and parenting shape the social networks of the young, older people are freer to choose their associates, and they often choose to associate with kin.

The family's contributions to a good old age extend beyond day-to-day companionship of a mate or the vicarious pleasure of a grandchild's accomplishments. Although many would count family membership as an essential element of a good and rewarding old age, it often determines the very life chances of older people. Married people, for example, enjoy greater economic security in later life than do their single counterparts. And when health fails, families forestall institutionalization. Among Americans aged 65+, 1 in 8 nursing home residents is married (at the time of admission) compared with 1 in 2 community residents; 1 in 3 nursing home patients is childless, but only 1 in 5 older people residing in the community has no living children.[12]

Parting Company: Marital Status of Older Americans

Elmer Carlson, 95, and his wife, Margaret, 96, celebrated their 75th wedding anniversary in 1993 with family and well-wishers.[13] They met on a dance floor in 1917, but Elmer now needed a cane to get about. Since 1987, they had resided in a retirement home. Despite the toll of advancing years, Elmer confided that tragedies, like the battlefield deaths of two sons in World War II, had only brought the couple closer together. When wished many more happy anniversaries, Margaret acknowledged that anniversaries like theirs are exceptional. "Don't say many more," she joked. "That's really overdoing it."

With advancing years, husbands and wives who grow old together run greater and greater risk that their marriage will be broken by the death of one partner or another. Although only 7 percent of men are widowers at ages 65–69, 53 percent are widowers at age 90 and older (see Figure 2.6). Among women, 30 percent are widowed at ages 65–69 as compared with 86 percent at ages 90 + .

Since women generally marry men who are older than themselves, it is usually the husband who dies and the wife who is widowed. Even if women were to wed men their own age, the husbands would usually be the first to die because of higher male mortality rates. Once widowed, most older people live out their lives without marrying again. Fewer than two older widows (and 15 older widowers) out of every thousand remarried in 1987.[14] A shortage of eligible bachelors in the older population is part of the reason for widows' lower remarriage rates. There are nearly four unmarried women for every unmarried man in the older population.

As a consequence of sex differences in mortality, most older men are married; most older women are widowed. Older men live with a spouse, but the women who survive them live alone. Among Americans aged 65 + , almost three-fourths of men, but only about one-third of women are living with a spouse. Since women are more likely to be widowed, they are at special risk in old age. Most men are cared for by wives; women must look to grown children for help. Most men continue to live in the community; women eventually live in nursing homes. Most men draw comfortable pensions; their widows often slip into poverty. For women, a good old age is still tied to a husband's health.

Happily, until the 1980s, each new generation arriving at old age was more likely to be married than was its predecessor. This trend was not sustained between 1980 and 1990. The percent "married, spouse present" among men aged 60–64 actually slipped from 82 percent in 1980 to 79 percent in 1990. For their female counterparts, the percent married flattened out at 63 percent, the same figure as a decade earlier.

To understand these changes, it helps to know what was driving previous gains in the percent married: Decreasing death rates led to lower proportions of both men and women widowed at the threshold of old age. While almost 30

FIGURE 2.6   Marital status, by age and sex: 1990.

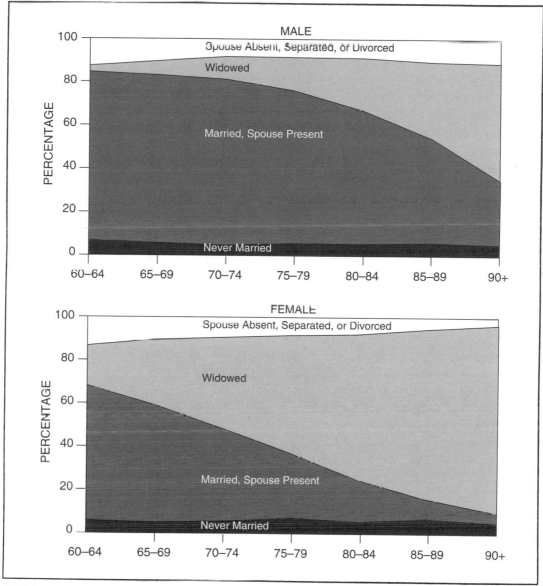

SOURCE: U.S. Bureau of the Census. 1990 Public Use Microsample Data, 5 percent file.

percent of women aged 60–64 were widows in 1950, only 20 percent were widows in 1990. In the 1980s, however, more men and women came to old age divorced. This rise in the divorced older population more than offset the decade's declines in the widowed. Consider women aged 60–64, for example. They were twice as likely to be widowed as divorced in 1990, but the divorced made up almost 10 percent of this population in 1990 versus less than 7 percent a decade earlier. Women were more likely to be divorced than were their male counterparts—in part because they were less likely to remarry after divorce.

Divorced Americans now arriving at old age have been caught in the changing cross-currents of marital formation and dissolution. Americans of all ages experienced higher divorce rates in the 1960s and 1970s than they had earlier (Cherlin 1992). But their prospects for remarrying sank after the mid-1960s (Norton and Moorman 1987). Although Chapter 1 in this volume shows that unmarried cohabitation partially offset greater singlehood among younger Americans, cohabitation never really caught on among the old. In 1990, for example, only two older women (and four older men) out of every thousand were reported as the unmarried partner of a householder of the same or opposite sex.

Because more recent generations of elderly were subject to higher risks of divorce over more of their married lives, a higher percentage of the young-old than the old-old are divorced. Older couples are not themselves prone to divorce. Fewer than two in every thousand married people aged 65 + divorced in 1987; the divorce rate for the overall married population was ten times higher.[15] However, with many middle-aged Americans now divorced and with recent rates forecasting divorce or separation for two-thirds of new first marriages (Martin and Bumpass 1989), we can expect more divorced older Americans in coming years.

Although divorced older Americans are still a small minority, this growing group comes to old age without the resources that many married couples take for granted. The financial well-being of older divorced women compares poorly with that of their widowed and married counterparts. For example, neither recent nor long-term divorcees are as likely to own their own home (Uhlenberg, Cooney, and Boyd 1990). Divorced men are less able to call on their grown children for support in old age (Cooney and Uhlenberg 1990). Even the mortality of divorced people is higher (Siegel 1993:314).

Another development limits marital advantage among the oldest-old. At least among men aged 85 and older, the percent married but living apart from their spouse for reasons other than marital discord has risen slowly and steadily. Only 2.3 percent were married, spouse absent in 1950, but this figure stood at 6.7 percent in 1990. Longer life expectancies have promoted intact marriages in later years, but poor health and frailty seem increasingly likely to come between the oldest men and their wives.

One's Own Home

Whether they live in a large house or a small apartment, older Americans place a high value on maintaining their own homes in the community. By running their own households, they can enjoy the comfort of familiar surroundings, keep control over their daily lives, and avoid the embarrassment of depending on others (Day 1991). Because frailties and impairments of advancing years make it harder and harder to maintain one's own home, some older people eventually live in the homes of relatives or in nursing homes. What is surprising, perhaps, is how many older Americans succeed in living independently.

Older Americans almost always live in their own households (see Table 2.3). In the population aged 65+, 91 percent of all men and 84 percent of all women were part of "householder units" in 1990. In other words, they were either the householder or the spouse of the householder. Even among those aged 85+, about half of women and three-quarters of men were still in their own households and often living alone. Older Americans became more likely during the 1980s to keep their own homes and less likely to live in the households of kin.

Residential independence did not always come so easily to older Americans. Among persons aged 65+ in private households (as opposed to institutions or other group quarters), there was a 17 percent increase between 1950 and 1990 in men living in their own homes and a 30 percent increase among women.[16] Some of this change, particularly for women, reflects the decline in widowhood, but even older, unmarried women became more likely to head their own households and less likely to live with others. Perhaps older Americans value residential privacy more than earlier generations did, but rising rates of homeownership (documented in Chapter 6, Volume 1) reflect the affluence that permits unprecedented numbers of aged to live independently.

TABLE 2.3   Living arrangements of aged 65+ population, by sex: 1980 and 1990.

	Male		Female	
	1980	1990	1980	1990
Households	96%	96%	93%	93%
Householder unit	90	91	81	84
Householder	86	87	48	49
Spouse of householder	3	4	33	34
Other relatives of householder	5	4	11	8
Parent or parent-in-law	3	2	8	6
Sibling or sibling-in-law	1	<1	2	1
Other	<1	<1	1	1
Nonrelative of householder	1	1	1	1
In Group Quarters	4	4	7	7
Group quarters resident	<1	<1	<1	<1
Institutionalized	4	3	6	7
Total	100.0%	100.0%	100.0%	100.0%

SOURCE: U.S. Bureau of the Census. 1990 and 1980 Public Use Microsample Data, 5 percent file.

NOTE: Numbers differ slightly due to rounding error.

Many who keep their own homes live by themselves. In 1990, 38 percent of women aged 65+ and 15 percent of their male counterparts lived alone. Because solitary living usually comes with widowhood, women and the oldest-old are more likely to live alone than are other older Americans. Whites account for the overall increase in solitary living during the 1980s; Asian elderly as well as young-old Hispanics, blacks, and Native Americans were actually *less* likely to live alone in 1990 than a decade earlier. Living alone is a mixed blessing. It means residential independence, but the lack of live-in support can be problematic for frail elderly who must worry about being able to get up after a fall or to a telephone in an emergency.

Although keeping one's own home is the norm, 9 percent of older men and 16 percent of older women do not live in their own households. Typically, they live either in institutions or in the households of kin. Some really prefer to live in someone else's home (say, with a favorite daughter), but others are just too sick or too poor to stay in their own homes. One percent of Americans aged 65+ who live in private households are *not* related to the householders; they are live-in housekeepers, boarders, roommates, and the like. Another tiny segment of older Americans live in noninstitutional group quarters like big roominghouses, religious convents, community-based group homes, or emergency shelters.

In the Home of Kin

Four percent of older men live as a relative of the householder but not the spouse; so do 8 percent of women aged 65+. By age 85+, the chances of living in the homes of adult children, siblings, or other kin have doubled. The oldest-old are especially likely to live in the homes of kin, because their increasing needs for physical assistance and economic support overwhelm preferences for privacy and independent living.

Women are more likely than men to be taken in by family members, because they are more likely to outlive their spouses, their health, and their resources. Figure 2.7 pictures the living arrangements of noninstitutionalized, unmarried women aged 60+. The percentage living alone rises, plateaus, and then declines with advancing age. Never-married, divorced, and widowed women not living alone typically live with relatives. In their 60s, their kin are readily available to share quarters; they have unmarried children, siblings, and even surviving parents with whom to share homes. At older ages, the supply of close surviving kin is smaller, but the needs of very old unmarried women prompt them to double up with others.

Older Americans who live in relatives' homes are usually a parent or parent-in-law of the householder; this arrangement accounts for about 2 percent of all

FIGURE 2.7   Living arrangements of older never-married, divorced, and widowed women, by age: 1990 (noninstitutionalized population).

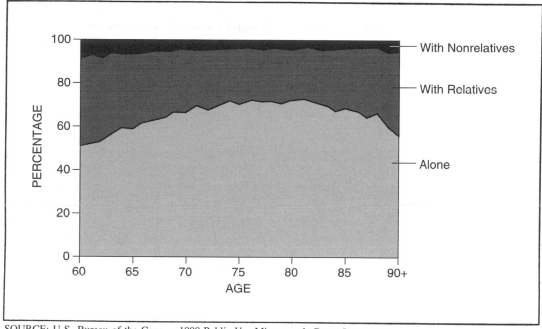

SOURCE: U.S. Bureau of the Census. 1990 Public Use Microsample Data, 5 percent file.

older men and 6 percent of their female counterparts. One percent of older persons are the brothers or sisters of either the householder or the householder's spouse. Then there are grandparents, aunts and uncles, cousins, and steprelations of the householder—an assortment of more distant kin who make up a tiny fraction of older Americans in private households. There are even 8,000 aging children (age 65+) who live in the homes of very old parents.

The Nursing Home

The association between age and debility leads most Americans to consistently overestimate the number of older people who are institutionalized. Only about 1 in 20 Americans aged 65+ lives in a nursing home or similar institution, even though the oldest-old face serious problems in living independently. Their needs for assistance often lead to institutionalization, especially for those without close kin. Among those aged 85+, nearly 1 in 4 was in an institution in 1990.

We think of institutions as a last home for older people who are no longer able to live in the community, but some seriously disabled Americans have lived their whole lives in institutional settings, and some older people manage to return to the community when their health or resources improve.

The oldest-old women are particularly likely to live in institutions because they are frail and seldom have a surviving spouse to care for them in advanced old age. Remarkably, 27 percent of women aged 85+ live in institutions as compared with 7 percent of all women aged 65+. For men, 15 percent of those aged 85+ live in nursing homes as compared with 3 percent of all those aged 65+. Despite the aging and the feminization of the older population, the percentage of institutionalized in the aged 65+ population has remained remarkably constant.

Older people living in nursing homes are typically too compromised by health problems to get by on their own. For example, 63 percent of nursing home residents aged 65+ in 1985 were disoriented or had memory impairments.[17] Surveys undertaken in the middle of the 1980s dramatically highlight the differences between older Americans who live in nursing homes and those who live in the community. Fully 91 percent in nursing homes need assistance to bathe versus only 6 percent living in the community (Dawson, Hendershot, and Fulton 1987). While 63 percent in institutions require help to get in or out of bed or a chair, fewer than 3 percent of noninstitutionalized older people need this help. These data offer reassuring evidence of the continuing capacities of most older Americans, but they also point out the serious plight of those who can no longer care for themselves.

But not all severely impaired individuals are institutionalized. In every community there are residents who are in worse shape physically, mentally, and functionally than some of their institutionalized counterparts. Being in a nursing home depends on many factors besides disability. People without family to care for them are at higher risk of institutionalization, for example. Cultural differences in the pervasiveness of protective attitudes toward the oldest-old, the supply of nursing home beds, and government willingness to pay for nursing home stays all affect nursing home utilization (Doty 1992:251–267). Although informative, institutionalization patterns probably tell us more about our societal response to disability among our older population than they do about the level or pervasiveness of impairments.

WORK AND RETIREMENT

In the 1950 census monograph on the older population, Sheldon captured the ambivalence many Americans once harbored toward retirement—a practice that had only recently "been given respectability as a reward for years of productive contribution." Retirement had a number of drawbacks: a late-life descent into economic insecurity, the loss of coworkers' sociability, the lack of intrinsic pleasure in a productive activity. Were this not enough, not having a job carried some taint of "uselessness, irresponsibility, and inadequacy." As Sheldon glumly intoned:

> Although retirement from one's career is coming to be looked upon as a normal phase of the work cycle, there still remain overtones of the negative attitude toward joblessness, along with other problems not solved by the rocking chair or fishing pole. The retired older man is often at odds with himself and with society. (Sheldon 1958:40–41)

From the vantage of the 1990s, these concerns seem quaintly irrelevant. No longer faintly distasteful, retirement, especially early retirement, has become a centerpiece of the American Dream, just like homeownership. The enthusiasm for retirement is understandable when one thinks of earlier generations of elderly who, lacking the resources to retire, had no choice but to settle for low wages at taxing jobs. Earlier generations also suffered the indignities of age-based mandatory retirement rules that sharply severed their ties to a career job. Workers approaching retirement age today want to give up the standard work week for more free time, but a majority say they would like to continue working with reduced and flexible hours (Harris 1981). Thus, older Americans have embraced retirement and, when they do work, work at part-time jobs.

The Trend Turns

In 1980, labor force participation of men aged 65+ in the civilian, noninstitutionalized population stood at 19 percent. By 1990, the figure was 16 percent. These numbers appear consistent with the long-run trend to lower rates of labor force participation by older American men. After all, almost half of men aged 65+ (46 percent) had been in the civilian labor force as recently as 1950. As Figure 2.8 shows, each new decade that followed 1950 recorded another drop in older men's work force involvement.

What actually went on during the 1980s could hardly have been predicted from the long-run trend. Nor was it captured by the decennial censuses. The annual Current Population Surveys (CPS) show that the trend turned. First, declines in older men's labor force participation slowed markedly in the early 1980s. After a low of 15.8 percent in 1985, their labor force participation began to creep upward. By 1989, it reached 16.6 percent. A gain of .8 point over 4 years may not seem momentous, since it added fewer than 100,000 people to the 1989 civilian work force of 124 million. After decades of late-life labor force declines, however, it was a newsworthy development. Official labor force projections quickly incorporated new assumptions of slowing declines and modest increases in labor force participation for men aged 55+ (Fullerton 1991).

FIGURE 2.8   Percentage of population aged 65+ in the civilian labor force, by sex: 1948–1992.

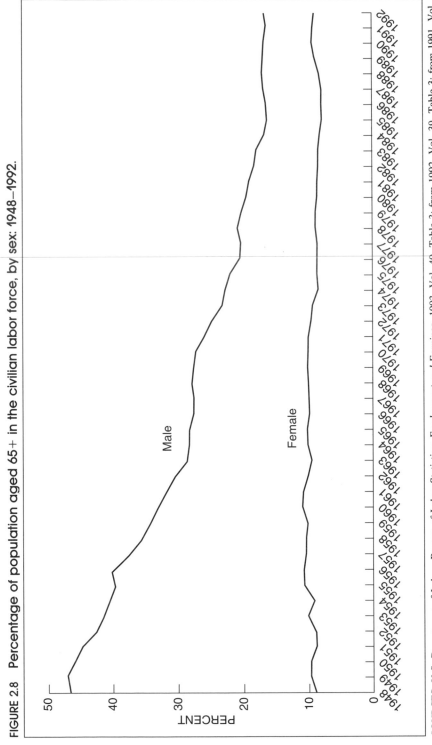

SOURCES: U.S. Department of Labor. Bureau of Labor Statistics: *Employment and Earnings*, 1993, Vol. 40, Table 3; from 1992, Vol. 39, Table 3; from 1991, Vol. 38, Table 3; from 1990, Vol. 37, Table 3; and from 1989, Vol. 36, Tables 3, 5.

74

The dominant force in the new trend was 65–69-year-old men, whose labor force participation rose 6.5 percent (from 24.5 to 26.1) between 1985 and 1989. They were not alone. Men aged 70 + experienced a 1 percent increase in labor force participation. Declines in overall unemployment undoubtedly made it easier for older Americans to find work, but their increases in labor force participation occurred in the face of well-entrenched institutional barriers to continued employment in old age (Herz and Rones 1989). The increase in late-life labor force participation also transpired without any increase in the average age at which men retired. Although the decline in men's retirement age began to slow as early as the 1970s, it certainly did not rise during the 1980s. Men's first receipt of Social Security retirement benefits showed an average age of almost 69 in 1950, whereas it stood at about 64 years of age in both 1980 and 1990 (Gendell and Siegel 1992).

In contrast to older men, trends in older women's employment had been flat, because higher labor force participation rates of successive generations of American women swamped their trend toward earlier retirement. For decades, the percentage of women aged 65 + in the civilian labor force moved within a narrow band—increasing fitfully in the 1950s before starting a slow decline in the mid-1960s. At the beginning of the 1980s, the 8 percent of women aged 65 + in the labor force was only a little lower than the 10 percent reported three decades earlier. A slow decline continued until the mid-1980s when older women, too, began to register greater labor force involvement. Between 1985 and 1990, their percentage in the labor force rose from 7 to 9. As with men, most of the gains were experienced by the 65–69 year olds, who had more recent job experience and fewer disabilities than their older counterparts. Between 1985 and 1990, these women saw their labor force participation climb from under 14 to 17 per hundred—a remarkable increase of 26 percent.

In the face of an upturn in unemployment in the early 1990s, labor force participation of men aged 65 + fell back to its 1985 level but showed signs of rebounding by 1992. Women aged 65 + held onto most of their gains. Higher late-life labor force participation is to be expected, because new cohorts of elderly, being better educated than were earlier ones, will certainly be more advantaged in the labor market. Even in 1990, 43 percent of men aged 65 + in the labor force had at least some college education, as opposed to only 26 percent of those not in the labor force. Those still working were more likely to be skilled workers in clean jobs that placed fewer physical demands on them, and provided higher wages for each hour of employment.

Workers and Retirees

Mandatory retirement was abolished for virtually all jobs between 1978 and 1986. Workers did not drastically change their retirement plans in response to changing laws, but they did gain considerably more discretion over the timing of their work force exits. Typically, workers chose to retire sooner rather than later. In 1989, 78 percent of women and 69 percent of men claimed first-time benefits from Social Security before they were 65 years of age.[18] A 1992 survey of new Social Security beneficiaries found that early retirees (i.e., those retiring between ages 55 and 61.5) were about as likely to say they retired just because they wanted to as to cite conventional health reasons (Packard and Reno 1989). What makes it possible for so many older people to quit work is greater retirement income from social security, private pensions, and savings.

Because retirement is universally accepted as a worthwhile goal, the issue now is largely one of timing. Ages for receipt of partial and full Social Security benefits—62 and 65—once dictated a worker's retirement plans. The 1983 Amendments to the Social Security Act will gradually increase the eligibility age for full benefits to 67 in 2027 while reducing the partial benefit payable at age 62 from 80 to 70 percent. Although these changes are supposed to buoy the finances of the Social Security system by encouraging later retirement, retirement timing is increasingly influenced by the provisions of private retirement plans. Today, employer pension plans typically allow retirement before age 62, albeit with reduced benefits (Wiatrowski 1993). Early retirement incentive plans, liberalizing eligibility and sweetening benefits, permit even earlier labor force withdrawals (Herz and Rones 1989). Mature men are likely to return to work after an absence from the labor force. By 1980, men could expect to retire more than once in their lifetime (Hayward et al. 1988).

Not everyone welcomes retirement. Some older people still leave the work force reluctantly: some because of health reasons; some accept early retirement plans only because they anticipate losing their jobs; others are really "discouraged workers" who stop looking for a job after long stints of unemployment. Although older workers are less likely to become unemployed, they face greater problems in finding new jobs than do younger workers. For older people without jobs, retiring to collect a pension can make the difference between living above or below the poverty line (Grad 1990).

Given the incentives to retire, it is surprising that anyone is to be found working after age 65, but 1 in 6 men and 1 in 12 women aged 65+ were working or looking for work at the time of the 1990 census. Their jobs were not necessarily what we think of as "career jobs." In fact, 69 percent of both men and women aged 65+ in the labor force in 1990 were already collecting Social Security benefits in 1989; 30 percent of men and 19 percent of women reported receiving other retirement pensions. Despite drawing a pension, they were engaged in the labor force at a life stage when many were not.

Older Workers' Jobs

A memorable McDonald's commercial of the 1980s introduced TV viewers to the "new kid," a senior citizen who straightened his bowtie, kissed his wife, and set off for a new job where he cheerfully peddled hamburgers in a cap under golden arches. Although McDonald's is not the mainstay of older workers, the fast food industry has long relied on part-time employees.

Most older Americans who work hold part-time jobs, jobs involving fewer than 35 hours of work per week. Among men aged 65+ at work in nonagricultural industries in 1990, 48 percent were part-timers—up from 30 percent in 1960.[19] As for their female counterparts, 59 percent worked part-time in 1990 as compared with 44 percent three decades earlier. In contrast, among workers aged 45–64, only 7 percent of men and 23 percent of women worked part-time in 1990.

Older people see part-time jobs as attractive on a number of counts. Shorter hours are less taxing physically and mentally, and they free up time to pursue other interests. Because too much income can trigger taxes on Social Security benefits, older workers have an incentive to make sure their hours do not boost their earnings too high. When there are caps on the years of service credited toward pension benefits, older people also have less to gain from a standard work week.

Part-time jobs are not usually very good jobs (Tilly 1991). Well-paid, part-time jobs are rare; they are less likely to offer pension plans and health benefits, perhaps because the employer's training and administrative costs are about the same whether one works 20 or 40 hours a week (Herz and Rones 1989). Not surprisingly, part-time work is unpopular among younger Americans, who cannot fall back on Social Security and Medicare to make ends meet. Although 9 of 10 older part-timers say that their reduced hours are voluntary, younger part-time workers are more likely to cite economic reasons like a partial layoff or not being able to find a full-time job.[20]

The number of part-time jobs has grown rapidly, because employment has shifted into retail trade and services that have long depended on part-timers (Tilly 1991). Employers in other industries have also embraced short shifts and part-time employment as a means of cutting labor costs, staffing peak hours, and even "busting" unions. Ironically, the economic restructuring that has fostered part-time jobs, temporary employment, and the use of low-wage contractors to supply parts or perform services has served the needs of older people, even while undermining the economic security of younger workers.

ECONOMIC WELL-BEING

At one time, the economic circumstances of older Americans were a national disgrace. Too poor to save, too old to work, they often lived out their days totally dependent on kin. Lacking employee pensions, private insurance, or Social Security, they were haunted by fears of being pushed into desperate poverty by a hospital bill, a bank failure, or the death of the family breadwinner. Lingering images of deserving old folks laid low by misfortune and illness now war with new views of the aged. By these new accounts, the aged are advantaged. Retirement, attacked as discriminatory unemployment when mandatory retirement was still the norm, is now regarded as enviable leisure time. Older Americans today are seen as so affluent that marketers target them for retirement condos, vacation cruises, and luxury cars. Political commentators, however, sometimes target them for criticism—charging them with self-serving defense of their privileges at the expense of younger generations. In fact, both poverty and affluence are found in the older population.

Four Income Groups

Painting the aged in broad-brush—whether as poor or as affluent—masks important differences in the economic well-being of the older population. To understand income differences, it helps to focus on four income groups within the elderly. The *poor* have incomes below the government poverty line; the *near-poor* have incomes that lift them no more than 150 percent above the poverty line. Those we call *comfortable* have incomes exceeding their poverty line by five times or more. Falling between the near-poor and the comfortable are *middle*-income elderly.

An older couple living alone was "poor" if its 1989 income was less than $7,495, and "comfortable" if it was $37,475 or more.[21] Although $37,475 for two people in 1989 is an admittedly arbitrary cutoff for admission to the comfort zone, it is roughly comparable (given inflation) to the $44,000 in 1993 that triggered new taxes on 85 percent of Social Security benefits under the Clinton budget. For an older person living alone or apart from kin, the poverty line was $5,947 in personal income, while the comfort threshold was $29,735. For other old people (say, a widow living with her daughter's family), the poverty line varied depending on the family's size and composition; if the family was not classed as poor on the basis of its members' total incomes, the widow would not be poor even if she had no income of her own.

Figure 2.9 shows how older men and women are distributed across the four groups based on their 1989 incomes. By our definition, the comfortable make up about 1 in 5 Americans aged 65+. Most older Americans fall squarely in the middle, that is, between 150 and 500 percent of the poverty line. About 1 in 8 is poor. For every older American who is poor, another is very near poverty. These near-poor could easily wind up poor if they suffered a minor setback (or if the poverty line were recalibrated to recognize a more adequate standard of income adequacy). Women are almost twice as likely as men to be found in poverty, and they are half again as likely to be counted among the near-poor. They are less likely to be middle income or to live in comfort. While 1 in 6 women aged 65+ lives in comfort, 1 in 4 men does.

Why are so many poor or nearly so? Social Security, the mainstay of retire-

FIGURE 2.9   Income groups of Americans aged 65+. by sex: 1989.

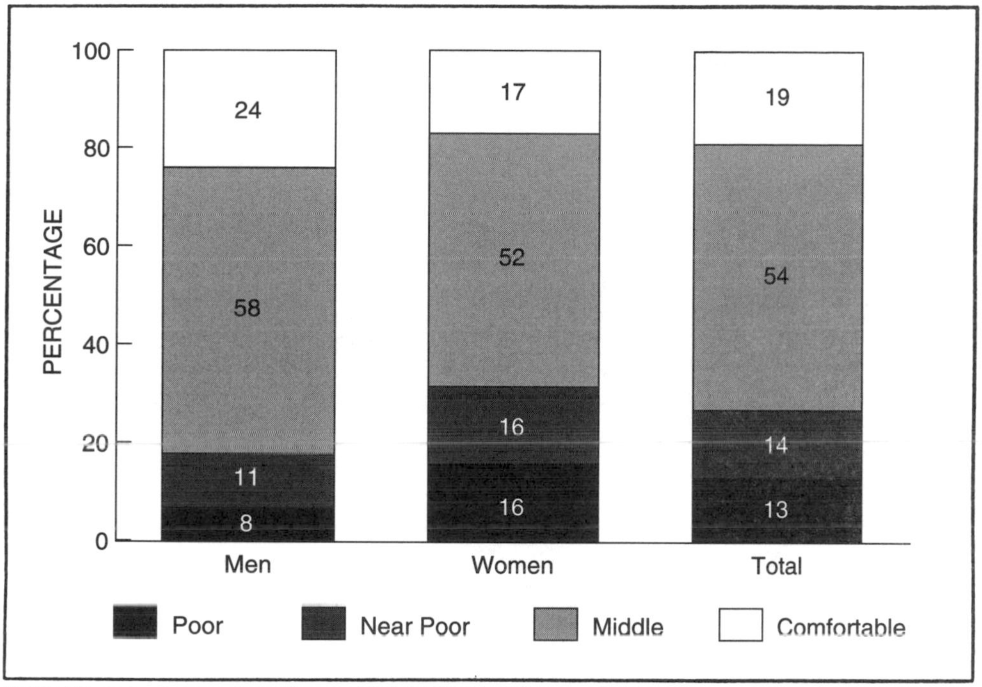

SOURCE: U.S. Bureau of the Census. 1990 Public Use Microsample Data, 5 percent file.

ment income, is not necessarily enough for those without other, substantial sources of personal income. In 1989, 88 percent of elderly poor living on their own were receiving Social Security or Railroad Retirement income.[22] At $488 per month, the *average* Social Security benefit for a female retired worker in December, 1989, was insufficient to keep a single person above the poverty line.[23] Many retirees received less than this average, and their incomes, even when augmented by Supplemental Security Income (SSI) and food stamps, were meager.

Income Portfolios of Older Men and Women

Social Security is the most important income source for older Americans, but Social Security was never intended to be the only source of retirement income. It was conceived to be one leg of a three-legged stool—with savings and private pensions also propping up incomes in old age. Compared with European countries, where a majority of the elderly's income comes from government programs, older Americans rely more on market income (i.e., earnings, investments, occupational pensions)—income characterized by great inequality (Achdut and Tamir 1990).

At least in the aggregate, a three-legged stool does characterize older men's

FIGURE 2.10   Income by source for persons aged 65 +, by sex: 1989.

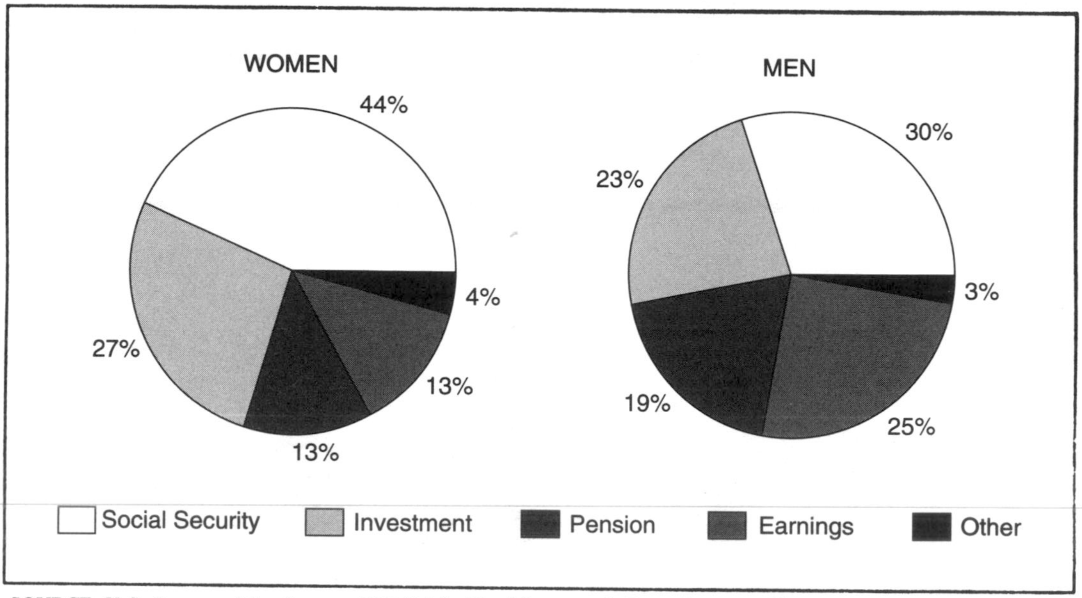

SOURCE: U.S. Bureau of the Census. 1990 Public Use Microsample Data, 5 percent file.

finances. In fact, since they count on Social Security, private pensions, invest-ments, *and* earnings, their financial base has all the stability of a four-legged chair (see Figure 2.10). Admittedly, few older people are "average," mirroring the personal income sources of the older population as a whole, but older men do demonstrate diversified income portfolios. Those with income beside Social Security are less likely to find themselves poor. Of men aged 65 + living com-fortably, 47 percent report earnings, 79 percent report investment income, and 54 percent report pensions; the figures for men aged 65 + living in poverty are only 8 percent, 10 percent, and 22 percent, respectively.

Nor can the economic security of older women be said to rest on a three-legged stool. Because older women get fully 44 percent of their income from Social Security, it is tempting to describe them as leaning precariously on a cane. If we take account of the 27 percent of personal income from investments, we may even picture them on crutches. Women's weaker ties to the work force have traditionally limited their earnings and private pensions, and Social Secu-rity is not sufficient to compensate for this disadvantage. To be sure, many women share in their husband's income, but their limited sources of personal income leave them vulnerable to poverty when they are widowed.

Who Are the Poor and Who Are the Comfortable?

A disproportionate share of the poor are old-old; in fact, more than half of older women in poverty are aged 75 + (see Table 2.4). The young-old, how-

TABLE 2.4   Percentage of poor and comfortable, aged 65+ population, with selected characteristics, by sex: 1990.

	Women		Men	
	Poor	Comfortable	Poor	Comfortable
Age 75+	53%	35%	45%	29%
White	76	94	68	95
Southern U.S.	46	32	49	32
Married, Spouse Present	14	58	51	83
High School Graduate	30	79	25	80
Mobility Limitation	27	13	22	6
Renter	43	11	34	9

SOURCE: U.S. Bureau of the Census. 1990 Public Use Microsample Data, 5 percent file.

ever, dominate the comfortable category. Their generation came to old age with a generally higher level of economic resources than did earlier cohorts of elderly who now make up the old-old. The young-old have suffered fewer of the late-life setbacks (institutionalization, widowhood) that are associated with poverty. Their retirement pensions have yet to be eroded by inflation, and some even continue to earn income.

Some characteristics, like race or educational attainment, embody lifetime legacies of advantage or disadvantage carried into old age. Although a majority of both the poor and the comfortable are white, racial and ethnic minorities are overrepresented among the aged poor just as they are among younger Americans living in poverty. Fully one-third of poor men aged 65+—and one-fourth of poor women aged 65+—are blacks, Hispanics, or others. By contrast, only about one-twentieth of men and women in the comfortable category belong to these minority groups.

Educational background also distinguishes the poor from those who are better off. During their work lives, their modest educational credentials tracked the aged poor into poorly paid jobs that offered little in the way of retirement pensions or opportunities to save for their later years. Among older poor men, only 25 percent finished high school as compared with 80 percent of those living comfortably. In contrast, 58 percent of financially comfortable older men had at least some college education versus 11 percent of the poor.

Although being white or a college graduate confers economic advantages throughout the life course, old age brings its own special risks. Mobility limitations and widowhood occur largely in later life, sometimes with disastrous consequences for people who were once economically secure. Those who avoid widowhood fare better than those who do not. Being married and living with one's spouse substantially reduces the risk of late-life poverty, particularly for older women. Among women who are comfortable, 58 percent are married and living with their spouse; among women who are poor, only 14 percent are married, spouse present. Many older women find that losing a husband also means losing a paycheck or a pension benefit. With limited resources of their own, it is hardly surprising that 66 percent of poor older women (versus 37 percent of their comfortable counterparts) are widowed.

Because the poor are especially vulnerable to illness and disability, late-life impairments are sometimes the result of earlier socioeconomic disadvantage. Old age, however, brings incapacitating health conditions to the affluent as well as the poor. Functional limitations affect income directly by reducing labor force participation, earnings, and ultimately savings and pension benefits. Only 13 percent of women aged 65+ in the comfortable category report a mobility limitation—a longstanding health problem making it difficult to go outside the home; 27 percent of poor women do.

Trends in Economic Well-Being

Although the 1990 Census of Population counted almost 4 million older people living in poverty, the 1980s brought the highest level of economic well-being ever known by older Americans. As Figure 2.11 shows, trends in poverty rates tell the story. In 1959, when the government first began to compute poverty statistics, fully 35 percent of Americans aged 65+ lived in poverty. The 1960s and early 1970s saw an expansion of private pensions coupled with increased coverage and benefits under Social Security. Poverty plummeted to 15 percent by 1974. With some gentle ups and downs, the percentage of aged who were poor stabilized at 12 percent in 1990—slightly above the 11 percent for adults aged 18–64. Poverty still plagued some groups. Of black women aged 75+, 4 in 10 (and 3 in 10 of their Hispanic counterparts) were poor at the end of the decade. On the whole, however, the 1980s witnessed unprecedented prosperity for older Americans.

As in older people, the poverty rate of children declined into the 1970s. Then it began to climb. By 1990, 21 percent of America's children—but only 12 percent of its aged—lived in poverty. To some, this looks like a zero sum game—public expenditures for senior citizens benefiting the old at the expense of children. When federal spending for the elderly was tallied for 1990, it amounted to $11,290 per older American; in contrast, federal expenditures for children came to only $1,020 per child aged 17 or younger, but these figures leave out substantial state and local expenditures for children's schooling, social services, and income support.[24]

Although the aged have benefited from federal programs like Social Security and Medicare, these programs cannot fully explain the diverging fortunes of America's children and its elderly. Both the young and the old became better off because of the Great Society programs (e.g., food stamps and Medicare) of the 1960s and early 1970s. Since then, each new generation of the aged came to old age with better financial histories and greater economic resources. But

FIGURE 2.11 Percentage of older adults and children in poverty: 1959–1992.

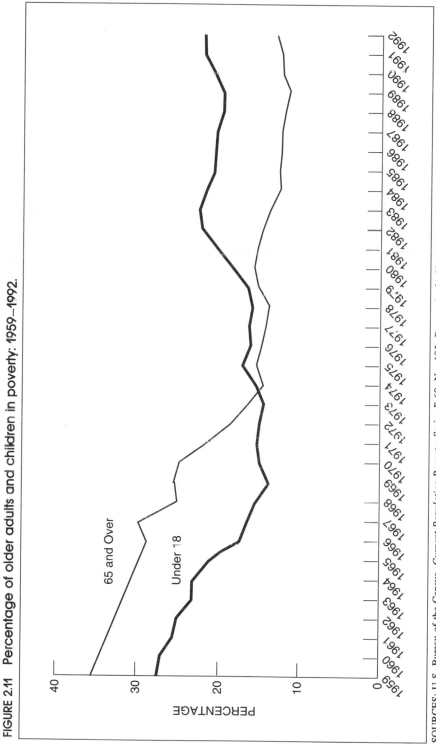

SOURCES: U.S. Bureau of the Census. *Current Population Reports*, Series P-60, No. 185, *Poverty in the United States: 1992*. 1993, p. x; and from No. 181, *Poverty in the United States: 1991*. 1992, p. vii; and from No. 175. *Poverty in the United States: 1990*. 1991, Table 7.

the lot of children deteriorated, in part because they spent more of their lives in single-headed families with limited financial means, as demonstrated by Hogan and Lichter (Chapter 3 in this volume).

Poverty trends may not be the best gauge of the economic standing of older people, if only because so many are near-poor. More telling are the shifts in the relative incomes of younger and older adults—the working age and retirement age populations. In 1950, the median income of young men aged 25–34 was three times larger than that of men aged 65 + . By 1980, it was two times larger, and by 1990, the median income for young men was just one-and-one-half times bigger. Figure 2.12 traces birth cohorts beginning when the men were aged 25–34 and ending in 1990. One can see that each new cohort started out with less of an income advantage vis-à-vis the aged than did the cohort that preceded it.

Many men aged 25–34 are still getting established in the job market. We might expect them to gain on retirees as they put schooling behind them, settle into career jobs, and get more work experience and seniority. Until the 1980s, this was a reasonable description of the experience of real cohorts of 25–34 year olds who, over 10 years, aged to become 35–44. During the 1980s, however, young men born in 1946–1955 failed even to hold their own, relative to men aged 65 + . When their incomes were stacked up against those of their grandfathers, they were no better off than at the start of the decade. And their younger brothers, born in 1956–1965, were off to an even worse start.

The situation for women was markedly different. The decade of the 1980s saw the end of older women's improvements in relative income. Older women actually began to lose out to younger women, who enjoyed higher labor force participation rates and earnings from the labor market of the 1980s, as shown by Bianchi (Chapter 3 in Volume 1). As younger cohorts moved through the decade of the 1980s, their growth in median income actually outpaced that of women aged 65 + . In 1980, the median income of women aged 25–34 was 165 percent of the median for women aged 65 + ; by 1990, these 35–44 year olds reported 180 percent.

Higher retirement income fueled the long-run gains in the relative income advantage of the old. In the 1980s, the growing disadvantage of younger men made the old look even better off. Workers encountered unemployment, slowing wage gains, and rising prices (see Levy, Chapter 1 in Volume 1), but cost-of-living adjustments in pensioners' Social Security checks insulated them from inflation and the vagaries of the job market. Higher housing prices shut young people out of the housing market, but they left many elderly homeowners with unanticipated wealth. As Myers and Wolch point out (Chapter 6 in Volume 1), older Americans in 1990 were more likely to own their own homes than the earlier generation of aged in 1980.

A study of "family units" (that is, families and individuals living apart from kin) suggests how developments in individual income played out in households

FIGURE 2.12   Median income of males in selected birth cohorts
as percentage of median for males aged 65+: 1950–1990.

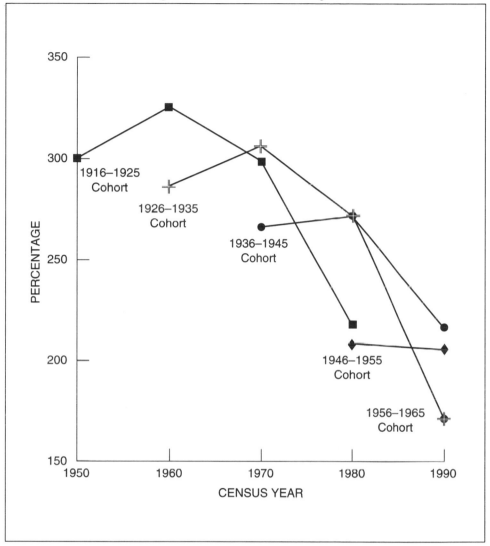

SOURCES: U.S. Bureau of the Census. *Current Population Reports,* Series P-60, No. 174, *Money Income of Households, Families, and Persons in the United States: 1990.* 1991, Table 24; and from Series P-60, No. 167, *Trends in Income by Selected Characteristics: 1947 to 1988.* 1990, Table 24.

over the 1980s (Radner 1987 and 1991). Between 1979 and 1984, aged units' median income (adjusted for needs implied by family size and composition) gained markedly vis-à-vis the recession-wracked median for younger units. Between 1984 and 1989, however, the relative advantage of the older units slipped. On the one hand, a drop in unemployment—from 7.4 to 5.2 percent—

benefited the young. But declining interest rates began to pare the investment incomes of older Americans; a one-year bank CD earning 9.73 percent in 1984 was paying only 7.88 percent in 1989.[25] The aged fared relatively well overall during the 1980s, although some older Americans still lived in poverty.

NEW AND OLD: ELDERLY IMMIGRANTS

Hinh Nguyen, 79, is an old man in a confusing, new country. Because he does not want to disappoint his children who worked hard to bring him from Vietnam to Southern California, he buoys his spirits with frequent visits to the Asian Senior Acculturation Center in Santa Ana. There, elderly immigrants like Mr. Nguyen read Vietnamese newspapers, socialize with others who speak their language, join in *tai chi* exercises, and attend classes to learn English.[26]

Most foreign-born elderly came to the U.S. as young people and grew old here. But immigration changed the face of many American communities in the 1980s (see Chapter 5). Although it is usually the young, not the old, who are willing to pull up stakes and move to a new land, many older people have been caught up in the new waves of immigration from Asia and the Western Hemisphere. A global diaspora of professional workers has even created a whole new class of bicontinental grandparents, commuting regularly between the homes of grown children in, say, California, Britain, and Pakistan. As Figure 2.13 shows, the foreign-born (not counting outlying areas of the U.S. like Puerto Rico) make up about 1 in 5 persons aged 65+ in California, Hawaii, and New York compared to 1 in 10 for the whole United States. Elderly newcomers who immigrated in the 1980s are concentrated in just a few states: 38 percent in California, 15 percent in New York, and 13 percent in Florida.

Elderly newcomers came to public attention in 1994. To save $6 billion over 5 years, an Administration task force proposed eliminating SSI benefits for future legal immigrants (except refugees) until they became citizens. Under the SSI program, the indigent who are blind, disabled, or elderly get food stamps and as much as $446 monthly for individuals and $669 for couples. Immigrants do not usually receive aid during their first 3 years in the United States, when eligibility formulas count the assets and income of kin who sponsored their immigration. Even so, the number of legal noncitizens collecting SSI has climbed from 128,000 in 1982 to 601,000, two-thirds of whom are elderly.[27] Whether American taxpayers should bankroll the retirement of an immigrant whose working life was spent in another country is a heated issue.

Because immigration law favors the relatives of adult U.S. citizens and resident aliens, 6 percent of immigrants admitted between 1980 and 1984 were foreign-born parents joining offspring in the United States (Jasso and Rosenzweig 1990). Elderly parents come to the United States to be close to grown

FIGURE 2.13   Foreign-born as a percentage of the aged 65+ population, by state: 1990.

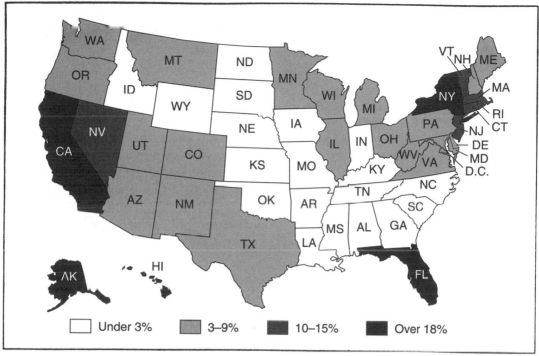

SOURCE: U.S. Bureau of the Census. 1990 Public Use Microsample Data, 5 percent file.

children or to help with family businesses and grandchildren. Some older people are refugees. Like younger immigrants, older people must cope with unfamiliar surroundings and an unintelligible language. Unlike their younger relations, they do not usually have jobs or schools where they can forge social ties and learn new customs.

Like Mr. Nguyen, 41 percent of older people who entered between 1980 and 1990 speak no English. Relatively few older immigrants learn enough English to become U.S. citizens and, hence, few would collect SSI if only citizens are to be eligible. Among persons aged 65+, fewer than one-half of Asians and one-quarter of Western Hemisphere immigrants entering the United States in the 1970s had become naturalized citizens by 1990. Because they lack a U.S. work history, only 21 percent of older newcomers received any Social Security benefits in 1989. The economic status of recent older immigrants is often precarious. Fully 23 percent live in poverty—a figure twice that of the general population aged 65+. Limiting assistance to citizens means that many elderly legal immigrants would never qualify for public assistance, no matter how long they resided in the United States; some would live out their lives poor, while others would be dependent on their relatives.

By virtue of poverty, limited English, and cultural traditions, the daily lives of new immigrants are already more intertwined with kin than are those of other older Americans. As we pointed out earlier, older Americans value residential independence and typically choose to live alone if they cannot live with a spouse. However, only 6 percent of the new immigrant elderly live alone. At the time of the 1990 census, more than 1 in 5 older persons immigrating since 1980 resided with kin as opposed to only 1 in 12 of their pre-1950 counterparts. Whether relatives or nonrelatives, those with whom the new immigrant elderly live are often themselves relatively new to the United States. Fully 42 percent of the recent immigrants live in households termed "linguistically isolated," that is, where no one over the age of 14 speaks English very well.

Recent immigrants make up only 1 in 10 foreign-born elderly. The majority have lived most of their lives in the United States; in fact, 54 percent immigrated before 1950 and have assimilated economically into the U.S. mainstream. For example, 84 percent of older, pre-1950 immigrants receive Social Security, and only 1 in 15 receives public assistance like SSI. These long-time residents are more likely to be among the old-old; while 71 percent of the foreign-born aged 75 + arrived in the United States before midcentury, only 38 percent of those aged 65–74 entered that early. Because Europeans dominated the earlier waves of immigration, 60 percent of immigrants now aged 75 + trace their roots to Europe as compared with 44 percent of those aged 65–74. Today, however, only a scant majority (52 percent) of all foreign-born elderly come from Europe. Another 30 percent were born in the Western Hemisphere, 13 percent in Asia, and 5 percent in other regions.

WHAT LIES AHEAD

The 1980s were a halcyon era of generational balance. The needs of a growing elderly population were offset by the relative decline in the population of dependent children. Moving into their middle years, an army of baby boomers stood ready to support both young and old. Of course, the baby boomers were themselves aging, and their old age promises to be unprecedented for America.

Of baby boomers, 6 in 10 report that they worry that they won't be able to afford to retire (Moore and McAneny 1993). Although they seem likely to arrive at old age with more assets than their parents had, boomers will come up short on spouses and children to support them in their later years (Easterlin, Schaeffer, and Macunovich 1993). Women of the baby boom generation will be more likely than earlier generations to reap the rewards of their labor: Working longer at higher pay than their mothers, they will be more likely to qualify for Social Security in their own right and to augment it with private pensions (Burkhauser and Salisbury 1993).

Not everyone can count on a big private pension, given the 1980s declines in pension coverage for full-time, wage and salary workers in the private sector. The adequacy of future pensions is also increasingly uncertain. More and more employers are switching from "defined benefit" plans guaranteeing a certain level of retirement income to "defined contribution" plans specifying only how much is paid in. With 401K plans offering an unfamiliar array of annuities, mutual funds, and other investments, workers themselves now bear the risks of inflation, bear markets, failed insurers, and their own feckless management of big, lump-sum payouts (Burkhauser and Salisbury 1993). For baby boomers, the only certainty is a longer wait to collect full Social Security benefits.

As the aging of the baby boom generation demonstrates, the decade of the 1980s marked only the latest chapter in the demographic saga of population aging dating from the earliest years of our nation. Between 1980 and 1990, the older population of the United States grew both bigger and older. Its ethnic and racial diversity increased. Its tilt toward women slowed. Improvements in mortality insured that most Americans would live to be old and even very old. Older Americans enjoyed unprecedented prosperity.

Although the 1980s were not always kind to the young, the decade brought a good old age within reach of more and more old people. More older Americans eluded poverty; more achieved the cherished goal of maintaining their own homes; more owned the homes they lived in. Benefiting from the growth of part-time jobs, more older people kept working on their own terms. After decades of decline, late-life labor force participation actually turned up.

But these improvements in older Americans' lives did not happen by chance. These gains were the consequences, both intended and unforeseen, of an array of postwar public policy decisions—beginning with the G.I. Bill that sent World War II veterans to college. Benefiting older people were expanded Social Security coverage and other benefits indexed to the cost of living. There were Medicare, government and private spending on medical research, anti-smoking campaigns, and OSHA efforts to make workplaces safer. Mandatory retirement was outlawed. Private pension plans were regulated so that money would be waiting for workers when they retired. There were HUD funds for senior housing, income tax deductions for homeowners, and property tax benefits for veterans. There was a federal tax code that mandated an extra standard deduction for those aged 65+, exempted some or all Social Security income from taxes, and provided a tax credit for those without much income from Social Security; remarkably, 46 percent of the elderly owed no federal taxes in 1993.[28]

In the 1990s, new policy developments may either benefit older Americans or put additional pressure on them. How, for example, will the aged fare under health care reform? Will the pensions and medical benefits of current and future retirees be made safe from the industrial restructuring transforming U.S. corporations? Will the federal deficit be plugged with means-tests, caps, and taxes on entitlements? The aged are not the only stake-holders in contemporary policy debates, but their well-organized lobbying and voting strength gives strong voice to their interests. Although they made up only 12.6 percent of the U.S. population, persons aged 65+ constituted 22 percent of Americans who reported voting in November 1990.[29]

There are some signs that the Gray Lobby may no longer be invincible. In the early 1990s, advocates for the elderly hoped to raise the limit on what pensioners can earn without having their Social Security benefits reduced; instead, lobbyists found themselves waging an unsuccessful fight to stop higher taxes on the Social Security of prosperous retirees. Special treatment for well-to-do aged is harder to justify in the face of federal deficits. Certainly, major new public initiatives on behalf of older Americans are unimaginable. Even among the aged, there is little enthusiasm for helping out the less fortunate. For example, legislation expanding Medicare benefits for catastrophic coverage was repealed in 1989 when privately insured, middle-class retirees rebelled at funding it. Meanwhile, the needs of some older people will undoubtedly be sacrificed to bigger causes. Elderly legal aliens seem likely to lose out in the interest of welfare reform and immigration politics.

Even if the economic anxieties of aging baby boomers prove to be excessive, a good old age continues to elude many older Americans today. One-quarter of older people are either poor or near-poor. Many of the oldest-old have outlived their resources, their kin, their ability to live independently and to care for their own needs. Women are at special risk for disability, widowhood, poverty, and assisted living. Ethnic and racial minorities face special challenges in old age; so do the "new and old" immigrants of the past decade. There is great diversity in the older population, and many older people remain vulnerable even after the gains of the 1980s.

Increasingly, we can expect public policy debates to question who among the elderly stands to win or lose. The older population has grown too diverse, the circumstances of successive generations too different, to ask how the monolithic "aged" will fare under new taxes, health care reform, or changes in public benefit programs.

This research was supported in part by the University of California through an allocation of computer resources. The authors are indebted to Michael Aguilera, Quan Nguyen, and Laura Xia for research assistance in the preparation of this chapter.

ENDNOTES

1. U.S. Bureau of the Census (1993). Current Population Reports, Series P-25, No. 1095, *U.S. Population Estimates by Age, Sex, Race, and Hispanic Origin: 1980–1990*, Table 1.

2. *Encyclopedia of Associations, 1993* (27th ed.), Vol. 1, Part 2, p. 1135; U.S. Bureau of the Census. 1993. *Statistical Abstract of the United States, 1993* (113th ed.), pp. 67–68.

3. U.S. Bureau of the Census (1992). International Population Reports, P-25, No. 3, *An Aging World II.*

4. United Nations Statistical Office (1991). *The World's Women 1970–1990: Trends and Statistics,* Series K, No. 8.

5. National Center on Health Statistics (1991). *Vital Statistics of the United States, 1989, Vol. III, Mortality, Part A,* Table 6-1.

6. U.S. Bureau of the Census (1992). Current Population Reports, Series P-23, No. 175, *Population Trends in the 1980s,* p. 4.

7. U.S. Bureau of the Census (1992). Current Population Reports, Series P-25, No. 1092. *Population Projections of the United States, by Age, Sex, Race, and Hispanic Origin: 1992–2050,* p. xv.

8. National Center for Health Statistics (1993). *Health, United States, 1992,* Table 26.

9. U.S. Bureau of the Census (1992). *Statistical Abstract of the United States 1992* (112th ed.), Table 103.

10. *Los Angeles Times,* August 4, 1993, p. B2.

11. U.S. Bureau of the Census (1992). *1990 Census of Population and Housing, Summary Social, Economic and Housing Characteristics, United States* CPH-5-1, Table 4.

12. U.S. Senate Special Committee on Aging (1991). *Aging America: Trends and Projections: 1991,* p. 163.

13. *Los Angeles Times,* July 30, 1993, p. B2.

14. National Center on Health Statistics (1991). *Vital Statistics of the United States, 1987, Vol. III, Marriage and Divorce,* Table 1.7.

15. National Center on Health Statistics (1991). *Vital Statistics of the United States, 1987, Vol. III, Marriage and Divorce,* Table 2-5.

16. U.S. Bureau of the Census (1953). *U.S. Census of Population.* Vol. II, *Characteristics of the Population.* Part 1. United States Summary, Table 107.

17. U.S. Senate Special Committee on Aging (1991), p. 163.

18. U.S. House of Representatives Committee on Ways and Means (1990). *1990 Green Book,* p. 38.

19. U.S. Department of Labor, Bureau of Labor Statistics (1991). *Employment and Earnings,* p. 202.

20. U.S. Department of Labor (1991), p. 202.

21. U.S. Bureau of the Census (1990). Current Population Reports, Series P-60, No. 171, *Poverty in the United States: 1988 and 1989,* p. 355.

22. U.S. House of Representatives Committee on Ways and Means (1991). *1991 Green Book,* p. 412.

23. U.S House of Representatives Committee on Ways and Means (1991). p. 412.

24. U.S. House of Representatives Ways and Means Committee (1993). *1993 Green Book,* p. 1564.

25. U.S. Bureau of the Census (1991). *Statistical Abstract of the United States, 1991,* Table 621, p. 834.

26. *Los Angeles Times,* April 10, 1992, p. B1.

27. *Los Angeles Times,* March 17, 1994, pp. A3, A20.

28. U.S. House of Representatives Committee on Ways and Means (1993), p. 1468.

29. U.S. Bureau of the Census (1991) Current Population Reports, Series P-20, No. 453, *Voting and Registration in the Election of November 1990,* Table C.

3

Children and Youth: Living Arrangements and Welfare

DENNIS P. HOGAN and DANIEL T. LICHTER

THE NEW REALITIES of American family life, coupled with the changes in economic opportunities and housing described in this series, have dramatically altered the experiences of childhood and young adulthood over the past decade. The family, in its myriad forms, provides a context for bearing and rearing children, attending to their physical and emotional needs, and ensuring the next generation of well-adjusted and productive citizens (Zill 1993). But these traditional functions are now being challenged in significant ways by the current transformation of the family and shifts in the American social and economic structure. This chapter documents this process and analyzes the impact of these changes on the living arrangements, school and work activities, and economic well-being of American children and youth.

As detailed by McLanahan and Casper (Chapter 1), marriage and marital instability have taken on new forms and occur at different rates and with less predictability than was the case just 30 years ago. The average age at first marriage has risen sharply since 1980, while unmarried cohabitation among young adults has become commonplace. By 1990, roughly one-half of all marriages ended in divorce. The link between marriage and parenthood has also been weakened: more than one-quarter of births occur out of wedlock. These out-of-wedlock births and the rise in divorce result in an increasing share of families with children that are headed by single women. And because remarriage has become increasingly common, a growing percentage of children now live or have lived in stepfamilies or blended families; that is, families involving formerly married men and women and their children from previous marriages.[1] For young adults, changes in living arrangements are often even more dramatic.

93

They move away from the families in which they grew up, form their own households, and then, sometimes, move back to their parental families (Goldscheider and Goldscheider 1993).

It is no longer possible to draw sound conclusions about the well-being of American children and youth from data on intact families. Nor can conclusions about the lives of children be based simply on information about the adults with whom they live. The race and ethnicity of children, and their residential and economic experiences, can differ considerably from those of adults in their families. This situation becomes even more complex because the immigration of young adults and entire families to the United States has added significantly to the population of children, and it has changed the background and characteristics of children relative to those of prior generations. To understand the interplay of these changes in the American social and economic structure and in patterns of family building on child outcomes, it is thus essential to look at the population of children.[2]

BACKGROUND

The well-being of American children is a key element of the pursuit of happiness by American families. Overwhelmingly, American families try to raise their children in a secure and nurturant environment. They hope that their children will become economically and residentially independent adults with families of their own. They socialize their children to meet these expectations while attempting to provide the family environment and economic resources needed for success (Hogan 1985). Although local, state, and federal governments leave the primary task of raising children to families, they intervene in a variety of ways to ensure outcomes that are favorable to the national future—in recognition that today's children must become tomorrow's healthy and skilled workforce, citizens who are intelligent, honest, and loyal, with a commitment to family life and the production of a new generation of children. These interventions include campaigns and legislation to improve prenatal and postnatal health, to support free public schools, to require school attendance and ban child labor, and to protect against neglect and abuse of children. Through juvenile justice systems, governments have even put in place protections from the full force of legal sanction by the state. Churches, youth groups, and other voluntary organizations also function to support families in attaining these goals for their children.

Differing approaches to family life and the well-being of children are among the most hotly contested issues of our time. Sharp disagreement exists over the extent to which governments should be involved in family life. If parents are the best judges of their children's well-being, the state, then, should not intrude in family processes. But the inadequacies of some families might necessitate state involvement.

One major contention involves the effects of one-parent households, especially those that are mother-headed, on the physical and emotional well-being of children. The debate often centers on the extent to which American families have failed because of a lack of individual responsibility, and whether societal shifts (e.g., changing premarital sexual behavior, increasing cohabitation, or the rise in maternal employment) and declining economic opportunities for young adults have weakened the traditional nuclear family. Why such changes in the family and declines in family well-being have often been more pronounced among blacks has added to the controversy (Uhlenberg and Eggebeen 1986; Gill 1992). These debates have been based on varying combinations of facts pertaining to only part of the issues, to partial analysis guided by political theories of the appropriate roles of the individual and the state, and various disciplinary methods of collecting and analyzing data among the social scientists.[3] The structure of government programs for families and, most important, the well-being of a generation of American children rest in the balance.[4]

NATIONAL GOALS

In the midst of these complex social science concepts and research, theories of the family economy, and policy disagreements, it is tempting to turn to other issues that are more simply addressed. Yet we cannot avoid these issues because the successful rearing of our children is essential for our continued individual and collective success. This debate over who and what are responsible for the current situation and policy responses must not obscure a basic national agreement on what constitutes well-being for children and the goals that will achieve it.

One of the first explicit statements of our national goals for children and youth was provided in 1930, at the onset of the Great Depression, under a Republican administration. The Children's Charter, produced by President Hoover's White House Conference on Child Health and Protection, lays out in precise language the national aims for the children of America.[5] Although the language is dated, The Children's Charter provides a statement of aims for our children against which we can measure our progress and identify needs. The aims in this Charter are expressed repeatedly (albeit in different language and terminology) in our contemporary public discourse on children, and they are consistent with the principles underlying the concerns of groups with far different political orientations.[6]

PRESIDENT HOOVER'S WHITE HOUSE CONFERENCE ON CHILD HEALTH AND PROTECTION RECOGNIZING THE RIGHTS OF THE CHILD AS THE FIRST RIGHTS OF CITIZENSHIP PLEDGES ITSELF TO THESE AIMS FOR THE CHILDREN OF AMERICA (1930)

I For every child spiritual and moral training to help him to stand firm under the pressure of life

II For every child understanding and the guarding of his personality as his most precious right

III For every child a home and that love and security which a home provides; and for that child who must receive foster care, the nearest substitute for his own home

IV For every child full preparation for his birth, his mother receiving prenatal, natal, and postnatal care; and the establishment of such protective measures as will make childbearing safer

V For every child health protection from birth through adolescence, including: periodical health examinations and, where needed, care of specialists and hospital treatment; regular dental examination and care of the teeth; protective and preventive measures against communicable diseases; the insuring of pure food, milk, and pure water

VI For every child from birth through adolescence, promotion of health, including health instruction and a health program, wholesome physical and mental recreation, with teachers and leaders adequately trained

VII For every child a dwelling place safe, sanitary, and wholesome, with reasonable provisions for privacy, free from conditions which tend to thwart his development; and a home environment harmonious and enriching

VIII For every child a school which is safe from hazards, sanitary, properly equipped, lighted and ventilated. For younger children nursery schools and kindergartens to supplement home care

IX For every child a community which recognizes and plans for his needs, protects him against physical dangers, moral hazards, and disease; provides him with safe and wholesome places for play and recreation; and makes provision for his cultural and social needs

X For every child an education which, through the discovery and development of his individual abilities, prepares him for life; and through training and vocational guidance prepares him for a living which will yield him the maximum of satisfaction

XI For every child such teaching and training as will prepare him for successful parenthood, homemaking, and the rights of citizenship; and for parents, supplementary training to fit them to deal wisely with the problems of parenthood

XII For every child education for safety and protection against accidents to which modern conditions subject him to those which he is directly exposed and those which, through loss or maiming of his parents, affect him indirectly

XIII For every child who is blind, deaf, crippled, or otherwise physically handicapped, and for the child who is mentally handicapped, such measures as will early discover and diagnose his handicap, provide care and treatment, and so train him that he may become an asset to society rather than a liability. Expenses of these services should be born publicly where they cannot be privately met

XIV For every child who is in conflict with society the right to be dealt with intelligently as society's charge, not society's outcast; with the home, the school, the church, the court and the institution when needed, shaped to return him whenever possible to the normal stream of life

XV For every child the right to grow up in a family with an adequate standard of living and the security of stable income as the surest safeguard against social handicaps

XVI For every child protection against labor that stunts growth, either physical or mental, that limits education, that deprives children of the right of comradeship, of play, and of joy

XVII For every rural child as satisfactory schooling and health services as for the city child and an extension to rural families of social, recreational, and cultural facilities

XVIII To supplement the home and the school in the training of youth, and to return to them those interests of which modern life tends to cheat children, every stimulation and encouragement should be given to the extension and development of the voluntary youth organizations

XIX To make everywhere available these minimum protections of the health and welfare of children, there should be a district, county, or community organization for health, education, and welfare, with full-time officials, coordinating with a state-wide program which will be responsive to a nation-wide service of general information, statistics, and scientific research. This should include: a) Trained, full-time public health officials with public health nurses, sanitary inspection, and laboratory workers b) Available hospital beds c) Full-time public welfare service for the relief, aid, and guidance of children in special need due to poverty, misfortune, or behavior difficulties, and for the protection of children from abuse, neglect, exploitation or moral hazard

For every child these rights, regardless of race or color, or situation, wherever he may live under the protection of the American flag

PRIOR ASSESSMENTS

Despite the early and widespread interest in the well-being of children and youth, the first studies to focus specifically on children, rather than on families, did not appear until the 1960s. Since then, social scientists have begun to collect and analyze data specifically about children. Historical studies of child life provide insights into the period before 1960.[7] We begin by providing an assessment of national progress on each of these aims, using data from these studies and from decennial censuses and periodic surveys. The detailed information available in the 1980 and 1990 censuses allows us to document recent trends and race and gender differences in the living arrangements, activities, and economic well-being of children and youth. We use demographic methods to determine the extent to which differences in poverty among children of diverse racial/ethnic backgrounds result from disparities in family living arrangements and parental work patterns. We also detail ways in which the demographic and social situations of youth affect their family, work, and poverty experiences, providing readers with a historically informed and comprehensive overview of the situation of American children and youth, while drawing attention to their current unmet needs.[8] We conclude with a discussion of the public policies that might address these issues.

Changes in the economic opportunities for young persons have made it more difficult for a single earner to support a family with an adequate standard of living. The traditional marriage form in which a woman is a mother, wife, and homeworker while her husband is the primary breadwinner is a more difficult arrangement for young persons to sustain in the 1990s than it had been in past decades. This traditional family form is beyond the reach of many young American men who lack sufficient education to obtain secure and well-paying jobs (see Chapter 1 in Volume 1). Yet college-educated men, whose wives also tend to be well-educated, might be better able to afford this lifestyle. Many of these wives work, and because they are better paid than less-educated women had been in the past, they would experience a considerable loss in income were they to be full-time homemakers (see Chapter 3 in Volume 1). These two forces— downward pressures on the earnings potential of young men and expanded career goals of young women—result in a growing percentage of mothers, both married and unmarried, with preschool age children who are employed outside the home. This has given rise to the pervasive use of formal and informal childcare arrangements for children.

All of these trends have dramatically altered the experiences and activities of young adult Americans, with implications for their abilities to become the self-supporting and able parents of the next generation of American children. We document these changes and discuss their implications for the future of American children.

THE LIVES OF CHILDREN

Living Arrangements

Table 3.1 provides several indicators of change in the lives of American children since 1950. The changes in living arrangements are perhaps the most dramatic. The percentage of children living in two-parent families declined from 86 to 72 percent over 1950–1990. Only about 50 percent of American children in 1990 lived with both biological parents (down from 70 percent in 1950), and 22 percent live with one biological parent and a stepparent. In part, the increase in one-parent households results from an increase in the percentage of children who are born to single mothers—from 4 percent in 1950 to 26 percent in 1990 (Hernandez 1993: Table 3.4). The increased likelihood of parental separation and divorce accounts for the balance of the increase in single-parent households among all children.

This decline in two-parent families was not offset by increases in the number of other adults in the household. For example, between 1950 and 1980 the percentage of young persons who lived with a grandparent decreased from 12 to 6. Nor, by the 1980s, were grandparents substituting for an absent parent—only 9 percent of children living in a mother-headed household had a grandpar-

TABLE 3.1 Living arrangements and well-being of American children aged 0–17: 1950–1990.

	Year				
	1950	1960	1970	1980	Circa 1990
Living Arrangements					
Percentage with two-parent families (including stepparents)	86%	87%	82%	77%	72%
Percentage with two parents (not including stepparents)	70	71	65	57	51
Economic Well-Being					
Relative poverty[a]	27	24	23	24	27
Official poverty	48	26	16	16	20
Family Experience					
Average number of children per family	—	2.3	2.3	1.9	1.8
Percentage with parent having high school diploma or higher	—	—	62	74	80

SOURCES: *Current Population Reports*, Series P-20, Nos. 106, 218, 366, 447, 450; "Marital Status and Living Arrangements"; Bianchi (1990); Hernandez (1993).

[a]Percentage in families with income less than one-half the median family income.

ent living with them.[9] In general, even when co-residence with a grandparent occurs, it is of relatively short duration (Parish, Hao, and Hogan 1991).

Socioeconomic Environment In the Home

As a result of fewer two-parent households and fewer households in which a grandparent was present, average household size declined over the past decade or so. This trend was accelerated by decreases in the average number of children that women bore: per family the decline was from 2.3 to 1.8 between 1960 and 1990. But these modest declines in the number of siblings did little to counter the negative impact of changes in family structure and grandparent residence on child : adult ratios.

The educational environment of the homes in which children grow up has been improving over time. Children living with a parent with a high school diploma or higher went up from 62 percent in 1970 to 80 percent in 1990. This has translated into better educational attainment among the children, with 96 percent of those aged 14–17 enrolled in school in 1989, compared to 83 percent in 1950.[10] But even for children living in two-parent households, the smaller number of siblings and better education of parents did not translate inevitably into superior day-long socialization. Increasingly, married mothers with children, even those with children under age 6, were working (44 percent in 1970 to 59 percent in 1990). By 1990, 28 percent of children under age 6 had mothers who worked full-time, year-round, with this figure increasing to 40 percent for children aged 6–17.[11] During the 1980s, children under age 5 with working mothers were in daycare centers or preschool (24 percent), or cared for by non-relatives (22 percent) or by fathers or other relatives (40 percent).[12] By the mid-1980s about 14 percent of children aged 5–13 with mothers employed full-time were without adult supervision after school.[13] Although it may not be an inevitable feature of early and extensive maternal employment, some childcare arrangements now in place tend to be associated with poorer adjustment of children as they age, with children raised in daycare centers being more prone to noncompliant behavior.[14] However, regardless of any possible developmental consequences, many parents have chosen to raise their children in families in which the mother works—to help increase the family income or to further the mother's career.[15]

Some additional information helps to clarify the dilemma faced by many families. Between 1960 and 1988 the median household income per child increased (in 1989 $) from $4,332 to $7,250. But this income growth, excluding the earnings of women in the household, would have been only from $3,906 to $5,100 (an increase of 31 percent instead of 67 percent). The situation is even more dramatic if one looks at households in the lowest quartile of the income distribution. For these families the actual growth in household income per child was 49 percent, but if women in the household had not worked, the increase in real income per child would have been less than 1 percent (Fuchs and Reklis 1992: Table 3). Wetzel (Chapter 2 in Volume 1) shows that the earnings of men were largely stagnant (increasing only 5 percent) over the 1980s, with the earnings of male workers with less than a high school education declining by 18 percent. At the same time, women were able to increase their average annual earnings by 25 percent between 1979 and 1989, by increasing the number of hours they worked and through a 14 percent increase in their average hourly wage. Although these female earnings gains were concentrated among the better-educated, even women with less than a high school education were able to keep their average annual earnings from falling (Wetzel: Tables 2.5 and 2.6). Thus, the 1980s were a time in which families adapted to the unfavorable economic conditions facing young fathers through increased *maternal* employment.

Another benefit to families during the 1980s was the decline in the rate of inflation as it applied to the cost of raising a family. Between 1981 and 1989 the estimated average cost (in constant dollars) of raising a child from birth to age 18 in Midwestern areas increased by only 1 percent (to $105,055 in urban areas and $97,838 in rural areas).[16] In contrast, over the same period, the cost of a college education (in constant dollars) went up 29 percent in public 4-year colleges and 45 percent in private 4-year colleges.[17] Families thus faced another dilemma—it became even more critical that their children get a college education to successfully enter the labor market and, thereby, be better able to support their own families; but this change occurred at a time of dramatically increasing costs for education and relatively stagnant family incomes. As we shall see below, both parents and young adults have used a variety of strategies to respond to this challenge.

Children in Poverty

Trends in the official poverty rate for children during the period immediately after World War II initially were quite positive. The 1970 poverty rate of 16 percent was only one-third as high as the poverty rate in 1950 (48 percent), marking dramatic progress against child poverty. But the picture since then has been more discouraging. The poverty rate for children stopped declining in the 1970s, and then increased during the 1980s. Thus, even though many families were able to capitalize on improvements in parental education and the greater labor force participation of mothers to maintain the economic status of their children, for many other families these strategies were not available or not selected. This has led to increases in the proportion of children living in poverty (Bianchi, Chapter 3, Volume 1).

It is not surprising that public policy discussions of poverty center on how best to help children. The root of the problem is the increased percentage of children who have only one adult in their household at a time when two earners are increasingly necessary. Coupled with this, mothers who work full-time, year-round can expect to earn 36 percent less than fathers, making it difficult to support their families with the income level enjoyed by the average American child. Children have borne a disproportionate share of the cost of the American family revolution and the consequences of national economic restructuring (Fuchs and Reklis 1992; Haveman and Wolfe 1993).

The poverty rates of children around 1980 (before the most recent increase in child poverty in the United States) illustrate this—the posttax and transfer poverty rate of children in the United States was 17 percent, compared to 10 percent among Canadians, 8 percent in West Germany, and 5 percent in Sweden. When the poverty rates of children in two-parent families were examined, these differences were much more modest, and poverty rates were low—9 percent in the United States, 7 percent in Canada, and 5 percent in West Germany and Sweden. For one-parent families, half (51 percent) of all U.S. children were poor, compared to 39 percent of Canadians, 35 percent of the Germans, and 9 percent of the Swedes. In all of these nations except Sweden economic restructuring has made it difficult for a single parent to adequately support a family, but this problem is most severe in the United States.[18] That is, children in single-parent families have unusually high poverty rates compared to other developed Western European nations, but children in two-parent families do not. This situation has been exacerbated by the dramatic changes in the structure of American families, particularly the increasing proportion of our children that were in disadvantaged one-parent families.

Changing family structure and children's current and future economic well-being are inextricably linked. By the 1990s, one-parent families and family poverty were common. Roughly 1.5 million American children experience a parental divorce each year, and another 1.1 million are born outside of marriage. The costs to children are most easily measured in economic terms. For example, an increasing share of children live with their mothers in father-absent families, while the poverty rate of female-headed families was 46 percent in 1992.[19] American children today are nearly twice as likely as the elderly to be poor, and child poverty rates have increased over the past 15 years (Corbett 1993; Galston 1993). In 1992 the poverty rate among children was 22 percent, a rate of economic deprivation higher than in any year since the 1982 economic recession. Indeed, the number of poor children today—14.6 million—exceeds that of any year since 1965.[20]

The preponderance of scientific evidence suggests that one-parent families are disadvantaged relative to two-parent families, both because of their poverty and through the socioeconomic and developmental conditions in one-parent families. For example, based on the 15-year experiences of children under the age of 4 first observed in 1968, the American child living with only one parent will experience 7.2 years of poverty compared to an average of 0.8 years of poverty for children who live with two parents (Duncan and Rodgers 1991). The most common and immediate effect of parental divorce is a dramatic reduction in family income of the mother and her children. This decline in the standard of living places many families at risk of poverty when a parental divorce occurs. We have seen that nearly one-third of children in two-parent families live with stepparents. This reflects the high rates of parental remarriage among the children of divorce. In strictly economic terms, these children may benefit on average from having two potential earners, but there is little evidence that children in stepfamilies parallel children of intact families on various socioeconomic or developmental outcomes (e.g., school dropouts).[21]

The implications of child poverty, especially long-term or chronic poverty, are clear. Poor children are more likely than nonpoor children to be in ill health, to perform below average in school (i.e., have higher dropout rates), and to be economically disadvantaged as adults (Children's Defense Fund 1991). The current economic situation of American children portends an uncertain future as they grow into adulthood. Indeed, 1 in 7 children today—roughly 14.2 million— receive public assistance income in the form of AFDC. Although not all of these poor children will grow up to be poor adults who remain dependent on welfare and only marginally attached to the labor force, children raised in poverty are much more at risk of becoming inadequately employed, impoverished adults.

Race and Ethnic Variations in the Well-Being of Children: 1990

The Hoover Commission and prior research draw attention to many dimensions of children's lives. Central to all of the aspects of children's lives, however, is a two-parent family structure and an adequate family income. Data from the 1990 census show that differences on these two dimensions of family life— parental structure and income—represent increasingly important axes of racial inequality in American society (Cherlin 1992; Eggebeen and Lichter 1991). Declining marriage rates and increasing unmarried childbearing have eroded additional socioeconomic gains among certain disadvantaged racial minorities. Roughly two-thirds of black children are born outside of marriage, and a minority of black children currently reside in two-parent families. These children face an extraordinary high probability of poverty, even if compared with the children of divorce.[22] The situation of Puerto Rican children parallels that of blacks (Landale and Huann 1993). The apparently growing racial divergence in family structure implies that racial inequality—economic or otherwise—is exacerbated by current family demographic trends. Unfortunately, the situation is likely to grow worse as the current cohort of disadvantaged children reach adulthood and the effects of childhood poverty are fully manifested (Bianchi and McArthur 1991; Hernandez 1993).

Children's living arrangements. Recent changes in family structure, especially the rise in single-parent families, have placed a growing percentage of American children at risk of poverty and economic deprivation (Duncan and Rodgers 1991; Eggebeen and Lichter 1991). But to fully understand this risk, it is necessary to comprehend the great diversity in their living arrangements. Table 3.2 provides the distributions in 1980 and 1990 of all children in various living arrangements.

In the current period of rapid demographic change in American families, it is perhaps not appreciated that most children—72 percent—resided in two-parent families in 1990. Another 20 percent lived in families headed by their mothers, up from the 15 percent observed a decade earlier. And, although children living alone with fathers increased substantially on a percentage basis over the past decade, only 4 percent of children currently live with their fathers (i.e., in mother-absent families). The percentages of children living with other relatives, nonrelatives, in group quarters, or heading their own households are very small (about 4 percent overall). Despite children's increasing exposure to parental divorce (Bumpass 1984), and that over one-quarter of all births occur outside of marriage, the overwhelming majority of children still live in married-couple families. Of course, these families may include both biological parents or some combination of stepparents and adoptive parents. For some children, their family life course will be complex, living first with two parents, followed by a period in a mother-headed family, and then life in a reconstituted mother-stepfather household.

Although most American children live in married-couple families, racial and ethnic variations in children's living arrangements are substantial. Over 80 percent of white children reside in two-parent families. Only 37 percent of black children reside with both parents (Table 3.2), while nearly 50 percent live with their mothers in father-absent families. These figures are much higher than those of other historically disadvantaged groups. Among American Indians, for example, 30 percent live with their mothers and 56 percent live with two parents. Among Latinos, nearly two-thirds reside in married-couple families.

Although the living arrangements of Latinos are intermediate between those of whites and blacks—if measured in terms of percentages living in married-couple and female-headed families—wide variations exist across the various Latino groups. Puerto Rican children, for example, approximate the family circumstances of African Americans. About 45 percent reside in married-couple families, and 42 percent live with mothers only. Cubans, on the other hand, more closely resemble the circumstances of white children; nearly three-quarters live in married-couple families.

TABLE 3.2   Percentage of children aged 0–17, by family living arrangements: 1980 and 1990.

	Total		1990				
	1980	1990	White	Black	Latino	Asian	American Indian
Living With							
Both parents	76%	72%	81%	37%	64%	84%	56%
Father	2	4	3	6	6	3	7
Mother	15	20	13	49	24	9	30
Relatives	5	2	1	6	3	2	4
Other	2	2	2	3	3	2	3
Total	100	100	100	100	100	100	100

Economic well-being.   How best to measure the economic well-being, i.e., poverty status, of families and children remains a topic of continuing debate (Ruggles 1990; Jencks 1987). Absolute measures of poverty are based on whether family money income from all sources is below poverty income thresholds determined by an "economy" food plan for families of various sizes. The *official* measure of poverty has been criticized on a number of grounds, including its failure to accurately reflect equivalent income levels for families of various sizes, to account for the relative improvement in real income over time (i.e., the average income of the poor has increasingly fallen behind the average family income overall), and to adjust for a changing mix of goods that provides the basis for year-to-year adjustments for inflation in the poverty thresholds. Despite its problems, the official poverty rate has been frequently used in public policy debates, and it therefore provides an appropriate basis for much of the analysis and discussion provided here.

Evidence of a changing age profile of poverty and low income in the United States is unequivocal (Easterlin 1987; Preston 1984). In 1969 the poverty rate among the elderly was well in excess of that of children, but by 1992 the elderly were underrepresented among the poor, while children experienced disproportionately high rates of poverty. Moreover, American children in the bottom quintile of the family income distribution experienced absolute declines in real income, while those at the top experienced real increases in (family size-adjusted) income.[23] The income gap between America's poorest and wealthiest children widened during the 1980s.

Our analysis, based on the 1980 and 1990 censuses, indicates that the poverty rate increased from 16 to 18 percent (Table 3.3, top two rows). And although poverty increased for all racial and ethnic groups during the 1980s, economic disparities among children remain very large. Whites had a poverty rate of 11 percent, for example, while the rate was 39 percent among blacks and American Indians and 31 percent among the Spanish-origin population. Among the various

Latino groups, Cubans had the lowest rate (14 percent), while the poverty rate among Puerto Rican children was over 40 percent. Nearly one-third of Mexican American children were poor, using the official government definition.

Table 3.3 also provides the median family income-to-poverty ratio in 1989 for each racial and ethnic group. A median income-to-poverty ratio of 1.0 means that average income for a specific group is exactly equal to the poverty threshold. A ratio of 2.0 means that median income is twice that of the poverty threshold. This ratio provides an easily interpreted summary measure of the extent to which various demographic groups exceed the poverty threshold. It also provides a family-size adjusted measure of income.

Overall, the median family income of American children was two-and-one-half times the poverty threshold. White children fared best with a ratio of 2.8, while black and American Indian children were only slightly above the poverty threshold on average (income-to-poverty ratio of 1.4 and 1.3, respectively). Asian children and some Latino groups, such as Cubans (data not shown), had median income-to-poverty ratios that were very similar to those of whites.

These child poverty rates and the income-to-poverty ratios also vary substantially by family living arrangements. The poverty rate among children living with both parents was only 9 percent and the income-to-poverty ratio was 2.9. On the other hand, children living with mothers only had a poverty rate of 46 percent, and an income-to-poverty ratio of 1.1. The economic deprivation experienced by children living with their mothers is substantially greater than for those living with their fathers only or with other relatives. There is a widespread misconception that children living with their fathers (in mother-absent families) do quite well economically (i.e., that their fathers have physical custody of children because they are economically well-off). These children are more often poor than those in two-parent families but less often than those who live only with their mothers.

Thus, the family living arrangements of children vary substantially across racial and ethnic groups. And the economic situations of these groups differ, implying a link between family living arrangements and economic deprivation. The problem is in determining whether economic deprivation undermines traditional family arrangements (i.e., married-couple families), or whether marital instability and nonmarital fertility exacerbate or even create the disadvantaged circumstances of some racial and ethnic minorities. This is a question of cause and effect that cannot be fully reconciled here.[24] But we can provide data that illuminate this issue as well as the extent to which racial and ethnic inequality in family income is located in patterns of family structure.

The link between family living arrangements and child poverty.   Recent studies indicate that changing family structure is only weakly linked to changes in poverty for the entire population (Bane 1986), but that it is strongly associ-

TABLE 3.3   Poverty rates and median income-to-poverty ratios of children aged 0–17, by family living arrangements: 1990.

	Total	White	Black	Latino	Asian	American Indian
Poverty Rate, 1979	16	10	37	29	15	23
Poverty Rate, 1989	18	11	39	31	17	39
Living With						
Both parents	9	6	15	22	14	25
Father	23	15	34	33	20	49
Mother	46	34	57	55	39	60
Relatives	34	21	47	36	35	46
Standardized Poverty Rate,[a] 1989	—	11	22	27	18	31
Median Income-to-Poverty Ratio, 1989	2.5	2.8	1.4	1.6	2.9	1.3
Living With						
Both parents	2.9	3.0	2.3	1.9	3.1	1.8
Father	2.0	2.4	1.5	1.4	2.4	1.1
Mother	1.1	1.5	.8	.9	1.5	.8
Relatives	1.5	2.0	1.0	1.4	1.9	1.1

[a]White children used as a standard.

ated with poverty among children at a specific time point (Duncan 1991; Eggebeen and Lichter 1991). For example, Eggebeen and Lichter showed that changing family structure accounted for roughly 50 percent of the rise in child poverty during the 1980s.[25] Family structure cannot be disassociated from children's current economic circumstances.

This point is supported by the data presented in Table 3.3, which gives poverty rates for groups of children distinguished by racial/ethnic background and family living arrangements. These data suggest several general points. First, for each racial/ethnic group, poverty rates were highest and median income-to-poverty ratios were lowest for children living with mothers only. For black and American Indian children, poverty rates among children living without their fathers were exceptionally high, often exceeding 50 percent. These high poverty rates are particularly unsettling because they persist at a time when an increasing share of American children live with their mothers. This is especially apparent among black children, where the large majority lived in female-headed families rather than with both parents.

Second, the results nevertheless indicate that poverty rates were highest for blacks and American Indians *regardless of children's family living arrangements*. The obvious implication is that racial/ethnic differences in family structure are not solely responsible for racial differences in children's economic well-being. Promoting two-parent families will reduce but not eliminate the child poverty problem for racial minorities. Indeed, for children living with both parents, the poverty rates varied from a low of 6 percent for whites to a high of 25 percent for American Indians. These are large differences by any standard.

Third, family living arrangements provide a more important axis of economic differentiation for some racial/ethnic groups than for others. Among whites, for example, the poverty rate for children living with mothers only was 5.5 times greater than that for children living with both parents. Among African American children, the children living with mothers were 3.9 times more likely to be poor than those children living with both parents. The differences were smaller yet among Mexicans, for whom children living with mothers were 2.2 times more likely to be poor than their counterparts living with both parents (data not shown).

Although the link between children's living arrangements and poverty is strong, the exceptionally high poverty rates observed among historically disadvantaged groups cannot be reduced to a "family question." This point is illustrated succinctly using demographic methods of direct standardization (Shyrock and Siegel 1976). Simply, what would the child poverty rates be if children from the various racial and ethnic groups experienced the family living arrangements of whites (i.e., had the same proportions living with both parents)? The answer is provided in Table 3.3, which gives poverty rates that are standardized for family living arrangements.

Actual child poverty rates varied from a low of 11 percent for whites to a high of 39 percent for blacks and American Indians (see line 2 of Table 3.3). But if black children had the same family living arrangements as whites, but experienced their own status-specific poverty rates (i.e., the poverty rate for children living in married-couple families, etc., as shown in Table 3.3), the poverty rate would drop to 22 percent. The ratio of the standardized-to-observed poverty rates is .56, i.e., $22/39 = .56$, which means that poverty rates among black children would be 44 percent lower if their living arrangements were like those of white children. The remainder of the difference in childhood poverty is due to the fact that blacks in each family living arrangement have higher poverty rates than whites in the same family living arrangements. In 1960, black-white differences in family structure accounted for virtually none of the black-white difference in child poverty.[26] Changes in the family structure (i.e., the rise in female-headed families) are significant factors accounting for racial inequality in children's economic well-being.

The large adverse economic effects of single-parent family structures are also apparent for Puerto Rican children (data not shown). The child poverty rate would drop from 40 percent to 25 percent—nearly a 40 percent decline—if Puerto Rican children had family living arrangements that were similar to those of white children. The effects of family structure are less salient for other Lat- inos and American Indians, though the greater proportion of single-parent fami- lies in these groups increases poverty somewhat. Asians present an interesting contrast, however. Their family situations actually reduce poverty below levels that would be experienced were they to have family patterns like the whites (since a larger proportion of Asian than white children live with both parents— the family living arrangement with the lowest poverty rates).

Thus, racial differences in the family structure, especially between black and white children, are cause for policy concern because they erode recent progress toward racial economic equality. Welfare policy and antipoverty legislation can no longer ignore the family question. Yet, 39 percent (i.e., 11 of 28 percentage points difference) of the excess poverty of black children is unaccounted for by differences in family structure. And differences in family structure account for only a small portion of the higher poverty rates of most Latino and American Indian children. Although the effects of family structure cannot be downplayed, policies that promote the two-parent family, if successful, will not completely eliminate racial differences in poverty or economic deprivation in America. We next turn to a consideration of another factor that plays a major role in race and ethnic variations in child poverty—the access of parents to earned income.

Parental work patterns and children's economic well-being.   Recognizing that recent changes in family structure are unlikely to be reversed any time soon, many policymakers now view participation in paid work as the only sure solution to family poverty. The JOBS provision of the 1988 Family Support Act views work as a potential panacea to the poverty problem—especially among single mothers and their children. To what extent are variations in parental em- ployment patterns responsible for differentials in child poverty across various racial and ethnic groups?

Table 3.4 provides the distribution of children living in families distinguished by various living arrangements and work patterns. In 1990 only 23 percent of American children lived in the so-called traditional family, one comprising a father employed full-time and a mother not in the labor force. In 1990 a more common pattern (25 percent) was one in which children lived with two full- time working parents. Another 17 percent included a father working full-time and a mother employed part-time (fewer than 35 hours per week). Most children now grow up with one or both parents working. In 1990 only about 9 percent of American children lived in a family in which their parent(s) did not work.

The traditional family is much less evident among certain racial and ethnic minorities. Whereas 26 percent of white children lived with a full-time em- ployed father and a nonemployed mother, only 7 percent of African American children had this arrangement. The percentages are also low for American Indi- ans (15 percent) and among certain Latino groups. Asian children, on the other

TABLE 3.4   Percentage of children, aged 0–17, by parental work patterns and family living arrangements: 1990.

	Total	White	Black	Latino	Asian	American Indian
Living With						
Both parents						
Both full-time	25%	27%	18%	20%	36%	19%
Father full-time, mother part-time	17	21	7	11	12	10
Father part-time, mother full-time	3	2	3	3	3	3
Both part-time	2	2	2	3	2	4
Father full-time only	23	26	7	23	21	15
Father part-time only	3	2	2	4	4	5
Mother full-time only	1	1	1	1	1	2
Mother part-time only	1	1	1	1	0	1
Neither in labor force	2	1	2	3	8	3
Single-Parent Families						
Father						
Full-time	3	3	3	4	2	3
Part-time	1	1	1	1	0	2
Not in labor force	1	0	1	1	1	2
Mother						
Full-time	9	7	20	9	4	12
Part-time	5	3	13	5	2	8
Not in labor force	7	4	20	12	4	13
Total	100	100	100	100	100	100

hand, had the highest percentage living with two full-time employed parents (36 percent). This contrasts with a low of 14 percent among Puerto Rican children.

The modal pattern for African American children is one of living with a mother who was not employed, but with an absent father (20 percent) or in a mother-only family where the mother worked full-time. For Puerto Ricans the modal pattern (28 percent) was for children to live with mothers who did not work. A different story emerges, however, if the distribution of work patterns is considered separately for married-couple families, father-headed families, and mother-headed families (Table 3.5). For all children in married couple families, about one-third had two parents who worked full-time. Almost one-quarter more had a father who worked full-time and a mother who worked part-time. Another 30 percent lived in families in which only the father worked full-time. Clearly, in two-parent families, full-time work by the father characterizes the lives of children (85 percent of the time), and a working mother is the statistical norm.

The pattern is much different for single-parent families. Among children liv-

TABLE 3.5   Percentage of children, aged 0–17, by parental work patterns within types of family living arrangements: 1990.

	Total	White	Black	Latino	Asian	American Indian
Living With						
Both parents						
Both full-time	33%	32%	44%	29%	41%	31%
Father full-time, mother part-time	23	25	17	16	14	16
Father part-time, mother full-time	3	3	7	4	3	6
Both part-time	3	2	4	4	3	6
Father full-time only	30	31	17	34	24	24
Father part-time only	4	3	4	6	4	8
Mother full-time only	1	1	3	2	2	3
Mother part-time only	1	1	1	1	1	2
Neither in labor force	2	2	4	4	0	6
Total	100	100	100	100	100	100
Single-Parent Families						
Father						
Full-time	68%	75%	57%	65%	68%	47%
Part-time	18	16	23	22	13	26
Not in labor force	13	10	21	14	19	27
Total	100	100	100	100	100	100
Mother						
Full-time	44%	52%	37%	34%	44%	36%
Part-time	22	21	25	20	17	23
Not in labor force	34	27	38	46	39	41
Total	100	100	100	100	100	100

ing with their fathers only, for example, the fathers worked full-time in about two-thirds of the cases. The mothers worked full-time in only 44 percent of the mother-headed families, while 34 percent were not in the labor force. In part, the lower employment rate of single parents is associated with the presence of young children and the attendant difficulties in childcare. It is not surprising that the children of single-parent homes experience a disproportionate share of child poverty in America. They are less likely to have a parent who works, and they lack access to the larger incomes provided by two working parents. This has undoubtedly contributed to the growing reliance on public transfer income (as opposed to earnings) among children living with their mothers.[27]

Patterns of racial variation in parental work are not always fully appreciated. Perhaps the most striking result is found among black children in two-parent families. Among the racial/ethnic groups considered, black children had the highest percentage in which both parents worked full-time: 44 percent compared to 32 percent among whites. The problem resides in the low percentage of black children who are in two-parent families and, as we see next, the lower labor force participation by black single parents.

Indeed, the parental work patterns of blacks living with both parents contrasts markedly with those of black children living alone with their mothers. Only 37 percent of the mothers of these black children worked full-time, a figure much lower than that of whites (52 percent). Overall, Latino children—especially Puerto Ricans—were most likely to have a mother who was not in the labor force.

The story here is clearly one of considerable racial and ethnic variation in parental work patterns. These patterns exacerbate—along with changing family living arrangements—the economic hardships faced by historically disadvantaged racial and minority groups. This is especially difficult for black children who, because their parents have lower average earnings, need the earnings of two parents to rise above poverty. Instead, they typically have only one parent, and that parent often is not employed. Indeed, as shown in Table 3.6, nearly 60 percent of children in two-parent families were poor if neither parent was in the labor force. The poverty rates were 54 and 75 percent, respectively, for children of nonworking single fathers and mothers.

The lowest child poverty rates in married-couple families were observed when both parents worked full-time (2 percent) or when the father worked full-time and the mother worked part-time (5 percent). Even if only the father worked full-time (and the mother was not in the labor force), the poverty rate was 10 percent. This is lower than the poverty rate for children living alone with fathers who worked full-time (13 percent). It is also considerably lower than that of children who lived alone with mothers working full-time (19 percent). The implication, of course, is that marital instability (and nonmarital fertility) is in part selective of those with the least economic security (i.e., hold full-time jobs that pay poorly).

Table 3.6 also provides these poverty rates, disaggregated by parental work status, for children of various racial and ethnic backgrounds. Clearly, poverty among U.S. children would be greatly reduced if every child lived in a two-parent family, and if both parents worked full-time.[28] On the other hand, historical disadvantages in job security and wage rates of minority workers, coupled with their larger family sizes, mean that even when family structure and employment patterns are the same, their income often is inadequate. For example, the rates of child poverty in two-parent families in which the father was the traditional breadwinner was 7 percent for whites, 21 percent for blacks, and 25 percent for Latinos and American Indians. Even when minority families included two parents working full-time, their children could not fully escape the legacy of economic disadvantage. Only 2 percent of white children in these families were in poverty compared to 4 percent of black children, 7 percent of

TABLE 3.6   Percentage of children in poverty aged 0–17, by parental work patterns and family living arrangements: 1990.

	Total	White	Black	Latino	Asian	American Indian
Living With						
Both parents						
Both full-time	2%	2%	4%	7%	3%	9%
Father full-time, mother part-time	5	3	12	13	6	15
Father part-time, mother full-time	10	7	14	23	8	23
Both part-time	23	17	38	38	32	49
Father full-time only	10	7	21	25	9	23
Father part-time only	38	32	50	52	49	57
Mother full-time only	16	13	16	32	11	33
Mother part-time only	37	33	43	44	46	67
Neither in labor force	58	52	63	65	67	71
Single-Parent Families						
Father						
Full-time	13	8	20	23	8	25
Part-time	37	29	45	45	34	67
Not in labor force	54	45	60	61	53	74
Mother						
Full-time	19	14	28	25	13	29
Part-time	55	43	66	59	36	69
Not in labor force	75	68	80	76	70	83

Latinos, and 9 percent of American Indians. The racial disparity in working poverty also is evident among children living in families with their fathers or mothers only (panels 2 and 3 of Table 3.6).

This point is made clearly with poverty rates standardized for work status of parents provided in Table 3.7. In this analysis, we calculate child poverty rates for each racial/ethnic minority based on the assumption that the parental work experiences are similar to those of white children's parents. We also provide the ratio of the standardized poverty rate to the actual poverty rate. Ratios of less than 1.0 indicate that the parental work patterns contribute to differentially higher poverty among the specific minority populations.

The data indicate the surprisingly small role parental differences in paid employment play in race and ethnic variation in child poverty. Among children living with both parents, the standardized rates were only slightly lower than observed rates because there are few race and ethnic variations in employment patterns of parents in two-parent families. Indeed, among black children living with both parents, the standardized and observed poverty rates are equal. This means that these black children, as an ongoing legacy of racial disadvantage,

TABLE 3.7 Poverty rates of children aged 0–17, standardized by work patterns of
white parents: 1990.

	Both Parents		Father	
	Standardized Rate	Standardized to Observed Ratio	Standardized Rate	Standardized to Observed Ratio
Race and Ethnicity				
Black	15%	1.0	28%	.8
Latino	18	.8	30	.9
Asian	9	.7	16	.8
American Indian	19	.8	36	.7
White Poverty Rate	6	1.0	15	1.0

[a] Standardized by work patterns and family living arrangements of whites.

would have poverty rates that were 2.4 times greater than their white counter-parts (15 versus 6 percent), *even if both of their parents had work patterns that were identical to those of white parents.* Among Latinos, the poverty rate would decline from 22 to 18 percent if work patterns mirrored those of whites. Work patterns of parents accounted for about 25 percent of white–Latino difference in child poverty. For American Indians, the parental work patterns accounted for about one-third of racial difference in child poverty.

Findings are different for children living with single parents. Among black children living with their mothers in father-absent families, the poverty rate would decline from 57 percent to 50 percent if black children's mothers had the same work patterns as the mothers of white children. Black–white differences in mothers' employment patterns account for nearly one-third of the black–white difference in poverty rates among children living with their mothers (i.e., 7 of the observed 23 percentage point black–white difference in poverty rates).

Family structure and parental employment are major factors accounting for the higher levels of child poverty among racial and ethnic minorities. Child poverty among blacks, whites, and Asians would be virtually eliminated if all children lived in two-parent families where both parents worked. Neither a change in either family structure nor a change in employment patterns would be sufficient to eliminate poverty. Changes in both, however, would go a long way towards reducing the poverty of all racial and ethnic groups (including that of whites).

On the other hand, even if the family and employment patterns of minority groups came to resemble those of whites, substantial race and ethnic differences in poverty would remain. Table 3.7 (last two columns) provides poverty rates standardized for the joint family-work distribution of white children's parents. If black children lived in two-parent families in the same proportions as whites and had parents exhibiting work patterns similar to those of whites, poverty

	Mother		Total[a]	
	Standardized Rate	Standardized to Observed Ratio	Standardized Rate	Standardized to Observed Ratio
Race and Ethnicity				
Black	50%	.9	20%	.5
Latino	46	.8	22	.7
Asian	33	.9	13	.8
American Indian	52	.9	24	.6
White Poverty Rate	34	1.0	11	1.0

rates among black children would still be nearly double those of whites (20 vs. 11 percent), but the poverty rate for blacks would be only one-half what it actually was in 1990. Poverty rates among Latinos would be more than double those of whites even with the elimination of differences in family and work patterns. The role of both family structure and employment cannot be discounted in explaining the high rates of poverty among these children, but other factors (e.g., low earnings) are also at work.

Age Variations in Children's Experiences

The developmental consequences of living in a single-parent family, experiencing family poverty, or residing in a family without a employed parent vary for children of different ages. Young preschool children, for example, may be most adversely affected by living with a single parent or with one who is working outside the home (Garfinkel and McLanahan 1986). From the parents' viewpoint, preschool children most often are seen as needing in-home care, which places serious constraints on work for at least one parent. We cannot address all of these complex factors, but we can show the extent to which there are age differences in these relationships for children in 1990.

The family living arrangements varied only slightly for children of different ages, although racial differences were substantial. For all preschoolers (aged less than 6), 73 percent resided with both parents, a pattern remarkably similar to that of children aged 7–12 and 13–17. Whether married-couple families of older children include a stepparent is another matter, however. Younger children were more likely to be living with their biological parents, while older children were more likely to be living with one biological and one stepparent. The majority (52 percent) of black children aged 6 or younger lived without a co-residential father. The uniqueness of the status of blacks is seen by comparing their percent to the national figure: 12 percent of preschoolers in father-absent homes.

Younger children have higher rates of poverty because (1) their parent(s) are on average younger and therefore face higher rates of unemployment and labor force nonparticipation, and, if employed, earn lower wages, and (2) a higher percentage of young children in single-mother families result from nonmarital fertility rather than from divorce, and the poverty rates among never-married mothers are higher on average than among ever-married mothers (Macunovich and Easterlin 1990). The 1990 census reveals that 20 percent of preschoolers were poor contrasted to a poverty rate of 18 percent among 6–12 year olds, and 16 percent among those aged 13–17. Regardless of whether children live with both parents or one parent, poverty rates declined with age of the child.

More substantial age differences are observed among children living with their mothers in father-absent families. Preschoolers living with their mothers experienced a poverty rate of 53 percent. The rate among adolescents is about one-third lower, although it was still high (36 percent). Young children living alone with their mothers thus are among the most economically disadvantaged groups in America. This is especially evident among certain racial and ethnic minorities. The poverty rate among black preschoolers living with their mothers was 61 percent (data not shown). Among American Indians and Latinos, the poverty rates were 67 and 59 percent, respectively. To the extent that poverty during early childhood has long-term negative effects on physical and emotional development, these high rates of poverty for young children in mother-headed minority families present a troublesome picture of child poverty in America.

Labor force participation rates have typically been relatively low for married women with young children who require substantial care. Indeed, for children living with both parents, 37 percent had a father working full-time and a mother who was not in the paid labor force (i.e., a homemaker). But even for young children, over 50 percent had two parents who worked at least part-time. Among older children, this figure approached 70 percent.

Substantial age variation in maternal employment also exists for children living with their mothers in father-absent families (data not shown). Among those aged 0–5, 45 percent were living with nonworking mothers. This contrasts with 31 and 24 percent among children age 6–12 and 13–17, respectively. These substantial age differences in maternal work patterns contributed to the disproportionately high rates of poverty experienced by preschoolers. Indeed, for all children with a nonworking unmarried mother, the poverty rate was 75 percent, a figure well in excess of the poverty rate of 19 percent among children living with a mother working full-time.

Growing Up in the American Family

American children and adolescents grow up with a variety of family experiences. A majority have two parents. But for many, one of these parents is a stepparent, while others are growing up in a single-parent family. Patterns of cohabitation and remarriage mean that many young people see their parents dating or living with a person of the opposite sex. They observe the employment patterns of their parents—who works, the kinds of jobs held, and the wages earned. Parents typically have aspirations for their children's educational and occupational attainments and for their family formation. These parental desires, as well as the parental behaviors that children and adolescents observe, influence but do not determine what their children will do as they make the transition to adulthood (Hogan 1985). As a result of this greater diversity in parent behaviors, children and youth enjoy considerably more autonomy and have more choices about school and work and about sexual behavior and family ties than prior cohorts of young persons did.

But these young people also face different social and economic circumstances and opportunities in 1990 than their parents faced in the 1960s and 1970s. Continued schooling is more important for economic success today than in the past. Persons with less education find it difficult to form and support a family. Increasingly, human capital investments and career achievements are critical to successful family life. As we have seen, many of the poor, preschool children documented above are the products of marriages in which the father earns an inadequate income to support the family or the mother is head of a one-parent household. In order to understand the social reproduction of poor families from one cohort to the next, we must understand how American children become adults, and the effects of these histories for the living arrangements and welfare of their children. This is the subject we now address.

THE LIVES OF YOUNG ADULTS

The early adult years are a time of dramatic change in the lives of young Americans, as childhood gives way to the assumption of adult roles (Hogan and Astone 1986). They leave home, establish their own households, and occupy different and often transitory adult roles that bear on well-being (e.g., employment). For example, a young person in poverty at ages 18–24 may be temporarily poor because of enrollment in school and the lack of a full-time job; poverty is expected to end as this transitory period passes. Or poverty may be coincident with single motherhood, which means that low income may be a longer-term reality. During these ages, the socioeconomic well-being of young adults becomes less contingent on that of their parents and more a function of their own activities. The fates of parents and children are connected because the socioeconomic resources that 18 year olds bring to their lives are a heritage of the families in which they grew up. And the family life and economic accomplishments of these young adults as they become parents determine the likelihood that their children will be in poverty.

Thus, as young persons grow up to become adults, a variety of life changes occur that eventually transform their lives. This process is strongly embedded in American culture and is expected by our major institutions. These changes are often different for young men and women. But as gender roles have changed, most young people—both men and women—complete school, take a job, and establish their own residences as part of growing up. The nature and timing of these transitions, however, depend on the educational opportunities available, on the creation of new jobs through retirements and economic growth, and on adequate income levels to afford housing (Hogan 1981). This also is the time in life when family building—marriage and childbearing—typically begins. Such decisions are influenced by the economic attractiveness of men as husbands, by the economic costs of family roles to women, and by attitudes about the desirability of marriage and the acceptability of single motherhood. Military service remains an important feature of young adulthood for many men and for increasing numbers of women. The 1980s was the first decade since World War II in which such military service was voluntary, and there were no major wartime demands for military manpower. This decade, then, was the first in which other roles (like marriage) became reasonably compatible with military service. Here we use the 1990 census to examine how the likelihood of each of these activities changes with age, and the ways in which roles are combined for young persons to become adults.

Young Adults in 1990

There were 4.5 million Americans aged 18–24 in 1990, a 24 percent decrease from 1980. The proportion of the total population in these young adult years also declined, from 13 percent in 1980 to 11 percent in 1990. This decline in the absolute and relative size of the young adult population is a result of the aging of the baby boom cohorts, and their succession by the smaller cohorts born during the low fertility years of 1966–1972. There was an approximate balance in the number of males and females aged 18–24 in 1990, with a sex ratio of 104 men for every 100 women.

These data have social implications. Because these cohorts are smaller than in the past, young adults in the 1990s will have less influence on the cultural styles, patterns of consumption, and political affairs of the nation than young persons had in the past. But these cohorts also tend to face less competition for schooling and jobs compared to bigger cohorts of young adults in the past (such as the baby boomers during the 1960s and 1970s). The decline in average family size over recent decades also means less competition from siblings for parental support and assistance. Basic demographic changes suggest that these young adults should have relatively good resources and a variety of opportunities as they enter adult roles.

Such a conclusion assumes that the social origins, skills, and experiences that

TABLE 3.8   Characteristics of persons aged 18–24, by race and ethnicity: 1980 and 1990.

			Race and Ethnicity			
Characteristics	Total	White	Black	Latino	Asian	American Indian
Population (percent distribution)						
1980	100%	77%	13%	8%	2%	1%
1990	100	71	14	12	3	1
Percentage Foreign-Born						
1980	7	3	4	38	62	2
1990	9	2	4	42	70	2
Percentage Resident in State of Birth						
1980	64	66	71	47	28	66
1990	63	66	72	41	17	70
Percentage with High School Diploma						
1980	82	85	73	61	86	66
1990	84	88	77	62	90	71
Percentage of Women with One or More Children Ever Born						
1980	29	25	44	40	20	49
1990	26	22	41	38	12	44
Percentage with Disability or Limitation						
1980	4	4	5	3	2	6
1990	6	5	10	7	6	10

young people bring to early adulthood have remained unchanging over time, and that the market demand for this human capital has not changed. Neither of these statements is accurate for young adults in the 1990s. As shown in Chapter 1 in Volume One, the pay of unskilled workers is inadequate to support a family, and the demand for better-paying skilled blue-collar labor has declined. The best strategy for a young adult during the 1980s to succeed financially was to invest in higher education (see Chapter 4 in Volume One). At the same time, rising levels of marital instability and divorce, the resulting one-parent families, and the inability of many single parents to provide adequate incomes for their families resulted in many young persons bringing disadvantageous family origins to college and the labor market. Earlier cohorts of young adults had benefited from successive increases in the educational level of the household heads, from decreases in farm origins, and from smaller numbers of siblings. But these historical sources of improving social origins did not continue apace during the 1980s (Hernandez 1993), removing factors in the improved social mobility of successive cohorts that had been effective for more than half a century. Thus, when it is economically vital that young adults earn college degrees, their ability to do so is uncertain. There are many strategies for disadvantaged young adults to attend college. These include working while in college, financial aid, and reducing costs by living at home.[29] Of course, early marriage and parenthood and especially single parenthood make this process even more difficult, and such events are far from rare, as shown by McLanahan and Casper (Chapter 1). In studying the lives of young adults in the United States we document how these competing factors play out in the lives of men and women. We also indicate how these personal histories are modified by such experiences as disability, interstate migration, and military service.

Race and ethnicity. In order to understand changes in the lives of young adults between 1980 and 1990, it is essential to note the dramatic changes in race and ethnic composition. Young Americans became much more ethnically and racially diverse over the 1980s (Table 3.8). In 1980, 77 percent of persons aged 18–24 were white. This declined to 71 percent in 1990, a remarkable change over a single decade. The biggest share of the growth in minorities was accounted for by the rapid growth of the Latino and Asian groups. By 1990, the number of young adults who were Latino was approaching that of blacks; and Latinos can be expected to exceed blacks by early in the twenty-first century (Hernandez 1993). While the overall size of the Asian population remains small, their proportion in the population of young adults more than doubled over the 1980s. But significant proportions of the most rapidly growing minorities—Asians and Latinos—are foreign-born, and this percentage has increased over time. By 1990, 70 percent of Asian and 42 percent of Latino young adults were foreign-born (Table 3.8).

For the first time since the 1920s the United States is faced with the task of integrating foreign-born young adults into its educational, labor market, and political institutions. Most of these foreign-born young adults have at least fair mastery of the English language, often because they migrated here as children. But a significant minority in each ethnic group—10 percent of the Asian and 22 percent of the Latino young adults—reported that their English language abilities were poor. This is a serious obstacle to their advanced schooling, and often a handicap in job-seeking.

While the migration experiences of the foreign-born are key to understanding the lives of Latinos and Asians, for whites and blacks geographic stability is the most common experience (Table 3.8). More than two-thirds of young whites and blacks enter their adult years living in their state of birth. This means that, for the majority of young adults, their birth, family life, schooling, and entry into adult roles occur in the same state. It is worthy of note by policymakers—the skill and quality of the adult workforce in a state is closely tied to the human capital investments that the state makes in its children and young adults. Most notable is the extent to which this is true even of some of the most recent immigrant groups. While Latinos are growing in numbers due to immigration, 58 percent of the Latino young adults were born in the United States, and 41 percent became adults in states where they were born and grew up.

Physical limitation and disability. Inadequate family socioeconomic origins, cultural differences, and economic discrimination are all factors that can influence the economic success of young adults. A different, but highly salient, barrier to assuming independent adult roles is disability. Overall, 94 percent of young persons lack any disability or limitation. But this means that more than 250,000 young persons (6 percent of all young persons) report that they are disabled, have a personal care or a mobility limitation. Although many of these persons may have special needs or challenges, 77 percent report that they can work. Of the 40,000 young adults who report that they cannot work because of a disability, half say that their disabilities do not create personal care or mobility limitations.

The census provides a unique and valuable resource for understanding how disability affects the lives of these young Americans.[30] Birth defects, poor preventive health care, poor access to medical care for the treatment of acute and chronic disease, and accidents and violence are all factors in the number of young men and women with limitations or disabilities. This leads us to expect that limitations and disabilities will be most common among American Indians, blacks, and Latinos. Blacks and American Indians report disabilities or limitations twice as often as whites do (Table 3.8). Despite their poverty and immigrant status in 1990, Latinos had rates of disability or limitation in young adulthood only slightly higher than whites.

Socioeconomic origins. Because many persons aged 18–24 have left the homes in which they grew up, we cannot describe socioeconomic *origins* with certainty. Nor, because many of these persons are still in school and have not yet entered the labor force, can we describe their socioeconomic accomplishments in the same way as one would older adults. The situation is further complicated by the strong age variations in each of these behaviors during this part of the lifetime. The best indicator that we have of the socioeconomic resources that these young people bring to the transition to adulthood is whether or not they have earned a high school diploma.[31]

There are substantial race and ethnic differences in the likelihood of having this basic educational credential (Table 3.8). By this measure, Asians and whites are best prepared for the assumption of adult roles, with more than 88 percent holding diplomas. Three-quarters of blacks are also high school graduates, indicating the narrowing of this once large racial disadvantage. American Indians and Latinos lag far behind. Almost 40 percent of Latinos lack high school diplomas as they enter adulthood. As Mare and Levy show in their chapters in Volume One, this lack of a high school diploma limits their potential for higher education and hampers their entry into the American workforce. While language and migration experiences play some part in this, the contrasting experiences of the Asian immigrants suggest that the picture is more complex, relating to parental decisions about investment in their children's education, the value placed by families on educational attainment, and opportunities for an adequate education.

Activities of Young Adults

Young adults' activities relate to their eventual assumption of adult career and family roles.[32] These include activities that improve the human capital of a young person—enrollment in college or other post-high school training, service in the military, and work for pay in the labor force. They also include actions relating to family life—living independently of the family in which they grew up, and getting married. Particularly salient for young women is whether they have become mothers. The census data are excellent for determining a young person's current situation.

The percentage of young persons of different ages engaged in several activities in 1990 is shown in Table 3.9. These activities are strongly age-related, becoming increasingly or decreasingly common with age. Some people are engaged in these activities at every age, although this can be a very small number, as with military service or marriage at age 18. Other activities are quite common at certain ages. For example, three-quarters of those aged 18 live at home, and three-quarters are enrolled in school. Three-quarters of those aged 23 and 24 work full-time.

Each person who lives from his or her 18th to 25th birthday will experience

TABLE 3.9   Percentage of persons aged 18–24 engaged in various activities, by age: 1990.

Age	Activity				
	School	Work	Military	Live at Home	Married
18	74%	48%	1%	74%	4%
19	58	56	3	58	7
20	49	62	3	50	12
21	43	65	3	44	18
22	33	70	3	39	24
23	24	73	3	34	31
24	20	76	2	28	37
Person Years in Activity, 18–24	3.0	4.5	0.2	3.3	1.4

FIGURE 3.1   Person years in activity, aged 18–24: 1980 and 1990.

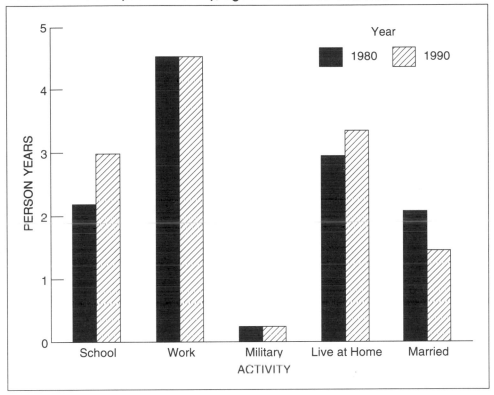

7 years of life at ages 18–24. During this time each individual could spend up to a maximum of 7 years in that activity. By looking at the average experiences of persons at ages 18 through age 24 in 1990, and summing these experiences over the ages, we can develop a picture of the life of a hypothetical person during this part of the life course.[33] This allows us to infer the amount of time a typical young person spent in each activity, and each combination of activities, from ages 18–24. This method assumes that a typical person becoming an adult at the conclusion of the twentieth century will have the same experiences at a given age as persons that age had in 1990.

Of the 7 person-years spent at ages 18–24, young Americans in 1990 spent an average of 4.5 years working, and 3.0 years in school (Figure 3.1). While time spent working did not change over the decade, school enrollment became increasingly common. On average, young people spend relatively few months of this part of their lives married, and person-years of marriage declined substantially over the 1980s. On the other hand, it was increasingly common for young persons to continue to live at home with their families (Goldscheider and Goldscheider 1993).

Gender and race and ethnic differentials.   Were race and ethnic differences in these early life experiences decreasing or increasing over the decade? Was there a convergence of the behavior of men and women over the decade? Did the age patterning of activities in these life domains increase over the 1980s? To provide more precise answers to these complex questions we used a statistical model (not shown here) to look at the likelihood that each activity occurred and the extent to which the likelihood differed by sex and by race and ethnicity in 1980 and 1990.[34]

We find that gender differences in residence with parents, schooling, and marriage were constant over the decade; changes observed in these transitions affected men and women equally. Work is the locus of gender differences in the transition to adulthood. While women in 1990 remained only 78 percent as likely as men to be working, this difference was one-fifth smaller than in 1980. Work was less common for both men and women at the *younger* ages (18, 19) in 1990 compared to 1980, but work was *more* common in 1990 among women aged 22–24. This pattern was strongest among white women; black and Asian women maintained their considerably lower likelihood of work relative to men of the same race.[35]

In contrast to the stability, and in some cases convergence, of the activities of men and women, race and ethnic group differences grew over the interval. In regard to both schooling and work, the other race and ethnic groups diverged from the whites over the decade. By 1990, blacks and American Indians became even less likely than whites to be in school or working. Latinos showed tendencies in the same direction. Over the decade, Asians became more likely to be in school and less likely to be working, relative to whites. There were no notable changes in the large racial differentials in marriage, and some convergence with whites in the likelihood of living in the parental home for blacks, Asians, and Native Americans. There are substantial race and ethnic differences in motherhood. Controlling for age, blacks, Latinos, and American Indians were all more than twice as likely to be mothers as white women, a difference that declined only slightly over the 1980s. In contrast, Asian women are even less likely than whites to be mothers, and this difference increased 74 percent between 1980 and 1990.

The 1980s were thus a time in which education continued to grow in importance. At the same time, workforce attachment remained common. This was a time of decreasing differences in the work of men and women. In contrast, the decade witnessed marked race and ethnic divergence, with a deterioration of the entry into work among blacks and American Indians. These young persons are more poorly prepared for work than whites, and this decline in the percentage of these young persons holding a job is one result. Among females, these ethnic differences have been accentuated by differences in motherhood.

Early Adult Roles

This discussion implies that the different activities of young adults are linked in various ways. There have been many studies of the linkages between education and marriage, marriage and motherhood, or motherhood and work (Hogan and Astone 1986). In our everyday conversations we characterize young people as "working moms," "in the service," "college student," "family man," and the like. In order to more fully understand the ways in which the activities in these life domains come together we produced a tabulation showing combinations of these activities corresponding to socially defined situations in 1980 and 1990 (Table 3.10).[36]

The most notable aspect of this table is the diversity of experiences of young adults during the early adult years. In 1990 nine different activity patterns were occupied by 5 percent or more of young persons. No activity pattern included more than 16 percent of the young adults. In part, this diversity results from pooling young persons of different ages. It also reflects the unpredictable and weakly structured life course of young Americans in 1990. But this early adult life course is not entirely without structure. In fact, as Table 3.10 illustrates, most activity patterns occur along well-defined lines that define familiar social roles. Between 1980 and 1990 there was an 11 percent change in the distribution of young people across these early life situations.[37] Over the decade there was an increase in students living with their parents (some working and some not) and an increase in single students who hold a job and live independently. There was a major decline in the percentage of young persons who were married and working.

There were systematic gender differences in these young adult roles. Fifteen percent of the women in 1980 but only 8 percent in 1990 were full-time home-makers, signifying a dramatic decline in this traditional situation. Changes in other young adult situations were in the same direction for men and women, but women showed a greater increase in the likelihood of being working students, either living at home or independently.

It is possible that the driving force behind the increasing proportion of women at work, then, is the need to work to cover the costs of postsecondary education. It certainly does not appear that stronger attachment to work per se is involved—it actually became less common for women to finish their schooling and work, either while living at home or living independently, because college enrollment typically occupies at least the early years of adult life considered here. Men showed similar, but smaller, increases in the likelihood of being working students.[38] For these young men, the traditional adult roles of husband and breadwinner declined dramatically over the decade.

Although the evidence is suggestive, it appears that young people have adjusted to the diminished economic opportunities for those with only a high

TABLE 3.10   Percentage of persons aged 18–24 with each combination of activity, by sex: 1980 and 1990.

	Living at Home	In School	In Military	Currently Working
Living at Home				
Dependent student	X	X		
	X	X		
Working student	X	X		X
	X	X		X
Working	X			X
Dependent	X			
Away at School				
Not working		X		
Working		X		X
		X		
Married		X		X
Military Service			X	X
	X			X
		X	X	X
	X	X	X	X
			X	X
	X		X	X
		X	X	X
	X	X	X	X
Independent Worker				X
Married				
Working				X
	X			X
Homemaker				
	X			
Other				
N				
Total Percent				

school education or less by emphasizing additional schooling during the young adult years. In the case of persons from less well off families, this schooling may require a combination of strategies, including reducing costs (by remaining in the parental household) and increasing income (through work while in school). This postponement of adult roles in effect enables many of these young people to escape their disadvantaged social origins through a college education (Hout 1988).

By 1990 the distribution of young men and women across different early adult roles differed by just 14 percent. This small gender difference is a result of the intercohort increases in college enrollment of women, higher levels of

Currently Married	All Persons		Men		Women	
	1980	1990	1980	1990	1980	1990
X	0.1%	0.1%	0.1%	0.1%	0.1%	0.2%
	8.0	10.5	8.5	11.1	7.6	9.8
X	0.0	0.1	0.0	0.1	0.0	0.2
	8.1	12.4	8.6	12.4	7.7	12.4
	17.1	16.1	20.1	18.9	14.2	13.2
	7.1	6.3	8.1	7.2	6.0	5.4
	7.3	8.4	7.7	8.6	7.0	8.2
	5.7	8.5	5.4	7.7	5.9	9.4
X	0.8	0.8	0.5	0.4	1.1	1.3
X	1.4	1.6	1.5	1.3	1.4	1.5
X	0.7	0.7	1.3	1.2	0.1	0.1
X	0.0	0.0	0.0	0.0	0.0	0.0
X	0.1	0.1	0.1	0.1	0.0	0.0
X	—	0.0	—	0.0	—	0.0
	1.8	1.4	3.2	2.4	0.4	0.3
	0.0	0.2	0.1	0.3	0.0	0.0
	0.2	0.2	0.3	0.3	0.0	0.0
	0.0	0.0	0.0	0.1	0.0	0.0
	12.2	12.2	12.4	12.8	11.9	11.6
X	15.8	10.0	15.5	8.7	16.2	11.3
X	0.5	0.6	0.6	0.7	0.5	0.6
X	8.1	4.4	2.0	1.2	14.2	7.6
X	0.4	0.4	0.2	0.2	0.6	0.5
	4.4	5.0	3.9	4.3	5.0	5.7
	296,465	224,903	147,899	114,531	148,566	110,372
	100.0%	100.0%	100.0%	100.0%	100.0%	100.0%

female labor force participation, and delays in family formation. Thus, we see that the demographic and socioeconomic trends discussed elsewhere in these volumes have dramatically changed the ways in which young Americans, especially women, become adults.

We made similar calculations of race and ethnic differences in these common activities (tabulations not shown). Latinos and whites were the most similar in their experiences (distributions differ by 16 percent). Asians experience their early adult years in ways that are distinctly different from the other race and ethnic groups (distribution differs by 24 percent from whites and 31 percent from blacks). They more often combine school enrollment with other statuses, especially work. Blacks and American Indians have greater difficulty than other groups in taking on adult roles—they more often are still living at home without being enrolled in school or working (both differ from the distribution of whites by 24 percent). They also disproportionately live away from their family but are not engaged in schooling, work, or other adult roles. Thus, there were substantially larger race and ethnic differences than gender differences in activities in early adulthood in 1990.

Human capital and adult roles.   Young adults vary in regard to the human capital—the resources, knowledge, skills, and abilities that they bring to adult life. These include many possible deficits or disadvantages—recent arrival in the United States and inadequate language skills, less than a high school education, and a disability or physical limitation. It includes geographic stability, which might help or hinder opportunities for taking on adult roles.[39] Veterans bring unique experiences to the workplace, and they may be entitled to educa-

TABLE 3.11   Percentage of persons aged 18–24 engaged in common combinations of activities, for selected groups: 1990.

Activity Pattern	All Persons	Migration Experience			Education	
		Foreign-Born	U.S. Mover	Nonmover	No High School Diploma	High School Diploma or More
Living at Home						
Dependent student	11%	6%	8%	12%	14%	10%
Working student	13	4	10	14	11	13
Working	16	12	11	19	14	17
Dependent	6	3	4	8	13	5
Away at School						
Not working	8	13	12	7	3	10
Working	9	5	12	7	1	11
Married	2	4	3	2	1	3
Military Service	3	1	7	0	2	3
Independent Worker	12	18	14	11	12	12
Married						
Working	11	11	11	11	10	11
Homemaker	5	14	5	5	9	4
Other	5	9	4	4	12	3
Total	100	100	100	100	100	100

NOTE: Percentages may not add to 100 due to rounding.

tional or employment benefits. Finally, women who have become mothers are likely to have a decidedly different mix of activities, since they primarily remain responsible for childcare, which may limit their options for schooling and work, especially if they are single parents.

Table 3.11 provides the distribution across combinations of life domains of young adults who differ in their human capital. Six percent of persons can be regarded as dependent on others: They are not integrated into such traditionally productive roles as student, worker, or homemaker. These statuses are less common among persons who immigrated to the United States or veterans, who more often live independently of the parental family. Veterans are less often in school (in part because they are generally older), more often working and married. Immigrants maintain a high level of enrollment in school and employment, confirming popular beliefs about their commitment to career success. Interstate movement between birth and adulthood has little impact on the educational or work activities of young Americans.

Persons with disabilities or limitations in physical functioning or mobility engage in activities that reflect difficulties in both their current situations and

Military Service		Women			Disability/Limitation	
Veteran	Not Veteran	With Children	No Children	With Children in Poverty	Yes	No
3%	11%	3%	12%	3%	13%	10%
5	13	2	16	1	6	13
17	17	7	16	3	12	16
8	6	8	5	8	19	6
3	9	3	10	7	7	9
7	9	2	12	3	4	9
4	2	5	2	3	2	3
—	—	0	1	0	0	3
19	12	10	12	14	9	12
22	11	22	8	6	6	11
6	5	25	2	19	8	5
5	5	15	3	36	15	5
100	100	100	100	100	100	100

their potential for successful adulthood. A substantial minority of the disabled—one-third—are neither in school nor working, 19 percent living at home and 15 percent living on their own. Young persons who are disabled are less likely to be married, and when they are they more often depend on their spouses for their income. But many of these persons do not regard their limitations or disabilities as preventing them from being employed in productive adult roles. Indeed, 58 percent of the persons with limitations or disabilities in 1990 aged 18–24 were either enrolled in school or working, investing in their human capital to attain economic independence.

One-quarter of women aged 18–24 have had a child, and this percentage approaches 40 percent or more of blacks, Latinos, and American Indians. Young women who become mothers have much more constrained choices than young women who have not (Table 3.11). They cannot, without giving up their child, undo the transition to parenthood. For most young women, motherhood means taking on caregiving responsibilities and maintaining a household for her family and sustaining these roles over the next two decades while her child grows. Sometimes these roles are made simpler by assistance from parents or coresidence with parents, but such assistance tends to be short-term (Parish, Hao, and Hogan 1991).

One-half of all young mothers are married, and one-half of these are single mothers (calculated from Table 3.11). About equal numbers of the *married* mothers are either in school or working or are traditional homemakers. Almost one-third of the *single* mothers are not in school or working, most living independently. These include some welfare mothers living in public housing, and other women depending on unmarried partners. But this is not the most common situation for single young mothers, popular stereotypes not withstanding. Almost two-thirds of young single mothers were working or in school in 1990. About half of these lived with their parents and half lived independently.

Young mothers who are in poverty tend to be either single and not working (36 percent) or homemakers (19 percent) whose husbands earn too little to support their families. Another one-quarter are poor even though they work. Again we see that being married and working are not guarantees against family poverty. Indeed, while single mothers who do not work often are heads of poor families, a majority of young women whose families are in poverty do not fit this stereotype.

Poverty in Early Adulthood

More than one-fifth of these young adults were in poverty in 1990. This figure was virtually unchanged from 1980, both overall and for the race and ethnic groups. While only 15 percent of whites were in poverty in 1990, roughly one-quarter of the Latinos and Asians and one-third of the blacks and American Indians were in poverty (Figure 3.2). Few whites and Asians are in

FIGURE 3.2   Distribution of young persons aged 18–24 according to poverty threshold categories, by race and ethnicity: 1990.

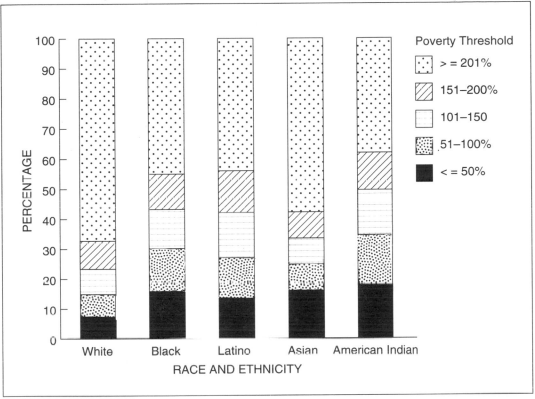

the marginally poor groups just above the poverty line. This contrasts sharply with the situations of the blacks, Latinos, and American Indians, whose inadequate employment and low wages keep many persons near poverty even though they work.

The relationship between adult roles and poverty can be seen clearly in Table 3.12, which shows the percentage of persons engaged in each activity pattern who are poor. The most effective way for these young people to avoid poverty is to stay in their parental homes and hold jobs. In this way, they have the advantage of other household members' contributions to the household income while also contributing themselves. One-third of young persons away at school are poor, and their situation is not greatly helped by work. Such work often will be part-time and provide too little income to rise above the poverty line. The inadequate wages often earned by young persons is evident in the 22 percent poverty rate of those unmarried men and women who have ended school and are working. The contrast in life chances for persons with and without a high school education is clear—33 percent of independent workers with less than a high school education are in poverty, compared to only 19 percent of those with a high school diploma or better.

Table 3.12 Percentage of persons aged 18–24 living in poverty, by common combinations of activities: 1990.

Activity Pattern	All Persons	No High School Diploma	High School Diploma or More	Women With Children	Women With No Children	Men With Children	Men With No Children
Living at Home							
Dependent student	12%	19%	9%	18%	7%	17%	6%
Working student	4	7	3	6	2	5	2
Working	5	11	3	8	2	7	3
Dependent	23	32	16	33	15	27	14
Away at School							
Not working	36	70	76	69	46	52	42
Working	30	46	45	43	24	28	18
Married	15	29	13	20	7	26	11
Military Service	3	12	8	6	3	14	3
Independent Worker	22	33	19	42	17	26	12
Married							
Working	8	20	6	9	3	16	5
Homemaker	25	36	18	26	13	43	18
Other	56	74	63	82	45	53	36

Unmarried mothers who work and remain in their parental households do much better than other unmarried mothers. In the case of the young marrieds, two incomes often are needed to make an adequate living for the family, whereas others opt for limited family income in order to have a traditional family life. This is most clear in the last four columns of Table 3.12, which show the poverty rates for 18–24-year-old mothers and fathers in each of the common activity groups. Here we see that the families of young mothers who are married have a poverty rate of only 9 percent if the wife works, compared to 26 percent if she does not. Married fathers who work are more likely to be in poverty than the mothers, since more of them will be in families in which a single worker is present (i.e., in which the wife does not work).

Race and ethnic differences in early adult activities worsen the immediate economic situations of young blacks and American Indians. Their future prospects are also diminished by the relative absence of investment in higher education and the failure to develop a history of labor force attachment. Among these minorities, the situation is further worsened for women who become mothers at early ages. Once children are born, many of these young parents are unable to keep their families from poverty. Only when the parents marry and both work is the probability high that young minority families will have an adequate income to raise their children.

CONCLUSIONS

Other chapters in this volume have documented the many changes in demographic, economic, and social behaviors of Americans during the 1980s, changes that have transformed the family life and welfare of American children and young adults. We have seen that the families in which American children grew up in the 1980s were diverse in terms of family structure, contact with adults, and access to a favorable socioeconomic environment. Living arrangements became disadvantageous for more children in the 1980s, as increasing numbers of families have only a single adult. Partly countering this were the smaller family sizes of recent cohorts of children and the readiness of mothers to work and provide a significant share of the family income. But these changes, too, have transformed the living arrangements and family experiences of children, many of whom now attend preschool, have after-school care, or have parents who are involved in shiftwork and are infrequently together (Presser 1989).

During the 1980s, changes in the economy made it more important than ever that young people receive post-high school education or training. We, in fact, find an increase in school enrollment among young adults. Coincident with this is a decline in the proportion of young adults in the labor force and married (Hogan 1981). Military service became a lesser option as the demand for military manpower declined. Changes in school benefits for veterans further diminished military service as an avenue to higher education.

But in 1990 more of the young persons in school were working and living at home than in earlier years. These were steps taken by young persons to enable them to afford post-high school educations (Goldscheider and Goldscheider 1993). Young people in 1990 postponed many of the transitions to adulthood (full-time work, independent residence, marriage, and parenthood) in order to complete the advanced education necessary for career success in the U.S. economy at the end of the twentieth century. Of course, the absence of good jobs for young people who had only a high school education was another force driving the trend.

It was easier for some groups of people to respond to these forces of social history. In particular, young persons with better socioeconomic origins did better, as did Asians. In this process blacks, Latinos, and American Indians lagged. The relatively difficult life course that minorities face in completing higher education as preparation for a successful career is further complicated by the tendency to have children at young ages and outside of marriage. One result is the formation of families in which both the young parent and the children are poor.

Poverty among American children cannot be understood without recognizing the central role of family structure and parental employment. If intact families were to again become dominant and new patterns of parental employment adopted, that is, full-time employment by both parents, poverty would be reduced significantly, but racial differences would remain stark. This is because the economic benefits of work depend not only on labor force participation and whether work is part-time or full-time but also on the type of job held, its wage or salary, and its benefit package.

Good jobs with extensive benefits often require the attainment of post-high school education and the postponement of family formation until a person's occupational career is underway. The lives of young adults in 1990, coupled with ongoing changes in the economy, provide little hope that minority groups will soon gain full access to American prosperity and a stable, economically secure family life. Instead, it appears that whites and Asians more often will succeed in adapting to the new American economy and the economic realities of family life in the 1990s.

In the past 20 years we have seen an increased proportion of all children in disadvantaged family structures and economic circumstances. This is especially prevalent among the minority groups that are historically disadvantaged, significantly increasing the likelihood of persistent race and ethnic inequality. In 1930 President Hoover's Conference on Child Health and Protection laid out ambitious national goals for our children. As a nation, considerable progress was made on many of these goals during the 40 years that followed. But reductions in many Great Society programs in the late 1960s, economic stagnation in the 1970s, and uneven economic expansion in the 1980s have severely undermined the economic prospects and family situations of young adults and American children. As the twentieth century draws to a close, changes in family processes and economic opportunities have combined to thwart improvement in the well-being of American children and youth. The nation thus remains a considerable distance from achieving the national goals for children adopted six decades ago.[40]

The authors gratefully acknowledge the computational assistance of Kristen Brocking, Jan Hendrickson-Smith, and Susan Kunselman, and the clerical assistance of Ramona King and Cassie Johnstonbaugh. This chapter also benefited tremendously from the comments of Reynolds Farley and Nancy Cunniff.

ENDNOTES

1. Bumpass and Sweet (1989b), Martin and Bumpass (1989); Schoen and Weinick (1993); U.S. Bureau of the Census (1993). *Current Population Reports*. "Poverty in the United States: 1992"; National Center for Health Statistics (1993). "Advance Report of Final Natality Statistics, 1991"; *Monthly Vital Statistics Report*. U.S. Bureau of the Census (1992). *Current Population Reports*. "Household and Family Characteristics: March 1991"; Bianchi and Spain (1986).

2. A common practice is to look at the well-being of families. While this provides useful information about family units, it cannot provide a true picture of the situation of children, insofar as the number of children differs across families that include at least one child. See Preston (1976).

3. For example, discussions of the negative impact of maternal employment have generally ignored the economic effects on families had the mothers not worked. A home environment in which the mother was present all day long might, for example, also have engendered a change of residence to less expensive housing in a more dangerous neighborhood with inferior schools.

4. For summaries of these debates see Reynolds (1992) and Whitehead (1993).

5. U.S. Department of Health and Human Services (1991), *Child Health USA '91*.

6. Most recently, The National Commission on Children filed a final report that describes progress on these goals and unfilled needs. Although the solutions they propose are quite dissimilar from those President Hoover might have adopted, the aims for our children are similar. See *Beyond Rhetoric: A New American Agenda for Children and Families*. The Final Report of the National Commission on Children (1991).

   The Children's Defense Fund lays out similar concerns for children's health, early care and development, income, housing, education, and youth development. See, for example, *The State of America's Children* (1991).

7. The most detailed and comprehensive view of the lives of children is provided by Hernandez (1993). For a description of youth, see Uhlenberg and Eggebeen (1986).

8. This is a conscious decision intended to keep this chapter as politically neutral as possible, while providing basic information and insights into the well-being of children and youth for policymakers of all perspectives. The National Commission on Children rejected such a strategy in its final report: (1991, p. xviii).

9. Calculated from data provided in Hernandez (1993): Tables 3.6 and 3.10.

10. See David L. Featherman and Robert M. Hauser (1975), *Opportunity and Change*. New York: Academic Press, for evidence on the intergenerational transmission of education. Data on school enrollment of children from U.S. Department of Education, Office of Educational Research and Improvement, *Youth Indicators 1991*. Washington, D.C.: U.S. Government Printing Office, Indicator 21.

11. Bianchi, Chapter 3, Table 3.4, in Volume 1.

12. U.S. House of Representatives Select Committee on Children, Youth, and Families, *U.S. Children and Their Families: Current Conditions and Recent Trends*, 1989, p. 91, Washington, D.C.: U.S. Government Printing Office.

13. U.S. House of Representatives Select Committee on Children, Youth, and Families (1989) *U.S. Children and Their Families: Current Conditions and Recent Trends*, p. 97.

14. See the evidence and debate on this issue in Belsky and Eggebeen (1991).

15. Taeuber (1991); and Bianchi, Chapter 3 in Volume 1.

16. U.S. Department of Education (1992) *Youth Indicators 1991*, Indicator 19.

17. U.S. Department of Education (1992) *Youth Indicators 1991*, Indicator 20.

18. Smeeding and Torrey (1988), "Poor Children in Rich Countries," Table 1. It is notable that Australia is the only nation in which the levels of child poverty approach those in the United States.

19. U.S. Bureau of the Census (1993). *Poverty in the United States 1992*, Current Population Reports. Series P-60–115. Washington, DC: U.S. Government Printing Office.

20. U.S. Bureau of the Census (1993). *Poverty in the United States 1992*.

21. See Zill (1993) for review; also Huston (1991); Sandefur, McLanahan, and Wojtkiewicz (1992).

22. Bianchi (1993). The poverty rate of children living with divorced mothers was 37 percent in 1991, compared with a poverty rate of 66 percent among children of never-married mothers.

23. See Lichter and Eggebeen (1993). The median family income-to-poverty ratio for children at the bottom of the income distribution declined from .78 to .68 between 1979 and 1989. It increased from 5.39 to 5.93 for children at the top of the family income distribution.

24. Using the data from the Survey of Income and Program Participation, Bianchi and McArthur (1991) showed that the income-to-needs ratio of children whose fathers eventually left the family was initially lower than the average for all children. But

the father's departure nevertheless also resulted in a 13 percent decline in this ratio over the period of study.

25. If children's living arrangements in 1988 mirrored those of children in 1960, the poverty rate would have declined from 25.7 percent in 1960 to 13.8 percent in 1987, instead of the observed decline to 20.3 percent. Thus, the child poverty rate in the late 1980s would have been about one-third lower in the absence of changes in children's family living arrangements since 1960.

26. See Eggebeen and Lichter (1991). In 1959 the observed poverty rate among black children was 66 percent, while the standardized rate, using white children as the standard population, was about 63 percent. In 1987 the observed and standardized rates were 45 percent and 26 percent, respectively. Racial differences in children's living arrangements account for an increasing share of the black–white difference in children's poverty rates. Similar results are reported by Hernandez (1993). He showed that if the post-1960 rise in female-headed families had not occurred, the black–white difference in child poverty would have been only 50–75 percent as large as the observed difference.

27. Donald Hernandez (1993), Table 8.1; Jensen, Eggebeen, and Lichter (1993). In the Jensen et al. study, the mean percentage of family income from parental earnings declined by 63.2 percent in 1969 to 46.3 percent in 1989.

28. See Lichter and Eggebeen (1994). They show that child poverty in married couple families would be reduced by 23 percent if employment rates among currently non-employed mothers increased to 50 percent. A 50 percent employment rate among currently nonworking poor mothers heading their own families implies a reduction in child poverty of 26 percent.

29. See Hout (1988). He showed that the association between origin and destination occupations declined by about one-third between 1972 and 1985. This was due in large part to the increasing proportion of young college graduates, a group whose family background status had little effect on occupational mobility.

30. The 1980 census data on disability are presented to illustrate how alternative measures of disability can change recorded levels. Because more refined questions about limitations were added to the 1990 census, it is not appropriate to compare the figures for 1980 and 1990.

31. Persons enrolled in their senior year of high school at the time of the April 1 census are counted among those with a high school diploma in this analysis.

32. See Rindfuss (1991). He describes the young adult years as a period of "demographic density," where many new adult roles occur more or less simultaneously or within a few years of each other (e.g., migration, first job, first marriage, etc.). At the same time, increasing diversity in the order of these events is now more apparent than in the past (e.g., childbearing that precedes marriage).

33. Demographers refer to this as a synthetic cohort calculation since no actual group of persons is followed from ages 18–24. Synthetic cohort methods are a sound way to describe these young adults since confounding factors associated with extremely rapid societal change or sharp differences in the earlier life experiences of the cohorts are largely absent.

34. Logistic regression models were used to calculate the likelihood that a person was

engaged in a particular activity, conditional on year of age, gender, and race and ethnicity. These models were done separately for 1980 and 1990. We then compared the coefficients of the models for the two years to determine the extent to which differentials had increased or decreased over the 1980s. By comparing behaviors within a census year we can determine the relative size of sex and race and ethnic differentials for each of the transitions. An advantage of these models is that they make no synthetic cohort assumptions; the observed behaviors of individuals are predicted. These models also permit the discussion of differences associated with one status (for example, sex) controlling for differences in other variables (for example, age and race or ethnicity).

35. These statements are based on a logistic regression model that tested sex and race and ethnic interactions on the age grading of work.

36. For the five activities we consider, a total of 32 combinations are theoretically possible. Under census procedures all persons on active duty were classified as being at work, excluding any combination involving military without work, leaving a total of 24 combinations. Twelve of these combinations each characterized less than 1 percent of young people. For this analysis, young people in these rare categories were pooled with young persons in the more common role combinations to which they most closely corresponded.

37. We compare differences in these activity distributions of groups using an index of dissimilarity. This measure gives the percentage of persons in a group who would have to be engaged in a different set of activities so that it would be exactly like another.

38. As Mare shows in Chapter 4 of Volume 1, 1990 witnessed more reports of school enrollment than in prior years. This may at least partly be an artifact of changes in the census questions about school enrollment between 1980 and 1990. The relatively high levels of work by persons enrolled in school in 1990, and the increase in this activity pattern between 1980 and 1990, are based on these changing questions about school enrollment. In particular, we may be picking up more marginal forms of part-time or non-degree school enrollment among young people whose activity pattern is really focused on work. However, a variety of other evidence shows that the life course of young persons is increasingly complex, leading us to believe that these increasingly complex ties between schooling and work are not simply artifacts of changes in the census questions.

39. Perhaps geographic stability may improve life chances by conferring more knowledge about schooling or job opportunities and permitting longer residence in the parental home while attending college. But such immobility may also restrict life chances by limiting the potential benefits to be gotten from moving to an area with a better labor or housing market.

40. This portrait of the living arrangements and well-being of children and young adults is far more negative in tone than that for many other groups covered in this series. This does not reflect a particularly dour approach on our part; rather we believe that the evidence for increased relative disadvantage of children and youth is overwhelming. Families are responding to the challenges now facing them, but these responses have proven inadequate to resolve their problems, and their adaptive strategies sometimes introduce other issues for families. While some might argue that children in the upper fifth of the income distribution are doing well, such a

comparison looks only at economic outcomes and is selective of those with favorable living arrangements and mother's pattern of work. In any case, for average families, and especially for those in poverty, the living arrangements and well-being of children have unquestionably deteriorated over the past two decades. These trends have worsened the situation of the young relative to that of the elderly, and they have marked the United States as a distinctly risky nation in which to be a young child.

4

Racial and Ethnic Diversity

RODERICK J. HARRISON and CLAUDETTE E. BENNETT

Among the most important and immediately visible of trends in the past two decades has been the increasing racial and ethnic diversity of the nation's population. America's so-called minority populations—defined to include blacks, American Indians, Asians, and Hispanics—have grown much more rapidly than the population as a whole. This growth reflects younger age structures and higher fertility rates and, most strikingly, the increased immigration of Asians and of Hispanics.

As a consequence, whites, who represented nearly 84 percent of the United States population in 1970, dropped to about 80 percent in 1980 and to just over 75 percent in 1990 (Figure 4.1). The trends are even more visible in many large urban areas and a few states: 6 of the nation's largest 10 cities, and 14 cities with over one-half million persons were "majority minority" in the 1990 census; New Mexico, with a minority population of 49.6 percent, nearly joined the District of Columbia (73 percent) and Hawaii (69 percent) as a "majority minority" state in 1990, and California (43 percent) is expected to do so by the year 2000.[1] The Census Bureau projects that if current trends continue, the white share of the population would steadily fall to 60 percent in 2030 and to 53 percent in 2050. The nation would thus approach a "majority minority" population around 2050.[2]

But what is new about these developments? This is scarcely the first time that people from different nations and cultures have represented a large and growing segment of this nation of immigrants. Why does the growth of racial and ethnic diversity seem to penetrate, in such new and deep ways, to the very heart of what the United States is or could become? Why do we seem filled with an almost palpable foreboding or hope that these changes will create an America quite different from ours, perhaps unrecognizable to many?

Few of us can pinpoint or articulate just why we feel this way. Perhaps more often than we care to admit, the difficulty involves feelings that disturb us— feelings about undeniable differences, however caused, in the educational and

FIGURE 4.1 Percentage of the population, by race or ethnicity: 1970 to 2050.

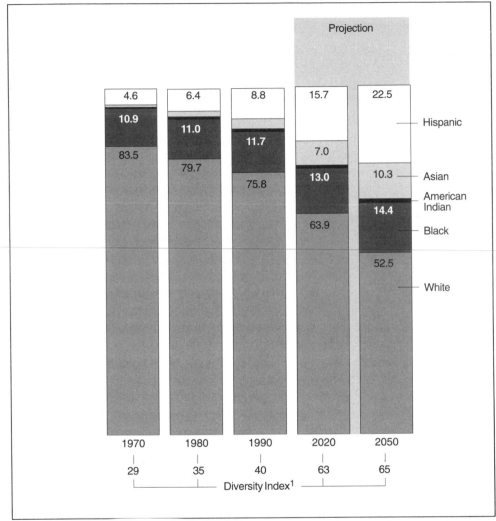

SOURCE: U.S. Bureau of the Census, Census of Population and Housing; Day, Jennifer Cheeseman, "Population Projections of the United States, by Age, Sex, Race, and Hispanic Origin: 1993 to 2050." U.S. Bureau of the Census, Current Population Reports P25-1104, November 1993.

NOTE: Bar segments for 2 percent or less are not labelled separately on figure.

[1] Diversity index reports the percentage of times two randomly selected persons in the United States would differ by race/ethnicity.

socioeconomic attainments of various groups and the safety of their neighborhoods. It almost certainly involves the moral tension and discomfort that surround our public discourse about race in America, and the painful absence of shared understandings about what we can and dare not say across racial lines without confirming each other's worst fears, and sometimes our own, about how we see race and inferiority in America. Discomforting as it is, our feelings and fears revolve closely around questions of inferiority and superiority.

Although today's increasing racial and ethnic diversity shares much with the great European immigration that gave us our national self-image as a "melting pot," there is a difference that we are not sure we can overcome. As the term itself suggests, the nation sees "minorities" very differently than its European immigrants. While many European immigrants faced hostility, prejudice, and discrimination on these shores, they were seldom assigned legally subordinate statuses before the law.[3]

Only America's nonwhites were considered sufficiently different and inferior to be so distinguished and subordinated, and thus denied the rights guaranteed to other Americans. For African Americans it was slavery,[4] and soon after the Civil War, Jim Crow segregation. The Supreme Court fully recognized and sanctioned racial segregation in 1896, when it upheld, in *Plessy* v. *Ferguson*, Louisiana's law requiring separate railway carriages for blacks, and through it, separate facilities in all areas of life, including public schools. For Asians it was the status, defined by the very first Congress in 1790, of "aliens ineligible for citizenship." This status was used in state and federal laws from 1850 until a century later to limit immigration from Asia and to prevent Asians from owning or leasing land. Indeed, Asian-born persons were denied citizenship until 1952, long after the 14th Amendment had guaranteed that right to blacks. For American Indians it was a long history as a conquered people, symbolized most dramatically by the Trail of Tears and their often coerced relocation from their tribal lands to reservations under the Indian Removal Act of 1830, despite the Supreme Court's recognition of their right as sovereign nations to decline relocation. Mexicans, Puerto Ricans, and Native Hawaiians, Guamanians, and other Pacific Islanders were never subject to legal subordination. However, they became American citizens through conquest—the annexation of the Southwestern states from Mexico in the Treaty of Guadaloupe-Hidalgo in 1848, and the acquisition of Puerto Rico and several Pacific Islands in the Spanish-American War of 1898.

The nation takes justifiable pride in the abolition of these *de jure* distinctions in the 1950s and 1960s. In 1952 the McCarran-Walter Act allowed Asians to become naturalized citizens, and the nation no longer excluded groups from citizenship based solely on their race. The 1954 Supreme Court decision in *Brown* v. *Board of Education* declared that separate facilities were inherently unequal and that the castelike segregation of blacks by state law was no longer constitutional. The arduous struggle of the civil rights movement reached its peak in the 1960s, and the nation determined that it would no longer recognize legal distinctions based upon race, color, creed, or national origin. The civil rights acts of the 1960s, sought to guarantee this new equality in employment (1964), voting (1965), and housing (1968); and new movements sought to strike down status distinctions based on gender, age, disability, and sexual preference. The 1965 Immigration Act finally removed the national origins quota system that essentially restricted immigration to Europeans, opening our gates to waves of immigration from Mexico, Latin America, and Asia.

Even as some celebrate the new diversity and the movement towards national ideals that engendered it, our nation still cannot visualize the new minority immigrants becoming "just like everybody else." We suspect that we—and our grandchildren—will still see "persons of color," even among "model minorities" who have matched and even exceeded the socioeconomic attainments of European immigrants, native-born whites, and their children. We suspect that we will always see them as minorities because even in post–civil rights America, the "everybody else" whom one could become like remains racially and ethnically white and European. We worry that whatever their accomplishments, minorities will always be distinctly "other." We sense this, and it disturbs us.

But if minorities cannot replicate the assimilation processes of European immigrants, we harbor fears that, like blacks, they might instead remain separate and unequal despite the removal of *de jure* discriminatory barriers to their inclusion. The suspicion lurks that the inequality lies deeply embedded in cultural inferiorities. Frustration has mounted over the past two decades as evidence suggested that conditions were not improving and often were worsening in many black neighborhoods. To many, the considerable national efforts undertaken in civil rights legislation, the War on Poverty, and affirmative action, and such successes as the emergence of a new black middle class, the exploding numbers of blacks elected to local and state offices, and gains in congressional and cabinet representation, seemed not to help. The nation is deeply troubled by the persistence of these problems and by the possibility that without great changes, the growth of more cities towards a "minority majority" will mean the spread of crime, drugs, poverty, and other social cancers to new minority slums—and even into previously white suburban rings.

Two riots in Los Angeles, 25 years apart, provide vivid and searing images of what has changed and what has not. The 1965 riots were the fiery harbingers of a rage that within a few short years swept all the nation's major cities. In trying to understand the wave of civil disorder, the Kerner Commission concluded, in an all-too-apt phrase, that we were becoming "two societies, separate and unequal, one black, one white." Nearly three decades later, these two societies seem no less separate and only modestly more equal, but in 1990 they together comprise less than half of Los Angeles' population. While the Watts riot of 1965 was a drama of blacks and whites, the cast in 1992 featured Hispanics and Koreans prominently, as rioters and as storeowners directly and vengefully targeted in many areas. Did the images of turmoil in this "Capital of the Third World," the images of Hispanics looting, blacks torching, and armed Koreans guarding their stores while sales of guns to whites skyrocketed, suggest we had become a balkanized society, fearing, hating, and fighting one another to protest wrongs that others saw as justice, to protect rights that others thought of as self-interest? Did it suggest that persons were striking out against the "haves" closest to the slights and strains of their daily lives?

The Kerner Commission saw unemployment, limited education, poor jobs, poverty, and beneath all these—racism—as causing the outbursts. Nearly 30 years later these conditions had not changed for black residents of Los Angeles' inner city. On the contrary, conditions worsened in many neighborhoods as Los Angeles lost over 70,000 manufacturing jobs to plant closings during the 1970s (Johnson and Oliver 1989). Did the nation fail in the commitments it made in the 1960s to overcome these problems, or did we instead find the limits to what government policy, rather than personal and group initiative, can accomplish?

Did the worsening conditions suggest the persistence of racism, or the ravages of economic dislocation, the apparent breakdowns in values reflected in burgeoning crime, drugs, violence, and gangs, in the crumbling of married-couple families, the rise in teenage motherhood and out-of-wedlock births, and an increasing isolation of an underclass in areas overwhelmed with these problems? Are we witnessing, 30 years later, the bitter harvest of a "culture of poverty"? Does the relative success of immigrants from a dozen or more Asian nationalities now show that opportunity is still sufficiently abundant and equal in America for those with the family and personal values needed to take advantage of it? If a new Kerner Commission were established to explain why, more than 25 years later, Los Angeles erupted in a multiracial riot, what might it conclude?

The 1990 census data can address only some of the issues, but these include several that have been central to efforts toward understanding race relations in the United States. We report important evidence that race remains persistently significant in America. Convergences in the earnings of comparably educated young blacks and whites in the 1970s and 1980s suggested that racial barriers were falling in American labor markets. Our analyses show parity in the earnings of comparably educated minority and white women but persisting differentials in the earnings of males in each of the minority populations, and at all educational levels. For males there is still a substantial cost—usually 10 to 20 cents on each dollar of earnings—to being a black, an American Indian, an Asian, or an Hispanic, in American job markets. There are no comparable differentials between the earnings of minority and white women.

These earnings differentials point to a disadvantage suffered by males in all minority groups. In contrast, residential segregation and interracial marriage patterns indicate that whites maintain a much greater social distance from blacks than from other minorities. They also maintain much greater distance from today's minorities than native-born whites did from the European immigrants when they were arriving in large numbers earlier this century. We seem far from overcoming the legacy of the unique, castelike segregation that distinguishes blacks from all other groups in American history. We are also far from integrating the new minorities in ways that would replicate Europeans' assimilation into a so-called melting pot. Neither European immigrants nor blacks provide useful analogues for the barriers that American Indians, Asians, and Hispanics have or will encounter. Each is likely to forge a path towards full equality as different and distinctive as the minority statuses and forms of exclusion each seeks to overcome.

We also find disquieting evidence of a pause in the steady and truly historic progress that young blacks, American Indians, and native-born Hispanics have made since 1940 in closing the gap between their high school completion rates and those of whites. Since our policy thinking has relied heavily, and perhaps too exclusively, upon gains in education to reduce socioeconomic differentials and improve conditions for these groups, we must be concerned that the 1980s was the first decade in at least half a century to not record such improvements.

Many have considered the growth of neighborhoods with high concentrations of poverty to be an explanation for the persistence of poverty and the growth of an underclass in our central cities. Popular and academic thinking has followed Wilson (1987) in suspecting that the isolation of poor minorities in these areas reduces their exposure to so-called mainstream values and behavior, and increases the risk that these youth will engage in such ghetto-specific behaviors as dropping out of high school or becoming teenage mothers. Surprisingly, we find no such neighborhood effects. The children of poor families maintained by single parents who are themselves high school dropouts are most likely to become teenage mothers or dropouts. These outcomes were *not* more likely in neighborhoods with higher poverty or dropout rates, with higher percentages of families maintained by females, or with lower incomes. Several neighborhood characteristics beyond those we tested might affect these or other behaviors. However, poverty and family disadvantages on their own may suffice to place youth at risk for such outcomes.

We present these and other findings in the pages that follow, examining trends in social and economic indicators that help in identifying (1) where we have and have not progressed in reducing discriminatory barriers and providing genuine equality of opportunity, and (2) how changing social and economic conditions, and personal, family, and neighborhood characteristics, acting independently of or together with discriminatory patterns, might promote or impede the full and equal inclusion of various sectors of minority populations.

We examine these trends in four sections. The first reviews the growth of the new diversity and its geography; the second examines residential segregation and interracial marriage as indicators of "social distance." Trends in educational attainment and in the occupations and earnings of comparably educated minorities and whites are discussed in a third section. Finally, we examine trends in family composition, income, and poverty, and analyze the effects of neighborhood characteristics on teenage motherhood and dropout rates.

THE GROWTH AND GEOGRAPHY OF RACIAL AND ETHNIC DIVERSITY

Our perception of ourselves as a melting pot of diverse peoples has revolved primarily around the peopling of the United States by slaves from Africa and by immigrants from Europe, especially the more than 27.6 million who arrived between 1880 and 1930. Half of these—14.5 million—arrived between 1900 and 1920, the largest influx in the nation's history.[5] This great wave of immigration transformed the nation. The foreign-born grew from 4 percent of the population in 1900 to 13 percent in 1920. While earlier immigrants primarily came from Northern and Western Europe, the new immigrants were predominantly Southern and Eastern Europeans. The ethnic composition of the white population thus changed substantially, and with it national self-images of the United States as a melting pot.[6]

Ironically, while the white population had become more diverse in its ethnic composition, the United States had become racially less diverse than at any prior point in the nation's history. Whites represented about 81 percent of the nation's population from its founding in 1790 until 1830. The nation of the Founding Fathers was 19 percent black, and in 1790 whites were only about 65 percent of the population inhabiting the territory the United States now encompasses. With the continued decimation of the American Indian population, the abolition of the African slave trade, and the continuing immigration from Europe, whites grew to about 86 percent of the population in 1860. The great immigration pushed this to 90 percent by 1920; blacks almost fully accounted for the remaining 10 percent.

Ever since, we seem to have thought of the United States as a predominantly white nation, with a 10 percent black minority. Native Americans, especially after their forced removal to reservations, seemed to enter the national consciousness primarily through the mythology we developed about the Old West in the movies and later, on television. Until recently, few Asians entered the lives of Americans outside of California, some Pacific coast cities, Hawaii, and New York City. Interaction with Hispanics was similarly limited to the Southwestern border states, New York City, and a few Midwestern industrial cities.

That America is gone forever. These populations, once small and localized enough to remain marginal in our thinking, are now too large, diverse, and dynamic for the national consciousness to ignore. And yet who are they? How did this happen? How will they change the country?

The racial and ethnic composition of the population changed more rapidly since 1960 than in any period of our history. Whites (including Hispanics) were about 89 percent of the population in 1960. Non-Hispanic whites fell from 84 percent of the population in 1970, to 76 percent in 1990 (Figure 4.1). The transformation would have been less rapid but for the confluence of two sweeping forces: the changes in immigration streams generated by the historic reform in immigration policy in 1965, and the simultaneous slowing of population growth to almost unprecedented lows in the nation as a whole (10 percent), and especially among whites (4 percent). Rates of natural increase have declined for whites and blacks since the 1960s, as each group has continued to bear fewer children; these rates have also declined for the other major groups since at least 1980. As a result of their declining fertility, the black and white populations have grown older. Because whites have both the oldest population and the lowest fertility rates—births to whites are below replacement levels—one would expect the white population to grow more slowly than other groups and to decline as a percentage of the population.

Differential rates of natural increase usually change a population's racial composition only gradually, however. Thus, for example, the black population has grown at more than twice the rate of the white population since the 1930s, but remained about 10 percent of the population until 1950, 11 percent until 1970, and 12 percent since 1980. In part, this is because prior to 1965, immigration tempered rather than reinforced the effects of the slower growth in the white population: two-thirds of all legal immigrants to the United States were from Europe and Canada. The national origins quotas, established in the 1924 Immigration Act, limited annual immigration from any country to 2 percent of that nationality's foreign-born population counted in the 1890 census. This and other laws effectively choked off immigration from Asia and Latin America, and favored Northwestern Europeans.

The 1965 Immigration Act replaced the national origins system with annual quotas of 20,000 per country, and it retained the occupational skills preferences established in the Immigration Act of 1952. The effects on immigration flows were immediate, striking, and unexpected. During the 1960s, immigrants from Europe and Canada fell from two-thirds to less than one-half of the total; the percentage from Mexico and Latin America grew from 25 to 40 percent. Asians increased from 6 percent of all immigrants in the 1950s to 44 percent in the 1980s, while Europe's and Canada's contribution fell to 14 percent. In only two decades, Asia almost reversed roles with Europe and Canada in their shares of the immigrant flow, and Latin America came to provide a stable 40 percent of immigrants.[7]

Boosted by these immigrants, the Asian population nearly doubled in each decade since 1960,[8] and grew to 7.3 million, or nearly 3 percent of the population, in 1990. Counts of Hispanics from 1960 to 1980 are not fully comparable,[9] but the general trend is unmistakable—the Hispanic population has grown by nearly 50 percent or more in every decade since 1940. It increased from less than 3.5 million in 1960 to over 9 million persons in 1970, and reached 22.4 million, or 9 percent of the population by 1990. The American Indian population also grew dramatically—by nearly 50 percent in the 1960s and 1970s, by 72 percent between 1970 and 1980, and by about 38 percent in the past decade.

The 1990 American Indian population of 2 million approaches, for the first time, lower estimates of its size when Europeans first arrived around 1500 (Thornton 1987). The growth of this population is notable because it is greater than natural increase, immigration, and improved census coverage can explain. It reflects changes in self-identity by persons who did not identify as American Indian in previous censuses, but did so in a later census.[10]

These developments have not only altered the nation's racial and ethnic composition, but also substantially increased the diversity of its minority population. For example, the probability that a nonwhite would also be black has sharply declined, from over 80 percent in 1960, to 65 percent in 1970 and just under 50 percent in 1990. The combined Hispanic, Asian, and American Indian population is now larger than the black. Similarly, the probabilities that an Asian was Chinese, Japanese, or Filipino, and that a Pacific Islander was Hawaiian, dropped from about two-thirds in 1980 to less than 60 percent in 1990.[11] This increased diversity can be more formally gauged by an interaction index that measures the probability that two persons drawn at random from a population will belong to different groups.[12] The index shows that in 1990, 4 of every 10 pairs would include persons from different groups, up from 3 in 10 in 1970.

The changes since 1960 have transformed a nation in which whites were the numerical majority as well as the dominant group in most places, into one in which whites are now the minority in many of the largest cities. They have transformed the nation, which has historically seen and defined its racial relations almost exclusively in terms of black and white, into one where several groups, neither black nor white, are the most rapidly growing components of the population. These trends are projected to make the United States, by 2010, a nation where Hispanics, rather than blacks, are the largest minority group, and by 2020, one where whites fall to their numerical representation in 1790 (65 percent) in the continent into which the United States has since expanded. By then, two persons drawn at random would be more likely to represent two different groups rather than a single group (Figure 4.1).

The new diversity is concentrated, however, in specific regions and areas of the country, often in a relatively small number of states or metropolitan areas. These concentrations reflect both the enduring legacy of each group's history in the United States and the ports-of-entry of recent immigrants. Many port and early industrial cities still retain ethnic populations and identifiable neighborhoods created by successive groups of immigrants, beginning with the Irish in the 1840s.

Despite massive outmigration over much of this century, more than one-half of all blacks still live in the South. The net "return" migration of blacks to the South in recent decades should preserve this distribution. Asians, American Indians, and Hispanics are similarly concentrated in the West, making this (with a diversity index of 51 percent), the most racially and ethnically diverse of the

FIGURE 4.2a   Percent minority, by region: 1990.

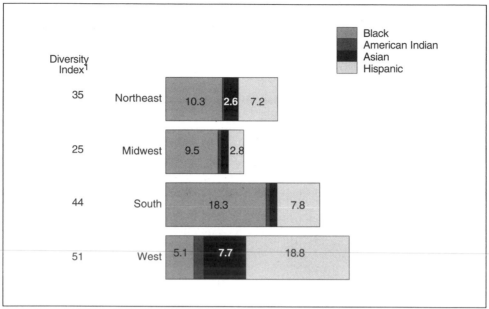

SOURCE: U.S. Bureau of the Census, Census of Population and Housing; and *1990 Census Profile, Race and Hispanic Origin,* Number 2, June 1991.

NOTE: Bar segments for 2 percent or less are not labelled separately on figure.

[1] Diversity index reports the percentage of times two randomly selected persons from the region would differ by race/ethnicity.

regions (Figure 4.2a). Each of these groups comprises more than twice the percentage of the West's population than they do of the nation's. The percentage of blacks (5 percent) is about half what it is elsewhere; and only two-thirds of Westerners are white. The West has moved farthest from a predominantly black and white region, to one whose composition suggests a new racial and ethnic diversity.

The concentration of these groups in the West, however, and the concentration of blacks in the South, leave the regions outside the West with less diversity (diversity indexes of less than 35 percent) than the nation as a whole, and with populations that are still predominantly black and white. The Midwest is almost as white as the nation was in 1970 (both over 86 percent), and its remaining population is largely black (10 percent) (Figure 4.2b). The Northeast and the South also remain 90 percent black and white. The South's substantial Hispanic population (8 percent) is barely visible (less than 3 percent) outside of Texas, Florida, and the District of Columbia.

As this suggests, the geography of minority concentration and diversity is more a state and metropolitan than a regional phenomenon. There are only a few states where the major groups are all represented in large numbers: Califor-

FIGURE 4.2b Population by region and race or ethnicity: 1990.

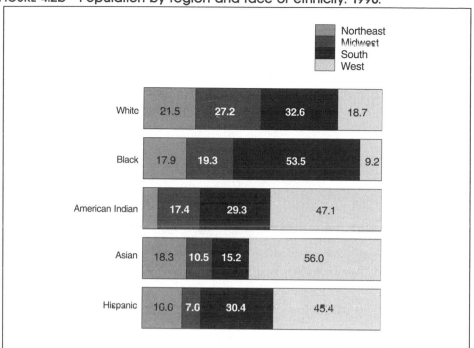

SOURCE: U.S. Bureau of the Census, Census of Population and Housing; and *1990 Census Profile, Race and Hispanic Origin,* Number 2, June 1991.

NOTE: Bar segments for 2 percent or less are not labelled separately on figure.

nia, Texas, Florida, New York, New Jersey, and Illinois.[13] Much of the diversity in the last four is attributable to three metropolitan areas: Miami, New York, and Chicago. American Indians combine with blacks in Oklahoma, and join Hispanics in Arizona and New Mexico, to create states with distinct racial and ethnic compositions.

More than three-quarters of all Hispanics lived in these "new diversity" states, and more than 70 percent of all Asians resided in these states or Hawaii in 1990. Key new diversity metropolitan areas (Figure 4.3)[14] were home to more than one-half of both the Hispanic and the Asian populations. Indeed, nearly one-fifth of all Asians lived in the greater Los Angeles area, which also had the largest concentrations of all but two Asian nationalities: the largest Chinese and Asian Indian populations are in greater New York; and Honolulu has the largest numbers of Japanese and of Pacific Islanders. Half of the Puerto Rican and Cuban populations lived in either New York or Miami. Almost 75 percent of all Mexicans resided in California or Texas, and 39 percent in metropolitan areas of these states.

In contrast, these new diversity states and metropolitan areas accounted for less than 40 and 35 percent, respectively, of the black population. The nation's

FIGURE 4.3   Percent minority for selected metropolitan areas: 1990.

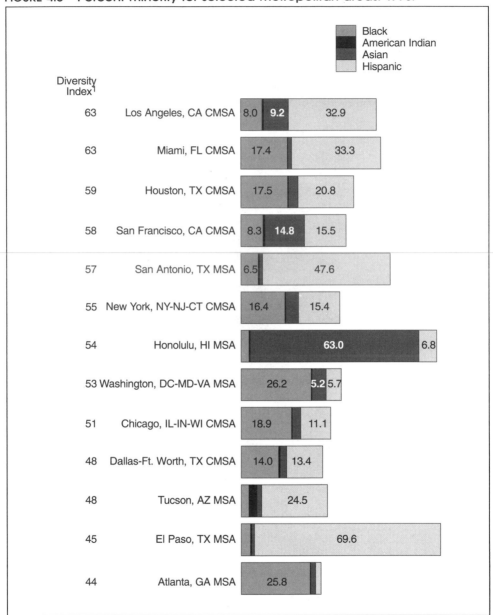

SOURCE: U.S. Bureau of the Census, *1990 Census of Population, General Population Characteristics for the United States,* November 1992.

NOTE: Bar segments for 5 percent or less are not labelled separately on figure.

[1] Diversity index reports the percentage of times two randomly selected persons from the metropolis would differ by race/ethnicity.

largest black populations live in new diversity areas, but large concentrations are also in Michigan and several southern states and in metropolitan areas such as Philadelphia, Detroit, and Baltimore, which are less diverse (interaction scores under 40 percent) than the nation. Blacks (16 percent) are also more likely than Asians and Hispanics (10 percent) to live in nonmetropolitan areas.

The geographic distribution of American Indians is unique: nearly one-half resided in nonmetropolitan areas in both 1980[15] and 1990, and about 37 percent resided on reservations and other American Indian and Alaska Native areas. Before 1980, the majority of American Indians lived on reservations; they are the only population whose current location in the United States still largely reflects governmental policies on where they could and could not live (Sandefur 1986).

Internal Migration Patterns

The concentration of minority populations means that relatively few states and metropolitan areas have fully encountered the new diversity. It also means that the growth and decline of these specific areas can have substantial effects upon the economic opportunities of minority groups. For example, the concentration of blacks in the South, which has had the lowest educational and income levels of the regions, has been an important component of national black–white differentials. Reductions in the regional differentials helped close the racial gaps in recent decades, and this may continue as the South grows (Heckman 1989). Conversely, the concentration of Asians in high-education, high-income metropolitan areas of the West has helped boost their educational and income attainments nationally, but now may have adverse effects as the California economy wrestles with dislocations arising from converting its defense industries.

With greater integration into American society, one might expect groups to migrate in patterns more like that of the general population and to disperse from areas where historic migration or immigration placed them (Sandefur and Jeon 1991). The return migration of blacks from the Northeast and Midwest in the 1980s to the South parallels a general population stream, perhaps suggesting a greater integration into national labor markets. Did other groups also follow the same migratory paths out from the deindustrializing states of the Northeast and Midwest into the West and the South Atlantic during the 1980s? The broad answer is that they did. However, blacks, Asians, and Hispanics were distinctively more likely to move, on balance, to the growth areas where they already had large populations and not to others.[16] The patterns suggest that rather than converging towards a single national pattern, each group has found, in the geography of economic and population growth, a "niche" destination where it was already concentrated.

The first difference in the migration patterns of the groups is the probability

TABLE 4.1 Selected characteristics of white, black, American Indian, Asian, and Hispanic movers to and from selected areas: 1990 (in 1989 dollars).

Race, Hispanic Origin, and Geographic Areas	Same House	Different House, Same State	All Interstate Movers
White			
Number	109,033,561	59,890,000	17,789,470
Net shift percent of all movers[a]	NA	NA	+11.8%
Percent some college or higher[b]	41.9%	52.7%	65.3%
Percent poor	7.2	11.4	10.7
Mean family income (dollars)	$39,492	$36,098	$37,467
Black			
Number	16,674,070	10,132,837	2,301,034
Net shift percent of all movers[a]	NA	NA	+14.2
Percent some college or higher[b]	30.8	38.9	54.3
Percent poor	27.6	33.1	24.8
Mean family income (dollars)	26,255	21,959	25,117
American Indian			
Number	1,055,447	777,182	215,585
Net shift percent of all movers[a]	NA	NA	+3.5
Percent some college or higher[b]	32.7	41.4	52.7
Percent poor	30.2	31.5	27.8
Mean family income (dollars)	26,043	22,590	24,252
Asian			
Number	3,152,104	2,315,961	797,513
Net shift percent of all movers[a]	NA	NA	+13.8
Percent some college or higher[b]	54.2	62.6	74.7
Percent poor	9.6	13.3	15.6
Mean family income (dollars)	51,192	43,775	39,097
Hispanic			
Number	10,725,243	7,878,793	1,365,016
Net shift percent of all movers[a]	NA	NA	+17.0
Percent some college or higher[b]	25.4	30.7	44.8
Percent poor	22.9	25.7	23.9
Mean family income (dollars)	30,762	26,746	26,859

SOURCE: U.S. Bureau of the Census, Census of Population and Housing: 1990 Public Use Microdata Samples.

NA = Not available.

[a]The net shift is the sum of the difference between the number of persons who entered and left each state in the specified area between 1985 and 1990. The percent reported is the net shift divided by the total number of interstate movers.

From Selected Net Loss Areas				To Selected Net Gain Areas		
Northeast	Midwest	South Central[c]	West[d]	California	South Atlantic[e]	Florida
−837,743	−758,538	−494,882	343,714	110,030	749,915	887,504
−4.7%	−4.3%	−2.8%	1.9%	0.6%	4.2%	5.0%
66.2	66.8	62.7	65.0	72.4	68.9	52.8
9.4	10.5	11.7	12.3	8.1	7.8	8.8
$41,822	$36,907	$35,769	$32,776	$42,882	$40,188	$35,138
−163,980	−72,429	−90,825	22,996	24,101	228,622	51,515
−7.1	−3.1	−3.9	1.0	1.0	9.9	2.2
51.8	55.6	53.5	62.5	59.6	55.7	50.0
23.1	30.5	26.7	21.9	20.0	19.2	22.6
27,005	23,406	23,457	23,585	27,889	26,438	23,935
−2,567	2,563	−7,484	3,893	−1,674	5,018	251
−1.2	1.2	−3.5	1.8	−0.8	2.3	0.1
51.8	55.0	52.1	54.0	56.6	53.5	46.8
21.5	32.1	22.8	31.1	21.2	19.4	20.4
26,105	21,271	27,314	22,326	27,998	27,702	23,527
−1,046	−49,580	42,788	−16,441	75,132	24,261	10,462
−0.1	−6.2	−5.4	−2.1	9.4	3.0	1.3
80.1	78.3	72.5	67.2	69.3	75.2	70.0
13.1	18.1	15.8	14.9	19.2	10.2	12.6
45,889	40,799	37,160	33,278	41,373	39,990	33,942
−114,551	−12,003	93,526	42,426	−12,933	49,654	140,933
−8.4	−0.9	−6.9	3.1	−0.9	3.6	10.3
43.9	46.0	41.5	43.8	42.3	55.3	44.0
24.4	23.9	26.4	26.5	22.0	15.0	20.2
27,735	29,628	25,437	23,315	28,232	31,945	27,605

[b] Persons 25 years old and over.
[c] Includes Kentucky, Tennessee, Alabama, Mississippi, Arkansas, Louisiana, Oklahoma, and Texas.
[d] Exclude data for California.
[e] Includes Delaware, Maryland, the District of Columbia, Virginia, West Virginia, North Carolina, South Carolina, and Georgia, but excludes Florida.

that one lived in the same residence or state in 1990 as in 1985. Immigration affected this: 1 in every 5 Asians and 1 in every 10 Hispanics, compared to about 1 in every 100 whites, blacks, or American Indians, entered the United States since 1985. Among those living in the United States in 1985, whites and blacks were most likely (over 57 percent) to reside in the same house. American Indians and Asians (about 50 percent), were more likely than whites and blacks to move, both within and across state lines. However, except for departures from the South Central division and entries into the South Atlantic states, American Indian moves to and from each area roughly counterbalanced, and hence led to relatively small net interregional shifts. Hispanics were the group most likely to have moved within states and the least likely to have moved between states. Both the American Indian and Hispanic patterns suggest less involvement in national labor markets.

With few exceptions, the interstate moves of each group between 1985 and 1990 (shown in Table 4.1) resulted in net movement out of the Northeast, the Midwest, and the South Central division, and net immigration into Florida, the other South Atlantic states, and the West, including California. The origins and destinations that dominated each group's net movement were distinctive, however. For example, about half of the black and Hispanic net outmigration flowed from the Northeast, while half of the net Asian outmigration was from the Midwest. Black outmigration from the Midwest was only half as large as outmigration from the Northeast, but it was still substantial. By comparison, the Midwest's net loss of Hispanics and the net outmigration of Asians from the Northeast were both negligible. White net outmigration from the Northeast was as great as from the Midwest.

The selectivity of migration is evident when one compares the mean family income, poverty rate, and college attainment of interstate migrants to those who stayed in the same residence or state. Compared to the other interstate movers in their groups, blacks, American Indians, and Asians who left the Midwest since 1985 had relatively high poverty rates in 1989. High proportions of the whites, blacks, and Hispanics who left the South Central states were also poor in 1989, and the adults were less likely to have attended or completed college by 1990. These characteristics are consistent with the economic dislocations in the manufacturing and petrochemical industries of the Midwest and South Central states.[17] There is evidence of bimodality, however, in the relatively high proportion of college-educated blacks and Asians who left the Midwest between 1985 and 1990.

The groups were even more distinct in the destinations of their net migration streams. About 80 percent of the net internal migration of whites and Hispanics, and 86 percent of that for blacks, went to the South Atlantic division (including Florida). Three of every four Hispanics that the South Atlantic gained went to Florida, while the other South Atlantic states (especially Georgia, North Carolina, and Maryland) were the destinations for blacks. White net immigration was more evenly divided between Florida and the other South Atlantic states.[18] Two-thirds of the Hispanics moving to Florida came from the Northeast, and another sixth from Texas and California. Those from California were more likely to be foreign-born (about 70 percent) than the Texans or Northeasterners (about 50 percent).

Each group's migrants to the South Atlantic states included relatively high proportions of adults who attended college. Ironically, despite vivid images of black professionals moving to Atlanta and the New South, blacks with some college were only marginally more represented among migrants to the South Atlantic than among black movers generally (54 percent vs. 56 percent).

Asian net migration into Florida and the South Atlantic was substantial, but their primary destination (nearly 70 percent) was California, which had very small net gains or losses of other groups. While whites and blacks who moved to California had higher percentages of adults with college experience than most of their other migration streams, Asian inmigrants to California were less likely than Asian movers to other regions to have attended college. Relatively disadvantaged Asians, particularly from the Midwestern and South Central states, seemed to seek better opportunities in California even as poor whites were leaving.[19] The movers were primarily foreign-born (over 75 percent), and strikingly bimodal in their educational levels: at least 30 percent did not have high school diplomas, while 25 percent or more, including half of the Northeastern Asians moving to California, were college graduates. Many were perhaps recent graduates of Eastern colleges starting careers in California.

Beneath the broad similarities in the net 5-year migration patterns of the groups lie distinctive patterns. All groups migrated out of the Northeast, Midwest, and South Central states, but in numbers that represented widely different proportions of their net streams. American Indian interstate movers tended to remain within regions rather than cross regional boundaries. Black, Asian, and Hispanic streams ended, disproportionately, in the population growth areas with previously high concentrations of each group—the South Atlantic states for blacks, California for Asians, and Florida for Hispanics. These areas provide group-specific niches for minority migrants, and the migration reinforced rather than attenuated the importance of extant population centers as distinctive features of racial and ethnic life in the United States.

SPATIAL AND SOCIAL DISTANCE

Millions of Americans living in a few key states and in several of our largest metropolitan areas have experienced the new racial and ethnic diversity. They have watched as newcomers, different in race or color, creed or tongue, swept toward their neighborhoods, their childhood homes, and the schools they attended, making the familiar strange. In making those new areas "home," the new residents created enclaves—a "Koreatown," a "Little Havana," a place to visit, to shop, or to eat "ethnic" foods. More often their neighborhoods became to others, alien worlds, where even shop signs suggest that outsiders are not expected. And all too often these enclaves are simply unknown worlds, other "ghettos," other "barrios," visited only via the evening news.

In addition to the crime, the poverty, the decay, our physical impressions of ghettos and barrios are often as inner city areas or as now-blighted zones in nearby suburbs, some densely populated, where everyone is black or Hispanic. Areas that are inhabited primarily by members of a single group show very clearly on the map of Los Angeles (map 4.1), especially the massive predominantly black and Hispanic areas south and east, respectively, of downtown. The black area—nearly 10 miles wide and 15 miles long—is the South Central Los Angeles of both the 1965 Watts riots and the 1992 Rodney King conflagration. The even larger Hispanic area grew eastward from East Los Angeles, and is often called by this name, although it has long since burgeoned beyond the bounds of this barrio into eastern suburbs. Asian concentrations, by contrast, appear as a few distinct enclaves, such as Chinatown, directly north of downtown, Monterey Park to the east, and Gardena to the south. Asians are not the majority, nor even the largest group in so-called Asian communities such as Koreatown, Sawtelle (long a Japanese community), Walnut, and Cerritos. Whites are virtually absent from South Central and East Los Angeles, and they never reach a majority of the population in tracts south of the Santa Monica and San Gabriel foothills, or west of the Long Beach freeway, except in the beach communities.

The map conveys powerful images of a racially and ethnically divided metropolis, the "separate societies" described by the Kerner report, where minorities seldom meet whites as neighbors or as classmates in public schools. The map also shows, however, that many predominantly white areas were substantially integrated, with populations that were 20 to nearly 50 percent "minority." How segregated or integrated are blacks, Asians, and Hispanics in Los Angeles and other metropolitan areas?

Answers are important for two reasons. First, residential segregation created an insuperable barrier to *de facto* integration of housing and public schools and trapped minorities in limited markets of the oldest and often the most decayed housing. Second, contact and interaction between groups in residential neighborhoods had seemed pivotal to the successful assimilation experiences of European immigrants in the United States; and many analysts considered this to be a key prerequisite to genuine racial integration.

The most widely used measure of segregation, the index of dissimilarity,

MAP 4.1 Racial and ethnic population concentration in Metropolitan Los Angeles and Orange counties: 1990.

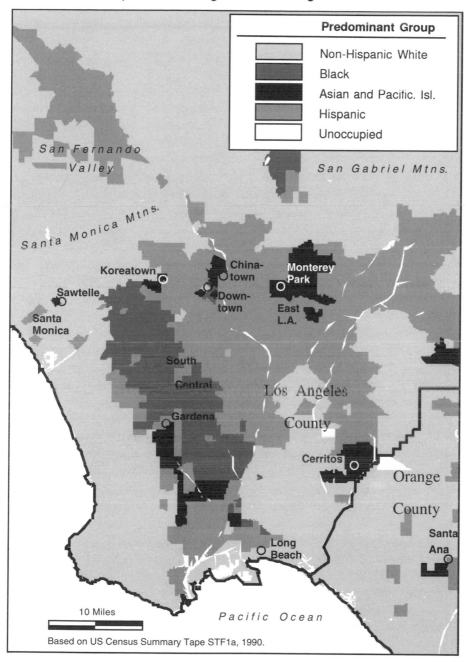

Predominant Group

- Non-Hispanic White
- Black
- Asian and Pacific. Isl.
- Hispanic
- Unoccupied

San Fernando Valley

San Gabriel Mtns.

Santa Monica Mtns.

Koreatown

China-town

Monterey Park

Sawtelle

Down-town

Santa Monica

East L.A.

South Central

Los Angeles County

Gardena

Cerritos

Orange County

Long Beach

Santa Ana

10 Miles

Pacific Ocean

Based on US Census Summary Tape STF1a, 1990.

TABLE 4.2 Mean residential segregation indices for minorities for all metropolitan areas in 1980 and 1990, and for Los Angeles in 1990.

Minority Groups	Dissimilarity	Isolation	Concentration	Centralization	Spatial Proximity	Distance-Decay Isolation
Los Angeles: 1990						
Black	0.728	0.693	0.925	0.817	1.672	0.612
Hispanic	0.611	0.715	0.794	0.749	1.377	0.668
Asian	0.463	0.405	0.915	0.718	1.190	0.349
United States: 1980[a]						
Black	0.736	0.659	0.899	0.778	1.449	0.508
Hispanic	0.500	0.451	0.831	0.724	1.199	0.381
Asian	0.397	0.205	0.891	0.698	1.053	0.161
American Indian	0.363	0.065	0.883	0.638	1.117	0.050
United States: 1990[b]						
Black	0.694	0.629	0.897	0.762	1.427	0.508
Hispanic	0.504	0.517	0.791	0.707	1.226	0.458
Asian	0.409	0.282	0.876	0.682	1.082	0.235
American Indian	0.349	0.069	0.885	0.626	1.128	0.054
Change: 1980–1990[c]						
Black	-0.042	-0.031	-0.002	-0.015	-0.022	0.000
Hispanic	0.004	0.067	-0.040	-0.016	0.027	0.076
Asian	0.012	0.077	-0.015	-0.015	0.030	0.074
American Indian	-0.014	0.005	0.003	-0.011	0.011	0.004
Percentage Change: 1980 to 1990[d]						
Black	-5.8	-4.6	-0.2	-1.9	-1.5	0.0
Hispanic	0.9	14.8	-4.8	-2.2	2.3	20.0
Asian	3.1	37.7	-1.7	-2.2	2.8	45.7
American Indian	-3.8	7.6	0.3	-1.7	1.0	8.4

SOURCE: U.S. Bureau of the Census, Census of Population and Housing: 1980 and 1990.

[a] 1980 indices for each group are means of metropolitan area indices weighted by the group's 1980 population.
[b] 1990 indices for each group are means of metropolitan area indices weighted by the group's 1990 population.
[c] Changes 1980 to 1990 are means of metropolitan area changes weighted by the average of the group's 1980 and 1990 population.
1980 to 1990 are the ratios of the 1990 mean changes to the 1980 mean indices.

indicates the percentage of each minority population that would have to move to other census tracts for the group to be proportionately represented in all tracts. The isolation index increases when a minority population in each tract is more likely to encounter its own members than whites. The distance-decay isolation index increases with greater geographic distances between minority and white areas, and with it, for example, the difficulty of integrating schools by bussing students from areas of racial isolation. The spatial proximity index measures whether predominantly minority census tracts cluster together in contiguous areas—as they do for blacks and Hispanics in South Central and East Los Angeles. Concentration indices increase when a minority population is concentrated in a relatively small number of compact tracts, and centralization indices measure whether or not a group resides close to the downtown area. Our images of "ghettos" and "barrios," particularly in older cities, involve concentrated minority populations clustered in dense inner city neighborhoods, and hence aspects of segregation that these indices seek to measure (Massey and Denton 1988).

The segregation measures (Table 4.2) confirm the map's image of black, Asian, and Hispanic populations in Los Angeles concentrated in areas very close to downtown (see top panel of Table 4.2). The means for all metropolitan areas (see middle panels in Table 4.2) in 1990 suggest similar, but somewhat less concentrated and centralized minority areas in the average metropolis, and less clustering into large contiguous areas like South Central and East Los Angeles. In New York, for example, blacks are more segregated than in Los Angeles on the dissimilarity index (.815 compared to .728), but they live in geographically separated areas, such as Harlem in Manhattan, Bedford-Stuyvesant in Brooklyn, and in several areas in Queens. The concentration and clustering of minority populations in Los Angeles make blacks, Asians, and Hispanics more isolated than in most metropolitan areas. Higher percentages of each group in Los Angeles would have to move to other tracts to eliminate dissimilarity; the distance-decay indices indicate that these moves would also involve longer distances.

The national averages on these and related measures of segregation reveal three unmistakable trends in residential segregation in the United States (Harrison and Weinberg 1992). First, no matter how segregation is measured, blacks were the most segregated group in both 1980 and 1990, usually by a substantial margin (e.g., 35 percent higher on the dissimilarity index). Hispanics were second on most indices, and Asians were more highly segregated than American Indians.

Second, all forms of residential segregation either remained stable or declined modestly (10 percent or less) for blacks during the decade. The declines in dissimilarity for American Indians and blacks were consistent with suburbanization or other moves from tracts of over- to under-representation. In contrast, Hispanics and Asians became slightly more segregated and notably more isolated from whites, both generally and when the distances to predominantly white neighborhoods are specifically considered (see isolation and distance decay indices). These increases, and those in clustering as well, can occur when a group grows rapidly as a proportion of the population, and when the new members establish residences closer to persons of their own group. The observed increases in segregation thus seem traceable to Asian and Hispanic immigrants settling near extant communities.

Third, the changes in residential segregation during the decade were relatively small and evolutionary. The decline in the dissimilarity index for blacks, for example, would leave blacks as segregated 50 years from now as Hispanics were in 1990. But if the increased segregation of Hispanics and Asians is not surprising given immigration, the trend is important: the residential segregation of Asians and of Hispanics might not decline so long as the centripetal forces of continued immigration counterbalance the residential dispersion of longer-term residents. This, and the modest declines in the residential segregation of blacks, more than two decades after the passage of equal housing opportunity laws and despite considerable suburbanization, suggest that present patterns of residential segregation may remain with us for decades to come. Suburbanization helped reduce the residential segregation of blacks during the 1970s, but suburbanization slowed in the 1980s, and its effects are often tempered as the "new" areas attract more blacks (Farley 1991). For example, in 1990 one in every five blacks lived in a block that had been less than 10 percent black in 1980 (Judkins, Waksberg, and Massey 1992). However, because this influx often pushed black representation above 10 percent, only 12 percent lived in blocks that were still less than 10 percent black in 1990.

Hopes and expectations that residential segregation would fall more rapidly with suburbanization also rested on the fact that lower incomes, rather than discrimination alone, often prevented minorities from renting or buying in many areas. Analyses of the greater New York metropolitan area showed that "acculturated" middle-income Asians and Hispanics (but not blacks) resided in tracts with racial compositions and household incomes similar to those of whites with comparable incomes.[20] Access to internal files used to generate the 1990 5 percent Public Use Microdata Sample (PUMS) enabled us to identify the census tract in which each individual and household in the file lived.[21] Regressions analogous to those conducted for greater New York were used to compare the percentage white and mean family incomes of tracts in which each group lived in 1990, when they had comparable family incomes, family types, educational levels, poverty statuses, and rented or owned units of similar value (Table 4.3).

Blacks and Hispanics lived in tracts in 1990 that had at best 60 percent of

TABLE 4.3   Regression of mean family income and percent white of census tract on selected family and household characteristics: 1990 (in 1989 dollars).

| | Dependent Variables | | | |
| | Mean Family Income of Tract | | Percent White of Tract | |
	Owners (dollars)	Renters (dollars)	Owners	Renters
Intercept	20,860	15,260	78.6	86.8
Regression Coefficients				
Metropolitan area	0	0	0.0	0.0
Value of housing unit or rent	570	1,260	−0.1	−0.1
Family income	0	0	0.0	0.0
Poverty status of family	−1,440	1,660	−2.2	−0.8
Educational attainment of householder	310	390	0.7	0.3
Family Type				
Male householder, no spouse present	280	580	−2.5	−3.0
Female householder, no spouse present	1,630	1,980	−3.2	−3.4
Single male living alone	1,670	2,040	−1.8	−2.9
Single female living alone	4,130	3,290	−1.1	−2.5
Race or Hispanic Origin				
Black	−5,390	−4,220	−41.6	−46.6
American Indian	3,550	−3,360	−15.6	−24.0
Asian	−1,440	1,430	−28.0	−27.0
Hispanic origin	−3,450	−4,030	−38.2	−38.3

SOURCE: U.S. Bureau of the Census, Census of Population and Housing: 1990 Public Use Microdata Samples.

NOTE: The omitted categories are "married-couple families" for family type and "whites" for race or Hispanic origin.

the expected percentage of whites. American Indian renters and Asian owners or renters lived in neighborhoods that had at least 25 percent fewer whites than expected, and American Indian owners lived in tracts with 16 percent fewer whites than expected. Blacks and Hispanics lived in tracts with mean family incomes $3,400–$5,400 lower than whites with comparable profiles. The corresponding figures for American Indians and Asian owners ranged between $1,400–$3,600 lower. The model shows that comparable educational attainments, family income, and expenditures on housing did not lead minorities to live in neighborhoods with incomes or percentages of whites as high as expected, were race and ethnicity not a factor.

The primacy of racial over income factors is especially striking for blacks. Dissimilarity measures of the segregation of poor and nonpoor persons in each group from nonpoor whites show that the black poor (.79) and nonpoor (.72) are the two most highly segregated groups, and poor whites (.34) the least. Notably, nonpoor blacks are more residentially segregated from nonpoor whites than poor Hispanics, Asians, or American Indians (from .62 to .67), who are in turn far more segregated than the nonpoor in their groups (.52, .41, and .38, respectively). Poor minorities were thus far more segregated than nonpoor in their groups, but the uniquely small differentials among blacks underscore the paramount importance of race rather than economic standing in their residential segregation.

While the high segregation levels of both poor and nonpoor blacks sharply distinguish them from other minorities, the segregation levels of Asians and of Hispanics similarly belie simple comparisons with European immigrant groups. Italians (.134) and Russians (.101) were the most isolated groups in the nation's 17 largest cities in 1910.[22] Both dropped below .093 by 1920, and the next highest value (Hungarians, at .030), was considerably lower. Only American Indians (.126) showed comparably low isolation among today's minorities. Even if Italian and Russian isolation were twice that estimated for 1920, Asians and Hispanics would remain considerably more isolated in 1990 than European immigrants 70 years ago. Residential segregation levels and the "social distance" they imply suggest that America's racial minorities today experience exclusion far beyond that of the European immigrants. Inclusion and assimilation processes that begin so differently might be expected to have very different trajectories and outcomes.

Intergroup Marriages and Children

Minorities have experienced greater residential segregation than European immigrants, but their histories of intermarriage differ even more sharply. Intermarriage has for some time been high enough among European ancestry groups for large percentages to either report complex mixtures or to find it impossible to fully identify or trace the strains (Waters 1990). In contrast, when Richard Loving, a white man, and Mildred Jeter, a black and American Indian woman, married in 1958, and returned to their home state of Virginia, they were promptly arrested for violating the state's miscegenation laws. The judge suspended the 5-year prison sentence they faced provided that they leave the state. The Lovings moved to Washington, D.C., but they were arrested again when they visited Richard's mother in Virginia 5 years later. Their appeal led the Supreme Court to strike down miscegenation laws in Virginia and in the 15 other states that still banned interracial marriages in 1967.

Such prohibitions, extant in 29 states as late as 1953, are a defining characteristic of caste. Conversely, intermarriage without regard to racial or ethnic distinction virtually defines complete assimilation and equality between groups. Students of assimilation have long seen residential propinquity as a necessary condition for social interaction and integration among racial and ethnic groups. A white might first accept minorities as co-workers or neighbors and perhaps later as friends. But the ultimate test of declining social distance and growing equality has been acceptability as marital partners.

In 1960 there were about 150,000 interracial couples in the United States. This number grew rapidly to more than 1.0 million in 1990. When marriages with Hispanics are added, the number of intergroup marriages totaled about 1.6 million in 1990. Couples like the Lovings were thus about 7 times more prevalent in 1990 than when they had won their case two decades earlier. Nevertheless, interracial couples still represented only about 2 percent, and intergroup couples 4 percent, of the 51 million married couples in the United States in 1990. Only 1 in 5 intermarriages involved a black and a white. Indeed, couples like the Lovings, with a white husband and black wife, remained rare, representing only 5 percent of intermarriages.

The two most striking features of interracial marriages in the United States (Figure 4.4) are that blacks and whites are proportionately least likely to marry outside their groups, and that whites are several times more likely to marry members of groups other than blacks. Over 93 percent of whites and of blacks marry within their own groups, in contrast to about 70 percent of Asians and of Hispanics and less than one-third of American Indians. Indeed, American Indians were more likely to have white spouses than to be homogamous.

When minorities marry outside their group, their spouses are very likely to be white: interracial marriages in the United States seldom involved the mixing of two minority groups. Nearly half of the 3 percent of white men who outmarry wed Hispanics, and most of the remainder have Asian (0.8) or American Indian (0.4) spouses; rarely (0.1 percent) do they marry black women. White women are also as likely to marry Hispanics (1.2) as the other three groups combined (about 0.3 percent each).

If persons married without regard to race or Hispanic origin and simply in proportion to each group's percentage of the married population, about 5.5 percent of white males and females should have Hispanic, and another 5.5 percent, black, spouses.[23] This is about 5 times as many marriages as actually occur between whites and Hispanics; about 20 times the percentage observed between white women and black men, and 50 times that realized between white men and black women. One would expect white men to marry Asian women about 4 times (2.6 percent) as often as they do, and Asian men to wed white women about 10 times more frequently (2.1 percent). However, 3 of every 5 marriages

FIGURE 4.4 Race or ethnicity of couples: 1980 and 1990.

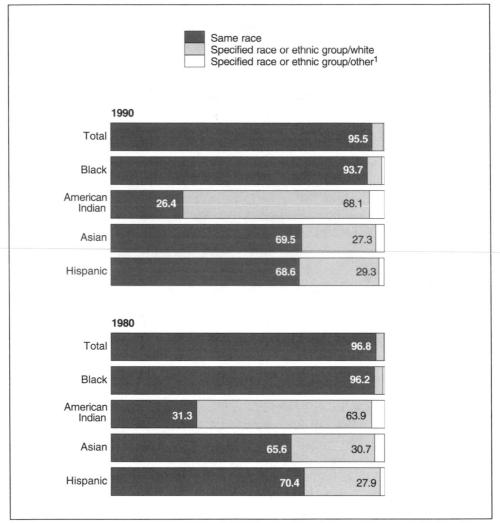

■ Same race
□ Specified race or ethnic group/white
□ Specified race or ethnic group/other[1]

1990

Total	95.5	
Black	93.7	
American Indian	26.4	68.1
Asian	69.5	27.3
Hispanic	68.6	29.3

1980

Total	96.8	
Black	96.2	
American Indian	31.3	63.9
Asian	65.6	30.7
Hispanic	70.4	27.9

SOURCE: U.S. Bureau of the Census, *1980 and 1990 Census of Population and Housing,* Public Use Micro-data Samples.

NOTE: Bar segments for 6 percent or less are not labelled separately on figure.

[1] Classified by the race of the female spouse or partner.

that one would expect between American Indians and whites actually occur. Homogamy, age, education, geography, and other factors not examined here affect intermarriage, and the patterns reflect much more than social distance alone. The strong *differentials* in the patterns nevertheless suggest that whites maintain far more "social distance" from black men, and especially black women, than they do from other groups.

Parallel to the intermarriage patterns, 92 percent or more of white and black children who lived with both parents shared the same race with both parents in 1990 (Table 4.4).[24] Only 185,000 children lived in households where one parent was black and the other white. The 126,000 who identified as black represented about 3 percent of black children, and the nearly 60,000 who identified as white, less than 1 percent of white children. In contrast, about 330,000 children lived in households with one American Indian and one white parent, 435,000 children with one Asian and one white parent, and 1.3 million with one Hispanic and one non-Hispanic white parent. Almost one-quarter of the 2.0 million children with at least one Asian parent, and of the 5.4 million with at least one Hispanic parent lived in interracial households with one non-Hispanic white parent or stepparent. More than half (59 percent) of all children with at least one American Indian, Eskimo, or Aleut parent live in such households.

Substantial percentages of Asians, Hispanics, and American Indians thus have a white parent. The implication of this might heavily depend on whether society at large defines such children by the race or ethnic group of the minority parent, as it did with blacks, or whether interracial children might, like European ethnics, have ethnic options, perhaps changing during their lives, over how they identify (Waters 1990). An emerging alternative, advocated by several organizations of multiracial families, is that society recognize that such children represent a new form of "diversity," and that we can no longer classify our population into mutually exclusive race and ethnic groups.

As prevalent as intergroup marriages and children were in 1990, they remained far below the levels for European immigrants, which suggests distinctions and social distances of an entirely different magnitude than Europeans experienced. The argument that interracial children should not be forced to belong to only one heritage suggests that the races of the parents matter in ways that the differing nationalities of European parents did not. The struggle against being forced into the group of one parent contrasts with the presumed desire of many European immigrants to "melt" into an Americanness where the origins of their parents were of personal significance only. Race has a significance in these matters that has only faint parallels among European ethnics. Today's minorities may be unlikely to follow the trajectory into a melting pot.

Levels of intermarriage and of residential segregation underscore the distinctive and castelike social distance that separates blacks from whites in our society. Despite modest changes on these indicators, we maintain social distances that for decades to come will keep us two societies, separate and unequal, one black, one white.

TABLE 4.4 Race or ethnicity of child, by race or ethnicity of householder and of spouse or partner: 1980 and 1990 (universe is children under 18 in married- or unmarried-couple households).

				Race or Ethnicity of Minority Parent			
	Total[a]	White	Black	American Indian	Asian	Hispanic
1980						
Total	51,437,700	40,496,320	4,567,480	544,560	1,193,300	4,556,320
Percent	100.0%	100.0%	100.0%	100.0%	100.0%	100.0%
Child same group as parents[b]	95.8	99.9	95.8	38.0	69.9	74.2
Parents/child(ren) different group						
Total	4.2	0.1	4.2	62.0	30.1	25.9
Child white: one parent specified group and one white	1.4	NA	0.8	29.3	15.4	7.6
Child specified group: one parent specified group and one white	2.0	NA	1.9	25.2	9.2	14.9
Child, one parent specified group and one other race[c]	0.3	NA	1.1	3.7	2.1	1.5
Child different group than both parents[d]	0.5	0.1	0.4	3.8	3.4	1.9

1990

	47,133,399	35,515,907	3,632,004	567,610	1,979,890	5,365,343
Total						
Percent	100.0%	100.0%	100.0%	100.0%	100.0%	100.0%
Child same group as parents [b]	93.9	99.8	92.3	31.7	71.4	72.3
Parents/child(ren) different group						
Total	6.1	0.2	7.7	68.3	28.6	27.7
Child white: one parent specified group and one white	2.1	NA	1.6	31.0	12.7	8.9
Child specified group: one parent specified group and one white	2.7	NA	3.5	27.7	9.3	15.0
Child, one parent specified group and one other race [c]	0.5	NA	1.7	4.6	2.2	1.7
Child different group than both parents [d]	0.8	0.2	0.9	4.9	4.3	2.1

SOURCE: U.S. Bureau of the Census, 1980 and 1990 Census of Population and Housing, Public Use Microdata Samples.

NA = Not Applicable.

[a] Total includes persons who identified in the other race category, not shown separately.

[b] Parents include unmarried partners and stepparents.

[c] Includes all other groups except white and the group specified. Classified by group of male partner.

[d] Classified by race of child.

EDUCATION AND LABOR FORCE

Educational Attainment

If there is a core American creed regarding what has enabled some individuals and groups to succeed and thrive while others have not, education lies at its heart. Americans hold a deep-seated moral, as well as policy, conviction that education is the key to success in the United States, and that the historical and current solutions to group disadvantage and poverty lie in acquiring the higher levels of education needed to compete in relatively meritocratic and ever more skilled labor markets. During the 1980s, the deteriorating job opportunities and earnings of men with high school degrees or less, and the contribution that this may have made toward the decline of married-couple families and the growth of an underclass, particularly in black communities, has underscored this fundamental tenet.

Most minority groups have shared this conviction, have struggled and even shed blood to eliminate barriers to equal educational opportunity. It is thus scarcely coincidental that the single most pivotal event in modern American race relations, *Brown* v. *Board of Education,* was fought over equality in education; or that the most heartrending battles for civil rights were fought literally at schoolhouse doors, by children and young adults requiring the fully armed power of federal marshals and federalized troops to cross thresholds guarded by angry defenders of the traditional segregated way of life. It is not surprising that reverse discrimination and efforts to delineate and delimit how race can be considered in remedying past discrimination came most prominently to national attention in *Bakke's* suit over admission to medical school (*Regents of the University of California* v. *Bakke*). Nor is it happenstance that the first skirmishes of the new racial diversity are being fought between advocates of multicultural curricula and those who fear this abandons the transmission of Western civilization to new generations.

Two sweeping historical trends have dominated educational attainment in the decades since 1940. The first has been the dramatic, relatively unheralded, reduction of racial and ethnic differentials in high school completion. The second was the rapid expansion of college and postbaccalaureate education, beginning in the 1960s in reaction to the Soviet Union's launch of Sputnik.

All groups have dramatically increased their high school graduation rates since 1940. In fact, black, American Indian, and Hispanic students have made the greatest gains, especially since 1960, and have therefore converged towards the rates of white and of Asian students. In 1940, more than 1 in 4 white adults (aged 25 and older) had completed high school. This doubled to over one-half in 1970, and had tripled to nearly four-fifths by 1990 (Figure 4.5). In contrast, fewer than 1 out of 10 black adults was a high school graduate in 1940, but 3 in 10 were in 1970, and 6 in 10 were by 1990. About 1 in 3 American Indian and Hispanic adults had graduated from high school in 1970; this grew to two-thirds and one-half, respectively, in 1990. As Mare shows in Chapter 4 in Volume 1, native-born Hispanics are almost as likely to complete high school as blacks and American Indians; the very low percentage of Hispanic immigrants with high school diplomas reduces the completion rates of the group as a whole.

FIGURE 4.5   Percentage of persons 25 years and over who have completed college, by sex and race or ethnicity: 1970 to 1990.

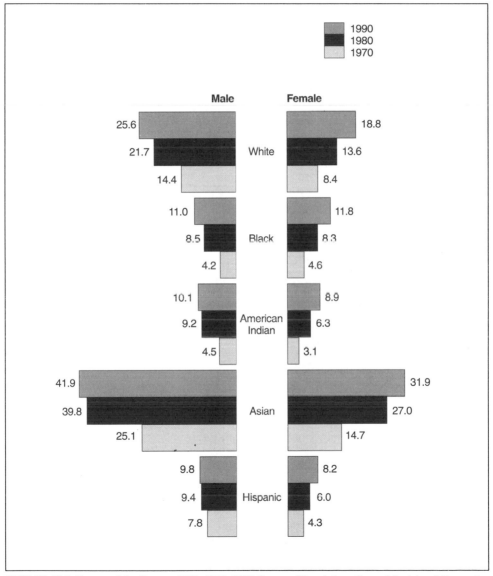

SOURCE: U.S. Bureau of the Census, 1970, 1980, 1990 Census of Population, *General Social and Economic Characteristics for the United States.*

NOTE: 1970 data for Asians are based on the 1 in 1,000 Public Use Microdata Samples.

The convergence is clearer when one compares persons who were aged 65 or older in 1990 with 25–44 year olds (Figure 4.6). High school graduates increased from about 50 percent of Asians and 60 percent of whites aged 65 or older to nearly 90 percent of those in the younger cohorts. Black, American Indian, and Hispanic cohorts aged 35–64 doubled or tripled the high school completion rates of their oldest cohorts, however, and moved progressively closer to white and Asian completion rates. One might therefore expect even higher percentages of high school graduates among 25–34 year olds; and this does occur for black women and for Asian and Hispanic men and women. Instead, the percentage of high school graduates among 25–34-year-old whites and American Indians fell from the previous cohort, and the proportions for black males scarcely differed.

Gains in completing high school thus leveled off in key groups after 1974, when the late baby boom cohorts (that is, persons aged 25–34 in 1990) began graduating from high school. Whites and Asians may be approaching a so-called ceiling, reflecting a pool of about 10 percent or so of students for whom high school completion is difficult. Black, American Indian, and Hispanic completion rates (and progress towards convergence) leveled off far short of this ceiling during the period, however. This problem differs from the alarming 50 percent attrition rates reported in some inner city schools.[25] The trend suggests a problem that is national rather than specific to minorities; one that arises from a halt in a historic march towards greater parity, rather than a lost generation floundering or succumbing to cultures or environments that insufficiently value or promote education. In a nation that has heavily relied upon gains in education to reduce the historic exclusion of minorities, this pause in decades of progress towards parity must be a matter for sober concern.

The steady advances of young blacks, American Indians, and native-born Hispanics toward the high school completion percentages of white and Asians suggested that the battleground would soon move to college and higher education. The percentage of college graduates among the population aged 25 years and older grew rapidly for all groups in the 1970s and showed some convergence. The percentages of white males and females with college degrees grew by 50 percent during that decade, while those of blacks and American Indians nearly doubled, to about 8.4 percent for black men and women and to 9.2 and 6.3 percent for American Indians.

This expansion continued but slowed considerably in the 1980s. Asians increased their already very high percentages of college graduates (Figure 4.5). The proportion of white male baccalaureates grew by nearly 20 percent, but non-Asian women registered 40 percent increases, and black males a 30 percent gain. Black men, who completed college in smaller percentages than American Indian and Hispanic men in 1980, passed these groups during the decade. They now have slightly higher percentages of college graduates than do American Indians and Hispanics. (See Figure 4.6 for trends in college completion from 1970 to 1990.)

FIGURE 4.6   Educational attainment of persons, by race or ethnicity, sex, and selected age groups: 1990 (in percent).

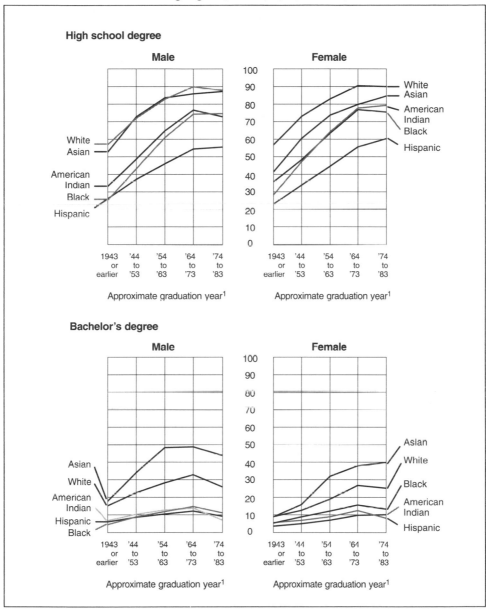

SOURCE: U.S. Bureau of the Census, Census of Population and Housing: 1990, Public Use Microdata Samples.

[1] Assumes high school graduation is at 18 years and college graduation at 22 years.

Despite important advances, blacks, American Indians, and Hispanics continue to complete high school and college at much lower rates than do whites and particularly Asians, whose educational attainments surpass those of all groups. Asians were about two-thirds more likely to have completed college than whites were, who, in turn, did so in proportions twice those of blacks, American Indians, and Hispanics. The high percentage of Asians with college degrees in part reflects selective immigration and the high proportion of foreign-born Asians who are college-educated (38 percent). Native-born Asians are still substantially more likely to complete college (32 percent) than are whites and other groups, but the differential is smaller. Intergroup differentials in earning college degrees declined modestly in the 1980s and gender differentials more substantially, suggesting some improvements in educational opportunities for blacks, Hispanics, and American Indians, and important gains for women in all groups. However, the historic progress that blacks, American Indians, and native-born Hispanics have made in reducing high school completion differentials with whites has levelled off.

Returns to Education

The thesis that race has declined in significance in the post–civil rights era stands on an empirical base almost entirely comprised of convergence in the earnings of young college-educated blacks and whites during the 1970s, and on strong theoretical expectations, most fully developed by economists, that competition should drive discrimination resulting from anything but differences in productivity from labor markets (Shulman and Darity 1989). The 1980 census provided important evidence of convergence for 25–34 year olds (Farley 1984). Adjusting for region, the hourly earnings of black and white men in this cohort were almost equal in 1980 (96 percent) among those with 4 or more years of college, and the gap had closed substantially (to 89 percent from 70 percent in 1960) among those with two years of college. The gap between black and white high school graduates remained large, but it had closed to 82 percent from 65 percent in 1960. Among women aged 25–34, black–white differentials had already disappeared in 1970, and in 1980 the earnings of black women were within 5 percent of parity at all educational levels.

What does the 1990 census tell us about these trends? With a few important exceptions, the earnings ratios (which do not adjust for region or residence) indicate parity for comparably educated minority and white women, but persisting and substantial differentials for all minority men.

The parity in both the annual and estimated hourly earnings of women was consistent across all educational levels except for American Indians and for Hispanics at some educational levels. American Indian women with less than college degrees generally earned only 83–88 percent of the wages that comparably educated white women earned annually and per hour (Figure 4.7). American Indian women with college and graduate degrees had earnings closer to those of white women (90–93 percent). Exceptions to parity among Hispanic women arose only in selected birth cohorts without high school diplomas or with associate degrees (data not shown).

The earnings ratios for men, by contrast, approached parity only in the annual and hourly earnings of Asians with associate and graduate degrees (92 and 97 percent). Men in each minority group otherwise earned considerably less than whites at each educational level. The annual earnings ratios were worst—at about 70 percent—for American Indian males with less than a college degree. Their hourly earnings ratios were comparable to those for similarly educated blacks and somewhat lower than comparable Hispanics and Asians. Below the associate degree level, annual earnings ratios were lower than the hourly values, ranging between 70 and 76 percent for black and American Indian males and from 76 to 83 percent for Hispanic and Asian males. Working fewer hours or weeks in 1989 than comparable white males thus contributed to the annual differentials. That is, the racial difference between the earnings of minority and white men is greater for annual earnings than for hourly earnings because white men typically work more hours per year.

The differences from whites were modestly smaller for minority men with associate, bachelor, or graduate degrees. American Indian men again had the lowest hourly and annual earnings ratios. Blacks, Hispanics, and Asians had earnings closer to those of white men. While American Indians' most favorable ratios were for college graduates, blacks', Hispanics', and Asians' highest annual and hourly ratios were among associate degree-holders. Among college graduates, the gaps for each group except American Indians were greater in the older cohorts. At other educational levels, the gaps were smaller for older blacks and Hispanics, suggesting modest convergence with greater work experience. There were no consistent age patterns for American Indians or Asians.

The 1990 earnings ratios strongly indicate that earlier trends towards parity in earnings for men have abated, and that minority men at all levels of educational attainment remained unlikely to obtain returns to their education equal to those of comparable white men. The earnings ratios usually, but far from invariably, improved at the higher educational levels. The differences are not dramatic, however, and scarcely suggest that higher education alone will reduce intergroup differentials. The contrast in male and female earnings differentials suggests attention to the occupations to which members of each group took their degrees: the occupational distributions of women of different races have been more similar than those for men, and this contributed to the parity in earnings evident among women.

Occupation

The occupational distributions of minority and white women were similar primarily because about 40–50 percent in each group worked in administrative

FIGURE 4.7 Median hourly earnings of minority group to white earners, by sex, educational attainment, and selected ages: 1990 (percentage of white median hourly earnings).

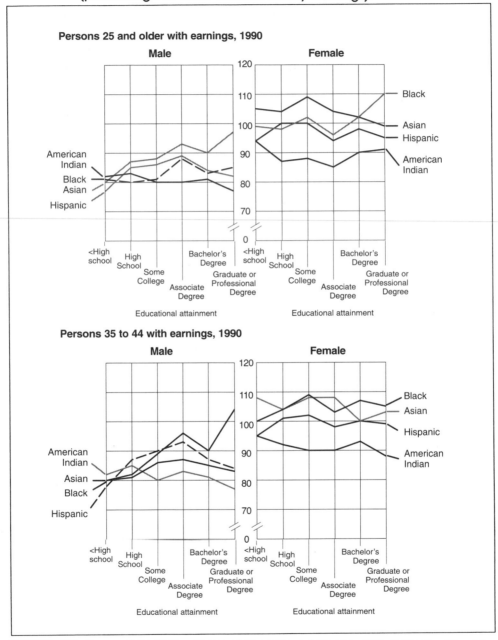

SOURCE: U.S. Bureau of the Census, Census of Population and Housing: 1990, Public Use Microdata Samples.

FIGURE 4.8   Occupational distribution of the civilian labor force, by sex and race or ethnicity: 1990 (16 years and over).

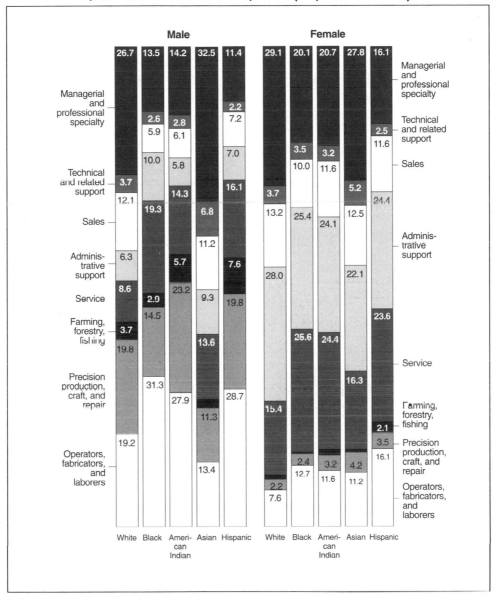

SOURCE: U.S. Bureau of the Census, 1990 Census of Population, Supplementary Reports, *Detailed Occupation and Other Characteristics from the EEO File for the United States.*

NOTE: Data for whites, blacks, American Indians, and Asians are for non-Hispanic persons only. Bar segments for 2 percent or less are not labelled separately on figure.

support and service occupations in 1990 (Figure 4.8). When added to the 10–13 percent of each group in sales jobs, more than half of all women shared the same broad occupations. The differences in the proportion of women in each group who worked as managers and professionals were greater, but they were still much smaller than among men. Among men, whites and Asians were twice as likely as other men to hold managerial, professional, and sales jobs.

For both men and women, the differences in the occupational distributions of the groups in part reflected differentials in education; they are smaller among comparably educated people (Figure 4.9a). The percentage of college-educated women in each group who held managerial (19 percent) or professional (about 40 percent) positions was remarkably consistent. Only Asian women differed, with fewer professionals (about 30 percent) and twice the percentage of technicians (9 percent). College-educated female managers in each group had comparable earnings close to the overall average of $29,800, but black and Asian professionals earned more ($27,440 and $31,510) than the overall average for professionals of $25,000 (Figure 4.9b).

The differences in the occupations and earnings of college-educated men were much larger. A consistent 25 percent of each group were professionals; but substantially higher percentages of white (29 percent) than of minority men (around 22 percent) worked as managers. The intergroup earnings differences for men in these occupations were striking, especially when contrasted with women's differentials: college-educated white men averaged about $55,000 in managerial and $48,000 in professional jobs, while Asians earned about $48,000 in each. Blacks, American Indians, and Hispanics averaged $43,000 or less in either occupation. The earnings of college-educated white men were higher than for similar minority men both because they took their degrees to higher paying management jobs, and because they earned more than minority men when they held jobs as managers or professionals.

Differences in the detailed occupations that minorities and whites held within the managerial and professional categories also contributed to the greater earnings differentials among men than among women.[26] Except among Asians, for example, over 70 percent of college-educated professional women worked as elementary and secondary school teachers, as registered nurses, as writers, artists, and entertainers, and as religious and social workers. Elementary and secondary school teaching attracted about 40 percent of black and Hispanic professional women, but one-third or less of other groups. Among teachers, black women earned more (around $31,000) than the average ($27,000). About 30 percent of Asian women, but less than 20 percent of other women were registered nurses. Notably, another 25 percent of Asians worked in about equal numbers as physicians, other health assessment and treatment professionals, mathematical and computer scientists, and postsecondary school teachers. With these exceptions, each group of women had similar distributions across and earnings within these detailed professions.

FIGURE 4.9 a Occupational distribution, by educational attainment, sex, race, or ethnicity: 1990 (in percent).

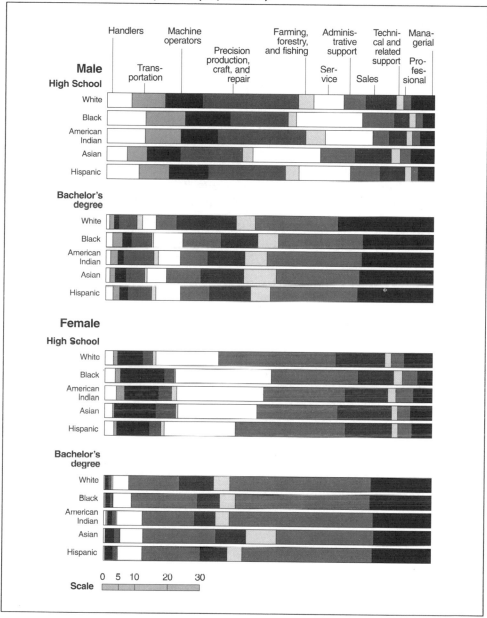

SOURCE: U.S. Bureau of the Census, Census of Population and Housing: 1990 Public Use Microdata Samples.

FIGURE 4.9 b   Mean money earnings in 1989, by selected occupations, education, sex, and race or ethnicity (in thousands of dollars).

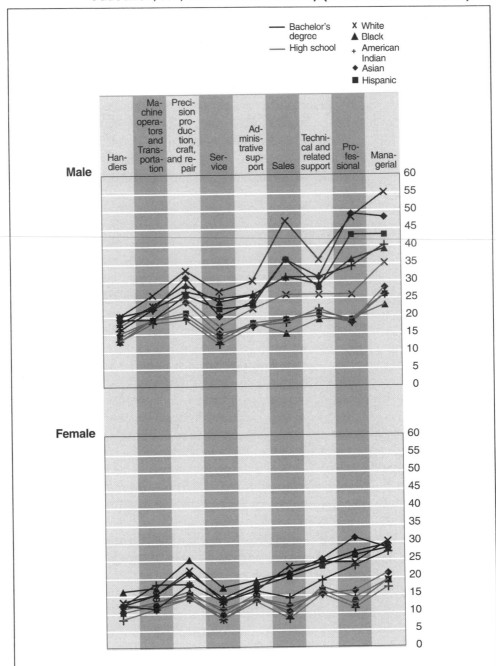

SOURCE: U.S. Bureau of the Census, Census of Population and Housing: 1990 Public Use Microdata Samples.

Among males, over 40 percent of black, American Indian, and Hispanic college-educated professionals worked as elementary and secondary school teachers, as writers, artists, and entertainers, and as religious and social workers. The average earnings in each of these occupations were less than $35,000. In contrast, about 37 percent of white and nearly 60 percent of Asian professionals held higher paying jobs (over $43,000) as engineers, mathematical and computer scientists, and physicians. Only a third of Hispanic and American Indian males, and only one in four blacks held such positions. Thus, white men tend to concentrate in the higher paying and minority men in the lower paid professions. Earnings within the detailed professions also differed substantially: white engineers averaged nearly $4,000 more than others, and white and Asian physicians at least $10,000 more. The much greater group differences in the detailed professions held by men than by women, as well as the greater earnings differentials within many of these, widened the gaps in returns that men received for their college degrees.

Similar patterns also help explain the greater group earnings differentials among male than female high school graduates. White and Hispanic women were more likely to hold administrative support jobs than service jobs (about 35 and 15 percent), while other women were about equally divided between the two. High school graduates earned much more in administrative support than in service occupations ($14,270 and $8,480). Black women's earnings were above the average in both occupations, and Asians' in service jobs, which partially compensated for their lower representation in higher paying administrative support occupations. However, black female high school graduates were also less represented and earned less than the average ($10,450) in sales occupations, where earnings fell between those in service and administrative support jobs.

Sales occupations are among the best paying for male high school graduates (about $25,000). Whites and Asians were twice as likely as black and American Indians to hold such jobs. White, Hispanic, and American Indian men were also more likely than blacks and Asians to work in the precision craft occupations, where high school graduates averaged around $24,000. In addition, white high school graduates earned substantially more (over $25,000) than others (usually under $20,000) in both sales and precision craft occupations. Conversely, minority men were twice as likely as whites to take high school diplomas to lower paying ($15,660) service occupations, where they were also less likely to hold higher paying police and fire jobs (over $27,500) than such lower paying jobs ($16,000 or less) as cleaning and personal service workers, as private guards, and, among Asians, as cooks and waiters (about $11,000). The higher earnings of white men results from their concentration in the better paying occupations and also because within many occupations they are paid more than minority men with high school diplomas.

Differences in the major occupations in which men and women in each group take their degrees, differences in their distribution across regions, across major

TABLE 4.5   Regression of annual and of hourly earnings on educational attainment, selected employment characteristics, region, and race or ethnicity, by sex: 1979 and 1989 (in 1989 dollars).

| | Men | | | |
| Dependent Variable | 1989 | | 1979 | |
	Annual	Hourly	Annual	Hourly
Intercept[a]	$16,170	$-5.40	$18,740	$1.60
Regression Coefficients				
Age	250	0.40	240	0.30
Educational attainment				
Less than high school	-1,410	-3.80	-2,860	-4.20
Some college	2,180	0.30	1,250	0.20
Associate degree[b]	2,970	2.10	NA	NA
Bachelor's degree	9,800	5.20	9,330	5.30
Advanced degree[a]	23,630	12.20	NA	NA
Weeks worked	450	-0.40	460	-0.20
Hours worked	360	-0.40	250	-0.50
Region				
Midwest	-2,760	-1.30	880	0.90
South	-3,870	-1.20	-1,470	0.30
West	-830	1.70	1,290	1.50
Class of worker				
Public sector	-4,360	-2.30	-3,410	-1.20
Self-employed	4,700	8.60	3,090	5.00
Occupation				
Managerial	12,760	11.10	10,060	8.20
Professional	7,370	7.90	7,440	6.40
Sales	5,680	6.10	3,690	4.40
Technical	3,660	5.80	3,260	3.70
Administrative support	270	3.60	510	1.00
Private household	980	-1.70	-340	-1.80
Protective service	5,260	6.30	1,230	2.70
Service	230	-0.50	0	-1.30
Precision	2,000	4.30	2,630	3.80
Machine operators	-190	3.50	300	2.90
Transport operators	-480	3.01	1,320	3.90
Industry				
Manufacturing	1,100	-0.20	-1,270	-2.10
Wholesale trade	2,410	2.00	-70	-0.80
Retail trade	-4,290	-4.40	-6,910	-6.40
Finance, insurance, and real estate	2,970	1.65	-3,130	-2.80
Repair service	-5,440	-4.60	-8,320	-6.70
Professional service	-1,640	-1.60	-5,090	-5.10
Public administration	0	0	-1,070	-1.90
Race and Hispanic origin				
Black	-2,180	-1.70	-2,220	-0.30
American Indian	-2,890	-3.10	-2,190	-0.40
Asian	-2,000	-3.40	-1,550	-0.80
Hispanic origin	-2,490	-1.80	-2,040	-0.10
Immigration				
Immigrant before prior decade	520	2.60	630	0.60
Immigrant during prior decade	-3,970	-0.30	-2,220	-0.10

SOURCE: U.S. Bureau of the Census, Census of Population and Housing: 1980 and 1990 Public Use Microdata Samples.

[a]Represents the expected annual and hourly earnings of a native-born white high school graduate working 40 hours per week for 50 weeks in the Northeast as a handler in a private sector agricultural, mining, or construction industry.

Women			
1989		1979	
Annual	Hourly	Annual	Hourly
$13.170	$-0.10	$12,700	$1.60
80	0.20	60	0.10
-470	-1.60	-870	-1.50
1,260	0.90	700	0.30
2.660	2.30	N.A.	N.A.
5,560	4.10	4,130	3.30
12,280	7.90	N.A.	N.A.
280	-0.20	260	-0.10
280	-0.10	200	-0.30
-2,300	-1.40	-180	0.10
-2,510	-1.50	-940	0.10
-530	-0.10	510	1.00
450	0.10	1,000	0.60
-190	5.40	-1,030	2.40
6,630	4.60	5,150	3.90
4,970	3.90	4,720	4.10
2,590	1.40	1,390	0.30
4,160	3.80	3,130	2.80
990	1.00	980	0.90
-950	-1.80	-1,170	-2.90
3,550	2.10	910	0.80
-120	-0.70	60	-0.60
1,800	1.90	1,470	1.30
1,180	-0.20	-640	0.10
540	0.40	320	0.10
2,140	1.40	1,270	0.40
3,560	2.30	2,620	1.50
-1,730	-1.80	-1,900	-2.80
2,020	1.60	-40	-0.40
-1,110	-0.80	-2,010	-2.20
-500	-0.50	-1,500	-2.00
0	0	-340	-1.10
660	1.20	790	2.20
-980	-0.80	-480	0.83
910	0.80	860	0.70
-580	0.30	-360	0.60
710	0.70	570	0.90
-1,910	-0.60	-750	0.40

[b] Included in "some college" category in 1979.
[c] Included in "bachelor's degree" category in 1979.

N.A. = Not Applicable.

industries, and across types of employment (self, public, or private)—all contributed to intergroup earnings differentials. Many of these influences are included in the regression results for 1989 and 1979 (see Table 4.5). The inter-
cepts represent the expected annual and hourly earnings in 1989 and 1979 of a
native-born white high school graduate working 40 hours per week for 50 weeks
in the Northeast as a handler in a private-sector job in agriculture, mining, or construction. Each coefficient represents the increase or decrease in earnings expected
in 1989 and 1979, given the worker's age, the hours or weeks worked, and his or
her region of residence, occupation, industry, or sector. The coefficients for each
group, and for immigrants entering during or prior to the previous decade, represent the differentials found after controlling simultaneously all these factors.

There were substantial costs to being a minority male in annual earnings in
1989 and 1979. These costs ranged from around $2,000 for blacks and Asians
to $2,500 for Hispanics and nearly $2,900 for American Indians. They grew as
high as $3,500 to $7,500 at the college and graduate levels.[27] Except for blacks,
these costs were higher than in 1979, when the disadvantages for all but Asians
(over $1,500) clustered around $2,000. The estimated costs in hourly earnings
in 1989 ranged from about $1.70 for blacks and Hispanics to more than $3.10
per hour for American Indians and Asians. These costs were all sharply higher
than in 1979, when only Asians ($0.80) lost more than 50 cents per hour in
expected wages. These relatively small hourly differentials in 1980 are consistent with the convergence reported for black and white men in 1980, adjusting
for region and metropolitan residence. Men who immigrated during the previous
decade showed substantial losses in expected annual, but not estimated hourly,
earnings in both decades, while those who had lived in the country at least
10 years actually earned more than the comparable native-born per year and
per hour.

In contrast, except for American Indian women in 1989, minority women
earned more per hour than white women with comparable education and region
and employment characteristics, perhaps reflecting unmeasured differences in
work experience. The advantage was less than 80 cents per hour of work, however, except for black women, who earned about $1.20 more in 1989 and $2.20
more in 1979. While black women, Asian women, and immigrants resident for
more than 10 years also earned more than comparable whites annually, American Indian and Hispanic women earned between $500 and $1,000 less, and
recent immigrant women earned almost $2,000 less in 1989.

The regression results are generally consistent with the earnings ratios for
men and women. Additional factors, such as metropolitan area wage differentials, detailed occupations and industries, and work histories, also affect earnings and might alter the coefficients presented here. The costs in earnings of
being a minority male nevertheless seem too substantial to discount. To the
extent that reductions in such differentials in earlier decades were taken as evi-

dence of declining discrimination in labor markets, their persistence in 1990 suggests that race remains a significant determinant of earnings opportunities. In assessing its enduring impact, we might imagine how a $2,000 pay cut—over $160 per month—might alter our personal budgets and lives. This was the approximate cost in 1989 of being a minority male.

Unemployment and Labor Force Participation

Higher educational attainments are usually compensated by better jobs and higher earnings, greater labor force participation, and reduced risks for unemployment. In 1990 the unemployment rates for white and Asian men were about 5 percent (Table 4.6). Unemployment was twice as high for Hispanics and nearly three times higher for blacks and American Indians than for whites. Non-Asian minorities have experienced unemployment levels at least twice as high as whites for decades: this did not change in 1990. The pattern for women was similar: around 5 percent of whites and Asians and 11 to 13 percent of Hispanic, black, and American Indian women were unemployed. Unemployment rates were lower at each higher level of educational attainment for every group. However, unemployment among black and American Indian men remained twice that of whites at almost all educational levels.

Labor force nonparticipation rates for black and American Indian men are also twice those of whites, except among college graduates on one end of the spectrum, and those who did not complete high school at the other. Completing high school substantially increases labor force participation for all groups, but it reduces unemployment rates for black and American Indian men only modestly compared to other groups. Additional education thus greatly reduces the employment problems of black and American Indian men, but it generally does not reduce the differentials between them and comparably educated whites. This finding, like that on earnings differentials, again indicates that despite its importance in improving social and economic outcomes in the United States, we cannot expect increased education alone to reduce racial inequalities in these outcomes. Differentials can arise as readily among the more- as among the less-educated, and they seemed to persist in key employment and earnings outcomes in 1989.

The high unemployment rates of black men and their declining participation in the labor force have drawn increasing attention and concern. Their problems seem to reflect the differential impact of economic transformation and dislocation on residents of central cities and persons with high school diplomas or less. But these employment problems are seen as a major contributor to the decline in black married-couple families and growth of out-of-wedlock births.

The greater prevalence of work disabilities among black men has affected their nonparticipation rate. The declining labor force participation of black men

TABLE 4.6 Labor force participation rates of men and women aged 16 years and over, by race or ethnicity: 1970–1990, and by selected educational attainments: 1990.

Race or Ethnicity	1990	1980	1970[a]	1990 Educational Attainment		
				Less than High School	High School	Bachelor's Degree
White						
In labor force						
Men	75.2%	76.1%	77.4%	69.2%	83.1%	88.9%
Women	56.3	49.4	40.6	35.0	62.8	76.7
Unemployed						
Men	5.3	5.9	3.6	10.9	5.9	2.5
Women	5.0	5.7	4.8	10.3	5.3	2.4
Black						
In labor force						
Men	66.5	66.7	69.8	53.7	78.1	88.6
Women	59.6	53.3	47.5	44.1	69.1	85.9
Unemployed						
Men	13.6	12.3	6.3	21.5	14.0	4.8
Women	12.2	11.3	7.7	21.0	13.3	4.0
American Indian						
In labor force						
Men	69.4	69.6	63.4	56.9	79.4	86.6
Women	55.1	48.1	35.3	39.4	63.1	80.7
Unemployed						
Men	15.4	14.1	11.6	23.1	15.9	4.7
Women	13.1	11.9	10.2	21.7	13.6	4.9
Asian						
In labor force						
Men	75.5	76.5	75.4	56.9	78.1	86.3
Women	60.1	57.7	48.5	44.4	61.8	74.4
Unemployed						
Men	5.1	4.3	2.4	10.8	6.4	3.2
Women	5.5	5.2	2.6	9.3	6.2	3.7
Hispanic Origin						
In labor force						
Men	78.7	78.0	78.2	74.9	85.1	90.2
Women	55.9	49.3	39.3	47.2	66.3	79.1
Unemployed						
Men	9.8	8.5	5.5	13.0	9.3	3.7
Women	11.2	9.6	8.0	17.0	9.8	4.8

SOURCE: U.S. Bureau of the Census: 1970, 1980, and 1990 Censuses of Population and Housing. The 1970 data for Asians are based on the 1970 Microdata Public Use Samples. Data for education are based on the 1990 Public Use Microdata Samples.

[a]Data are not completely comparable with 1980 and 1990 for whites, blacks, and American Indians. The 1970 data for whites and blacks include Hispanics. The 1970 data for American Indians exclude Eskimos and Aleuts.

also reflects, however, long-term trends for men generally. Men's labor force participation has declined continuously since 1940, but it has been counterbalanced by the increasing participation of women. White men reduced their labor force participation from about 81 to 77 percent in the 1960s, and then more slowly to 76 percent in 1980. Black men's participation dropped more sharply in both decades, from 76 to 70 percent in the 1960s and to about 67 percent in 1980 and 1990. The participation rates of American Indian men also remained stable, but at the low level of 70 percent in 1980 and 1990, while white and Asian participation declined slightly to about 75 percent. Only Hispanic men increased their participation—to nearly 79 percent—the highest among men.

The labor force participation of women in each group has increased by at least 3 percentage points in each decade since 1960. White female participation grew most rapidly, especially during the 1970s, and converged upon the rates for blacks and Asians. The largest increases during the 1980s were for American Indian and Hispanic women, from below 50 percent to levels comparable to those of white women (56 percent) in 1990. Sixty percent of black and of Asian women were in the labor force in 1990.

The declining labor force participation of black men and the high participation rates of black women have created a perhaps historic gender differential: there were more black women than men in the labor force in 1990, and they outnumbered black men in all major white collar occupational categories. Future generations may retrospectively view this as the vanguard of gender equality or reversed differentials in the labor force experience of other groups. Today, however, it seems to strike many as yet one more troubling indicator of differences in gender responsibilities and family patterns that seem unique to blacks.

To many Americans, the separation of blacks from white society, and perhaps from other minorities, does not seem rooted in the persistence of residential segregation and castelike social distance, or in equally stubborn racial differentials in earnings and employment. These key indicators of exclusion showed important improvements during the 1960s and 1970s. Many instead attribute the growing separation to what they see as the virtual collapse of the black married-couple family in the 1960s and 1970s, the abandonment of fatherhood and family responsibilities by black men, and the resulting cancerlike spread of a culture involving welfare dependency, out-of-wedlock births, drug and alcohol abuse, and murderous black-on-black violence and crime. Could one accuse the hard-working residents of Yonkers or Crown Heights of racism, if they fought low-income housing projects which they felt would bring these problems into their schools and streets? To many there seemed to be something not just different, but frankly "wrong" with black family and social life, and a longstanding need to take a probing look at it.

FAMILY AND NEIGHBORHOOD CHARACTERISTICS

. . . there is a considerable body of evidence to support the conclusion that Negro social structure, in particular the Negro family, battered and harassed by discrimination, injustice, and uprooting, is in the deepest trouble. While many young Negroes are moving ahead to unprecedented levels of achievement, many more are falling further and further behind. After an intensive study of the life of central Harlem, the board of directors of Harlem Youth Opportunities Unlimited summed up their findings in one statement: "Massive deterioration in the fabric of society and its institutions." At the heart of the deterioration of the fabric of Negro society is the deterioration of the Negro family (Moynihan 1965).

Moynihan's unflinching look at the black family in 1965, despite all the problems and controversies surrounding his explanation for its "pathology," now seems tragically prophetic of the drop, perhaps more rapid than even he expected, in black married-couple families in ensuing decades. Writing in 1965, Moynihan could contrast the highly unstable family structure of lower income blacks with the "high degree of stability" maintained by white families. A quarter of a century later, pummeled by an economy undergoing fundamental restructuring, by burgeoning divorce rates, and by changing values concerning marriage, family, and the roles of women, the American family now strikes us as an institution in the midst of a dizzying revolution. The decline of black married-couple families now seems more like a particularly devastating form of these instabilities than a phenomenon entirely unto itself.

The percentage of family households has declined for each of the major races and for Hispanics since 1970. Delays in marriage and increases in the numbers who were never married have increased the number of households in all groups with single people living alone or with others. While marriage rates have fallen among all groups, the decline has been especially sharp for blacks. (The statistics for blacks and for whites in this paragraph include Hispanics who identified themselves as black or white by race.) In 1975, for example, 94 percent of white women and 87 percent of black women aged 30–34 had married. This fell to 86 percent for similarly aged whites and to only 61 percent for black women in 1990. One-quarter of these young black women may never marry, compared to perhaps 10 percent of whites in this cohort (Norton and Miller 1992).

The growth in single-person households has reduced household sizes, but families have also had fewer children and become smaller. The average white family had 3.5 persons in 1970, but 3.0 in 1990, while other groups dropped from over 4 persons to about 3.5 for blacks and American Indians, and to about 3.8 for Asians and Hispanics. Despite all the social changes, married-couple families remain predominant among all groups, except for blacks (Figure 4.10). Fifty percent of all black families were married-couple families, compared to 66 percent of American Indian, 70 percent of Hispanic, and over 80 percent of Asian and white families. The percentage of married-couple families dropped

FIGURE 4.10   Family type, by race or ethnicity: 1970 to 1990.

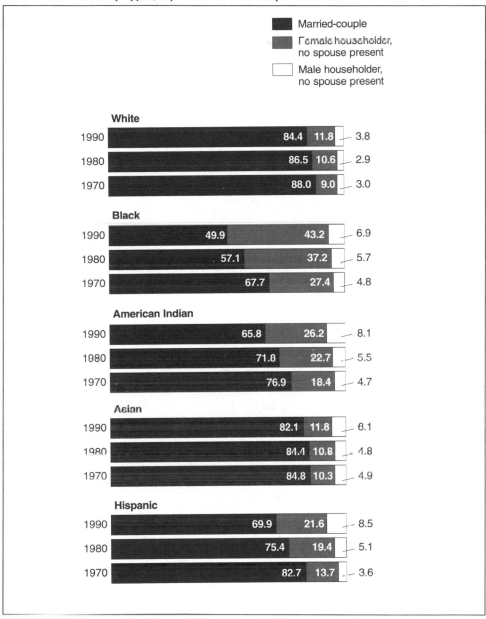

SOURCE: U.S. Bureau of the Census, 1970, 1980, and 1990 Census of Population, *General Social and Economic Characteristics for the United States*.

NOTE: 1970 data for Asians are based on the 1 in 1,000 Public Use Microdata Samples.

FIGURE 4.11   Percentage of children living in two-parent households, by race or ethnicity: 1970–1990 (under 18 years).

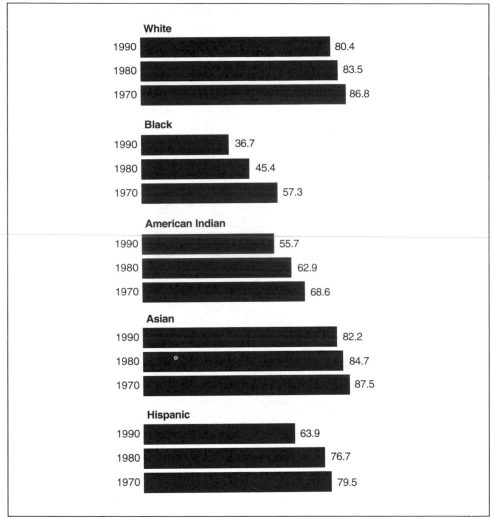

SOURCE: U.S. Bureau of the Census, 1970, 1980, and 1990 Census of Population, *General Social and Economic Characteristics for the United States.*

NOTE: 1970 data for Asians are based on the 1 in 1,000 Public Use Microdata Samples.

more in the 1970s for blacks (from 68 to 57 percent) and Hispanics (from 83 to 75 percent) than in the 1980s. The declines among American Indians and whites (from 77 and 88 percent, respectively) were more evenly divided across the decades.

With the decline in married-couple families, the probability that a child resided with two parents also dropped in all groups, but most dramatically for blacks (Figure 4.11). Thirty-seven percent of black children lived in two-parent families in 1990 compared to 57 percent in 1970, but the decline was smaller (from 45 percent) in the 1980s than in the 1970s. About 56 percent of American Indian and 64 percent of Hispanic children lived in two-parent families in 1990, down from about 69 and 80 percent 20 years ago. Over 80 percent of white and of Asian children lived in two-parent families in 1990, but these had fallen from about 87 percent for both in 1970. The percentage of children in two-parent families is now higher among Asians than among whites. The overwhelming majority of children raised by single parents lived with their mothers, but the small percentages raised by male householders grew in every group during the decade. Because of remarriages, the percentages living with two parents hide the full magnitude of instability in children's living arrangements: an estimated 60 percent of children born today will spend some time in a single-parent family (Saluter 1989). Family life is thus no longer "stable" in America.

Relatively little attention has been given to the growth of subfamilies as an alternative living arrangement for children. (A subfamily is a married couple with or without never-married children under 18, or one parent with one or more children under 18, living in a household with and related to either the householder or the householder's spouse.) Subfamilies have been particularly prevalent in the black population: there were about 3.7 million black families with children in 1980, and about one-tenth as many subfamilies with children (373,000) (Table 4A.1). If one added the numbers of black families and sub-families with children, subfamilies would have represented 9 percent of the combined number for blacks in 1980. The comparable percentages for American Indians and for Hispanics (7 and 5 percent, respectively) were not inconsiderable, while those for Asians and whites (4 and 3 percent) were lower.

By 1990, however, subfamilies represented 16 percent of the combined number of black family units with children, more than 10 percent of American Indian and of Hispanic units, and about 6 percent of Asian. By comparison, subfamilies grew modestly for whites, to 4 percent. Over 80 percent of black subfamilies with children, but only 56 percent of the Asian subfamilies, were mother-child units. These comprised about 65–70 percent of the subfamilies in the other groups. Hispanic, white (about 15 percent), and especially Asian (30 percent) subfamilies with children were much more likely to be married-couple units than those of American Indians and blacks (7 and 3 percent).

The great concern with the decline in married-couple families stems from the lower income and strikingly higher poverty rates of single-parent families and their effects on the family income distributions of the groups. Intergroup differentials have, in fact, changed very little except for Hispanics, whose median family income fell from 75 percent of the white median in 1969 to 70 and 66 percent in the next two decades. Black and American Indian median family incomes remained a relatively stable 60 percent of the white median, except for an improvement to 65 percent for American Indians in 1979. The median income of Asian families was 8 and 9 percent more than the white median in 1979

TABLE 4.7 Median family income in 1989 and ratio of minority to white median family income, by family type and educational attainment: 1979 and 1989 (in 1989 dollars).

| | Race or Ethnicity | | | | |
| | Median Family Income in 1989 | | | | |
Family Type and Educational Attainment	White	Black	American Indian	Asian	Hispanic
Family Type					
Married couple	$39,915	$33,000	$27,936	$47,579	$30,000
Male householder, no spouse present	30,000	21,000	16,679	35,260	22,000
Female householder, no spouse present	21,023	13,500	12,000	27,000	14,374
Educational Attainment of Householder					
Less than high school					
Married couple	24,500	22,644	19,360	31,933	23,740
Male householder, no spouse present	21,703	16,264	13,700	29,908	19,500
Female householder, no spouse present	15,339	10,000	9,231	18,000	11,560
High school					
Married couple	35,022	32,258	27,949	40,127	32,000
Male householder, no spouse present	28,200	21,600	15,987	34,000	24,000
Female householder, no spouse present	20,064	13,000	11,900	24,700	15,480
Some college					
Married couple	42,505	40,000	33,000	46,684	39,000
Male householder, no spouse present	32,271	26,040	19,900	34,000	27,766
Female householder, no spouse present	22,900	18,000	14,500	27,981	19,800
Bachelor's degree or higher					
Married couple	60,000	55,000	46,600	60,000	51,570
Male householder, no spouse present	47,500	37,200	33,122	45,834	35,778
Female householder, no spouse present	34,019	31,000	25,500	40,476	30,000

SOURCE: U.S. Bureau of the Census, Census of Population and Housing: 1980 and 1990 Public Use Microdata Samples.

1989				1979			
Ratio Black/ White	Ratio American Indian/ White	Ratio Asian/ White	Ratio Hispanic/ White	Ratio Black/ White	Ratio American Indian/ White	Ratio Asian/ White	Ratio Hispanic/ White
0.83	0.70	1.19	0.75	0.79	0.75	1.11	0.77
0.70	0.56	1.18	0.73	0.65	0.66	0.93	0.71
0.64	0.57	1.28	0.68	0.62	0.61	1.04	0.58
0.92	0.79	1.30	0.97	0.85	0.79	1.05	0.89
0.75	0.63	1.38	0.90	0.71	0.71	0.93	0.81
0.65	0.60	1.17	0.75	0.64	0.64	0.95	0.62
0.92	0.80	1.15	0.91	0.86	0.80	1.02	0.84
0.77	0.57	1.21	0.85	0.72	0.73	0.87	0.77
0.65	0.59	1.23	0.77	0.66	0.65	0.96	0.71
0.94	0.78	1.10	0.92	0.92	0.82	0.99	0.87
0.81	0.62	1.05	0.86	0.75	0.73	0.85	0.82
0.79	0.63	1.22	0.86	0.72	0.69	0.99	0.76
0.92	0.78	1.00	0.86	0.92	0.85	0.98	0.85
0.78	0.70	0.96	0.75	0.74	0.90	0.82	0.78
0.91	0.75	1.19	0.88	0.85	0.74	1.06	0.78

and 1989 because of their higher educational attainments and because about 20 percent of Asian families had three or more earners. The latter reflects both family composition and size. When their larger family size is considered, Asian per capita income ($13,640) is actually only 85 percent of whites' ($16,070).

The ratios varied considerably by family type, however, and so have trends in closing differentials. The income gaps for black (0.83), American Indian (0.70), and Hispanic (0.75) married-couple families were much smaller than for female householders in each group (Table 4.7). The differentials were even smaller for black, American Indian, and Hispanic families when the wives worked as well. Black married-couple families and those with working wives both converged towards whites since 1979 (0.79 and 0.84), but the gaps for American Indian and Hispanic married-couple (0.75 and 0.77) and dual-earner families (0.79 and 0.81) actually grew larger in this 10-year span (Table 4A.1). The great increase in working wives among whites (from 48 to 59 percent) and a comparable decline among Hispanics (from 48 to 40 percent) contributed to the growth in the ratio for Hispanic married couples.

The gaps were even narrower among black and Hispanic married-couple families in 1990 and 1980 when similarly educated householders are compared. The ratios exceed 0.90 at the college level, except for Hispanics (0.86). The differential remained wider, at about 0.80, for American Indian married-couple families at all educational levels. The smaller differentials among comparably educated householders points to the role that educational differentials play in higher median family incomes of whites and of Asians. The failure of the ratios to reach parity and their relative invariance across educational levels also indicate, however, that additional factors, such as region, age, and the number and earnings of workers in the family, contribute to the differentials. Such factors help explain the consistent advantages that the ratios for Asian families show.

Poverty

The percentage of families and of individuals in poverty rose for all groups except blacks between 1979 and 1989, after falling for all groups except Hispanics during the 1970s (Figure 4.12). Notably, blacks were thus the only group with reductions in poverty levels in both decades—from 30 to 24 percent of families, and from 35 to 29 percent among individuals. The increases in poverty during the 1980s were smaller than the declines in the 1970s for whites, and especially for American Indians, leaving their 1989 rates lower than in 1969. Indeed American Indians had the highest family and person poverty rates in 1969, but dropped to about the same level as blacks in 1989 (27 and 31 percent). Only Hispanics had higher family and individual poverty rates in 1989 (22 and 25 percent) than in 1969 (20 and 24 percent). This may in part reflect immigration.

These trends still left Hispanics, American Indians, and blacks with strikingly

FIGURE 4.12   Poverty rates for persons and families, by race or ethnicity:
1969–1989.

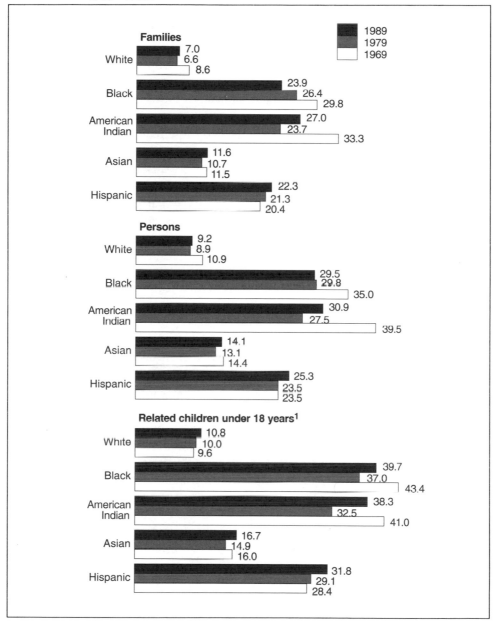

SOURCE: U.S. Bureau of the Census, 1970, 1980, and 1990 decennial censuses, *General Social and Economic Characteristics for the United States.*

NOTE: 1970 data for American Indians and Asians are based on the 1 in 1,000 Public Use Microdata Samples.

higher family and individual poverty rates (ranging from 22 to 31 percent) than Asians (12 and 14 percent) and whites (less than 10 percent). Although the poverty rate for black families declined in the 1980s, the poverty rate for black children increased, just as it did for other groups. Poverty rates increased from 10 to 11 percent for white children, and grew by 2 to 3 percentage points for Asians and for Hispanics (to 17 and 32 percent). American Indian children suffered a sharp increase in poverty—from 33 to 38 percent. The growing poverty among children of all the major groups is clearly one of the nation's most ominous problems.

It is nevertheless important that blacks and American Indians were able to reduce their overall poverty rates despite the recessions and economic dislocations of the past two decades and their declines in married-couple families. For blacks, a contributing, and perhaps surprising, factor has been a modest declined in poverty among families maintained by females, from 46 percent in 1980 to nearly 44 percent in 1990. This includes families with and without children and others without. Poverty rates for Hispanic female-householder families dropped as well (from 48 to 46 percent) despite the rise in poverty for all Hispanic families during the decade. Increases in the labor force participation and earnings of women, as well as in the higher educational attainments of female householders, have contributed to these declines among blacks and Hispanics. If the wages of black and Hispanic women continue to increase, poverty rates should decline among the families they head. Such trends did not, however, reduce poverty rates for families maintained by women in other groups. Poverty remained stable, at about 25 percent, for such Asian families, and increased for whites (from 21 to 24 percent) and American Indians (from 46 to 50 percent).

The very high poverty rates suffered by families maintained by women, the frightening effects seen nightly in television coverage of the crime and violence perpetrated by youth in our poorest slums and ghettos, and more broadly in the perceived explosion of dropout rates, teenage motherhood, illegitimacy, and welfare dependency, have again vividly raised in the public and policy minds the specter of a people trapped in a cycle of persistent and self-perpetuating poverty.

In an era where the racism that the Kerner Commission saw as an underlying cause of inner-city problems seemed to be declining, explaining just how the "cycle of poverty," or "tangle of pathology," perpetuates itself has become increasingly important. Wilson's seminal and influential effort (1987) argued that the growing number of neighborhoods with high and increasing concentrations of poor minorities created isolated worlds where youth have few remaining opportunities to interact with such bearers of mainstream values and behaviors as married-couple families or adults with "good" educations, stable jobs, and high aspirations for their children (see also Anderson 1992). This isolation, and the loss of many key institutions with the departure of the middle class for better neighborhoods, has increased the likelihood that youth will fall into behaviors that plague life in the ghetto and perpetuate poverty. These include joining gangs, committing crimes, dropping out of school, or becoming teenage mothers.

The absence of national data sets that would enable researchers to combine information on individuals and families with characteristics of their neighborhoods has made empirical examination of these hypothesized effects difficult. A special neighborhood file provided information on such characteristics as the racial, educational, occupational, employment, income, and family type distributions in the tracts in which individuals and households resided in the 1970 Public Use Microdata Sample (PUMS) (Crane 1991). More recently, the census tracts of respondents were attached to records in the Panel Survey of Income Dynamics. Researchers using this file to examine 35 neighborhood measures found the "insignificance of virtually all the neighborhood measures" striking (Brooks-Gunn et al. 1993). However, both studies found some beneficial effects for young adults associated with the presence of professional and managerial workers and affluent neighbors.

Our access to internal versions of the 1990 5 percent PUMS enabled us to identify the census tract in which each individual and household in the file resided and to estimate several neighborhood characteristics from the sample, including the poverty and male unemployment rates in each tract, the percentage of households maintained by females, the percentage of adults who did not complete high school, the percentage of whites, and the mean family income. In addition, dummy variables were created to identify high (20 to 29 percent), "very high" (30 to 39 percent) and "extremely high" (40 percent or more) poverty tracts. (Some of these characteristics did not meet minimum statistical criteria for entry into the model and are not included in Table 4.8.)

Does living in a census tract with lower mean family incomes and higher concentrations of poverty, families maintained by women, dropouts, the unemployed, and minorities make a 15–20 year old more likely to have had a child or drop out of school than a teenager raised in a comparable family but in a "better" neighborhood? The effects of these neighborhood characteristics, of several relevant characteristics of the teenager's own family, and of the teenager's own race on the probability of these outcomes were examined using a step-wise regression procedure that identifies variables in the order of their ability to predict the outcomes of interest. The procedure is useful in examining neighborhood effects because it shows whether each variable had a significant effect on the outcomes, and also whether that variable adds explanatory power beyond those already in the regression. This provides a statistical criterion for assessing whether additional variables actually improve our understanding of a phenomenon.

TABLE 4.8   Step-wise logistics regression of teenage motherhood and of not completing high school on selected individual, family, household, and census tract characteristics: 1990.*

	Estimate	Concordant Percent[c]	Somer's D[d]	Odds Ratio
Model One: Teenage Motherhood				
Variables Entered in Order[b]				
Intercept	−11.4	N.A.	N.A.	0.0
Dropout	1.5	29.3	0.25	4.4
Black	0.9	52.7	0.44	2.4
Age	0.5	78.0	0.62	1.6
Number of persons in family	0.3	82.2	0.66	1.3
Family type	0.3	83.6	0.69	1.4
Mean family income	0.0	84.5	0.70	1.0
Family income	0.0	84.7	0.70	1.0
Asian	−0.7	84.8	0.70	0.5
Poverty status of family	0.2	84.8	0.70	1.3
Poverty rate under 20 percent	0.0	84.8	0.70	1.0
Percent female householder	0.0	84.8	0.70	1.0
Householder dropout	0.1	84.8	0.70	1.1
American Indian	0.3	84.9	0.71	1.4
Poverty rate 40 percent or higher	−0.3	84.9	0.71	0.8
Percent unemployed	0.0	84.9	0.71	1.0
Percent white	0.0	84.9	0.71	1.0
Poverty rate 30–39 percent	−0.1	84.9	0.71	0.9
Hispanic	0.0	84.9	0.71	1.0
Model Two: Male Dropout				
Variables Entered in Order[a]				
Intercept	−9.3	N.A.	N.A.	0.0
Householder dropout	0.8	37.5	0.26	2.2
Age	0.4	66.7	0.42	1.4
Family income	0.0	72.4	0.46	1.0
Percent high school dropout	0.0	72.7	0.46	1.0
Family type	0.2	73.0	0.47	1.2
Number of persons in family	0.1	73.1	0.47	1.1
Asian	−0.1	73.2	0.47	0.5
Black	−0.4	73.3	0.47	0.7
Mean family income	0.0	73.4	0.47	1.0
Percent female householder	0.0	73.4	0.48	1.0
Poverty rate under 20 percent	0.0	73.5	0.48	1.0
Poverty status of family	0.0	73.5	0.48	1.1
Percent unemployed	0.0	73.5	0.48	1.0
Hispanic origin	−0.1	73.5	0.48	0.9

SOURCE: U.S. Bureau of the Census, Census of Population and Housing: 1990 PUMS.

*Only the independent variables that meet criteria for entry into each model are presented, and these differ for the two models.

[a]Census tract characteristics are indented.

[b]The step-wise regression procedure enters variables in the order of their ability to explain variance in the dependent variable.

[c]The concordant percent is the percent of cases whose outcomes can be predicted correctly using the variables entered to that point.

[d]Somer's D is a measure of the rank correlation between observed and predicted outcomes.

The results for teenage motherhood indicate that knowing the age and poverty status of teenagers and whether they are black or high school dropouts, enables one to correctly predict whether they have or have not had a child in about 83 percent of the cases (see concordant percent). Some of the effects of being black reflect correlations with family type and size. Adding these variables to the regression reduces the apparent influence of blackness and helps increase the correlations between observations and predictions. The mean family income of each tract, the first neighborhood effect to enter the model, only marginally improves the fit of the model. None of the other neighborhood characteristics has any significant effect upon whether a teenage woman has a child.

Similarly, knowing four variables about a teenage male: his age, his family income, and whether the householder completed high school, enables one to predict dropping out in about 73 percent of the cases. Knowing the dropout percentage in the tract increases this only marginally. The other neighborhood's characteristics also have no significant influence upon whether a young man drops out of high school.

The key factors in teenagers' risks for motherhood and dropping out are such personal and family characteristics as their own age, their household's poverty status, their family type and its income and size, and the education of the householder. (Model available upon request.) For teenage mothers, being black and for female dropouts, having had a child, are also important. Black teenage mothers were more likely to drop out than those who did not have a child. The tract variables examined here add interesting details at the margins, and hence are not totally inconsistent with the cited findings of some significant effects, but they can scarcely be included in parsimonious models of these behaviors. The important explanatory factors are at the individual and family level, not at the census tract or neighborhood level.

Neighborhood characteristics beyond those modeled may have effects on these or other behaviors. Brooks-Gunn et al.'s (1993) interpretation of the 3 significant effects they found among their 35 neighborhood measures suggests modest support for the positive effects of affluent neighborhoods, particularly for whites. However, their investigation does not support the hypothesis that poor areas have negative effects. These surprising results remind us, however, that teenage motherhood and dropping out are common in poor, inner-city neighborhoods simply because they are home to large numbers of families with the characteristics that increase risks for these outcomes. Insofar as statistical models inform us about these matters, we can no more expect to reduce teenage motherhood or dropout rates by dispersing "at risk" families to less problem-ridden neighborhoods than we could expect to reduce illness and death by breaking up retirement communities.

CONCLUSION

> What then is that problem? We feel the answer is clear enough. Three centuries of injustice have brought about deep-seated structural distortions in the life of the Negro American. At this point, the present tangle of pathology is capable of perpetuating itself without assistance from the white world. The cycle can be broken only if these distortions are set right (Moynihan 1965).

A new Kerner Commission would certainly agree, 25 years later, that poverty, employment problems, economic dislocation, and family instability are barriers at least as important as racism and discrimination to the exclusion, not only of blacks, but also of Hispanics, American Indians, and some Asians, from full and equal participation in American society. It is clear that these problems are severe enough in the most disadvantaged segments of our minority population—and among the oft-forgotten poor of white America—to perpetuate themselves for generations to come, even if groups were no longer subjected to discriminatory or inequitable barriers. We are perhaps approaching the end of the era in which we can expect further improvements from the removal of *de jure* discrimination alone.

But 1990 census data also tell us that if we took improvements in measures of residential segregation and in occupational and earnings differentials among comparably educated young workers as evidence of declining discrimination in the 1960s and 1970s, then we must recognize that these barriers remain critical factors in the disadvantages and exclusion that minorities suffer today. If we must think in terms of cycles and tangles, discrimination remains inextricably interwoven in their perpetuation.

There is also, however, something peculiar about our efforts over the past half-century to identify or discover specific mechanisms that would keep individuals or groups in poverty. We seem to operate from a deep and unexamined assumption—perhaps uniquely American, perhaps arising from our history of abundant and overflowing opportunity, but almost certainly embodied in the mythic functions that the European immigrant experience serves in our culture—that people and groups would and should, in the course of events, naturally rise up out of poverty. When this does not occur, something must be "wrong"; and if opportunities are available, something must be wrong with the people or group.

We acknowledge the history of restricted opportunities for some groups—and sometimes even the persistence of those limitations. We discuss dislocations in an economy that for decades has been unable to generate enough jobs, much less "good" jobs, for everyone seeking and qualified for work. And yet when we frame our research and policy questions, we seem to implicitly assume that blacks, Hispanics, and American Indians should have climbed out of poverty in much higher numbers, and that they might have done so were they not trapped in a cycle of poverty or enmeshed in a tangle of pathology. We act as if we really expected the removal of *de jure* barriers alone to free disadvantaged minorities to follow the upward trajectory that we think European immigrants took towards socioeconomic success and full inclusion in American society.

What levels of poverty would we really expect today, given the educational, occupational, and earnings differentials between these groups in 1970 and the performance of the economy since then? Do we have any realistic baseline expectations that their poverty rates exceed? Or is our baseline simply our impression that the European immigrants climbed from "rags to riches" in a few brief generations? If we did set realistic baselines, would we really need any mechanism more complex than serious competitive disadvantages in a difficult economy to explain why poverty rates have not fallen more dramatically among some groups? Might we not even find that some groups have done better than we expected, given their differentials in 1970?

And if we expected economic dislocations and declines in married-couple families to proliferate and perpetuate poverty, how do we confront the evidence of falling poverty rates for black and other minority families, including female-householder families in the 1980s? We must, in part, do so by identifying and analyzing the problems more carefully: by distinguishing the problem of high poverty rates, primarily involving different people and families who fall in and climb out of poverty, from problems of long-term, chronic poverty among an important fraction of those who are poor at any given time; by distinguishing problems of educational attainments that are rising, but perhaps not rapidly enough, from actual increases in failure to complete high school. We must recognize that despite a modest rise in recent years, teenage motherhood has dropped dramatically among blacks (Wilson 1987:67) and other groups since 1960; that the proportion of births that are to such youth has risen not because they are increasingly likely to engage in such self-defeating behaviors, but because older cohorts have reduced their fertility even more rapidly.

Doing so is not "flinching," nor is it casting a favorable light on very serious problems. It does not imply that children raised by children are any less disadvantaged. It does not deny that a crisis exists in schools where teachers spend much of their time battling to maintain order, and when graduating seniors read at ninth grade levels. It acknowledges that the social fabric is disintegrating in neighborhoods where a teenage boy's death is most likely caused by another teenager's handgun. It recognizes that these problems are serious, even deadly, enough to be posed and framed more carefully and precisely.

But perhaps too, until we can say what, beyond a metaphor, a social fabric is, and can recognize its fraying and unraveling, its mending and repair, we must pose our questions more humbly. Culture and cultural differences are involved in the creation and persistence of the problems we face, and they will

TABLE 4A.1 Selected social and economic indicators
of exclusion for the racial groups: 1990
(numbers in thousands; data are based on sample tabulations).

Characteristics	White			Black		
	1970[a]	1980	1990	1970[a]	1980	1990
Total Persons (000)	178,107	180,603	188,425	22,550	26,092	29,285
Age and Sex						
Percent under 5 years	8.1%	6.5%	6.6%	10.7%	9.1%	9.1%
Percent under 18 years	33.4	26.1	23.3	42.3	35.5	31.9
Percent 65 years and over	10.3	12.4	14.4	7.0	7.8	8.4
Median age	28.9	31.7	34.9	22.4	24.9	28.4
Males per 100 females	95.3	94.8	95.0	90.8	89.5	89.3
Families by Presence of Children						
Families with own children under 18	24,967	23,824	23,184	2,968	3,696	3,902
Percent	100.0	100.0	100.0	100.0	100.0	100.0
Married-couple families with own children under 18 years	89.7	85.9	82.9	66.8	54.3	46.8
Female householder, no husband present with own children under 18 years	8.4	11.9	13.6	29.8	41.7	47.8
Male householder, no wife present with own children under 18 years	1.9	2.2	3.5	3.4	4.0	5.4
Number of subfamilies	829	790	1,219	319	397	772
Percent with own children under 18 years	69.5	73.7	82.1	87.1	93.9	96.7
Persons per family	3.51	3.16	3.03	4.15	3.69	3.46
Fertility						
Children ever born per 1,000 women	1.6	1.2	1.2	1.9	1.6	1.4
Educational Attainment						
Percent high school graduates						
Males 25 years and over	54.0	70.3	79.6	30.1	50.8	62.3
Males 25–34 years	74.1	87.0	87.8	51.0	73.2	74.6
Females 25 years and over	55.0	68.9	78.5	32.5	51.6	64.0
Females 25–34 years	73.7	86.6	90.0	52.6	75.1	79.1
Occupation						
Employed persons 16 years and over	68,282	80,792	91,447	7,361	9,207	11,185
Percent	100.0	100.0	100.0	100.0	100.0	100.0
Managerial and professional specialty	20.0	24.3	28.5	9.1	14.1	18.2
Technical, sales, and administrative support	30.4	31.3	32.6	18.2	25.2	29.4
Service	11.0	11.5	11.5	27.8	23.1	22.1

American Indian			Asian			Hispanic Origin		
1970[a]	1980	1990	1970	1980	1990	1970[b]	1980	1990
764	1,534	2,015	1,369	3,726	7,227	9,295	14,604	21,900
12.0%	10.1%	9.8%	9.8%	8.6%	7.9%	12.5%	11.3%	10.6%
45.2	38.1	34.3	37.5	30.2	28.4	45.0	38.6	34.9
5.7	5.2	5.8	8.4	5.9	6.1	4.1	4.6	4.8
20.4	23.4	26.9	28.1	28.4	30.1	20.7	23.2	25.5
97.6	97.6	98.2	94.6	93.5	95.8	96.4	99.2	103.3
98	226	282	187	507	938	1,447	30,472	3,081
100.0	100.0	100.0	100.0	100.0	100.0	100.0	100.0	100.0
78.5	71.5	63.4	76.6	88.5	86.9	84.1	76.5	71.4
18.3	24.2	28.7	16.8	9.5	10.1	13.7	20.4	22.2
3.2	4.3	7.9	6.5	2.0	3.0	2.2	3.1	6.4
12	18	37	21	39	125	84	144	422
91.7	86.7	91.8	57.1	51.4	51.8	78.6	77.6	82.4
3.5	3.83	3.57	4.0	3.75	3.74	4.28	3.87	3.84
2.0	1.7	1.6	1.5	1.2	1.1	1.9	1.6	1.5
33.6	57.0	65.8	64.8	78.8	81.5	37.9	45.4	49.8
49.2	73.2	71.7	86.9	89.6	87.2	50.4	57.5	55.4
33.0	54.1	65.3	64.2	71.4	74.0	34.2	42.7	49.9
44.8	71.0	74.9	80.6	83.4	84.7	45.7	57.0	60.4
267	508	729	859	1,689	3,412	3,904	5,457	8,982
100.0	100.0	100.0	100.0	100.0	100.0	100.0	100.0	100.0
12.7	16.1	18.3	24.8	28.8	30.6	11.8	12.2	14.1
13.9	24.2	26.8	25.6	30.8	33.2	21.8	24.5	25.9
24.7	18.1	18.5	19.0	15.6	14.8	15.9	16.3	19.2

Characteristics	White			Black		
	1970[a]	1980	1990	1970[a]	1980	1990
Farming, forestry, and fishing	3.7	2.9	2.4	4.2	1.9	1.5
Precision production, craft, and repair	14.6	13.4	11.6	9.6	8.9	8.1
Operators, fabricators, and laborers	20.2	16.7	13.4	31.0	26.7	20.8
Workers in Family in 1989						
Families	45,770	48,742	51,337	4,863	6,022	6,927
Percent	100.0	100.0	100.0	100.0	100.0	100.0
No workers	8.8	12.3	12.9	12.7	17.5	16.6
1 worker	40.5	32.8	27.1	35.6	34.5	33.2
2 workers	39.2	42.5	47.3	38.7	36.0	36.9
3 or more workers	11.6	12.4	12.8	12.9	12.0	13.3
Income						
Median income						
All families	$31,400	$34,910	$37,630	$19,130	$21,110	$22,470
Married-couple families	33,100	36,940	40,720	23,200	29,320	33,630
Husband and wife worked	36,220	42,540	47,270	28,100	35,750	41,610
Median income by number of workers						
No workers ($)	9,230	15,100	17,780	5,490	6,910	5,310
1 worker ($)	27,100	29,390	28,710	14,840	16,280	15,760
2 workers ($)	35,120	40,240	46,120	25,670	31,450	36,990
3 or more workers ($)	47,410	55,330	47,270	31,030	42,530	41,610
Median income, 15 years and over						
Males ($)	21,160	21,830	22,070	12,800	13,130	12,970
Females ($)	7,470	9,010	10,750	6,300	7,840	8,840
Median, year-round, full-time workers						
Males ($)	28,510	30,430	30,760	19,060	21,240	21,690
Females ($)	15,910	17,700	20,050	12,760	16,070	18,020
Per capita ($)	10,430	13,310	16,070	5,720	7,630	8,890
Income in 1989 Below Poverty Level						
Families in poverty	3,922	3,218	3,573	1,450	1,588	1,505
Percent	8.6	6.6	7.0	29.8	26.4	23.9
Married-couple families in poverty	2,530	2,030	1,845	678	477	347
Percent	6.6	4.8	9.2	21.1	13.9	10.0
With related children under 18 years in poverty	1,419	1,122	1,085	249	288	221
Percent	8.2	5.5	5.4	19.1	14.3	12.0
Female householder, no husband present in poverty	1,063	1,086	1,518	707	1,034	1,073
Percent	25.7	21.0	23.7	53.0	46.2	44.5

	American Indian			Asian			Hispanic Origin		
	1970[a]	1980	1990	1970	1980	1990	1970[b]	1980	1990
	7.1	3.7	3.3	5.0	2.1	1.2	6.4	4.7	5.0
	12.0	15.0	13.7	7.1	8.4	8.0	12.1	14.0	13.1
	29.6	23.0	19.4	18.5	14.2	12.1	32.1	28.4	22.9
	127	341	464	330	818	1,578	2,017	3,274	4,776
	100.0	100.0	100.0	100.0	100.0	100.0	100.0	100.0	100.0
	15.0	13.0	14.5	6.4	7.8	8.3	8.8	12.6	11.2
	40.9	35.5	33.2	35.2	29.2	26.2	42.1	35.0	31.2
	32.3	39.5	40.5	36.7	45.7	45.7	37.9	38.5	40.1
	11.8	11.9	11.9	21.8	17.3	19.8	11.2	13.9	17.5
	$18,430	$23,000	$21,750	$34,180	$38,060	$41,250	$23,130	$24,650	$25,060
	20,320	27,720	28,290	35,120	41,000	44,970	25,340	28,460	29,930
	25,830	33,710	35,390	41,420	45,760	52,730	29,590	34,500	37,010
	6,620	7,670	6,070	8,820	8,710	9,050	6,780	7,290	5,980
	17,170	17,670	15,530	25,830	28,220	27,860	19,960	18,690	16,910
	22,210	30,220	32,980	41,420	42,260	50,710	28,820	31,120	34,880
	32,600	36,440	35,390	45,200	57,700	52,730	37,330	44,240	37,010
	11,040	13,530	12,180	17,800	19,640	19,400	18,440	15,210	13,500
	5,340	7,140	7,310	9,610	11,200	11,990	8,660	7,930	8,350
	21,890	23,360	22,080	27,880	29,160	30,080	22,210	21,730	20,320
	14,960	15,650	16,680	18,900	19,270	21,340	14,330	14,950	16,310
	4,950	7,670	8,330	9,970	11,790	13,640	6,500	7,690	8,400
	50	81	125	38	87	183	415	696	1,067
	33.3	23.7	27.0	11.5	10.7	11.6	20.4	21.3	22.3
	23	41	52	27	57	120	260	355	510
	25.8	16.8	16.2	9.6	8.3	9.3	15.4	14.6	15.3
	5	30	40	10	42	91	55	275	424
	17.2	18.9	20.6	12.2	9.5	10.7	11.3	16.4	18.2
	16	36	61	10	23	48	139	306	470
	55.2	46.4	50.4	29.4	25.7	25.7	49.9	48.2	45.7

TABLE 4A.1 *(continued)*

Characteristics	White			Black		
	1970[a]	1980	1990	1970[a]	1980	1990
With related children under 18 years						
in poverty	841	945	1,330	633	943	958
Percent	35.7	30.5	34.4	59.5	52.5	53.9
Residence						
Total	100.0	100.0	100.0	100.0	100.0	100.0
All metropolitan areas	67.7	72.7	74.7	74.3	81.0	83.5
Inside central cities	27.8	24.0	24.5	58.2	57.7	57.0
Outside central cities	39.9	48.7	50.3	16.1	23.3	26.5
Nonmetropolitan areas	32.1	27.3	25.3	25.7	19.0	16.5
Tenure						
Total	100.0	100.0	100.0	100.0	100.0	100.0
Owner-occupied	65.4	68.5	69.1	41.6	44.6	43.8
Renter-occupied	34.6	31.5	30.9	58.4	55.4	56.2
Persons in Unit						
Median, owner-occupied units	3.00	2.51	2.34	3.30	3.09	2.79
Median, renter-occupied units	2.00	1.85	1.86	2.80	2.33	2.33
Median Housing Values						
Owners ($)	59,063	81,605	80,300	33,360	45,578	50,500
Renters ($)	299	350	381	223	260	310

SOURCE: U.S. Bureau of the Census, 1970 and 1980 decennial Census of Population and Housing, *General Social and Economic Characteristics,* and the 1980 and 1990 Public Use Microdata Samples.

play a role in their amelioration. Would we now expect years, or even a generation, of full employment in well-paying jobs to restore married-couple family patterns where they have eroded? Under what conditions might we expect such families to maintain the lifelong commitments of the past, and for children to find single parents, stepparents, and step-siblings an unusual arrangement?

If we doubt that we will ever return to earlier forms of lifelong marital and family commitments because our national culture and values have changed, can we treat the declining tendency among our least advantaged to even make such commitments as entirely their own distinctive cultural problem? A "culture" is more than a list of things we "value"—family, education, self-reliance, initiative. We cannot identify what is distinctive and what is common about our lives and problems if our understandings of culture and social fabric are limited to such lists, and if our comparisons of groups primarily serve to invidiously assert and reaffirm that these are the values that promote success and failure in the United States.

American Indian			Asian			Hispanic Origin		
1970[a]	1980	1990	1970	1980	1990	1970[b]	1980	1990
11	33	55	8	19	40	127	283	428
61.1	51.8	57.6	44.4	34.8	35.6	57.4	56.3	54.7
100.0	100.0	100.0	100.0	100.0	100.0	100.0	100.0	100.0
38.8	51.1	51.4	87.7	91.3	93.8	82.8	87.6	90.4
19.9	21.7	23.3	54.1	46.4	46.5	49.9	50.3	51.5
18.9	29.4	28.0	33.5	44.9	47.4	32.8	37.3	38.9
61.2	48.9	48.6	12.3	8.7	6.2	17.2	12.4	9.6
100.0	100.0	100.0	100.0	100.0	100.0	100.0	100.0	100.0
49.8	53.4	53.8	44.2	51.4	52.2	43.7	43.4	42.4
50.2	46.6	46.2	55.8	48.6	47.8	56.3	56.6	57.6
3.60	3.31	2.96	4.00	4.00	3.58	4.00	3.67	3.49
3.20	2.65	2.61	2.00	3.00	2.60	3.30	2.89	3.14
28,325	62,850	51,900	94,500	142,460	178,300	63,860	74,903	77,200
230	394	300	302	469	484	387	315	393

[a]Data for 1970 are for white and black only. No attempts were made to get data for non-Hispanic whites or blacks. Data are shown for the American Indian population only.
[b]Data based on sample only using the Spanish heritage identifiers.

Finally, we cannot pose our questions and frame our problems as carefully as effective policy demands, if we see the unsatisfactory scores of our "good" students in international comparisons as a national problem, and the problems of the poorest and most disadvantaged students as a minority problem. Would a system that fails to meet our standards for "good" students not have even greater difficulties educating students with serious problems to overcome? Have we separated our thinking about these problems as we have our society? Can we make, out of many, one, if the many remain distinctly different? Can we think of each other as "us" only if we are, or become, all alike? Can we do so if the "other" is a drunken, perhaps drug-crazed, black man driving at reckless speeds and responding poorly to police instructions when he is finally caught? Can we, in his shy and halting words, even "get along"? Can we stop all the fighting? Can we stop killing each other?

It is apt that someone we might not respect, someone we might rightly fear, someone whom police treat harshly, perhaps out of disrespect or fear, shocking a nation and eventually engulfing Los Angeles in flames of outrage, should pose the ultimate questions that racial difference and diversity raise, not only in our country, but everywhere and throughout time. These are the questions that unite Buchenwald and Birmingham, Soweto and Sarajevo, Tiananmen Square and the Trail of Tears; it is the ultimate, and still unresolved, issue of the civil rights movement, which we reduce at our own peril to questions of class interests and benefits. It is not simply the movement of groups towards socioeconomic success and full inclusion. These tasks will prove difficult enough: the poor as well as the "different," may always be with us. It is instead the problem of how we can see and recognize differences—in race, in gender, in education, in all that makes us people—without these also carrying distinctions in status and human worth. It is a prize that has eluded this nation and many others: a society where we do not have to be alike in our attributes or accomplishments to be treated with the full and equal worth and dignity with which we are endowed.

We are grateful to the staff of the University of Michigan Population Studies Center and to the Computer Applications Staff and Rachel Hall of the Population Division for helping extract and mount the PUMS and internal geography files on the Census Bureau's computer system. We owe special thanks to James Johnson, Jorge Chappa, Reynolds Farley, Suzanne Bianchi, and other Russell Sage chapter authors, and to Robert Kominski, Arthur Norton, Martin O'Connell, and Dan Weinberg for valuable comments on earlier versions of this chapter. We are especially appreciative of pivotal comments and suggestions from Paul Siegel and Nampeo McKenney, and of the support and resources provided by Arthur Norton, Chief of the Population Division, Nampeo McKenney, Assistant Division Chief, and the staff of the Racial Statistics Branch of the Population Division.

ENDNOTES

1. U.S. Bureau of the Census. 1991. *1990 Census Profile, Race and Hispanic Origin,* No. 2, June. One might note that Louisiana, Mississippi, and South Carolina were "majority minority" for over a century, and Hawaii has been since it was Sandwich Island.

2. J. D. Cheeseman, Current Population Reports, P25-1104, *Population Projections of the United States, by Age, Sex, Race, and Hispanic Origin: 1993 to 2050.*

3. Up to Reconstruction, the constitution of North Carolina denied Jews the right to vote.

4. The enslavement of African Americans was sufficiently embedded in the Constitution for the Supreme Court to rule in *Dred Scott* (1854) that the national constitution could not exclude slavery from any states or territories.

5. U.S. Department of Justice, Immigration and Naturalization Service. 1991. "An Immigrant Nation: United States Regulations of Immigration, 1798 to 1991." Appendix C.

6. All statistics in this section for whites prior to 1960 and for blacks prior to 1970 include Hispanics. Unless otherwise noted, statistics for whites for 1960 and subsequent years are for non-Hispanic whites, and statistics for blacks in 1970 and subsequent years are for non-Hispanic blacks.

7. See Chapter 5, Tables 5.1 and 5.2.

8. 1960, 1970, and 1980 census counts for the total Asian and Pacific Islander population are not fully comparable to 1990 data; 100 percent counts in these censuses did not include write-in groups.

9. Indicators of Hispanic origin changed in the 1970 and 1980 censuses. See Bean and Tienda (1987:36–55) for a discussion of these changes and of the counts obtained from using ancestry, language, and surname indicators of Hispanicity.

10. In the 1990 census, nearly 9 million persons reported an American Indian ancestry or ethnic origin. This contrasts with the 2 million in 1990 who reported their race as American Indian.

11. U.S. Department of Commerce, Commerce News Bureau of the Census. 1991. Press release. "Census Bureau Releases Census Counts on Specific Racial Groups." CB91-215. June.

12. See Lieberson (1980:253–257) for the formula and use of this index in measuring residential segregation. We are indebted to Paul Siegel for suggesting its use here to measure diversity.

13. California, New York, Texas, and Illinois are among the six states with the largest black, Asian, and Hispanic populations. New Jersey is among the six largest for Asian and Hispanics, and Florida for blacks and Hispanics.

14. The figure presents the metropolitan areas that have the ten largest populations of each minority group which also have diversity scores over 44, the diversity score for the entire metropolitan population in the United States.

15. The 1980 census was the first decennial census to identify all federal and state American Indian reservations and areas and all Alaska Native villages.

16. To show these differences, Table 4.1 and the discussion present data for California and the rest of the West separately. It also divides the South into the South Central division, the South Atlantic division excluding Florida, and the state of Florida.

17. See Chapter 6 in this volume and Chapter 1 in Volume 1.

18. These and other statistics in this section that are not presented in Table 4.1 are from more detailed tabulations, available upon request from the authors, on the origins, destinations, and characteristics of movers.

19. See Chapter 6 in this volume.

20. See Logan and Alba (1993:243–268 and 1992:367–397).

21. To protect the confidentiality of individual records, tract and other geographic information below counties, metropolitan areas, and/or sampling areas of 100,000 or more are not available in publicly available versions of the PUMS.

22. See Lieberson (1980:268–277). His mean isolation values and those in Table 4.2 are not strictly comparable. His were for 17 cities and could not distinguish native-born members of each group from other native-born whites. Since isolation values tend to increase with the size of the minority population, the selection of cities does not underestimate immigrant segregation levels.

23. Expected percentages are from a log-linear model of a cross-tabulation of the race or Hispanicity of the male and female partners. The analysis is available from the authors.

24. Because one cannot identify the race of parents who no longer live in the household in census data, our tabulations probably underestimate this number.

25. These rates are often the lowest in the distribution, and include students who moved or transferred to other schools. Census data also include students who earned GEDs.

26. The statistics for detailed occupations are from additional analyses, available upon request from the authors.

27. The education = specific estimates are from additional analyses, available upon request from the authors.

5

The New Immigrants

BARRY R. CHISWICK and TERESA A. SULLIVAN

IMMIGRANTS AND THE CENSUS

F ROM THE COLONIAL period to the present, and we can expect far into the future, immigration has posed persistent economic, social, and political issues for the United States. The nature of the concerns may change over time, but the issue is seldom far from America's consciousness. Three themes emerge sharply in an analysis of immigrants in recent decades.

- The increased numbers of immigrants and an increase in the proportion foreign-born in the population, especially since 1980.

- The increased diversity among immigrants and the foreign-born population in terms of country of origin, skills, and labor market adjustment, among other characteristics.

- Converging characteristics with duration of residence between the foreign-born and the native-born populations, although the gap may not be closed. Characteristics that converge include fertility, English language fluency, occupational status, and earnings.

Introduction

Immigration has played a vital role in the development of the American population, society, and economy. Since the start of recordkeeping in 1820, over 60 million people have immigrated legally to the United States. The total number since 1820 is even larger because the early data do not include those crossing the land borders with Canada and Mexico, and the data do not include illegal immigrants. Not all immigrants remained in the United States permanently, but without reliable data on emigration, it is difficult to estimate how many returned to their countries of origin. The flow of immigrants to the United States, adjusted for those who have left the country or have died, constitutes the stock of the foreign-born or immigrant population of the United States. According to the 1990 Census of Population there were about 20 million foreign-born persons in the United States (excluding those born abroad of American parents and those born in dependencies of the United States), comprising 8.0 percent of the total population.[1] In recent decades immigration has become an important national and local issue because of both perceptions and misperceptions regarding the immigrants' characteristics and their impact. This chapter uses data from the 1990 Census of Population to explicate the demographic, social, and economic circumstances of the foreign-born population of the United States.[2]

The Census as a Source of Immigration Data

Every decennial census since 1850 has included a question on place of birth that identifies those born outside the United States and classifies them by their country of birth. The decennial census is the best data source available for the study of the foreign-born population. Its nearly universal coverage of the population permits identifying relatively small nationality groups that would otherwise be difficult to survey. Other questions in the decennial census provide a wealth of information about the demographic, social, and economic characteristics of the foreign-born for describing them (e.g., by gender, country of origin, and duration of residence), and then for comparing them with the native-born population.

Yet, the 1990 census has limitations. Immigration is a dynamic process that involves adjustments over time at the destination. The census, however, provides information about individuals only at a single point in time. Although there are some retrospective questions in the 1990 census (e.g., where the respondent was born, where he or she was living in 1985, and if foreign-born, when the respondent came to the United States), they are rather limited.[3] As a result, some aspects of the dynamic adjustment process of immigrants must be inferred from the cross-sectional census data or by tracking cohorts of immigrants from one decennial census to another.

By its very nature the census focuses on measuring the characteristics of individuals and households. Thus, the empirical analysis of the macroeconomic impact of immigrants, and their impact on the distribution of income of either families or persons cannot be addressed here (see Chiswick, Chiswick, and Karras 1992). The absence of data on parental nativity (except for those living with their parents) and the inability to identify illegal aliens or recently legalized aliens pose additional limitations in using the census data. Parental nativity, which had been asked in every census from 1870 through 1970, would provide information for analyzing the longer term adjustment and impact of immigrants in the first and second generations.

The administrative records of the Immigration and Naturalization Service (INS) provide additional information concerning the flow of immigrants and the characteristics of those entering during a year.[4] The INS data are, however, largely confined to the self-reported characteristics of legally admitted aliens when they apply for permanent alien status, and hence the reporting may be influenced by the applicant's desire to maximize the probability of obtaining a visa. There is no regular INS follow-up survey on immigrants, and so INS data are not directly useful for analyzing either the characteristics or impact of the foreign-born population or the adjustment process of immigrants. INS obtains data on the characteristics of illegal aliens at the time of apprehension, but these data are quite limited in terms of the information solicited.

Illegal immigration has returned as a major policy concern, in spite of the provisions of the Immigration Reform and Control Act of 1986.[5] The 1986 Act was intended to "wipe the slate clean" by offering amnesty to certain illegal aliens already in the United States and to discourage future illegal migration by imposing penalties on employers who knowingly hire illegal aliens.[6] It is reasonable to assume that most beneficiaries of amnesty were enumerated in the 1990 Census, but it is unclear to what extent the illegal aliens who could not satisfy the provisions of the 1986 Act or who arrived after 1986 appear in the 1990 census data. Census data are likely to include some, but not all, illegal aliens.

IMMIGRATION, IMMIGRATION LAW, AND DIVERSITY

Anyone who walks the streets of Los Angeles today, or who walked the streets of Chicago or New York at any time in this century, would conclude that America's foreign-born population has grown rapidly and that they come from "everywhere." Just how true this observation is, and why it is prompted by visiting our largest cities, is the theme of this section.

Trends Over Time

Data from the INS indicate that after the great wave of immigration from the 1880s up to World War I, there was a period of decline and then very low immigration during the 1930s and early 1940s (Table 5.1). The difficulties in leaving Europe and the dangers of ocean transport during World War I, the restrictive immigration legislation enacted in the 1920s, the Great Depression of the 1930s, and World War II limited immigration from Europe, which was until

TABLE 5.1 Immigration and proportion foreign-born
in the United States: 1871–1990.

Decade	Number	Immigration Rate[a]	Foreign-Born[b]
1981–90	7,338,062[c]	3.2	8.0%
1971–80	4,493,314	2.2	6.2
1961–70	3,321,677	1.9	4.7
1951–60	2,515,479	1.7	5.4
1941–50	1,035,039	0.8	6.9
1931–40	528,431	0.4	8.8
1921–30	4,107,209	3.9	11.6
1911–20	5,735,811	6.2	13.2
1901–10	8,795,386	11.6	14.7
1891–00	3,687,564	5.9	13.6
1881–90	5,246,613	10.5	14.7
1871–80	2,812,191	7.1	13.3

SOURCES: *Statistical Yearbook of the Immigration and Naturalization Service, 1991*, Table 1, *Statistical Abstract of the United States, 1992*, Tables 1 and 45. *Historical Statistics of the United States: Colonial Times to 1957* (1960) Table Series A 5, 53, 57, 62, 63, 68, 69.

[a] Annual immigration in the decade, per 1,000 of the population in the census year preceding the decade.
[b] Percentage of the U.S. population that is foreign-born (excluding those born abroad of American parents) at the end of the decade.
[c] Includes 1,359,184 former illegal aliens who received permanent resident alien status in 1989 and 1990 under the Immigration Reform and Control Act of 1986. Some may have come to the United States to stay in an earlier decade.

then the primary source of immigrants to the United States. Following World War II, and particularly following the relaxation in 1965 of immigration barriers enacted earlier against Southern and Eastern Europeans and Asians, immigration has increased decade by decade both in absolute numbers and relative to the size of the United States population.

Was immigration to the United States during the 1980s large by historical standards? The answer depends on the criterion selected—absolute numbers or the number of immigrants relative to the population. In terms of absolute numbers, the 7.3 million new immigrants in the 1980s is second only to the peak immigration in the first decade of this century (8.8 million), although relative to the population, the immigration rate of 3.2 per 1,000 population is only about one-quarter of the rate in 1901–1910.

Immigration in the past few decades has been characterized not merely by a rise in the numbers but also by a dramatic change in the source countries. Whereas, during the nineteenth century and the first half of the twentieth century, immigrants came primarily from Europe and Canada, immigration is now predominantly from Asia, Mexico, and other parts of Latin America, including the Caribbean (Table 5.2). The "new immigration" from Asia, Mexico, and other parts of Latin America is having a profound effect that perhaps rivals the

TABLE 5.2   Region of origin of immigrants, by decade of immigration: 1921–1990.

Decade of Immigration	Europe/ Canada[a]	Mexico	Other Latin America	Asia	Africa	Total	Number (1,000s)
1981–90[b]	13%	23%	25%	37%	2%	100%	7,338
1971–80	23	14	26	35	2	100	4,493
1961–70	47	14	26	13	<1	100	3,322
1951–60	69	12	13	6	<1	100	2,515
1941–50	78	6	12	4	<1	100	1,035
1931–40	87	4	6	3	<1	100	528
1921–30	83	11	3	3	<1	100	4,107

SOURCE: *Statistical Yearbook of the Immigration and Naturalization Service, 1991*, Table 2.

NOTE: Detail may not add to total due to rounding.

[a]Includes Australia, New Zealand, and Oceania.
[b]Includes nearly 1.4 million former illegal aliens receiving permanent resident alien status in 1989 and 1990 under the Immigration Reform and Control Act of 1986.

effects on the United States of the "new immigrants" of a century ago, who were from Southern and Eastern Europe.

Changes in the flows of immigrants affect the proportion of immigrants in the population, but only after a time lag. For the three decades starting with World War I, while the large number of turn-of-the-century immigrants gradually died and new immigration flows remained small, the proportion of the foreign-born in the population dwindled from its peak of nearly 15 percent in 1910 to about 7 percent in 1950 and less than 5 percent in 1970. The proportion of foreign-born in the population has since increased to 8.0 percent in 1990 (Table 5.1). Despite the recent rise, however, the proportion foreign-born remains substantially below the levels recorded in the late nineteenth and early twentieth centuries.

Just over one-quarter of the total foreign-born population of the United States in 1990 was born in Europe and Canada, with another one-quarter coming from Asia (Table 5.3). Mexico and other parts of Latin America each account for one-fifth. Less than 2 percent of the foreign-born were from Africa. Reflecting trends over the past few decades, among the most recent arrivals, those immigrating between 1985 and the 1990 census, only 13 percent were born in Europe and Canada, whereas 26 percent came from Mexico, 31 percent from Asia, 22 percent from other parts of the Americas, and only 2 percent from Africa. Thus, the foreign-born population is increasingly Asian and Latin American in origin.

A population of particular interest is the primary working-age population, those aged 25–64 years. This group of 12.5 million forms the core of the immigrant labor force and household decision makers. This group also shows the effects of changes in the flow of immigrants over time (Table 5.4). Among the adult foreign-born, those from Asia, Mexico, and other parts of Latin America are far more likely to be recent immigrants, while the European/Canadians have, on average, been in the United States for a longer period of time.

Where They Came From: Policy and Geography

Immigrants to the United States have not always come from "everywhere." Through the first two-thirds of the nineteenth century, the principal immigration to the United States came from the Northwest European countries of Great Britain, Ireland, Germany, Scandinavia, France, and the Low Countries. The Constitution barred the importation of slaves after 1808 (although some were smuggled in illegally), and even voluntary immigration from Africa was virtually nonexistent until recently. Immigration from Eastern Europe and Asia was also very small.

After the Civil War, however, the immigrant flows changed in composition. On the West Coast, Japanese, Chinese, Korean, and Filipino workers came as contract laborers. On the East Coast, a shift occurred toward the so-called new

TABLE 5.3 Foreign-born population of the United States, by region of birth and period of immigration: 1990.[c]

Period of Immigration	Europe/ Canada[b]	Mexico	Other Latin America	Asia	Africa	Other[c]	Total	Number (1,000s)
1985–90	3.2%	6.5%	5.6%	7.8%	0.6%	1.2%	24.9%	4,895
1975–84	3.6	8.3	7.6	11.1	0.8	1.5	32.9	6,464
1965–74	4.2	4.2	5.0	4.2	0.3	0.7	18.6	3,662
1960–64	2.5	1.0	1.7	0.7	0.1	0.2	6.1	1,198
1950–59	5.3	1.0	0.8	0.8	0.1	0.2	8.1	1,588
Before 1950	7.3	0.8	0.4	0.5	0.0	0.4	9.4	1,841
Total	26.1%	21.9%	21.0%	25.0%	1.8%	4.3%	100.0%	19,649
Number (1,000s)	5,128	4,293	4,124	4,913	354	836	19,649	

SOURCE: 1990 Census of Population, Public Use Microdata Sample.

[a] Excludes persons born abroad of American parents or born in U.S. territories.
[b] Includes Australia and New Zealand.
[c] Includes foreign-born with country not specified.

TABLE 5.4 Foreign-born population aged 25–64, by region of birth and period of immigration: 1990.[a]

Period of Immigration	Europe-Canada[b]	Mexico	Other Latin America	Asia	Africa	Other[c]	Total	Number (1,000s)
1985–90	12.6%	17.9%	19.7%	26.4%	26.5%	23.4%	19.7%	2,466
1975–84	17.6	40.7	37.2	45.0	48.6	38.8	35.6	4,462
1965–74	22.3	26.5	28.5	20.3	17.7	22.4	23.9	2,999
1960–64	14.0	6.7	9.7	3.7	3.4	6.5	8.3	1,037
1950–59	24.9	6.3	4.1	3.8	3.2	6.1	9.5	1,196
Before 1950	8.6	1.9	0.9	0.8	0.6	2.7	3.0	375
Total	100.0%	100.0%	100.0%	100.0%	100.0%	100.0%	100.0%	12,536
Distribution by Region of Birth	24.1	20.7	22.6	26.5	2.1	4.0	100.0	
Number (1,000s)	3,019	2,592	2,830	3,327	262	507	12,536	

SOURCE: 1990 Census of Population, Public Use Microdata Sample.

[a] Excludes those born abroad of American parents or born in U.S. territories.
[b] Includes Australia and New Zealand.
[c] Includes other areas not separately listed and country not specified.

immigrants from the city-states of the Italian peninsula, from Poland and Russia, from Greece and the Balkans. They differed from the earlier immigrants in language, religion, and appearance. Less likely to be literate or to be skilled laborers, they also came from countries with more autocratic forms of government (Lieberson 1980; Carpenter 1927). Fears mounted on both the East and West coasts that these immigrants could not be assimilated.

In a reaction to racial prejudice and economic competition in the West Coast states where most Asian immigrants lived, measures were taken by the federal government as early as the 1870s to exclude the Chinese, and in 1907 immigration from Japan was halted through diplomatic means (Bonacich 1984). To restrict Southern and East European immigration, legislation enacted in the early 1920s attempted to force the nationality composition of the immigrant population of the United States to be the same as the distribution of the origins of the white population. Throughout this time, however, immigration continued from Canada, Mexico, and the Caribbean. Immigrants from the Western Hemisphere were technically subject to the same qualitative restrictions that were applied to the Eastern Hemisphere—for example, the exclusion of criminals and persons with communicable diseases—but they were exempt from numerical restrictions (Cafferty, Chiswick, Greeley, and Sullivan 1983).

The National Origins Quota Act of 1924, which barred some nationalities entirely and subjected others from the Eastern Hemisphere to quotas, continued with some modifications until the major changes wrought by the 1965 Amendments to the 1952 Immigration and Nationality Act. An important feature of the 1965 legislation, which took effect in 1968, was to make people from all independent countries of the world eligible for visas. Although it was first applied only to the Eastern Hemisphere and then to all countries, there was an overall numerical quota and a uniform country limit for certain categories of immigrants, but admission of individual immigrants was determined by a preference system. Preference was given primarily to persons being reunited with family members already residing in the United States (i.e., spouse, parents, children, and siblings) and secondarily to persons based on their skills. Provision was also made for some refugees and for investors, persons making job-creating investments in businesses in the United States (Keely 1971 and 1975).

This legislation had three important ramifications. First, Asian and African immigrants were again permitted to enter the United States, and most of the initial entrants came under the skilled-worker preferences and the investor category because they did not have immediate relatives in the United States. They were now identified as the "new" immigrants. Second, Latin American immigrants came under numerical restriction for the first time. As a result, many workers who had previously migrated back and forth across the U.S.–Mexico border legally suddenly found themselves redefined as illegal immigrants. Third, to a much greater extent than had been anticipated, family reunification visas came to swamp the visas for skilled workers and investors. The framers of the legislation had anticipated that family reunification would apply principally to the European relatives of the now-aging immigrants already resident in the United States. By linking new visas to kin already residing in the United States, family reunification would merely replicate the countries of origin of the foreign-born population. Instead, family reunification was extensively used by the relatives of the newly arrived skilled workers, investors, and refugees, creating new patterns of chain migration (Jasso and Rosenzweig 1986). And, seemingly, the more immigrants admitted under family reunification provisions, the more new applicants there are for those family-based visas.

The pressures on the U.S. immigration system were intensified by a number of overwhelming pull and push factors. American higher education, reputed to be the world's best, attracted thousands of international students who were the best and brightest of their countries, and who received a first-hand taste of the world's most vigorous economy. Population pressures in the rapidly growing countries of Asia, Africa, and Latin America outstripped the abilities of many of their economies to generate good jobs and made emigration attractive to young adults. Wage rates for unskilled workers in the United States that might seem very low by U.S. standards seemed very attractive to those with even poorer labor market opportunities in their country of origin. Especially for Mexicans, an undetected entry across the southern border of the United States was easy, resulting in a large number of illegal entrants. Even for Asians and Africans, for whom the cost of air travel declined, overstaying a tourist or student visa proved easy to accomplish. Events abroad, such as government instability, wars, and revolutions, created streams of refugees, many of whom sought ultimate asylum in the United States.

Tensions over the illegal portion of the immigration stream led to a legislative compromise in the Immigration Reform and Control Act of 1986 (IRCA) (Bean, Vernez, and Keely 1989; Chiswick 1988). This legislation initiated sanctions against employers for knowingly hiring undocumented immigrants, while providing that legally resident workers, regardless of their origin or citizenship status, could not be legally discriminated against in hiring. The intent of these provisions was to dry up the demand for undocumented workers without harming legally resident workers with a similar national or ethnic background.

As a result of confusion over the employers' legal responsibilities neither to hire illegal aliens nor to discriminate against those with legal rights to work, minimal funding for enforcement of employer sanctions, and the virtual absence of any penalties against illegal aliens who are apprehended by the authorities, the illegal alien flow into the United States continues. By 1992, apprehensions of illegal aliens increased to 1.3 million, the level that had been attained prior to the 1986 legislation. The law has apparently failed to eliminate the flow of illegal aliens attracted by jobs and other benefits, although there is some indication that the flow would have been even larger in the absence of employer sanctions.

The 1986 Act provided for amnesty for undocumented workers who could prove that they had resided continuously in the country since January 1, 1982. An alternative provision permitted those who had worked at least 30 days in seasonal agriculture to apply for amnesty. As of 1992, over 2.6 million persons out of 3.1 million applicants had been granted legal permanent resident status under the 1986 Act. Of the remainder, about half have had their applications denied while the applications of the others are still pending. These amnesties have created the expectation of future amnesties, and some limited amnesty provisions have been written into subsequent legislation.

The Refugee Act of 1980 redefined the terms under which a person could be admitted to the United States as a refugee. Under the 1952 legislation a refugee had to be fleeing persecution in a communist country or be a refugee from certain parts of the Middle East. The 1980 Act required merely that the person have a well-founded fear of persecution for political, religious, ethnic, or other related reasons. Among its provisions was the requirement that the United States not be the country of first asylum. Almost immediately, the Mariel boatlift to Southern Florida challenged the first-asylum provision. Later in the 1980s, large numbers of Haitians entered the country claiming an "economic refugee" status because of the poverty in their country. Other novel claims of asylum have been made, including claims by Chinese nationals that their country's one-child policy is a form of persecution against them, a claim by a Nigerian woman that her U.S.-born daughters would be subjected to ritual genital mutilation if she were deported, and a claim by a Mexican national that he was persecuted for sexual orientation. The instability in Eastern Europe and the former Soviet Union that has followed the collapse of communism may generate new refugee flows.

The Immigration Act of 1990, which modified the provisions for issuing visas based on kinship and skills and opened other opportunities for new flows of immigrants, did not affect the characteristics of the immigrant population in the 1990 census. Nor is it likely that the 1990 Act will be the last major legislative initiative on immigration. Legislative controversies for the 1990s include the definition of refugees and the mechanisms for granting asylum. Moreover, the increased public interest in the economic dimensions of immigration is likely to keep open the debate on allocating visas on the basis of the applicant's own level and type of skill rather than on kinship. Illegal immigration has again become an important political issue, with many observers arguing that current enforcement mechanisms, at the border and in the interior, have been ineffective in stemming the flow of undocumented workers. More effective enforcement of employer sanctions and penalties against the illegal aliens themselves will be subject to legislative debate.

Geographic Diversity of Origins

The foreign-born population enumerated in the 1990 census is the most diverse in our history, and yet one out of every five immigrants comes from only one country, Mexico. The claim that Americans "come from everywhere" was by 1990 almost literally true. Table 5.5 shows the twenty sending countries that account for the largest number of the foreign-born population, excluding those born abroad of American parents and those born in U.S. territories. These twenty countries together accounted for 69 percent of the total foreign-born population of 20 million enumerated in 1990.

Mexico was the leading country of origin for immigrants in both 1980 and 1990, and the proportion of the total foreign-born who are from Mexico increased from 16 percent to nearly 22 percent over the decade. Journalistic accounts of immigration occasionally lose sight of the fact that Mexico is a major source of legal immigrants. According to INS data, nearly one in every four legally admitted immigrants during the 1980s were from Mexico. Many Mexicans seeking legal entry are already familiar with the United States (Portes and Bach 1985; Hirschman 1978). Moreover, the family reunification preferences, applied to the Western Hemisphere since 1976, have made many Mexicans eligible to immigrate legally to rejoin family residing on the U.S. side of the border. The Mexican migration stream is large for several reasons: the large gap in real wage rates and employment opportunities between the U.S. and Mexico; the long-standing circulatory movements of Mexican workers between the two countries; and the development of chain migration, as residents of Mexican villages learn more about life in the United States and receive migration assistance from friends and relatives who migrated previously (Massey et al. 1987).

An important issue in the census taking of both 1980 and 1990 was the extent to which the illegal immigrants were enumerated. Analysts claimed that substantial numbers of illegally resident Mexicans had been counted even in the 1980 census.[7] By 1990, some 2.3 million Mexicans had applied for legalization through the amnesty program enacted in 1986, presumably reducing their hesitation to be counted. The issue remains, however, as to how many illegally resident foreign-born persons were missed in 1990. Ethnographic studies conducted in conjunction with the census suggest that illegal immigrants were missed in the census—Mexicans as well as undocumented entrants from other countries (De la Puente 1993).

The Philippines moved to second place on the list from seventh in 1980, accounting for 4.5 percent of the total foreign-born population in 1990 (Table 5.5). The Philippines is a country with direct ties to the United States since the Spanish-American War of 1898, and even when other Asians were barred from immigrating, some Filipinos could immigrate legally. The Philippines has many well-educated workers, and their admission both as skilled workers and as fam-

TABLE 5.5   Top twenty countries of birth among the foreign-born, and selected demographic characteristics 1990.[a]

Rank in 1990	Country[b]	Rank in 1980	Number (1,000s)	Percent Distribution	Median Age	Ratio Males to Females	Percent Naturalized	Percent Immigrated Since 1985
1	Mexico	1	4,297	21.8%	29	123	23%	30%
2	Philippines	7	882	4.5	38	77	54	26
3	Canada	3	755	3.8	53	71	53	11
4	Cuba	6	735	3.7	49	94	53	7
5	Germany	2	713	3.6	53	53	74	6
6	United Kingdom	5	633	3.2	49	71	49	14
7	Italy	4	583	3.0	59	98	75	3
8	Korea	10	575	2.9	34	79	38	34
9	Vietnam	12	552	2.8	30	113	44	25
10	China	11	524	2.7	45	99	42	32
11	India	16	446	2.3	36	114	35	32
12	El Salvador	28	446	2.3	29	109	14	34
13	Poland	8	378	1.9	58	88	61	20
14	Jamaica	18	344	1.7	35	83	39	24
15	Dominican Republic	19	341	1.7	33	86	25	32
16	USSR	9	332	1.7	55	82	59	30
17	Japan	13	279	1.4	37	61	27	45
18	Colombia	23	277	1.4	35	85	29	28
19	Taiwan	33	244	1.2	33	87	40	33
20	Guatemala	39	228	1.2	30	104	19	39
—	All Others		6,160	31.2	38	98	42	26
Total			19,724	100.0%	37	96	40%	25%

SOURCE: 1990 Census of Population, Public Use Microdata Sample.

NOTE: Native-born: median age 33; ratio males to females 95.

[a] All data refer to 1990, except rank in 1980.

[b] Germany includes East and West Germany. United Kingdom includes all constituent units. USSR includes all areas of what was the former USSR. China includes Hong Kong but not Taiwan.

223

ily members has led to a total foreign-born population of nearly 1 million people. The majority of the Filipinos reside in California (53 percent), with smaller numbers living in Hawaii (8 percent) and other states. The Philippines ranked second in the number of permanent resident alien visas received in 1992.

Three countries each account for about 3.5–4.0 percent of the foreign-born: Canada, perennially a major sending country; Cuba, a major source of refugees since the beginning of the Castro regime in 1959; and Germany, a traditional source of immigration since Colonial times. Although these countries were major contributors to the stock of the foreign-born, they are less important in the recent flow; none of these three countries is among the top ten countries of origin for immigrants admitted to the United States in recent years. There is actually another group that could be considered the third-largest source "country": that is, the 856,000 foreign-born who reported only that they were "born abroad" or gave similarly vague answers as to their foreign birthplace, so vague that the Census Bureau could not code their country of birth.

Of the remaining countries listed in Table 5.5, many have contributed immigrants because of recent refugee streams. Entrants from Vietnam, El Salvador, the former Soviet Union, and Guatemala have sought asylum from political, religious, or ethnic persecution. For example, the persecuted ethnic Chinese of Vietnam and Jews from Russia received asylum. Many entrants from El Salvador and Guatemala seek refugee status because of armed violence in their home countries, although it appears that others from these countries are undocumented entrants (Hagan and Rodriguez 1992; Rodriguez 1987). The significance of these sending countries increased after the census of 1990. Among the countries of origin for immigrants admitted during 1992, Vietnam had moved to second place, the Soviet Union to fourth, and El Salvador eighth.

Some of the remaining top 20 countries listed in Table 5.5 are there because immigrants survive from migrations that took place much earlier in this century. Their median age is therefore considerably older than the median age for more recent immigrant groups. For example, the median age of the Italian foreign-born is 59, and the median age of the Polish foreign-born is 58, in contrast to 37 years for all of the foreign-born. Between 1985 and 1990, only 23,309 foreign-born persons entered the United States from Italy and 69,209 from Poland. Italy's rank in Table 5.5 results principally from immigration earlier in this century, including survivors of the immigrants who arrived prior to the restrictive legislation enacted in 1924. Polish immigration is being renewed in the wake of the collapse of communism and the Iron Curtain. In 1992, over 25,000 immigrants were admitted from Poland. By contrast, median ages are much younger among the foreign-born from some of the newer sending countries, 36 for persons born in India, and 29 for El Salvador.

The degree of heterogeneity among immigrants may well be typified by the group born in Africa, of whom 45 percent reported their race as black or African, 44 percent as white, 7 percent as Asian, and 3 percent as other and mixed races. By region within Africa, 50 percent were born in Central Africa (of whom over two-thirds were black and 13 percent Asian), 36 percent in North Africa (three-quarters white), and 14 percent in Southern Africa (three-quarters white).

The evident diversity of the immigration stream is manifested by the great number of origins listed by nearly one-third of the remaining foreign-born. The Census Bureau coded the foreign places of birth that were reported on the census forms into more than 250 areas, including Antarctica. Some of the codes are subnational entities; for example, the Channel Islands, Guernsey, and Jersey are coded separately from England, and United Kingdom is yet a different code. On the other hand, with the breakup of the USSR, Czechoslovakia, and Yugoslavia, country categories would exist today that did not exist in 1990.

Sometimes, however, the respondents' self-identifications proved to be prescient of later political developments. In addition to country of birth the census asked for ethnic origin (ancestry). Of the nearly 140,000 people who listed Yugoslavia as their place of birth, only 30 percent claimed to be Yugoslavian by ethnicity or ancestry, 19 percent reported themselves Croatian, 13 percent German, 12 percent Serbian, 4 percent Slovak, 4 percent Slovene, 3 percent Macedonian, 1.5 percent Hungarian, and 14 percent reported other ancestries or did not respond to the question. Among the nearly 86,000 persons born in what used to be Czechoslovakia, only 17 percent identified their ancestry as Czechoslovakian, while 30 percent reported themselves to be Slovak, 27 percent Czech, 19 percent Austrian, and 6 percent reported other ancestries or did not respond.

Perhaps most interesting of all are the 330,500 foreign-born who reported that they had been born in what was then the Union of Soviet Socialist Republics. They reported 71 different ancestries, and 15.5 percent were coded in one residual category that included any response that might reveal religion. The most numerous of the specific ancestries were Russian (45 percent), Ukrainian (15 percent), and Armenian (10 percent). By 1992, the former Soviet Union ranked fourth in the number of immigrants admitted; and the continued entry of immigrants from this multiethnic region seems likely.

These combinations of birthplace and ancestry data point to processes of ethnic identification and reidentification. Social scientists have previously documented the disappearance of ethnic identification, such as the replacement of Germans by "Austrians" in the Canadian census after World War I (Ryder 1955). But censuses also document the emergence of ethnic identification. For example, the idea of a unified Italy gained impetus from immigrants who, once in America, no longer considered themselves Sicilian nor Milanese but rather

"Italian" (Glazer 1954; Greeley 1971, Lieberson and Waters 1990). As the political maps of the world change, the continuity of census data becomes more complex, but in the detailed coding categories may lie useful clues.

WHERE IMMIGRANTS LIVE AND THEIR CITIZENSHIP

The Geographic Location of Immigrants

Immigrants are attracted to a locality for much the same reason that the native-born are, and so from the beginning of our history there have been distinctive geographic clusters of immigrants (Portes and Rumbaut 1990; Bartel 1989). The availability of jobs (or in earlier times, of farmland) and amenities attract migrants. Immigrants also tend to settle, at least initially, in ports of entry. Finally, they also tend to settle near earlier entrants from their place of origin. Explicit government policies to channel immigrants to specific areas have seldom been adopted in the United States, and when attempted, they have failed because of subsequent internal migration.

Americans are deeply interested in the local economic impacts of immigration, but these impacts are difficult to measure. Because these localities are often growing through internal as well as international migration, it is technically difficult to identify a separate effect of the foreign-born within a labor market. As the number of migrants attracted by jobs rises, local wages should fall and unemployment may rise, but this effect occurs whether the migrants were born in the United States or abroad. Some recent work indicates that the internal migration of native-born workers may slow, cease, or be reversed in response to international migration, even though immigrants and native-born workers tend to be attracted to areas with growing employment opportunities (Filer 1992; Frey, Chapter 6 in this volume).

Even if the effect on individual workers cannot be precisely determined, however, there remains a strong interest in the collective effect of immigration on the public sector. Admission to the United States is a matter of federal law; and as a matter of constitutional right, the states are not permitted to limit migration, neither into nor from their territory. This is not true in all receiving countries; in Canada, for example, a potential immigrant can receive extra "points" in the visa allocation process by promising to settle in a relatively less populous part of the country, and the Province of Quebec can apply somewhat separate immigration criteria. Earlier in American history some states sent recruiters to Europe to encourage the migration of workers with technical skills. Much like the native-born population, however, once immigrants have entered the United States they are entitled to settle and resettle at will, moving from city to city and from state to state. Indeed, federal government efforts to distribute Cuban and

Vietnamese refugees throughout the country proved fruitless as they tended to concentrate themselves through secondary migrations within the United States.

Immigrants benefit from government infrastructure, such as highways, and from government services, such as public education and police protection, just as do the native-born. To the extent that immigrants cluster in only a few states or localities, the impact of immigration, both costs and benefits, will also be concentrated. Thus, while the federal government makes immigration policy, much of the impact may fall disproportionately on certain states and localities that have no control over the influx of immigrants into their areas. This imbalance between where policy is made and where the policy may have its largest impact has resulted in tension between the federal government and states and localities that have received the largest numbers of low-skilled immigrants.

Nearly three-quarters of the immigrants are clustered in only six states, with California the leading destination. One-third of the nation's foreign-born population lived in California in 1990. New York, which had been the leading destination in 1960, when 24 percent of the foreign-born lived there, was home to 14 percent of the immigrants in 1990, a distinct second place. Florida and Texas each accounted for about 8 percent of the foreign-born in 1990, and New Jersey and Illinois for 5 percent each. The remaining 27 percent of the foreign-born are scattered among the other 44 states and the District of Columbia.

Figure 5.1 shows the distribution of the foreign-born by county. The darkest shading represents counties with at least 16 percent of the population foreign-born, or twice the national proportion of 8 percent. Of the 3,141 counties in the nation, 95 percent of them have fewer than 8 percent foreign-born in their population, or less than the national average. Only 47 counties, or 1.5 percent of the total counties, have twice the national proportion of foreign-born; the highest proportion of foreign-born population, in Dade County, Florida, is 45 percent. The map concretely displays the uneven distribution of the foreign-born population.

Within California, the immigrants are concentrated in the largest metropolitan areas, particularly Los Angeles and the San Francisco Bay Area. Of all immigrants admitted to the United States in 1992, 129,000 or 13.3 percent intended to reside in the Los Angeles–Long Beach Area. Another 3.5 percent intended to reside in the neighboring Anaheim–Santa Ana Area; 2.4 percent in San Jose; 2.2 percent each in San Francisco and in San Diego. Among the top 20 metropolitan areas of intended residence, 8 were in California. California has attracted large numbers of immigrants from many different countries, including Mexico, Central American, China, Korea, the Philippines, Iran, and other parts of Asia and the Middle East.

Other major destinations included Miami, the fifth-ranked residence for those admitted in 1992, and Houston, which was seventh. Linguistic communities add to the appeal of these particular cities. In Houston, for example, the large Spanish-speaking community of Mexican origin helped attract new immigrant groups

FIGURE 5.1 Percentage of foreign-born, by county: 1990.

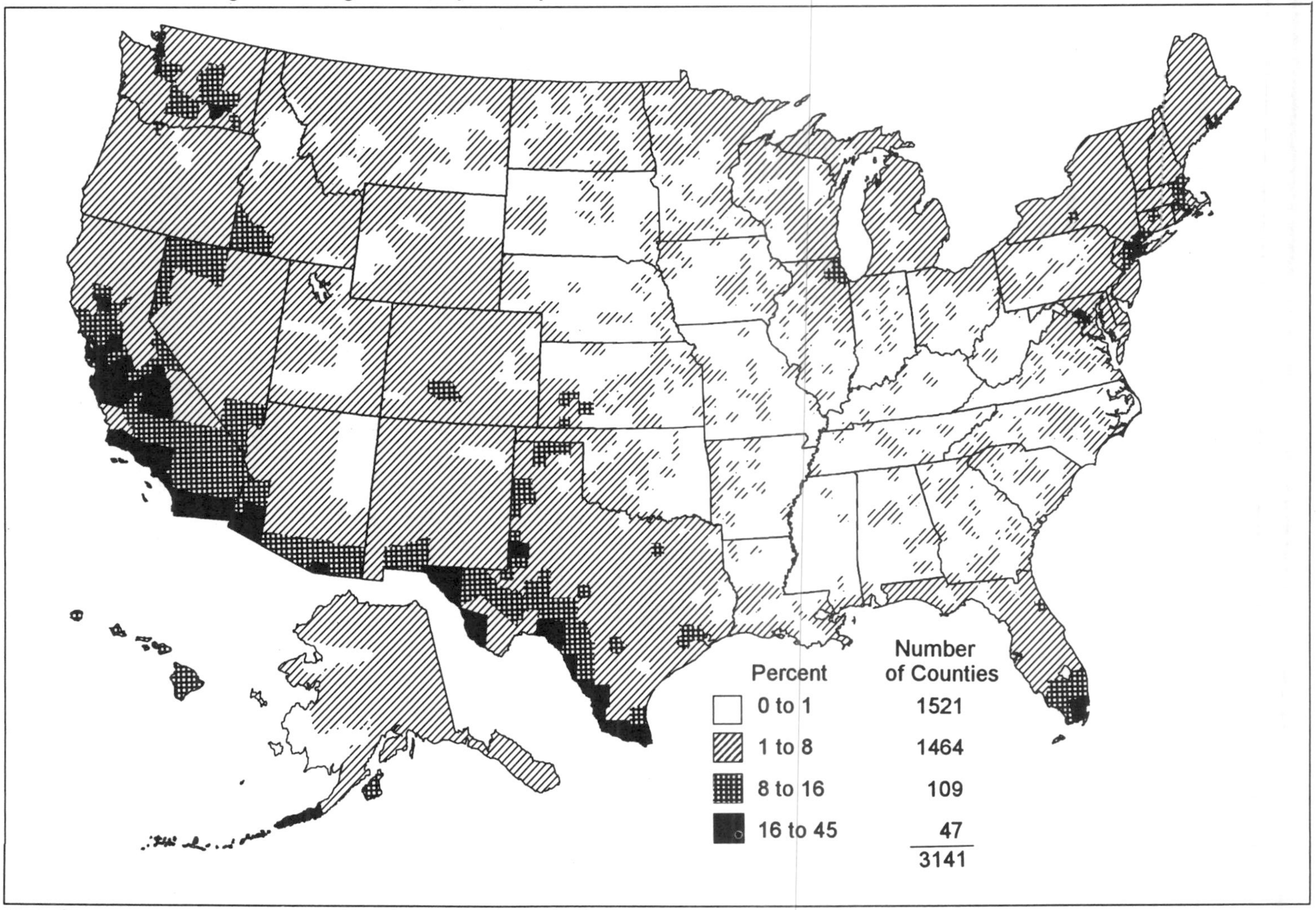

Percent		Number of Counties
0 to 1		1521
1 to 8		1464
8 to 16		109
16 to 45		47
		3141

SOURCE: 1990 Census of Population, Summary Tape File, 3C.

NOTE: National percentage: 8 percent.

from Guatemala, El Salvador, and other Central American locations, even if the newcomers preferred to speak one of the indigenous languages of their home country rather than Spanish.

The Local Impact

Besides absolute numbers of the foreign-born, it is useful to consider the relative impact of immigration on the state and locality. California is, after all, the nation's most populous state, and thus it could be expected to absorb a large number of immigrants. Even in relative terms, however, California stands out as a host state. Over 22 percent of the residents of California are foreign-born, compared with 16 percent of New Yorkers. Inevitably, the fact that one of every five Californians is foreign-born has a profound impact on the social, economic, and political life of the state.

Some states without large absolute numbers of immigrants nevertheless receive a large number in relative terms. In Hawaii, for example, 16 percent of the population is foreign-born, and in the District of Columbia almost 10 percent of the population is foreign-born. At the other end of the distribution, in 16 states fewer than 2 percent of the population are foreign-born. These states include Southern states, such as Mississippi (0.9 percent) and Kentucky (1.0); Midwestern Farmbelt states, such as Iowa (1.7 percent) and Nebraska (1.8 percent); Mountain states, such as Montana (1.9 percent); and Northern Plains states, such as South Dakota (1.2 percent). The political salience of immigration in the Farmbelt may be quite different from its salience in California, New York, and Florida.

One political issue is the expense borne by cities and states to provide services to immigrants. The cost of providing many public services may differ little for an immigrant or for a native-born migrant with the same level of income, age, and family structure (except perhaps for bilingual education for immigrant children); and the immigrants and migrants bear the costs of many of these services through sales taxes and user fees. There is little evidence that immigrants are able to avoid such taxes. Moreover, immigrants are specifically barred from receiving some types of welfare benefits until after some years of residence in the country (Jensen 1989).

The tension over providing services to immigrants is enhanced, however, in programs whose costs have been shifted to states and cities. When fewer federal dollars are available, states become concerned about the immigrant as a "free rider," especially for costly services such as Medicaid. Although the federal government disburses some impact payments for refugees and for immigrants legalized under the 1986 amnesty provisions, for the most part the states cannot recover the additional costs of providing public services for immigrants, except through their normal taxing mechanisms.

The impact that the immigrants have on state and local services varies according to how many immigrants there are—and with what characteristics. One important characteristic is age. Immigration has traditionally been undertaken by young adults. Although the host country has not clothed, fed, and educated them as children, the host country will reap the benefit of their productive years. Adults in their prime working years are usually self-supporting and taxpayers. Longer life expectancies, the family reunification policy, and the influx of refugees, however, have increased the likelihood that immigrants of all ages will inhabit American communities, and at some ages people are more likely to need government services. Children, for example, require public education, and the elderly are more likely to require medical care. We examine these groups in some detail because of the likelihood that their presence may increase the demand for government services.

Children and Education

More than 2 million children and teenagers were born outside the United States, or about 3 percent of those aged 19 and younger enumerated in 1990. California and New York also led the country in the proportion of children who are foreign-born. One in every nine children in California, and 1 in every 14 children in New York, was born in another country. Hawaii, Rhode Island, Nevada, District of Columbia, and Massachusetts, although not mentioned previously as having large numbers of immigrants, have a high proportion of children who are immigrants. In addition, immigrant parents may also have children born to them in the United States. They are native-born children, but they are the consequence of international migration. In the area of education, for which states and localities have responsibility, the uneven distribution of immigrants may be a problem.

One service that schools must provide, as a consequence of federal court rulings, is bilingual education. Consequently, schooling for immigrant children or the native-born children of immigrants may cost more than providing the same service to native-born children raised in English-speaking homes. This cost rises with the diversity of the immigrant stream. A school system whose immigrant population speaks many different languages faces a greater challenge than a school system whose immigrant children speak but one language other than English. These nuances are often lost in the debate, however, and immigration itself is seen as the driving force behind the need to provide bilingual (or multilingual) services in schools, courts, public hospitals, and other service agencies.

The magnitude of the bilingual education debate is illustrated by the fact that 1 in 7 school-age children speaks a language other than English at home. Along the Southwestern border (California, Arizona, New Mexico, Texas) and in New York, one-fifth or more of the school-age population can speak a language other than English (Pollard 1993). For two-thirds of these students, the home language is Spanish. But in areas such as Southern California, where the children have come from many different groups and speak many different languages, offering bilingual education and communicating with parents becomes problematic. In Los Angeles, for example, school children speak 80 languages at home. Emergency 911, fire and police dispatchers, and hospital trauma groups are among the services that need quick and accurate translations. And, when dozens of languages are routinely used, translation services can become a substantial public expense.

Senior Immigrants

At the other end of the life cycle, the distribution of the elderly immigrants may have policy significance. In the 1990 census, 13.2 percent of the foreign-born population were aged 65 or older, and 2.2 percent were aged 85 or older. As is the case with the native-born, there were fewer men than women among the aged. Among those aged 65 and older, there were 64 men for every 100 women among the foreign-born and 67 among the native-born.

Although some elderly immigrants have entered the United States recently through family reunification procedures, most have been residents for decades. Only 5.3 percent of the elderly foreign-born have entered the United States since 1985. Many of the states with the highest proportion of elderly immigrants, including Middle Atlantic and New England states (New York, New Jersey, Massachusetts, Connecticut, Rhode Island) and Illinois, have been destinations for immigrants for decades. The presence of older immigrants has potential implications for local health care and other services (Treas and Torrecilha 1994).

Naturalization and Politics

Naturalization is the process by which immigrants become citizens of the United States. The immigrant who wishes to become a U.S. citizen must apply for naturalization, which generally requires a 5-year residence in the United States as a permanent resident alien, demonstration of good moral character, and passing a simple test in English and U.S. history and civics. Naturalization confers many benefits on immigrants, including the right to vote, to hold elected public office (except president and vice president), and to serve on juries. Additional benefits include greater privileges for sponsoring the immigration of relatives (spouse, parents, children, siblings), the opportunity for employment in the Federal Civil Service and certain other government jobs (including police officers and teachers in many states), and certain government subsidies and transfers.

Among the foreign-born aged 18 and over in 1990, 43 percent were naturalized citizens. Naturalization rates vary systematically by demographic and other characteristics. For example, naturalization rates vary by duration of residence. It was very low (7 percent) among immigrants aged 18 and older who entered the United States between 1985 and 1990, largely because of the 5-year residency requirement for most immigrants. The rate was 31 percent for those who immigrated during 1975–1984, and the rate rose to 90 percent among those who immigrated before 1950. The increase with duration of residence arises, in part, because naturalization involves a waiting period and passing examinations on the English language and history/civics. More important, however, may be the delay until the immigrant decides to make the commitment to the United States, with the reduced ties to the country of origin that are implied by naturalization. Moreover, naturalization rates increase with duration because of the greater likelihood that those who have not made this commitment will return to their countries of origin.

But naturalization patterns differ sharply by region of origin. For example, among those in the United States 15–25 years in 1990, naturalization rates ranged from a high of 76 percent among Asian immigrants (for whom naturalization has been an important step in sponsoring relatives), to 65 percent for African immigrants, 53 percent for European/Canadian immigrants, 50 percent for non-Mexican Latin American immigrants, but only 31 percent for Mexican immigrants. The low rate among Mexican immigrants may be related to their higher-than-average rate of circular migration; that is, migration to and from Mexico and the United States. The ease of illegal immigration from Mexico may reduce the incentives for relatives legally in the United States to naturalize so as to serve as immigrant sponsors. Lower levels of schooling and English fluency may also account for the low naturalization rates among Mexican immigrants. Finally, compared with other source regions, the Mexican-born population in 1990 included a larger proportion of individuals whose status was recently legalized under the 1986 Immigration Reform and Control Act, thereby lowering the naturalization rate among the foreign-born from Mexico.

Naturalized immigrant voters may represent an important interest group in a ward or congressional district. To the extent that immigrants cluster within relatively few states and live within relatively few cities or neighborhoods within those states, their potential political power is enhanced. Even the immigrants who do not naturalize or who do not vote affect local politics through the redistricting process. One-person, one-vote requirements include all of the enumerated population, including the enumerated foreign-born, whether legally or illegally resident, and whether naturalized or resident alien. The Census Bureau was challenged in court because it attempts to enumerate illegal aliens in the census. Challengers argued that persons illegally residing within the country should not be given political influence through inclusion in the enumeration.

The courts have so far agreed with the Census Bureau, stating that the Constitution requires the enumeration of everyone within the national boundaries.

During the earlier migrations of this century, Congress and the courts had not yet reformed the process of redistricting. In fact, there was no redistricting at all after the 1920 census, in part because of concern about how immigration had swelled the population of cities (Anderson 1988). In many states, the dramatically unequal distribution of the population among districts allowed rural areas to maintain control of state legislatures (and, of course, the redistricting process), even after the population had largely shifted to the cities. One-person, one-vote became the law in *Baker* v. *Carr* (1962), and subsequently Congress passed the Voting Rights Acts, the most recent version of which provides that redistricting *not* dilute the votes of certain protected minority groups; e.g., blacks, Hispanics, American Indians, and Asian-Americans.

A large nonvoting population of immigrants can be useful to the existing voters in a district, for in effect their vote is enhanced. In California, for example, there are voting districts in which the majority of the population is Hispanic, but the majority of the voters are white (Clark and Morrison 1993). The reason for the apparent anomaly is that many of the Hispanic residents are immigrants who have not become naturalized, or if they are citizens they have not registered to vote or simply do not vote. As a result, the potential impact of the registered white voter is increased.

There has recently been a suggestion in California that permanent resident aliens (i.e., legal immigrants who have not become citizens) should have the right to vote, at least in local elections. There is precedent for this suggestion, but voting rights were usually offered by less populous states as a way to attract immigrants as settlers. For example, as recently as 1924, aliens could vote in Arkansas. The current context differs because it is not the less populous states with small numbers of immigrants, but rather the most populous state, where more than one in every five residents is foreign-born, where the issue of voting is being raised.

Although immigration policy is federal in scope, the patterns of geographic distribution have also affected public opinion differently in different parts of the country. Consensus about immigration policy has never been easy to reach in the United States: the geographic concentration and the increased diversity of the immigrant stream are likely to give the policy debate in the 1990s a distinctly regional and local flavor.

THE SKILLS OF IMMIGRANTS

The skills that immigrants bring with them or acquire while living in the United States affect not only many facets of their own lives but also the impact that their presence has on others.[8] Immigrants with more schooling and with greater English-language fluency in general have higher occupational attainments, higher earnings, lower unemployment, higher rates of internal geographic mobility, higher rates of naturalization, and lower fertility. It is, therefore, important to understand the level and temporal changes in the skills of immigrants.

The 1990 census provides data on the number of years of schooling and educational qualifications, current school enrollment status, language used at home, and English-language fluency. Data on other important dimensions of skill are, unfortunately, not available in the census. For example, there is no direct information on literacy in English or in another language, the place of the schooling, apprenticeship or other craft training, or investments in on-the-job training. Occupational attainment is sometimes perceived as a measure of skill and sometimes as an outcome of a labor market process that is influenced by skill level. In this chapter, occupational attainment will be treated as a measure of adjustment to the labor market and will be analyzed in the next section.

Educational Attainment

Possible answers to the question on educational attainment in the 1990 Census of Population are a mixture of years of schooling completed through grade 12 and, at higher levels, educational qualifications or type of degree completed. For simplicity of presentation, the categorical educational attainment data were recorded into equivalent years of schooling completed. Table 5.6 reports the mean and standard deviation of schooling among the foreign-born aged 25–64, by sex, country of birth, and period of immigration. Those currently enrolled in school are deleted from the analysis since many of them are in the United States on foreign student visas rather than as immigrants, and they cannot be separately identified in census data.

Several patterns emerge from these data. Immigrants have a lower mean and a greater dispersion (or variability) in their schooling than do the native-born. Adult foreign-born men have 11.5 years of schooling and the women 11.1 years, in contrast to 13.1 years and 13.0 years, respectively, for native-born men and women (Table 5.6). Among immigrants the proportion with 16 or more years of schooling is 24 percent for the men and 18 percent for the women, compared with 24 percent and 20 percent, respectively, for the native-born; that is, the proportion with college degrees is identical for native-and foreign-born men. While men have a wider dispersion in schooling attainment than women among both immigrants and the native-born, the dispersion in schooling is greater for immigrants than it is for the native-born, both within gender and overall.

A second important pattern is that the educational attainment of immigrants

TABLE 5.6 Schooling attainment among the foreign-born aged 25–64, by sex, region of birth, and period of immigration: 1990[a]

| | Mean Years of Schooling | | | | | | | | | | | | | Standard Deviation | |
| | Europe/Canada[b] | | Mexico | | Other Latin America | | Asia | | Africa | | Total[c] | | Total[c] | |
Period of Immigration	M	F	M	F	M	F	M	F	M	F	M	F	M	F
Mean														
1985–90	14.1	13.3	7.5	7.2	10.3	10.4	13.2	12.0	13.9	13.6	11.3	10.9	5.3	5.1
1975–84	13.4	12.8	7.1	6.9	10.8	10.5	13.4	12.2	15.3	13.7	11.1	10.7	5.1	4.9
1965–74	11.9	11.8	7.4	7.5	11.8	11.5	14.9	13.3	15.7	14.2	11.4	11.2	4.9	4.5
1960–64	12.7	12.2	8.3	8.1	13.1	12.5	15.1	13.1	15.3	13.2	12.3	11.8	4.5	4.0
1950–59	12.9	12.3	8.9	8.4	13.1	12.5	14.5	12.7	14.5	12.9	12.5	11.8	4.2	3.7
Before 1950	13.3	12.3	7.7	7.8	13.5	12.3	13.0	10.9	12.9	13.6	12.4	11.7	4.5	3.8
Total	12.9	12.3	7.4	7.3	11.3	11.1	13.8	12.4	15.0	13.7	11.5	11.1	5.0	4.6
Standard Deviation	4.0	3.5	4.7	4.6	4.4	4.2	4.4	4.6	3.5	3.5	5.0	4.6	—	—

SOURCE: 1990 Census of Population, Public Use Microdata Sample.

NOTES: M = Male, F = Female.
Native-born: Mean (standard deviation): Males 13.1 (2.9),
Females 13.0 (2.6).

[a] Excludes those currently enrolled in school.
[b] Includes Australia and New Zealand.
[c] Includes other areas not separately listed and country not specified.

235

varies less by period of arrival within countries of origin than it varies across countries (Table 5.6). As a result, the change in the source countries of immigrants has had a profound effect on both the overall level and dispersion of the schooling distribution of immigrants. Mexican immigrants have the lowest educational attainment, around 7½ years for both men and women, compared with nearly 14 years for Asian men and 15 years for very small groups of immigrant men from Africa.

The change in source countries of immigrants, with the European/Canadian component declining and the Asian and Mexican component increasing, among other factors, contributes to a decline in the level of schooling and a rise in the inequality of schooling among more recent immigration cohorts. Throughout the postwar period, among men, and since the 1960s among women, the level of schooling has declined with succeeding immigrant cohorts, except for the most recent group. Among male immigrants who arrived before 1960 the mean schooling level was nearly 12.5 years in contrast to only 11.1 years for those who arrived after 1975. Among female immigrants the schooling level declined from about 11.8 years (1950–1964) to about 10.8 years in the post-1975 cohorts. These declines in schooling level are not likely to be significantly mitigated by immigrants' attending school in the United States, because we are describing the population aged 25 and over. Postmigration schooling among adult immigrants is small and more likely among those who arrive with a higher level of schooling (Chiswick and Miller 1992).

Moreover, the shift over time in the countries of origin of immigrants has changed the shape of the distribution of schooling. Immigrants from Europe and Canada have a relatively high, homogenous schooling distribution (68 percent with 12–16 years of schooling and 11 percent with higher levels of schooling). Immigration is now heavily concentrated, however, in two other source regions, Asia and Mexico. Asian immigrants also have high educational attainments (66 percent with 12–16 years of schooling and another 15 percent with higher levels), but Mexican immigrants have a very low level (60 percent with 8 or fewer years, 27 percent with 12–16 years, and 1.4 percent with higher levels). As a result, recent immigrants are more diverse in that they bring both very high level and relatively sketchy educations to the United States.

The proportion of the foreign-born with very low educational attainment has increased sharply. Among the adult immigrants in the United States in 1990 who arrived in the 1950s, nearly one-quarter (23 percent) had 10 or fewer years of schooling, while among those immigrating from 1985 to 1990 over one-third (34 percent) had 10 or fewer years. Thus, at a time of increasing skills among the native-born population and when industrial restructuring requires greater schooling levels to compete successfully in the labor market, an increasing proportion of the immigrant stream has very low levels of schooling.

Language Skills

The 1990 census asked if a language other than English was currently spoken in the home. If so, respondents were asked to identify the language and to indicate their ability to speak English. The emphasis is on fluency, with no information on literacy in English or in another language. Figure 5.2 shows the English-language proficiency of immigrants aged 5 and over; that is, those who are school age and adult immigrants. Of these, 21 percent reported that they spoke only English at home, 32 percent lived in a home in which another language was spoken but reported that they spoke English very well, 22 percent reported that they spoke English well, 17 percent reported not well, and 8 percent reported that they did not speak English at all.

Among immigrants aged 25–64, 80 percent reported that a language other than or in addition to English was spoken in the home. This bilingualism was most common among immigrants from Mexico (96 percent) and Asia (92 percent), and less common among immigrants from Europe/Canada (56 percent). Among those reporting a language other than English, Spanish was the language most frequently cited (47 percent). Three Asian languages then followed—Chinese (7.0 percent of those reporting speaking a language other than English at home), Tagalog (5.3 percent), Korean (3.8 percent)—followed by German (3.3

FIGURE 5.2   English-language proficiency of the foreign-born: 1990.[a]

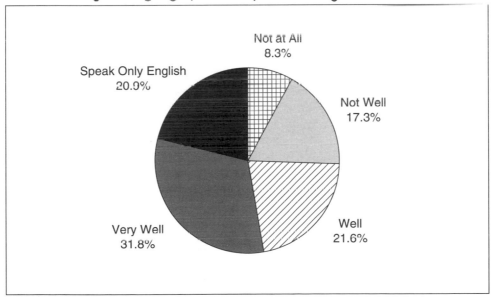

SOURCE: 1990 Census of Population, Public Use Microdata Sample.

[a] Persons aged 5 and over were asked if they spoke a language other than or in addition to English at home and, if so, to report their fluency in English.

percent), Italian (2.9 percent), French (2.7 percent), Vietnamese (2.6 percent), Hindi (2.2 percent), and Portuguese (1.8 percent). A total of 32 percent reported speaking these nine languages. The remaining myriad languages were reported by the 21 percent listing another language.

Reflecting the changing source countries of immigrants, the European languages, other than Spanish, were predominantly spoken by older immigrants who came to the United States in earlier decades. Spanish and the Asian languages, on the other hand, were more prevalent among newer cohorts of immigrants.

Retention of one's mother tongue may not be of much importance for understanding the social and economic adaptation of immigrants, although for some people retention might retard acquiring fluency in English. Speaking English is an important aspect and determinant of adjustment in the United States. Table 5.7 reports by period of immigration and country of birth the proportion of the foreign-born aged 25–64 who speak only English at home or who speak another language but speak English very well. The data are not reported by gender because the gender differences are very small.

English-speaking fluency varies by country of origin and duration in the United States, among other variables (Table 5.7). Among adult immigrants who lived in the United States 6–15 years by 1990 (i.e., immigrated 1975–1984), 68 percent of the European/Canadian immigrants spoke only English or spoke English very well, as did 45 percent of Asian immigrants, 44 percent of other Latin American immigrants, and 20 percent of Mexican immigrants. The extent of exposure to English, whether it is a primary, secondary, or a language little used in the country of origin, is an important determinant of these differences by country of origin.

Exposure to English in the United States, measured in part by duration of residence, is another major determinant of English language skills. In general, fluency in English increases, but at a decreasing rate, with duration of residence. Among all immigrants, those who spoke only English or spoke English very well increased from 36 percent among immigrants in the United States 5 or fewer years to 57 percent among those here 16–25 years, to 77 percent for those in the United States 40 or more years. The increase with duration is also found when the data are disaggregated by country of origin: the increase with duration occurs for immigrants from all regions of origin.

The use of English and the degree of fluency in English are also influenced by other dimensions of exposure to English and efficiency in acquiring English-language skills (Chiswick and Miller 1992). The immigrant's demographic characteristics and other dimensions of skill can be proxies for exposure and efficiency factors. Other measured variables held constant, immigrants who arrive in the United States at an older age, with less schooling competed, who immigrate with a spouse with the same "mother tongue," or who live in an area

TABLE 5.7   English-language fluency of the foreign-born aged 25–64, by region of birth and period of immigration: 1990.[a]

Period of Immigration	Europe/ Canada [b]	Mexico	Other Latin America	Asia	Africa	Total [c]
1985–90	60%	15%	34%	34%	66%	36%
1975–84	68	20	44	45	80	42
1965–74	71	29	59	66	84	57
1960–64	83	42	68	73	89	71
1950–59	86	46	70	75	85	77
Before 1950	90	51	83	70	100	83
Total	76%	25%	50%	49%	78%	51%

SOURCE: 1990 Census of Population, Public Use Microdata Sample.

[a] Proportion who speak only English at home or who speak English very well.
[b] Includes Australia and New Zealand.
[c] Includes other areas not separately listed and country not specified.

where many others speak their "mother tongue" are all less likely to speak only English at home and are more likely to have poorer fluency in English. By contrast, immigrants who anticipate attaining greater labor market earnings from greater fluency in English have been found to become more fluent in English.

School Enrollment Rates

The 1990 census asked respondents whether they are currently enrolled in school. It is therefore possible to study the school enrollment of immigrants. Unfortunately, because there is no question on visa status it is not possible to identify those on student visas who may comprise a significant component of the foreign-born enrolled in college or university programs.

An alternative approach is adopted here. There are relatively few exchange students (e.g., youths on student visas) enrolled in secondary school. As a result, this factor is not likely to generate statistical bias in an analysis of school enrollment patterns among youths aged 15–18 years. Those aged 15–18 years in 1990 were born in 1972–1975; the more recently they immigrated to the United States, the older their age at immigration.

Overall, 81 percent of the foreign-born youths aged 15–18 in 1990 were enrolled in school, in contrast to 88 percent among the native-born.[9] The immigrant youths who arrived in the United States as infants or toddlers have enrollment rates comparable to those of the native-born. On the other hand, among the youths who arrived in the 3¼ years prior to the 1990 census (1987–1990); that is, as preteens and teenagers, enrollment rates were 66 percent for the males and 69 percent for the females, far below the comparable percentages for the native-born.

The school enrollment rates also varied by country of birth. Much of this disparity by country of birth is attributable to duration in the United States. In general, for the same period of arrival in the United States, enrollment rates for the foreign-born aged 15–18 are highest for those born in Asia (93 percent), followed by European/Canadian immigrants (89 percent), and lowest among those born in Mexico (64 percent). Although Mexican immigrant youth consistently have lower enrollment rates than youths from the other major source regions, the gap is small among those who arrived in the United States as toddlers and infants and is very large among the most recent cohort. For example, among those who immigrated in 1987–1990 the enrollment rate of 15–18 year olds born in Mexico was 40 percent, in contrast to over 87 percent for Asian and European/Canadian immigrants.

The lower enrollment rates of new immigrant teenagers may result from difficulties in adjusting to the language and curriculum of the American schools. Moreover, given the very low educational attainment of immigrants from Mexico, many of the new immigrant youths may have dropped out of school in Mexico prior to their migration. Additionally, economic factors may come into play among low-income immigrant families. It is not the out-of-pocket cost of secondary schooling so much as the foregone earnings of teenagers that may affect the decisions of low-income new immigrant families from Mexico.

IMMIGRANTS AND THE LABOR MARKET

Immigrants play an important role in the labor market, and the labor market, in turn, has profound effects on the flow of immigrants to the United States and on their adjustment once they are here. Most immigrants come to the United States either because of their own (or some close relative's) labor market opportunities. Even refugees who may have noneconomic motives for leaving their country of origin choose among alternative destinations partly on the basis of labor market opportunities.

This section focuses on three key issues: employment status, class of worker, and occupational status.[10] Employment status refers to the classification of an immigrant as employed, unemployed, or not a member of the labor force. Class of worker refers to the status of the employer—private sector, government, or self-employment. Occupational status refers to the type of work that is performed. No single all-encompassing measure of adjustment in the labor market is available, but earnings are as close as one can get.

Employment Status

The 1990 census asked about the employment status of noninstitutionalized respondents aged 16 years and older during the week before the enumeration:

employed, unemployed, or not in the labor force. The employed are working for pay (employees) or for profit (the self-employed), or are unpaid workers in a family-owned business, even if they were temporarily absent from work during the reference week. The unemployed are either workers who have a job but are on a temporary job lay-off, or those without a job who are available for work and have been looking for work during the past 4 weeks. Respondents are not in the labor force if they do not have a job and are either unavailable for work or have not looked for work during the past 4 weeks.

Our analysis of the employment status of immigrants is limited to those aged 25–64. Older immigrants are likely to be retired, and younger immigrants are often enrolled in school or job training programs, so that their employment status reflects a temporary situation. Employment analyses are most appropriately performed separately by gender, because women tend to have lower rates of labor force participation. For example, among native-born men and women (aged 25–64) in the 1990 census, 87 percent of the men but only 70 percent of the women were in the labor force.

Recent immigrants are similar to other new entrants to the labor market in many of their characteristics. Compared with native-born workers, new immigrants tend to have fewer skills that are specific to the U.S. labor market, their industry, and their employer. They have less experience, shorter job tenure, and lower job seniority than other workers. As a result, both the new immigrant worker and the employer may perceive a weaker attachment between the worker and the job, with the result that recent immigrants experience higher job turnover, higher rates of lay-off and discharge, and higher quit rates. This greater labor market turnover need not be dysfunctional, because the employment of new immigrants involves a learning experience for both the worker and the employer. Indeed, one effective way for new workers to learn about jobs is to experience several jobs, which involves job turnover. Job turnover may entail periods of unemployment from the time of the quit/layoff until the new job is found. New immigrants are also often making investments in school or in special language training programs to facilitate the transferability of the skills they acquired abroad to the U.S. labor market or to acquire new skills. These investments are sometimes made full-time, thereby reducing their labor force participation.

The labor force participation rates of immigrant men aged 25–64 are slightly higher than the native-born, 89 percent compared with 87 percent. Among women, the immigrant labor force participation rate of 63 percent was lower than the 70 percent among the native-born. Thus, while immigrant men are somewhat more likely to be labor force participants, immigrant women are less likely to be participants than their native-born counterparts. Immigrant men and women are similar to the native-born in having labor force participation rates that vary systematically with demographic and skill variables. Participation rates increase with level of schooling and vary by marital status. Marriage is associated with higher participation rates for men and substantially lower participation rates for women. Children living at home, particularly young children, are associated with lower female participation rates.

Of particular interest for understanding the labor market status of immigrants are the variations in labor force participation rates by duration in the United States, region of origin, and gender (Table 5.8). Immigrants in the United States for fewer than 5 years have lower participation rates than those of longer duration immigrants. Among men aged 25–64, for example, the participation rates of those entering the United States in 1985–1990 was 84 percent, but it was 92 percent for the 1965–1974 cohort. Among women aged 25–64, the participation rate was 53 percent for the most recent (1985–1990) cohort, compared with 69 percent for the 1965–1974 cohort. Labor force participation among the most recent immigrants may be reduced because they are making relatively larger investments in skills specific to the United States, such as schooling, job training, and language training. The immigrants who arrived before 1950 (the longest duration cohort identifiable in census data) also have lower labor force participation rates, but they are disproportionately in their 50s and early 60s, and many have taken early retirement.

Immigrants' labor force participation rates vary systematically by region of birth and by gender. Mexican-born men tend to have higher rates of participation than other immigrants, particularly during the first few years in the United States. On the other hand, Mexican-born women have lower rates than other foreign-born women in the same immigrant cohort, only in part because of their larger number of children.

Labor force participation includes both employment and unemployment, and immigrants experience higher unemployment than the native-born. In 1990 the economy was close to "full employment," where full employment means the lowest unemployment rate attainable at a low and nonaccelerating rate of inflation. The unemployment rate in the census data among the native-born (aged 25–64) was 4.8 percent for men and 4.7 percent for women. The foreign-born experienced higher unemployment rates, 6.1 percent for men and 7.8 percent for women.

Viewing new immigrants as new workers, not just to the labor market but in the country itself, puts their unemployment experience into perspective. It is therefore not surprising to find higher unemployment rates among the newest of immigrants; and this differential seems to be largely dissipated after a few years in the country. Among the adult immigrant men in 1990, the unemployment rate was 7.9 percent for those in the U.S. 5 or fewer years, compared with 6.2 percent for those in the U.S. 6–14 years, and 5.2 percent for immigrant men in the U.S. for more than 14 years. For women, the gap is larger: an unemployment rate of 12.2 percent for the recent cohort compared with 8.3 percent for immigrants in the U.S. 6–14 years and to the 5.7 percent for those in the U.S. for more than 14 years.[11]

TABLE 5.8   Labor force participation rates of the foreign-born aged 25–64,
by sex, region of birth, and period of immigration: 1990.

Period of Immigration	Europe/ Canada[a]		Mexico		Other Latin America		Asia		Africa		Total[b]	
	M	F	M	F	M	F	M	F	M	F	M	F
1985–90	84%	53%	92%	46%	89%	65%	78%	52%	83%	63%	85%	55%
1975–84	92	67	93	56	91	71	91	67	93	72	91	66
1965–74	92	69	91	57	90	73	94	76	95	81	91	69
1960–64	90	67	87	56	89	70	92	70	98	67	89	66
1950–59	87	58	85	52	88	66	90	60	88	56	87	59
Before 1950	79	51	76	56	81	56	80	45	77	60	78	51
Total	89%	62%	91%	54%	90%	70%	88%	64%	91%	70%	89%	63%

SOURCE: 1990 Census of Population, Public Use Microdata Sample.

NOTES: M = Males, F = females.
Native-born (percent in labor force): Males 87, Females 70.

[a]Includes Australia and New Zealand.
[b]Includes other areas not separately listed and country not specified.

The highest unemployment rates are experienced by the Mexican immigrants, both overall and controlling for periods of immigration. Among adult men, the Mexican immigrant unemployment rate of 8.3 percent exceeded the overall immigrant rate of 6.1 percent, while among women the rates were 14.3 percent and 7.8 percent, respectively. To some extent this higher rate arises from the larger proportion of Mexican immigrants in the U.S. for 5 or fewer years. Yet unemployment rates are higher for Mexican immigrants even for the same period of arrival. Among the Mexican men, the unemployment rate was 9.3 percent in the recent (1985–1990) cohort and 7.9 percent among those in the U.S. for 6–14 years. Among the Mexican women the rates were 19.2 percent and 14.7 percent, respectively. Unemployment rates vary systematically by level of education, with the least educated having the highest rates. The low level of schooling of the Mexican immigrants is partially responsible for their higher rates of unemployment for the same duration of residence in the United States, but some of the differential remains unexplained.

The employment–population ratio, perhaps the least understood of the three labor force statistics, is the proportion of the relevant population that is employed. Some labor market analysts view this as the most relevant labor force statistic because it avoids the perhaps arbitrary boundary between being unemployed and outside the labor force. The employment–population ratios for immigrant and native-born men (aged 25–64) are quite similar, 84 percent and 83 percent, respectively, compared with the ratios for women, 58 percent and 67 percent, respectively. As would be expected from the lower labor force participation rate and higher unemployment rate among the recent (1985–1990) immigrants, this group had a relatively low employment ratio, 78 percent for men and 48 percent for women. The employment–population ratio shows little variation by country of origin for men. Among women, however, there are larger differences. In particular, Mexican women have a very low employment–population ratio (47 percent compared to 58 percent for all immigrant women), reflecting their low labor force participation rate and high unemployment rate.

In summary, the employment status of immigrants reflects patterns similar to those of the native-born (e.g., with respect to the effects of schooling and marital status), but also reflects effects from two characteristics unique to immigrants, duration of residence and country of origin. In general, unemployment rates are higher and labor force participation rates and employment-population ratios are lower during the first few years in the United States as immigrants make formal (schooling and language training) and informal (on-the-job training) investments to increase their skills relevant for the U.S. labor market and to acquire information about the labor market through job searches and experiencing jobs. Many are also using this period to find out about employment opportunities and where they fit in best. This adjustment process seems to be complete by about 5 years in the United States. Thus, labor force statistics show little variation by duration among immigrants in the United States for more than 5 years.

There are few differences in the employment status data by country of origin among immigrants in the United States for many years. Differences do emerge among more recent immigrants. Mexican immigrants have higher unemployment rates than other immigrants, although the employment ratio is higher for Mexican men and lower for Mexican women than for other immigrants.

Type of Employer: Class of Worker

Another way of looking at the employment of immigrants is termed "class of worker" by the Census Bureau, which actually refers to the status of the employer. The 1990 census provides detail on whether an employed person is working for a private company, a private not-for-profit organization, a government agency (by level of government), is self-employed, or is an unpaid family worker in a family-owned business.

Employed immigrants are more likely than native-born workers to be working in the private sector (i.e., for a private company or a not-for-profit organization) than for a government agency, but are equally likely to be self-employed. Among those aged 25–64 who were employed, 78 percent of the immigrants, in contrast to 72 percent of the native-born, were private sector employees, with only a trivial difference by gender.

In the public sector, from the local level up through the federal level, many jobs require U.S. citizenship. For example, in many jurisdictions public safety jobs, such as police and fire-fighting, require U.S. citizenship, and by a Presidential Executive Order employment in the Federal Civil Service requires citizenship. Moreover, some government jobs require passing proficiency tests in English, which are not required in their private sector counterparts. As a result, whereas 18 percent of the employed adult native-born men and women (16 percent and 19 percent, respectively, by gender) work for the government at all levels, among immigrants only 11 percent (10 percent for men, 12 percent for women) are government employees.

There is, however, a very strong relationship between government employment and duration in the United States as well as region of origin. Among the most recent immigrants, those who arrived between 1985 and 1990, only 10 percent were employed by government, with the proportion increasing with duration until a peak of 16 percent for the pre-1950 cohort of immigrants. With a longer duration of residence, the two primary barriers to new immigrant employment in the government sector become less formidable—proficiency in the English language and U.S. citizenship.

Country of origin also matters. Although differences in government employment by country of origin are slight among immigrants who arrived before

1950, they are very large among more recent immigration cohorts, reflecting important differences in education, English language fluency, and U.S. citizenship. Among employed immigrants who arrived in the United States in 1975–1984, by 1990, 10.4 percent of the Asian, 9.6 percent of the European/Canadian, 8.6 percent of the Other Latin American, and only 3.5 percent of the Mexican immigrants were in government employment. The small proportion of Mexican immigrants in government employment may arise from their low level of education and low proportion naturalized.

Among both immigrants and the native-born, 11 percent of the employed are self-employed. This similarity in overall rates masks important differences in self-employment patterns. Among the immigrants who are self-employed, 52 percent are in service, sales, and managerial occupations, and only 3 percent are in agriculture (including forestry and fishing), in contrast to 43 percent and 12 percent, respectively, for the native-born.

Rates of self-employment vary by duration of residence and country of origin. Overall, and for all country groups, self-employment increases with duration of residence. For immigrants aged 25–64 in 1990, it is 8 percent for the newest immigration cohort (immigrated 1985–1990), rising monotonically to 16 percent for the pre-1950 cohort. To some extent this reflects the rise in self-employment with age observed even for the native-born. It also reflects an independent effect of the exposure and experience that enhance self-employment opportunities through increased knowledge of the United States and easier access to capital from lending institutions. Presumably, many immigrants begin as employees, but after some years amass enough capital to start their own businesses.

As Tables 5.9 and 5.10 indicate, self-employment tends to be lower among Latin American immigrants (7 percent for Mexican immigrants and 9 percent for Other Latin American immigrants), and is higher for Europe/Canadian and Asian immigrants (14 percent each). Among Asian immigrants who arrived prior to 1950, one-fifth were self-employed in 1990.

Occupational Attainment

Occupational attainment is a measure of the outcome of the labor market process in which workers, with various skills and demographic characteristics, sort themselves out among the myriad types of jobs in the economy. The Census Bureau coded detailed occupational categories based on the information provided by the respondent on the type of work performed. The detailed occupations were then grouped into nine broad occupational categories used in this analysis. Data on the occupational distribution of those aged 25–64 are presented for the foreign-born and the native-born for men and women in Tables 5.9 and 5.10, respectively.

TABLE 5.9 Occupational attainment and self-employment status of men aged 25–64, by region of birth: 1990.

Occupation	Foreign-Born						Native-Born	Foreign-Born in Occupation
	Europe/ Canada[a]	Mexico	Other Latin America	Asia	Africa	Total[b]		
Managerial	18%	4%	9%	15%	16%	11%	14%	8%
Professional	16	2	8	21	25	12	13	10
Technical	4	1	3	7	4	4	4	10
Sales	9	3	9	12	11	8	11	8
Clerical and Adm. Sup.	4	3	8	8	8	6	6	10
Craft	24	22	20	12	8	19	21	9
Service	9	14	17	12	14	13	8	15
Agriculture[c]	2	16	2	1	<1	5	4	14
Operative/Laborer	14	35	24	12	13	21	20	11
Total	100%	100%	100%	100%	100%	100%	100%	10%
Self-Employed[d]	18%	8%	10%	16%	13%	13%	13%	

SOURCE: 1990 Census of Population, Public Use Microdata Sample.

NOTES: Detail may not add to total due to rounding. Index of dissimilarity between native-born and foreign-born = 7.8.

[a] Includes Australia and New Zealand.
[b] Includes other areas not specified and country not specified.
[c] Includes fishing and forestry and farm managers.
[d] Percent self-employed among those who are employed.

TABLE 5.10 Occupational attainment and self-employment status of women aged 25–64, by region of birth: 1990.[a]

| Occupation | Foreign-Born | | | | | | Native-Born | Foreign-Born in Occupation |
	Europe Canada[b]	Mexico	Other Latin America	Asia	Africa	Total[c]		
Managerial	13%	4%	7%	11%	12%	9%	13%	8%
Professional	16	4	11	17	22	13	19	8
Technical	3	1	3	6	4	4	4	9
Sales	12	6	8	12	11	10	10	10
Clerical and Adm. Sup.	22	10	20	18	24	19	28	7
Craft	4	6	3	5	2	4	2	19
Service	19	30	31	18	19	23	14	16
Agriculture[d]	<1	8	<1	<1	<1	2	<1	20
Operative/Laborer	11	32	15	13	6	16	8	20
Total	100%	100%	100%	100%	100%	100%	100%	9%
Self-Employed[e]	10%	6%	7%	11%	11%	9%	8%	9%

SOURCE: 1990 Census of Population, Public Use Microdata Sample.

NOTES: Detail may not add to total due to rounding. Index of dissimilarity between the native-born and foreign-born = 19.8.

[a] Among women who worked in the previous year or in the reference week in 1990.
[b] Includes Australia and New Zealand.
[c] Includes other areas not specified and country not specified.
[d] Includes fishing and forestry and farm managers.
[e] Percent self-employed among those who are employed.

The occupational distributions of foreign- and native-born men are quite similar. Fewer than 8 percent of the foreign-born men would have to change their occupation to have the same occupational distribution as the native-born men. The differences for the women are larger: nearly one in every five of the immigrant women workers would have to change her occupation for the foreign-born women to have the same occupational distribution as native-born women.

Not surprisingly, differences in occupational attainment reflect relative differences in education and levels of skill. Asian, African, and European/Canadian male immigrants have a high occupational attainment, higher even than the native-born; that is, they are more concentrated in the prestigious professional and managerial jobs, while Latin American immigrants, particularly those from Mexico, have a very low occupational status. Among the men, the professional, technical, and managerial occupations employ 43 percent of the Asian immigrants (including 1 in 5 Asian immigrants in professional occupations), 45 percent of the African immigrants, 38 percent of European/Canadian immigrants, 31 percent of the native-born, 20 percent of non-Mexican Latin American immigrants, and only 7 percent of Mexican immigrants. Among women the proportion employed in professional, technical, and managerial occupations ranged from 38 percent of the immigrants born in Africa to 9 percent of those born in Mexico, with 36 percent of the native-born women reporting one of these high-level occupations.

The ranking is reversed at the lowest end of the skill distribution. Operative and laborer jobs outside of agriculture employ one-third of male Mexican immigrants, but only 12–14 percent of Asian and European/Canadian immigrants. Including agriculture in the lower-skilled occupations, since most immigrants in agriculture are laborers, raises the proportion for Mexican immigrants to around one-half compared with only 13 percent and 16 percent, respectively, for Asian and European/Canadian immigrants. Similar patterns emerge for women, where 70 percent of women born in Mexico were in operative, laborer, agricultural, and service jobs, in contrast to 32 percent for Asian immigrant women and 30 percent for European/Canadian.

Another way of looking at the occupational attainment of immigrants is to consider their concentration in broad occupational categories. Although immigrants constitute 10 percent of all adult males reporting an occupation (Table 5.9), they are most heavily concentrated in service (15 percent) and agricultural jobs (14 percent) and have the lowest representation in managerial and sales jobs (8 percent each). Among the women, immigrants are most heavily represented in all of the lower-skilled jobs, particularly craft, service, and operative/laborer employment. Although one in five women in agriculture is foreign-born, relatively few women work in this sector.

Much of the public debate over immigration has centered on the issue of what kinds of jobs immigrants take. Are they clustered in the jobs that the native-born do not want, or are they dominating high-paid jobs in industry, universities, and health care? One reason that the debates are confusing is that, as the data indicate, these alternatives are not mutually exclusive. The diversity of the immigrants' impact on the occupational structure is shown by their dispersion across the occupational spectrum—because they take all sorts of jobs—as well as by their concentration in certain occupational groups.

To demonstrate this point, Figure 5.3 depicts graphically the proportion of workers in certain occupations who are foreign-born. Immigrants figure prominently in some professions, such as medicine (especially women physicians) and nursing, while they are much less likely to be found in the legal and teaching fields. Skilled craft jobs show much the same pattern, with immigrants comprising a very large proportion of some occupations, such as tailors and dressmakers, but much less numerous among others, such as electricians. Finally, as the preceding discussion indicated, immigrants are heavily concentrated in agriculture. Yet even within agriculture there is an uneven distribution, as immigrants are concentrated in farm laborer jobs for perishable crops (fruits and

FIGURE 5.3 Proportion of foreign-born in selected occupations ages 25–64, by sex: 1990.

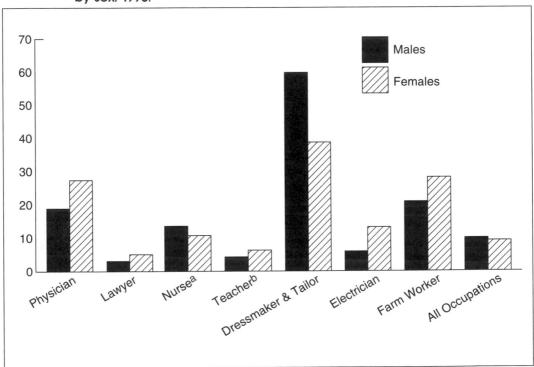

SOURCE: 1990 Census of Population, Public Use Microdata Sample; Employment and Earnings, Jan. 1991.

[a] Only registered nurses.
[b] Only primary and secondary educators.

vegetables). Generalizations about the immigrant impact on the labor market must take into account both patterns, the general pattern of dispersion across the occupational spectrum and the concentration within certain occupational groups and specific occupations.

HOUSEHOLD STRUCTURE, MARITAL STATUS, AND FERTILITY

Immigration inevitably entails a transition period for the immigrant, followed by a reorganization of family and household. The family reunification preferences that affected immigration since the 1965 Amendments were intended to assist the reconstitution of families within the United States. The process of reorganization, however, is by no means uniform. Some immigrants come with the intention of sojourning for a limited period of time and then returning to their home countries; for others, the relocation to the United States is permanent. For some families, the dislocation is temporary and adjustment is quickly made; for others, the period of dislocation may be lengthy.

In the sojourner stage, for example, the characteristic household may be made up of unrelated individuals. An ethnographic study of Mexican immigrants in San Diego depicted this type of organization:

> A total of eleven men, all undocumented Mexican immigrants, lived in this [one] unit. These men were all employed and worked different shifts, thus not all of them were in the housing unit at the same time. Their work schedule permitted them to sleep in shifts. [Velasco 1992]

In this type of household, the unrelated workers have not yet brought any family members to join them. Eventually, the entire family may be reconstituted within the United States. One of the incentives to naturalization offered by U.S. immigration law is the greater ability of citizens to sponsor relatives to enter the United States. Studies of the Mexican-origin population have indicated that by combining its efforts, the family experiences social and economic benefits from this reconsolidation (Briody 1987; Tienda 1980). Immigrants from other nationality groups may experience similar benefits.

During the family reunification process, various relatives may live together in extended families. The family reunification provisions in the 1965 Amendments tended to favor both generational extensions, through the immigration of the spouses, parents, and children of U.S. citizens and resident aliens, and horizontal extensions, through the immigration of brothers or sisters of U.S. citizens. It should be noted, however, that immigrants sponsored by their relatives need not live in the same household as their sponsor. Unfortunately, there are no data on the physical proximity of sponsoring relatives.

Diversity in Household Structure

The staging of family immigration over a period of years implies another type of diversity among immigrants: a diversity in the size and composition of their households. Complex households are further encouraged by the high rents typical of such large cities as Los Angeles and New York City, in which many immigrants reside. Sharing living quarters may offer one means to economize while the family members adjust to labor market conditions and seek to earn a living.

An ethnographer who assessed census coverage in San Francisco describes one complex household:

> Alejandro and his wife were Salvadoran immigrants employed in low wage service jobs. In order to meet the relatively high rent in the sample area Alejandro and his family rented a three bedroom apartment and took in nine other Salvadoran immigrants to help with the rent. . . . Alejandro, his wife and two children shared one of the three bedrooms. The other bedroom was occupied by a woman in her 30's with her twenty-one year old partner, their six month old child, two children from the woman's previous marriage and the nineteen year old brother of her partner. Three recent Salvadoran immigrants occupied the remaining bedroom. Two were in their twenties and unrelated and the third was a man in his forties who was the father of Alejandro's partner. [De la Puente 1993]

This household, made up of both related and unrelated family groups and non-relatives, is complex and difficult to enumerate. Only six of the thirteen residents of this apartment were reported in the 1990 census.

Table 5.11 illustrates some of the differences that can be found in household types using census data. Recently immigrated males have the most varied household structures, with nearly 1 in 5 living without any family members. Foreign-born males who are naturalized are more likely to be in married-couple households and less likely to be in nonfamily households than those who have recently immigrated. The prevalence of the male householder with no wife present also declines with length of residence. For women, the findings are quite different. Possibly because of family reunification, the most recent women immigrants are most likely to be living in married-couple households. Women who are naturalized citizens are most likely to be in nonfamily households. The female householder with no husband present is most likely to be an alien who immigrated before 1985. Mexican immigrants exhibit little difference from other immigrants in these household patterns.[12]

Table 5.12 investigates the extent to which family reunification among recent immigrants affects the composition of extended family households. Although the census does not provide information on the preference category used for obtaining a visa, it does have information on the relationship of each person to

TABLE 5.11 Household type of persons aged 18 and over, by nativity and immigrant status: 1990.

Household Type	Males				Females			
	Aliens				Alien			
	Immigrated 1985–1990	Immigrated pre-1985	Naturalized Citizens	Native-Born	Immigrated 1985–1990	Immigrated pre-1985	Naturalized Citizens	Native-Born
Married Couple	57%	71%	77%	72%	70%	69%	66%	63%
Male Householder, No Wife Present	16	10	6	5	8	4	2	2
Female Householder, No Husband Present	8	6	3	6	13	17	13	16
Nonfamily	20	13	13	17	9	10	19	20
Total	100%	100%	100%	100%	100%	100%	100%	100%
Number (1,000s)	1,682	3,125	3,405	79,875	1,583	3,277	3,940	87,214

SOURCE: 1990 Census of Population, Public Use Microdata Sample.

NOTE: Totals may not add to 100 because of rounding.

253

TABLE 5.12   Recent immigrants residing with relatives, by relationship, age, and hemisphere of birth of the immigrant: 1960–1990.[a]

Hemisphere/Year	Parents of Household Head Ages			Siblings of Household Head Ages		
	45–54	55–64	65+	25–34	35–44	45–54
Eastern						
1960	3.5%	18.6%	51.5%	2.7%	2.2%	2.1%
1970	4.2	20.4	48.0	2.9	4.1	4.1
1980	7.8	30.2	55.4	5.2	3.9	4.5
1990	6.6	36.3	54.6	6.7	5.3	5.0
Western						
1960	5.4	20.2	40.9	4.3	4.1	5.4
1970	7.1	24.9	47.9	4.5	3.7	3.9
1980	10.2	25.0	50.4	8.3	7.5	6.7
1990	11.7	33.9	49.3	12.5	10.0	6.5

SOURCES: Adapted from Jasso and Rosenzweig, 1991: Table 5.2, pp. 204–205; 1990 Census of Population, Public Use Microdata Sample.

NOTE: Native-born respondents—1990.

	Parents of Household Head			Siblings of Household Head		
Age	45–54	55–64	65+	25–34	35–44	45–54
Percent	1.6%	3.0%	12.1%	0.01%	0.3%	1.4%

[a]Percentage of recent immigrants (i.e., immigrated in the 5 years prior to the census year) who are the parents or siblings, including parents-in-law and siblings-in-law of the household head, by age, in the census year. Data from decennial censuses, 1960 to 1990.

the householder, that is, the person who rents or owns the housing unit in which he or she resides. Parents and siblings are two groups of relatives who may be sponsored under the kinship provisions. If the kinship provisions of the 1965 Amendments applicable to the Eastern Hemisphere and the extension a decade later of the preference system to the Western Hemisphere affected family-based migration, the proportions of parents and siblings living with household heads should rise with each successive census year. The data in Table 5.12 indicate that in 1990 over half the immigrants from the Eastern Hemisphere aged 65 and over were parents of householders, with a third of those aged 55–64 also parents of the householder. As expected, the proportions, especially for the 55–64 age group, have generally increased from 1960 to 1990. What is perhaps more revealing is the proportion of parents living with their children among Western Hemisphere immigrants. It increased from 41 percent in 1960 to 49 percent in 1990 among the older group (age 65 and over) and from 20 percent to 34 percent, respectively, among parents aged 55–64. Thus, for both hemispheres the proportion of elderly immigrants who are parents of householders has risen, suggesting that there are more older immigrants coming to the United States to be reunited with their adult children.

The pattern for siblings is not as startling as that for parents, but there has been a steady increase among the proportion of immigrants who are siblings of householders, particularly among Western Hemisphere immigrants in the 1980s. For example, 13 percent of the 1985–1990 cohort of immigrants from the Western Hemisphere aged 25–34 were living with a householder who was their brother, sister, brother-in-law, or sister-in-law. Of course, other siblings and parents have immigrated who do not live in the same household with their relatives.

Table 5.12 is revealing, not only because it shows the strength of family reunification policies, but also because it demonstrates the prevalence of extended family households for the most recent immigrants. These data undoubtedly also reflect the need of low-income immigrants to double up because of economic circumstances.

Marital Status and Fertility

Figure 5.4 shows the marital status of foreign-born and native-born adults in 1990. The two pie charts look remarkably similar except for the larger proportions of immigrants who report themselves married, spouse absent and sepa-

FIGURE 5.4   Marital status of the foreign-born and native-born populations ages 18 and over: 1990.

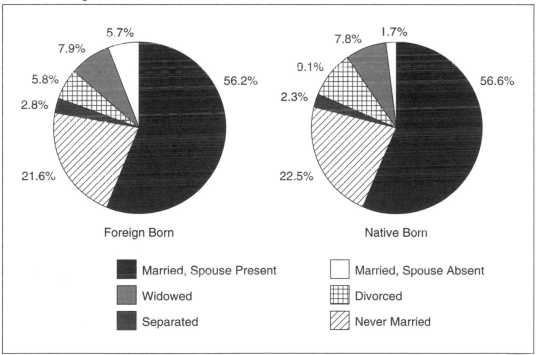

SOURCE: 1990 Census of Population, Public Use Microdata Sample.

rated, presumably because one spouse has yet to move to the United States. Immigrants are slightly less likely than the native-born to be widowed or married, spouse present. The dislocation of the immigration experience may lead to delayed or disrupted marriages, although some marriages of foreign nationals to U.S. citizens occur to facilitate the legal immigration of the former.

One heated immigration issue is the extent to which immigrants increase population growth through high fertility. Although many recent studies have indicated that immigrant fertility converges, after several generations, to American norms, the concern has been renewed because so many of the sending countries have current high levels of fertility (Rindfuss and Sweet 1977; Bean and Swicegood 1985). The total fertility rate is a measure of the number of children a woman would have, on average, if current fertility rates persisted throughout her entire childbearing years; the current rate in the United States is about 1.85. A total fertility rate of about 2.1 is required for a population to remain at about the same size. In major sending countries, such as Mexico, the total fertility rate is about 3.3 children per woman; in El Salvador the figure is 3.9, and in Guatemala it is 4.9. In other sending countries the fertility level is either low or it has been dropping. For example, in China the total fertility rate is 1.9, and in Korea it is only 1.6.[13] The question then arises, will the immigrants' fertility be typical of their home country, or will it be more typical of the United States?

Recent studies in both the United States and Canada of women immigrants from high-fertility countries have found their overall fertility rates to be very close to those of native-born women (Blau 1992; Sullivan 1992). The explanation for this finding may be found in the selectivity of immigration. Men and women who are better educated and have more "modern" attitudes are more likely both to migrate and to have lower fertility. Furthermore, migration is less expensive in terms of out-of-pocket costs and nonmoney (psychic) costs if there are fewer children in the family. Those anticipating immigration may delay childbearing; those with large families may be less likely to move. Moreover, just as immigrants adapt to the United States in other dimensions, they may also adjust their fertility in response to the same incentives that affect the native-born population. Thus, even immigrants who come from high-fertility countries may converge to the low-fertility norms of the United States.

Data on completed fertility confirms the reduced fertility of immigrant women. Completed fertility is the average number of children born per woman for a birth cohort of women at the end of their childbearing years. For U.S. native-born women over the age of 45 in 1990, the mean completed fertility (i.e., total number of children ever born) was 2.7. For the 2.4 million immigrant women over the age of 45 who were naturalized citizens, the number was *lower*, 2.4 children per woman. For 1.6 million immigrant women over the age of 45 who were not naturalized citizens, the number was *higher*, 3.3 children per woman. The lower fertility for naturalized citizen women, compared with alien women, can be attributed to the differences in their age structure, duration in the U.S., education, labor market opportunities, and other characteristics.

Table 5.13 presents detailed data on completed fertility and on childlessness by region of birth and by period of immigration. The data indicate that the immigrant women of European/Canadian origin have consistently low completed fertility (2.1 to 2.3, depending on period of immigration). The Mexican women present the strongest contrast to this pattern; their completed fertility is an average of 4.6 children, with a still higher number for the most recent immigrants, 5.5.

Immigrant women from Latin America, Asia, and Africa also show the highest completed fertility among the recent immigration cohorts. It would, however, be erroneous to assume any implication of a little baby boom among the foreign-born. These women are unusual because, having immigrated within the past 5 years, they must have entered the United States at age 40 or older. Their childbearing, therefore, was largely completed in their home countries. As the data in Table 5.5 showed, the median age at immigration for the largest sending countries is much younger, and so these women are atypical in the timing of immigration, and perhaps more than others they reflect the fertility norms in their origins rather than in the United States.

TABLE 5.13   Fertility of foreign-born women, by region of birth and period of immigration: 1990.

Period of Immigration	Europe/ Canada[a]	Mexico	Other Latin America	Asia	Africa	Total[b]
A. Mean Number of Children Ever-Born for Women Aged 45 and Over						
1985–90	2.2	5.5	3.7	4.0	3.9	3.8
1975–84	2.1	5.2	3.2	3.8	2.9	3.5
1965–74	2.2	4.6	2.4	2.5	2.5	2.7
1960–64	2.2	4.1	2.2	2.3	2.2	2.5
1950–59	2.3	4.1	2.2	2.5	2.4	2.5
Before 1950	2.3	4.5	2.3	3.2	2.3	2.5
Total	2.3	4.6	2.6	3.2	2.7	2.8
B. Percentage of Women Aged 15–30 Who Are Childless						
1985–90	72%	48%	59%	71%	65%	62%
1975–84	64	39	54	69	61	55
1965–74	64	46	54	76	78	69
1960–64	43	28	42	52	46	40
Total	66%	44%	56%	70%	65%	58%

SOURCE: 1990 Census of Population, Public Use Microdata Sample.

NOTE: Data for native-born women: panel A, 2.7 children ever-born; panel B, 65 percent childless.

[a] Includes Australia and New Zealand.

[b] Includes other areas not specified and country not specified.

The distribution of women by the number of children they have borne seems quite similar for the native-born and the foreign-born. Foreign-born women as a group are somewhat less likely to be childless, and somewhat more likely to have had a larger number of children. Of the foreign-born women aged 15 and over, 38 percent had no children compared with 48 percent of the native-born, and 18 percent had one child versus 16 percent of the native-born. Another 23 percent had two children, compared with 20 percent of the native-born. Fully 21 percent reported three or more children, compared with 16 percent of the native-born.

The lower panel of Table 5.13 provides a closer view of childlessness. Although not quite as likely as the native-born to be childless, a relatively high proportion of immigrant women aged 15–30 are childless. This figure is significant because a delay in childbearing past age 30 will result in a low completed fertility. Mexican women are the least likely to be childless, but 44 percent of them, and 48 percent of the most recent Mexican women immigrants under age 30, are still childless. Over half the Mexican immigrants are below the age of 29, and so this proportion of childlessness could have a significant impact on eventual completed fertility. The figure for Asian women rises to 70 percent childless, including 71 percent of the most recent immigrants. These women, because of their age, are more typical of all immigrants in the timing of their immigration as young adults.

The long-term effects of immigrant fertility on population growth are difficult to project. First, not all of the immigrants' children may be in the United States, so the population growth may occur in another country. Because the average age at migration is often in the young adult years, it is likely that young children will accompany (or follow) their immigrant mothers or be born in the United States. Family reunification preferences make it possible for children born abroad to rejoin their mothers in the United States. Second, the effect that these children will have on future growth depends on how rapidly they adopt the prevailing American fertility norms.

To summarize, census data indicate that immigrant households are likely to be larger and more complex than the households of the native-born, although the differences may diminish with duration of residence. There are substantial variations in fertility by duration in the United States and region of birth. Although immigrant fertility is somewhat higher than native-born fertility, the 1990 census data confirm findings from earlier censuses of a convergence in fertility to the U.S. norms. Mexican immigrant fertility shows high variability, with the most recent immigration cohorts having high completed fertility among the older immigrants, but nearly half of the younger immigrants are still childless.

IMMIGRANT INCOME

The incomes of immigrants are of interest for two fundamental reasons.[14] Data on income (including income transfers) provide information on the economic well-being of immigrant households, including the extent to which they are in poverty, as well as being strong indicators of the productivity of immigrant workers.

The decennial census contains separate questions on various sources of money or cash income, but it lacks direct information on the value of in-kind benefits, including the economic value of food stamps, public housing, Medicaid, Medicare, and employer-financed health insurance. Moreover, the reliability of reporting of money income in the census varies by type of income. Wage and salary incomes have been shown to be accurately reported in census data, but there is substantial underreporting of self-employment income, rental and investment (interest and dividends) income, and public and private transfer income. In the aggregate, wage and salary disbursements (and other labor income) were nearly 65 percent of total personal income in 1990 and 76 percent of personal income from sources other than income transfers.[15] Thus, the largest component of income and the primary source income for most households are well reported in census data.

Labor Market Earnings

Labor market earnings constitute an important measure both of immigrant adjustment and of their economic well-being. Earnings are defined in the 1990 census as the sum of wage, salary, and self-employment income in the previous year, 1989. Annual earnings are the product of two factors: units of time worked during the year and remuneration per unit of time worked. Among men aged 25–64 with earnings, most variations in earnings are due to variations in rates of pay. Among women, on the other hand, the variations in time worked are substantial and are dominant causes of differences in earnings. Because of the greater complexity of the analysis for the determinants of earnings among women, including variations in past and present labor market experience, the discussion of earnings that follows focuses on foreign-born men.

As indicated in Table 5.14, among adult immigrant men who had earnings, the mean earnings were $27,600, 14 percent less than the $32,100 earned by native-born men. Immigrant earnings increased with duration in the United States, rising from $20,000 among those in the United States for 5 or fewer years to nearly $38,900 among those who immigrated in the 1950s. The 1965–1974 cohort of immigrants had earnings ($31,100) comparable to the native-born. Immigrants who have lived in the United States a longer period of time

TABLE 5.14 Earnings of foreign-born men aged 25–64, by region of birth and period of immigration: 1990.[a]

Period of Immigration	Mean Earnings						Standard Deviation Total
	Europe/ Canada[b]	Mexico	Other Latin America	Asia	Africa	Total[c]	
1985–90	$32,771	$11,082	$15,660	$22,369	$22,157	$19,966	$23,161
1975–84	39,148	14,494	19,878	29,363	30,610	24,086	24,877
1965–74	36,939	18,915	26,667	43,911	46,244	31,140	31,108
1960–64	39,242	21,620	38,818	42,946	42,615	35,945	33,171
1950–59	41,318	24,660	36,799	47,097	58,140	38,883	33,891
Before 1950	46,620	22,378	41,272	39,671	14,387	41,705	41,123
Total	$38,891	$16,139	$23,615	$32,028	$32,388	$27,647	$28,933
Standard Deviation	$34,972	$13,902	$23,786	$32,562	$35,341	$28,933	

SOURCE: 1990 Census of Population, Public Use Microdata Sample.

NOTE: Native-born earnings: mean $32,057; standard deviation $28,330.

[a]Excludes those with zero earnings.
[b]Includes Australia and New Zealand.
[c]Includes other areas not separately listed and country not specified.

are likely to be older than more recent immigrants. Yet, even when analyses that hold current age constant are performed, the pattern persists of earnings rising with duration in the United States, with the sharpest increases in the first few years, thereafter increasing at a slower rate. The increase in earnings with duration in the United States reflects the favorable effects on employment and pay rates of greater experience in the United States labor market, enhanced English-language fluency, and postmigration schooling, among other factors.

Earnings also varied systematically by country of origin. Overall, among the major regions, earnings are highest among the European/Canadian immigrants (over $38,800), closely followed by the Asian immigrants ($32,000). The earnings of other Latin American ($23,600) and Mexican ($16,100) immigrants lag behind. Within each origin category, earnings increase with duration of residence, at least until the oldest cohort (pre-1950 immigrants). The steepness of this increase varies across country groups. It is flattest for the European/Canadian immigrants, since this group arrived with skills most readily transferable to the United States, including a high level of English-language fluency. The steepness of the profile is roughly similar for the other major source regions.

The pattern in earnings by region of origin reflects the impact of several factors. Differences in duration in the United States; for example, the longer duration of residence of the European/Canadian immigrants, account for some differences in earnings. Yet sharp differences exist even among immigrants who arrived in the same time period (Table 5.14). Immigrant earnings also increase with their level of education, although the effect of schooling on earnings is larger for the group (European/Canadians) with the more highly transferable skills. Their higher-than-average level of schooling also gives the European/Canadian immigrants an earnings advantage. Geographic location in the United States, preimmigration labor market experience, and marital status also influence earnings and vary across the birthplace groups.

Using European/Canadian immigrants as the benchmark, with other measured variables (age, education, time in the United States, marital status, region of residence, and urban/rural location) held constant, earnings are lower by about 15 percent for Asian immigrants, by about 26 percent for other Latin American immigrants, and about 34 percent for Mexican immigrants. The differences in earnings by country of origin when other measured variables are the same reflect many unmeasured or unmeasurable factors, including the lower transferability of skills from countries whose economies and/or language differ from that of the United States, and differences in the quality of schooling in the origin, refugee status, English-language fluency, and training or licenses specific to the U.S. labor market. Discrimination may also account for part of these differences.

The earnings of immigrants can also be compared with the earnings of native-born men, when other variables are the same. When this is done it appears that recent immigrants have lower earnings than comparable native-born men, but that their earnings increase sharply with duration in the United States. As a result, other things the same, the earnings gap between immigrants and the native-born decreases with the duration of residence of the former. The earnings of male immigrants from nonrefugee countries reach parity with native-born men at 10 to 20 years' duration in the United States, while those from countries where many of the migrants are refugees tend to have lower earnings and a later "catch-up," if it occurs at all. This finding of an earnings "catch-up" of economic migrants compared to native-born men, and the lower earnings of refugees, when other variables are the same, is not unique to the 1990 census. Similar patterns were found in analyses for the 1970 and 1980 censuses (Chiswick 1986). This suggests that although there may have been a decline in immigrant skills, as measured by years of schooling, and a shift in the source regions of immigrants, when schooling, country of origin, and other measured variables are the same, there does not appear to have been a decline over time in the unmeasurable dimensions of immigrant quality.

Public Assistance

Some observers fear that continued immigration will constitute a disproportionate drain on the welfare system. The 1990 census includes information on public assistance programs that provide cash benefits, such as Aid to Families with Dependent Children (AFDC), Supplemental Security Income (SSI), and other cash welfare programs. AFDC provides cash assistance to poor families with children, while SSI provides assistance to the poor who are aged or disabled. About 3.6 percent of the immigrants (2.6 percent for males, 4.7 percent for females) reported receiving any cash public assistance benefits in 1989, a proportion remarkably similar to the 3.9 percent (2.5 percent for males, 5.2 percent for females) among the native-born.[16]

There is no clear pattern in the receipt of cash public assistance benefits by duration of residence. Although incomes are lower during the early years in the United States, the major cash programs require either the presence of children in the family or a waiting period before benefits can be received. Among the major regions of origin, the proportion of immigrants receiving cash public assistance varies from 4.2 percent among Mexican immigrants to 1.6 percent for African immigrants. The variation by country of origin reflects differences in income and household structure. In general, these data seem consistent with a conclusion that immigrants use the welfare system at roughly the same rate as do the native-born.

Household Income

Household income is an important index of economic well-being. It is a complex measure because it combines the labor market earnings, property income, and money income from public and private transfers of all the household members. The fragmentation or consolidation of households can dramatically change the level and distribution of household income, even if the income of each household member does not change.

Overall, the income in 1989 of households in which the household head (householder) is foreign-born was only 1 percent larger than the native-born ($38,100, compared with $37,800 for the native-born). This difference does not arise from a larger proportion of aged, and hence lower-income households, among the native-born, because the proportion of the population aged 65 and older is about the same for the native-born and foreign-born (about 13 percent). There is, however, a different household structure among immigrants, with a larger number of workers per household.

Among both immigrant and native-born households, the lower the earning potential of the individual member, the larger the number of household members who work. If household members have low incomes, the household tends to have a larger number of adults living together and higher rates of labor force participation. Moreover, households with lower income from wages, salaries, and self-employment are more likely to be eligible for income transfer programs, including unemployment insurance, disability insurance, and welfare payments. As a result, the relative differences in household income are smaller across countries of origin and across immigrant cohorts than are the relative differences among the earnings of foreign-born men.[17]

The mean and standard deviation of household money income in 1989 are reported by region of origin and duration in the United States in Table 5.15. In general, household incomes increase with a longer duration of residence in the United States of the foreign-born head, but this generalization is tempered by declines among the longest duration immigrants, the cohorts with the largest proportion of aged. Differences exist by country of origin. Overall, Asian households have higher incomes than European/Canadian households, but the difference varies by duration of residence. More recent arrival cohorts of Asian immigrants have lower household incomes, but the cohorts that arrived in 1974 and earlier have substantially higher incomes than European/Canadian immigrants of the same duration in the United States. The larger number of workers per household and the steeper rise in labor market earnings with duration in the United States account for this pattern. The household income of the Mexican immigrants ($27,300) and other Latin American immigrants ($34,800) are far below the European/Canadian ($41,000) and Asian ($45,600) levels, and this pattern holds even when duration in the United States is the same.

TABLE 5.15 Household income of the foreign-born, by region of birth and period of immigration: 1990.[a]

Period of Immigration	Europe/ Canada[b]	Mexico	Other Latin America	Mean Income Asia	Africa	Total[c]	Standard Deviation Total[c]
1985–90	$41,062	$23,227	$27,581	$31,859	$29,383	$30,981	$29,379
1975–84	49,685	25,714	30,823	43,333	43,594	36,701	33,077
1965–74	46,848	29,261	36,733	60,018	59,579	42,880	39,084
1960–64	47,868	33,545	46,307	56,959	51,046	46,050	40,164
1950–59	46,039	33,502	43,486	58,259	57,655	45,226	41,054
Before 1950	30,531	23,187	34,045	38,851	30,778	30,341	35,244
Total	$41,046	$27,328	$34,820	$45,617	$44,204	$38,104	$36,389
Standard deviation	$40,664	$22,328	$30,117	$41,032	$45,542	$36,389	

SOURCE: 1990 Census of Population, Public Use Microdata Sample.

NOTE: Native-born: mean $37,838; standard deviation $33,785.

[a]Income of households in which the household head is foreign-born. Excludes those living in group quarters, those with no income, and vacant households.
[b]Includes Australia and New Zealand.
[c]Includes areas not separately identified and country not specified.

Immigrants in Poverty

Although household money income is a useful measure of the household's capacity to purchase consumer goods and services in the marketplace, it is deficient because it does not take account of household structure, as measured by the number and age composition of household members. The 1990 census data provide an index of household money income relative to family size and structure. On the basis of the number of family members and their ages, the Census Bureau calculated the threshold poverty level income for that household. The household poverty index is the ratio of the household's reported money income divided by its calculated poverty threshold.

For the foreign-born population as a whole, 18.0 percent lived in households with money income below the poverty line, with little difference by gender (17.3 percent for males and 18.7 percent for females). This was substantially greater than the poverty rate for the native-born, which was 12.4 percent (10.8 percent for males and 13.9 percent for females). The higher poverty rate for females arises from the prevalence of single mothers, who have lower earnings and a larger number of children per household than do single fathers, and also from the prevalence of widows, who are more numerous and have lower incomes.

The poverty rate of the foreign-born reflects patterns seen above in the components of the poverty index, such as income and household structure. Overall, the poverty rate declines with duration in the United States until the oldest cohort of immigrants, those who arrived before 1950 (see Table 5.16). The pre-1950 immigrants are disproportionately elderly, many of whom are in retirement. For others, the poverty decline reflects both increased employment and increased wage rates that occur with duration of residence.

TABLE 5.16   Poverty rates of the foreign-born, by region of birth and period of immigration: 1990.

Period of Immigration	Europe/ Canada[a]	Mexico	Other Latin America	Asia	Africa	Total[b]
1985–90	22.7%	37.3%	28.1%	27.4%	24.6%	29.8%
1975–84	8.1	28.9	18.3	14.4	13.2	18.7
1965–74	6.4	23.6	12.0	6.6	6.4	12.5
1960–64	5.2	17.3	9.6	5.7	6.9	8.7
1950–59	5.8	17.8	10.9	5.5	9.6	7.9
Before 1950	9.0	20.5	11.2	10.6	3.1	10.6
Total	9.1%	29.0%	18.3%	16.5%	15.4%	18.0%

SOURCE: 1990 Census of Population, Public Use Microdata Sample.

NOTE: Native-born (percent): 12.4.

[a] Includes Australia and New Zealand.
[b] Includes other areas not specified and country not reported.

The variations in the poverty rate by country of origin are striking (Table 5.16). Among the foreign-born, the poverty rate varies from a low of 9 percent for European/Canadian immigrants, which is below the rate for the native-born (12 percent), to a high of 29 percent for Mexican immigrants, more than twice the rate for the native-born. These large differences in the incidence of poverty can be understood in terms of the differences in the underlying components of the index. For example, the higher level of education and greater English-language fluency of the European/Canadian immigrants compared with Mexican immigrants translate into higher earnings among those who work. The greater female labor supply and smaller family size of the European/Canadian immigrants compared with those of Mexican origin also results in greater household income and a smaller poverty threshold, and hence a lower poverty rate.

The highest poverty rate is experienced by females born in Mexico. Nearly one-third (32 percent) of Mexican-born females live in households with incomes below the poverty threshold. This extraordinarily high rate compared with other immigrant women is not limited to particular immigration cohorts, but rather appears to be a feature of all the cohorts. Such a high poverty rate stems, in part, from the lower skills, lower labor supply, and larger family size (higher fertility) of women born in Mexico.

THE CONSEQUENCES OF IMMIGRATION: SUMMARY, CONCLUSIONS, AND IMPLICATIONS

This chapter has analyzed the demographic and economic characteristics of the foreign-born population of the United States as reported in the 1990 Census of Population. The strengths of census data include the large sample size and the rich array of questions asked in 1990. Its limitations include the inability to identify visa status, illegal aliens, and recipients of amnesty; the loss (after the 1970 census) of information on parental nativity; and the virtual absence of retrospective questions that address the dynamic nature of immigrant adjustment.

Three dominant themes emerge: immigration has increased absolutely and relatively; the diversity of immigrants has increased on nearly every measured characteristic; and immigrants converge impressively with the native-born in their demographic and economic characteristics. Over the past few decades immigration has been increasing, and in the most recent decade (1981–1990), 7.3 million individuals received permanent resident alien status, the equivalent of 3.2 percent of the population in 1980. By 1990 the foreign-born were 8.0 percent of the U.S. population (20 million people). This is the highest percentage of foreign-born in five decades. Even more dramatic has been the change in the source countries of immigrants. During the nineteenth and much of the twentieth centuries, immigrants came primarily from Europe and Canada. In recent decades immigration has been primarily from Asia, Mexico, and other parts of Latin America. In the 1980s, 85 percent of the immigrants were from Asia or Latin America, and by the 1990 census they were 67 percent of the foreign-born population.

The new immigration from Asia and Latin America shows more diversity in skills than the recent immigrants from the traditional (Europe/Canada) source countries. They occupy both high-skilled and low-skilled occupations. Many Asian immigrants in particular have high levels of education. More dramatic is the increased proportion of immigrants with very low levels of education, particularly among Mexican immigrants. The new immigrants are also less likely to arrive with English-language fluency.

As did the new immigrants from Southern and Eastern Europe at the turn of the century, the new immigrants of the late twentieth century tend to settle initially in a small number of metropolitan areas. With the passage of time, immigrants tend to spread out from their initial ports of entry. Their geographic concentration does, however, create a large disparity in the direct local area impact of immigrants.

The two basic conclusions from the analysis of the various demographic, skill, and economic characteristics of immigrants are diversity and convergence. In part because of the increased diversity in source countries, there is now greater heterogeneity among immigrants in nearly all demographic and economic characteristics, including fertility, education, English fluency, earnings, and household income. With a longer duration in the United States there tends to be a convergence in many of these characteristics among immigrants and with the native-born. With the passage of time immigrant fertility for those from high-fertility countries declines to the norm, all else the same, in the United States. Immigrant employment, English-language fluency, and earnings also increase with duration, and in the case of employment and earnings, even reach levels comparable to the native-born with similar measurable characteristics. The high unemployment and poverty rates of new immigrants decline with duration of residence.

The convergence of many characteristics of immigrants with the native-born is the optimistic side of the story. The pessimistic side exists as well. An increasing number and proportion of immigrants have been arriving with very low levels of skill, and even though there are improvements with a longer residence in the United States, these low levels of schooling, job training, and English-language fluency inhibit successful adjustment in the labor market. The results are very low earnings, often low employment, and hence very low household income and a high incidence of poverty. Moreover, these low-skilled immigrants are in direct competition for jobs, housing, and income transfer resources with the low-skilled population either born in or long-term residents of the

United States. These problems are exacerbated by the geographic concentration of immigrants.

The American economy is undergoing a major restructuring in which higher skills and labor market flexibility are increasingly essential for employment at high wages. The opportunities are bleak for the successful employment at incomes significantly above the poverty level for the increasing number of lower-skilled immigrants. Nevertheless, the demand for immigrant visas is high and likely to increase because of even more limited job opportunities and high rates of population growth in many source regions. Moreover, the potential exists for large refugee flows from the former USSR, Eastern Europe, parts of Africa, and perhaps from China. Meanwhile, the strength and the stability of the United States will continue to attract economic migrants and refugees from all over the world.

The challenge to America in the past was the successful absorption of a large immigration of primarily unskilled workers into the economy. Although that challenge was successfully met at the end of the nineteenth century and earlier this century, the American economy and society have changed. The economy now offers far fewer opportunities for low-skilled workers. In addition, public policy has changed, and providing assistance to those in economic need has become an important role of government. Finally, the skills and other characteristics of potential immigrants are more heterogeneous than in the past. This situation necessitates continuous rethinking of all aspects of immigration policy—legal immigration, enforcement of immigration law, and refugee policy—to be sure that U.S. immigration policy and practice are consistent with the economic, humanitarian, and other goals of the United States. If this reevaluation is done, the United States will continue to meet the challenge and opportunities offered by immigration.

We are indebted to the Russell Sage Foundation and the U.S. Bureau of the Census for invaluable support for this project. Additional funding came from the Venture 2000 project of the College of Business Administration, University of Illinois at Chicago and the Population Research Center of The University of Texas at Austin. Without the skillful research assistance of Michael Hurst and Grant Mallie, this project could not have been completed. Given the incompatibilities of our word processing programs, we are especially indebted for the assistance of Yvonne Marshall and Winona Schroeder. Additional technical support was provided by the Social Science Data Archive, University of Illinois at Chicago and the Office of Graduate Studies, The University of Texas at Austin. Finally, the essay has benefited substantially from the comments we received from our colleagues in this project and from the students in the sociology focus groups at The University of Texas at Austin. We are especially indebted to Reynolds Farley for his comments and assistance throughout this project. It should be noted, however, that the views expressed in this chapter and any errors of omission or commission are attributable solely to the authors.

ENDNOTES

1. Technically, "immigrants" refers to those who are awarded "legal permanent resident" status in the United States, which is a prelude to naturalization for the foreign-born. Immigrants may be economic migrants or refugees and enter the United States under kinship, skill, amnesty, or refugee provisions in U.S. immigration law. There are, however, other foreign-born individuals residing legally in the United States on tourist, student, temporary worker, and other temporary visas. In addition, there are illegal immigrants or illegal aliens, those in the United States without a lawful visa and those who have violated a condition of a lawful visa. Although the 1990 census provides information on whether a foreign-born person has become a U.S. citizen, there are no data in the census on the visa status of aliens. Nor are there reliable data on the extent to which immigrants and illegal aliens were underenumerated in the census. Throughout this study persons born abroad of American parents or born in Puerto Rico, the U.S. Virgin Islands, and other dependencies of the United States are treated as if they were neither foreign-born nor native-born.

2. Earlier census monographs on immigrants include Carpenter (1927); Hutchinson (1956); and Jasso and Rosenzweig (1990).

3. By way of contrast, the 1970 census included several important retrospective questions dropped from subsequent censuses, including questions on economic activity 5 years ago (employment status, occupation, and industry) and birthplace of parents.

4. The *Statistical Yearbook of the Immigration and Naturalization Service,* U.S. Department of Justice, is an invaluable source of administrative data on immigrants and illegal aliens. It is the primary source of data on annual flows of immigrants, apprehended illegal aliens, and beneficiaries of amnesty reported in this study.

5. Apprehensions of illegal aliens have increased since the late 1950s when they were fewer than 100,000 per year. There were about 161,000 per year in 1961–1970, 832,000 per year in 1971–1980, and 1.2 million per year in 1981–1992 (including 1.3 million in 1992). *Statistical Yearbook 1992:* Table 59.

6. There were 3.0 million applicants for legalization under the 1986 Act, of whom 74.7 percent were from Mexico, 5.5 percent from El Salvador, 2.3 percent from Guatemala, 2.0 percent from Haiti, and 1.1 percent from Colombia *Statistical Yearbook 1991:* Table 22). Nearly every country had at least some representation among the other 14.4 percent of applicants. For an analysis of the Immigration Reform and Control Act of 1986 and the characteristics of the applicants for amnesty, see Chiswick (1988) and *Statistical Yearbook 1991:* 70–73.

7. Passel and Woodrow (1984): 642–671; Passel and Woodrow (1987): 1304–1323; Bean, King, and Passel (1983): 99–109; Bean, Browning, and Frisbie (1984): 672–691; U.S. General Accounting Office (1993).

8. For a detailed analysis of the educational attainment and school enrollment of the population, see Mare, Chapter 4 in Volume One.

9. There is little difference by gender. For an analysis of the school enrollment of immigrant children using the 1976 Survey of Income and Education, see Schultz (1984): 251–288.

10. For an analysis of labor force statistics in the 1990 census and trends over time for

the population as a whole, see Wetzel, Chapter 2 in Volume One, and Kasarda, Chapter 5 in Volume One. For an analysis of the employment of immigrants using the 1976 Survey of Income and Education and the 1970 census, see Chiswick (1982).

11. For a detailed analysis of the employment and unemployment experiences of immigrants using census data, see Chiswick (1982).

12. For a similar analysis for 1980, see Frisbie et al. (1986): 74–99.

13. *Statistical Abstract of the United States: 1993:* Table 1376.

14. For a detailed analysis of income and poverty for the population as a whole using the 1990 Census, see Levy, Chapter 1 in Volume One.

15. *Statistical Abstract of the United States, 1993:* Table 682.

16. Analyzing data from the 1980 census, Jensen (1989) also reports a low incidence of receipt of cash public assistance.

17. Furthermore, the household income data include aged households. For the aged in a particular household, income may be a poor measure of their ability to consume since many are living in owner-occupied dwellings, receive large noncash transfers (e.g., Medicare), and are drawing down their savings.

6

The New Geography of Population Shifts: Trends Toward Balkanization

WILLIAM H. FREY

NEW DIVISIONS ACROSS SPACE

URBAN GROWTH and migration patterns continue to shift in unexpected ways and are creating sharper divisions across space. Back in the 1970s, urban scholars were baffled by the so-called rural renaissance, when rural and small communities in most parts of the country grew faster than large metropolises—reversing decades of urban concentration. Later, a broad review of that period's reversals concluded that the 1970s were really a transition decade for U.S. population redistribution, where the "transition" referred to new *social and economic contexts* for redistribution rather than to specific geographic patterns (Frey and Speare 1988). Since then, the geography of growth has again shifted, as industrial restructuring and the global economy have created more fast-paced and unpredictable distribution dynamics for the 1980s and 1990s (Frey 1990).

Just as these new redistribution forces began to take shape, increasingly large waves of immigrants from abroad, dominated by racial and ethnic minorities from Latin America and Asia, began to pour into selected parts of the country. They impact heavily on the sizes, diversity profiles, and economies of their destination areas and add vibrancy and vitality to these communities. However, they also contribute to dislocations and increased government spending.

These new population shifts do not necessarily adhere to familiar classifications—Snowbelt and Sunbelt, rural and urban, or even city and suburb. Minority segregation is no longer confined to individual neighborhoods or communities. In fact, there is emerging a new type of "demographic balkanization"—a spatial segmentation of the population by race, ethnicity, class, and age across regions and metropolitan areas, driven by both internal and international migration.

While recognizing the ever-dynamic state of the nation's population geography, this review of 1990 census findings emphasizes the following trends which emerged over the 1980s and are likely to characterize the 1990s as well.

1. An uneven urban revival.   A return to urbanization has countered the redistribution reversals of the 1970s (see Figure 6.1). No longer considered a rural renaissance, the 1970s redistribution reversals are now viewed as the product of period economic and demographic forces, which favored nonmetropolitan area growth and an industrial restructuring, which reduced the job-generating capacities of northern manufacturing centers. Yet the new metropolitan growth patterns since 1980 are not simply a replay of 1950s- and 1960s-style urbanization. They reflect a continuing national industrial restructuring that favors areas with diversified economies and, in particular, those engaged in advanced services and knowledge-based industries. Recreation and retirement centers also fared well. Many small metropolises and nonmetropolitan areas, especially in the nation's interior, fared poorly as a result of the adverse 1980s' influences as

FIGURE 6.1   **Metropolitan-nonmetropolitan growth.**

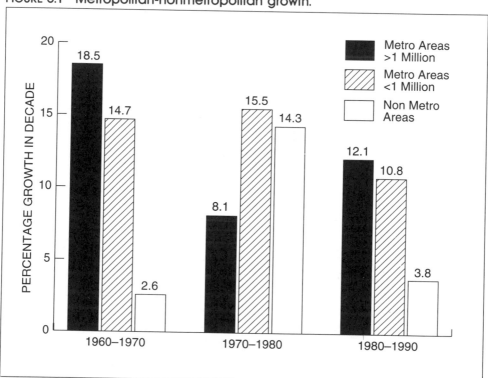

well as their dependence on less than competitive economic bases. The new urbanization has created sharp economic and demographic growth distinctions across regions and places.

2. Regional racial divisions. A second emerging trend is the increased regional separation of minorities and whites that has accompanied a more diverse national population. The heightened immigration from Latin America and Asia, as well as the population gains among native-born minorities, have led to a growth advantage for the minority versus the majority (non-Hispanic) white population. Yet these national growth disparities play out differently across regions, states, and metropolitan areas. In the 1980s, more than two-thirds of minority immigrants were directed to only seven states—led by California, New York, and Texas (see Figure 6.2a). Not only do these immigrants impact upon the race-ethnic profiles of these states' populations, they represent increased competition with native residents for jobs and housing, since most states that received large numbers of immigrants also lost white internal migrants to other parts of the country (see Figure 6.2b) (Frey 1993a and 1994d). While each minority group exhibits different distribution tendencies, the sharp majority–minority distinction across regions and metropolitan areas will affect the social and political character of these areas.

FIGURE 6.2a Migration from abroad: 1985–1990.

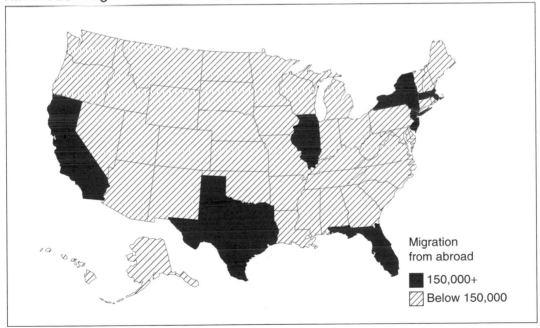

FIGURE 6.2b   Net Interstate migration: 1985–1990.

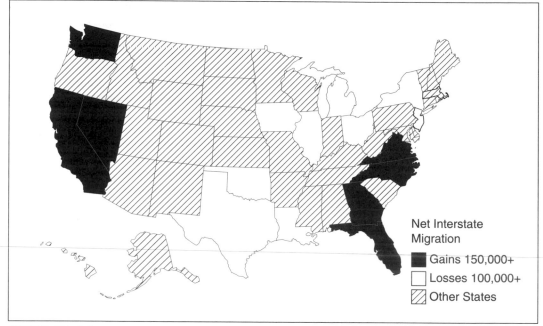

SOURCE: Tabulations of "Residence 5 Years Ago" question from 1990 U.S. Census of Population.

3. Regional divisions by skill level and poverty.   Income disparities widened between college graduates and those with lesser educations in the 1980s. This trend complements the geographic labor market disparities in industrial structure, in which areas that specialize in advanced services and knowledge-based industries are differentiated from those that are engaged in production and manufacturing activities. Together, these trends are creating different redistribution patterns, respectively, for the more- and less-educated segments of the population—for which the geographies of opportunities have become quite different. More so than other population groups, the poverty population is even less likely to follow mainstream redistribution patterns.

4. Baby boom and elderly realignments.   Although not as severe as for race and ethnic groups, segmented redistribution patterns are also evident among cohorts and age groups. As early baby boom cohorts entered the labor market in the mid-1970s, the deindustrialization in large northern metropolitan areas sent them scurrying to selected South and West destinations. Later baby boom cohorts (born after 1955) followed different paths as they entered the job market during the 1980s. A different redistribution pattern from both boomer cohorts is displayed by the elderly population, whose numbers and incomes have risen substantially over the past two decades. For them, amenities and low living costs take preference over an area's economic vitality. Especially during the 1980s, the retired elderly became a unique and important segment of the overall redistribution pattern.

5. *Suburban dominance and city isolation.* The suburbs achieved the un-disputed dominance as the locus of population and jobs in the 1980s. The broad expanse of territory outside of central cities became the primary activity space for the majority of metropolitan residents (see Figure 6.3). Particularly telling was the new practice of statewide or national political candidates appealing to suburban—rather than to traditional central city—constituency voters. Political analysts attribute the 1992 election of Democratic presidential candidate Bill Clinton to his success with suburban voters (Usdansky 1992). Garreau's *Edge City* (1991) points to the emergence of suburban office and commercial complexes.

Suburban areas have captured the bulk of employment and residential growth in the 1980s. The modal commuter now both lives and works in the suburbs, and several suburban cities have begun to rival their historically dominant central cities in the production of export goods and services (Pisarski 1987; Cervero 1989; Stanback 1991). America's suburbs are no longer the homogeneous bed-room communities of the 1950s. At the same time, the race and class divisions between central cities and suburbs have intensified.

A RETURN TO THE METROPOLIS—WITH VARIATIONS

A renewed metropolitan growth is evident from Figure 6.1, which shows that the nation's metropolitan population grew at a faster rate over the 1980s than did the entire nonmetropolitan population. In this sense, it is a return to the

FIGURE 6.3   City–suburb shares of metropolitan populations.*

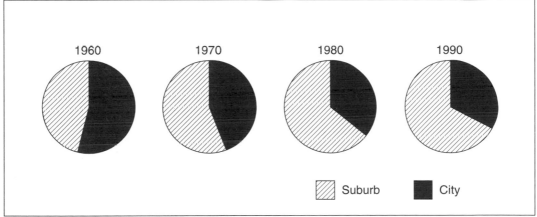

*Using central city and suburb definitions at each census.

well-established urban growth advantage of prior decades. Yet, underlying these broad metropolitan gains are fairly sharp differences in the growth rates of individual metropolitan areas as a result of the economic restructuring and immigration.

Regional Restructuring

Although several explanations were proposed to account for the redistribution reversals of the 1970s, the regional restructuring explanation appears to account best for both those reversals and for the selective urban revival of the 1980s and 1990s.[1] This explanation saw the deindustrialization-related metropolitan declines of the 1970s as only a temporary episode leading toward a new spatial organization of work. This new organization is associated with expanding worldwide markets, improved communications, and the rise of multinational corporations. According to this view, new urban growth should emerge after the industrial "downsizing" had taken place. Key metropolitan areas in this resurgence were expected to be headquarters for corporations, banks, and other "advanced service" activities (Noyelle and Stanback 1984). Growth was also expected for areas with knowledge-based industries associated with high-tech research and development. These kinds of industries still benefit from agglomeration economies; that is, having many firms performing similar or linked functions in the same place. On the other hand, metropolitan areas that were not diversified or that could not make the production-to-services transformation were predicted to experience unstable growth prospects. These areas' growth or decline are dependent on external economic conditions, where decisions are made at faraway corporate headquarters (in the case of branch plant downsizing) or government agencies (in the case of obtaining state or federal contracts for defense work and the like). This explanation contrasts sharply with a prevalent 1970s prediction that a rural renaissance-type population deconcentration would continue.

Major Metro Areas

Major metropolitan areas are typically considered to be those with populations that exceed one million.[2] In 1990, 39 such areas achieved major metro status, and for the first time in the country's history, a majority of the population resided in these major metros. What was most significant about these metros during the 1980s were the changes in their patterns from the previous decade.

Heavily affected by the period's deindustrialization, eight major metros—located primarily in the Rustbelt—actually lost population in the 1970s. Of these, only Pittsburgh and Cleveland continued to lose population in the last half of the 1980s. This suggests that the deindustrialization-driven losses for those areas have run their course, lending support to the industrial restructuring explanation of urban growth.

This restructuring explanation is also supported when individual areas' 1970s 1980s growth changes are linked to their respective industrial structures. Figure 6.4 displays both decades' growth rates for the 25 largest metropolitan areas in the country. For the most part, metro areas with diversified economies and those that serve as corporate headquarter and advanced service centers tended to improve their growth prospects in the 1980s. This was the case with New York, Philadelphia, and Boston in the Northeast; with Minneapolis–St. Paul and Kansas City in the Midwest; with Washington, D.C., Dallas-Ft. Worth, and Atlanta in the South; and with Los Angeles, San Francisco-Oakland, and Seattle in the West. An exception to the rule is Chicago, a major metro with a diverse economy that continued to decline in the late 1980s. The patterns in Figure 6.4 also make plain that the seemingly large 1970s gainers were not necessarily consistent ones. Metro areas whose economies were heavily dominated by particular industries ran the risk of experiencing boom-then-bust periods. This was the case with Houston and Denver, whose economies were strongly tied to oil and extractive industries.

Contributing to the different growth levels of these metro areas was immigration from abroad, which tended to be directed to a selected number of port-of-entry areas, contributing substantially to their population gains. All of the 1985–1990 migration gains for Los Angeles, New York, and San Francisco can be attributed to migration from abroad. In contrast, the lion's share of migration gains for Atlanta, Seattle, and Phoenix drew from internal migration from other parts of the country

Metro vs. Nonmetro, "The Belts" and "The Coasts"

The growth and later decline of the nation's nonmetropolitan territory were driven largely by economic trends concentrated in a specific period. The interplay of industrial restructuring and short-run economic trends also altered the geographic character of Snowbelt-to-Sunbelt redistribution since 1980.

Snowbelt to Sunbelt in the 1970s. The broad tapestry of these changes can be seen in Table 6.1, which displays growth rates across regions and metropolitan categories over the 1960s, 1970s, and 1980s. These data demonstrate the strong link that existed between population shifts across the metropolitan–nonmetropolitan dimension and those that existed across the regional dimension. Most of the nation's metropolitan area losses during the 1970s were borne by large metropolitan areas in the North, while most national small-metropolitan and nonmetropolitan gains were concentrated in the Sunbelt (South and West) regions.

FIGURE 6.4 Percent decade change for largest metropolitan areas: 1980–1990 as compared to 1970–1980.

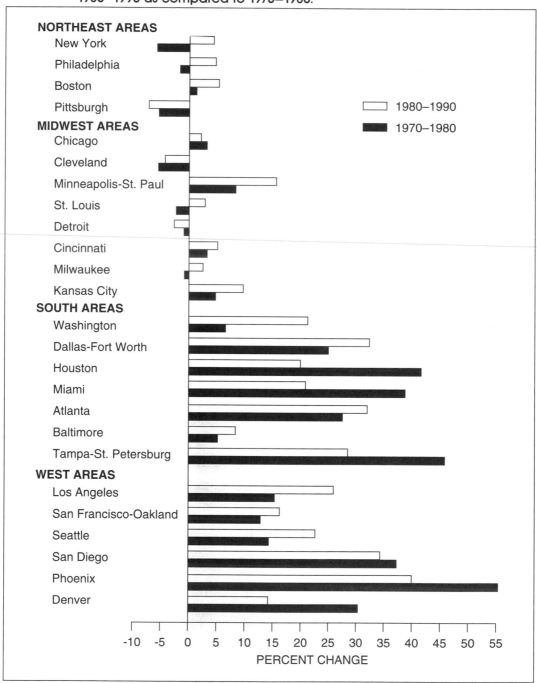

TABLE 6.1 Population change, by metropolitan status and region.

Region and Metropolitan Status	1990 Size (millions)	Percent 10 Year Change			Interior Percent 5 Year Change		Coastal Percent 5 Year Change	
		1960–1970	1970–1980	1980–1990	1980–1985	1985–1990	1980–1985	1985–1990
Northeast and Midwest								
Large metropolitan	62.9	12.0%	−0.9%	2.8%	0.8%	2.2%	1.8%	0.9%
Smaller metropolitan	25.6	11.1	5.2	3.3	0.5	1.6	1.6	3.6
Nonmetropolitan	22.6	2.6	8.0	0.1	0.2	−2.0	1.9	3.5
South								
Large metropolitan	28.2	30.9	23.4	22.3	16.0	4.6	10.1	11.5
Smaller metropolitan	31.9	15.5	20.9	13.4	7.8	1.3	10.3	8.1
Nonmetropolitan	24.9	1.1	16.3	4.6	4.5	−3.0	5.4	3.5
West								
Large metropolitan	33.8	29.1	20.0	24.2	16.4	7.3	10.0	12.8
Smaller metropolitan	10.8	24.8	32.2	22.8	11.6	11.7	11.3	9.3
Nonmetropolitan	8.1	9.0	30.6	14.1	9.2	2.1	8.9	7.8

SOURCES: Compiled at University of Michigan Population Studies Center from decennial census data and 1985 estimates prepared by the Census Bureau Population Division.

NOTES: Interior and Coastal portions of Regions are defined in terms of Census Regions and Divisions:

North Coastal: Northeast Region

North Interior: Midwest Region

South Coastal: South Atlantic Division

South Interior: East South Central and West South Central Divisions

West Coastal: Pacific Division

West Interior: Mountain Division

Large Metropolitan status includes metropolitan areas with 1990 populations exceeding one million.

279

The Snowbelt major metro declines in the 1970s were generated by the industrial restructuring influences discussed earlier. At the same time, a variety of period-specific economic "pulls" made smaller Sunbelt areas particularly attractive destinations. Among these influences were the mid-decade energy crisis which spurred extractive energy development in the Southwest, Mountain West, and Appalachia; recession-related relocations of manufacturing jobs to low-wage, nonunion communities in the Southeast; and a surprising worldwide food shortage which temporarily stunted outmigration from rural farming areas in all parts of the country. During this period, particularly large birth cohorts entered their retirement ages and gravitated to warmer amenity-laden communities in the Sunbelt. Together, these period influences forged a link between northern large metro declines and Sunbelt small area gains.

Bicoastal gains in the 1980s.   Just as the northern metropolitan declines served to fuel increased population growth in the Sunbelt during the 1970s, the urban revival served to slow the pace of this growth in the 1980s. The nation's Sunbelt regions still showed a considerable growth advantage over the Northeast and Midwest, but this margin became reduced, especially for the South as the 1980s decade wore on. The 1970s link between northern large metro declines and Sunbelt small area growth had reversed itself. Within the Sunbelt, the greatest 1970s–1980s slowdowns in growth occurred for smaller metropolitan and nonmetropolitan areas. Seventy-three of 85 small Sunbelt metros grew at slower rates (or declined) in the 1980s than in the 1970s. At the other extreme, 15 of the 18 northern major metro areas grew faster in the 1980s.

Restructuring influences turned to favor growth in several large Snowbelt (and Sunbelt) metros, and new period influences adversely affected small-town and rural growth through parts of the South and West. Ironically, these were reversals of the same period influences that spawned 1970s growth in these areas. Small-town manufacturing jobs dried up during the early 1980s as the strong dollar reduced demand abroad. The agricultural shortages of the 1970s became surpluses in the 1980s, leading to outmigration in rural farm communities. But perhaps most important was the fall of worldwide petroleum prices in the mid-1980s, which very quickly turned boom to bust for large stretches of the "oil patch region" of the Sunbelt—including Texas, Louisiana, and Oklahoma (Beale 1988).

These effects were most devastating for the interior portions of the South and West, particularly over the late 1980s (see Table 6.1 and Figure 6.5). During the 1985–1990 period, interior South small metro areas grew negligibly, nonmetropolitan areas declined, and the entire region's population growth grew by less than 1 percent. Oil-dependent Odessa, Texas, shifted from a growth rate of 17 percent in the first half of the 1980s to a decline of -12 percent in the decade's last 5 years.

FIGURE 6.5   Fast growing and declining metropolitan areas: 1985–1990.

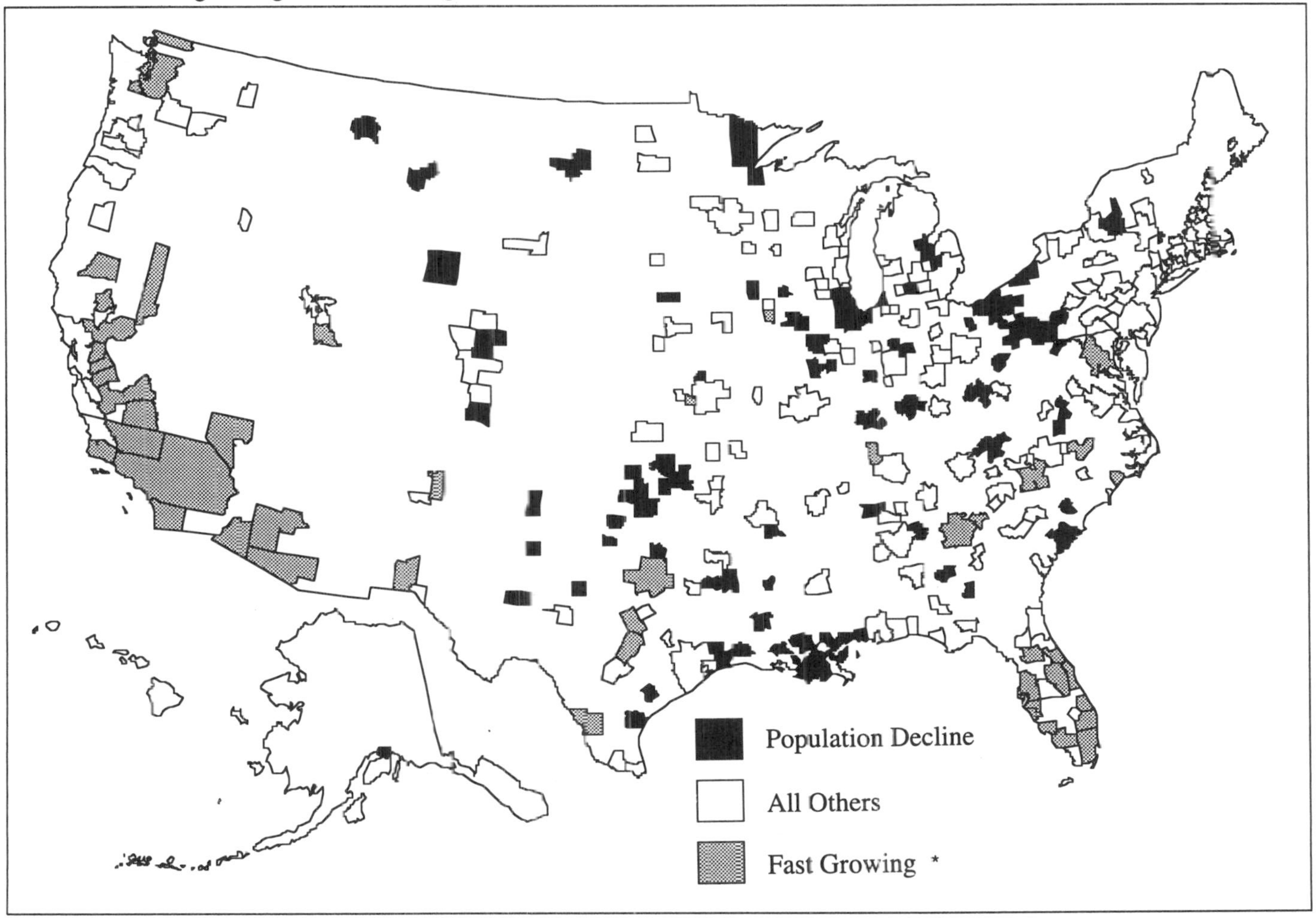

Population Decline

All Others

Fast Growing *

*Growth rate 2.5 times the national growth rate.

In contrast, coastal Sunbelt areas fared far better than the interior regions during this period. The generally higher levels of growth can be attributed, in part, to amenities and recreation, but also the emergence of growing regional centers with diversified economies (e.g., Atlanta) and the rise of knowledge-based industries (e.g., in the Research Triangle area of North Carolina). During the late 1980s, 15 of the nation's fastest growing metropolitan areas were located in the South Atlantic region or in California. Orlando, Florida, increased its metro population by more than one-fifth over this 5-year period. These patterns point up not only the emergence of new growth locations but also the volatility of growth and decline in response to national and global industrial restructuring.

The Rural Renaissance: A Postmortem

In retrospect, the rural renaissance was an aberration of the 1970s. When initially detected, many observers felt that technology and the loosening of distance constraints would free both employers and workers from the noose of locating in high-density, congested urban environments (Wardwell 1980; Fuguitt 1985). They thought that Americans' long-held preference for living in small communities could finally be achieved, and the eventual downsizing of large metropolitan areas was forecasted. But this stress on environmental preferences in explaining these earlier trends was overemphasized. Most of the 1970s non-metropolitan growth, as well as the 1980s slowdowns and declines, were driven by period-specific economic forces related to low-tech manufacturing, oil extraction, and agriculture. The former growth was further fueled by the wholesale elimination of manufacturing jobs in the nation's largest urban centers. In short, the rosy rural renaissance predictions of the 1970s failed to consider the mix of period and restructuring influences that helped provide the illusion of a new era of dispersed settlement.

Still, there are parts of nonmetropolitan America that continued to attract growth all through the 1980s. Some of these can be classed as retirement counties in all parts of the country, but especially in Florida, the upper Great Lakes, the Southwest, and the West. Flagler County, Florida, increased its elderly population by 266 percent over the 1980s—topping the country in elderly growth. (Fuguitt et al. 1989; Johnson 1993). A substantial number of nonmetropolitan areas increased their elderly populations significantly in Nevada (Nye County at 166 percent), Alaska (Kenai Peninsula at 147 percent), Arizona (Mohave County at 126 percent), and other western states. Owing to their high amenities and low costs of living, these counties attracted retirees with discretionary incomes that have contributed to their further economic development. (Crispell and Frey 1993).

A second kind of rural area that sustained growth during the 1980s were exurban counties that lie adjacent to metropolitan areas and show strong connectivity via commuting. This is linked to the growth of edge cities at the periphery of large metropolises.

Both the footloose elderly residents of retirement counties and the commuting residents of exurban counties are able to benefit from the amenities of rural life without necessarily depending on their economies for employment. Yet many more interior nonmetropolitan counties were beset by selective outmigration, population aging, limited infrastructures, and poverty. The future for them is less than rosy, and their further revival will require greater industrial diversification that extends far beyond the resource-based and temporary manufacturing growth that buoyed them in the 1970s.[3]

NATIONAL MINORITY GAINS—REGIONAL DIVISIONS

A significant ingredient of American demographic change over the 1980s was the growth of its minority population. Over the decade, the combined minorities (blacks, Hispanics, Asians, and American Indians) grew by almost one-third— more than seven times the 4.4 percent growth of the non-Hispanic white population. (Unless otherwise indicated, "whites" pertain to non-Hispanic whites.) If these trends continue, it is possible that the nation would become almost 50 percent minority by the year 2050 (Day 1992). Much of this growth, particularly for Asians and Hispanics, owes to immigration from abroad. Primarily due to fertility differences, black growth also exceeded that of whites by a ratio of 3:1. What is important for population redistribution *within* the U.S. is the fact that most of the nation's minority growth over the decade was directed to selected regions and to a relatively small number of metropolitan areas—which differed substantially from the areas of white gain. The potential long-term impact of these trends cannot be overlooked. Just as past racial and ethnic segregation took place at the neighborhood and community levels, these trends portend a broader-based segregation across large areas of the country.

Uneven Racial Gains

Even at the regional level, whites and minorities show distinctly different distributions. For example, close to half of the white population resides in the nation's Northeast and Midwest, as contrasted to less than one-third for the combined minorities. This is because immigrants as well as second-generation Asians and Hispanics are more likely to settle in or near West Coast or Southwest port-of-entry areas than are whites. For blacks, the modal region of residence is still the South, followed by the two Northern regions.

Across metropolitan-nonmetropolitan categories, whites are far less likely to reside in major metro areas, and far more likely to reside in nonmetropolitan areas than each of the three largest minority groups. Again, major ports-of-entry for recently arrived Asians and Hispanics tend to be larger metropolitan areas, accounting for the fact that about 7 of 10 members of each group reside in such areas. The figure drops to 6 of 10 for blacks, who are more likely to reside in (southern) nonmetropolitan areas than these two groups, but who are still more urbanized than whites overall.

What is important to note is that these white–minority differences have not moderated, as a result of redistribution over the 1980s (Frey 1993b). The high immigration-driven growth of Asians and Hispanics actually reinforced these differences. Among blacks, there was a relocation away from large northern metro areas toward major metros in the South, along with some movement to the West. These patterns represent the ascendancy of more blacks into the middle class and, hence, participation in a more nationwide migration network, as well as some return migration to the South. Whites were the one group whose 1980s redistribution patterns did not reinforce existing location types. There was a modest shift away from the Northeast and Midwest regions, resulting from employment dislocations linked to various boom and bust areas, as well as strong flows of elderly whites to selected Sunbelt retirement areas. Still, the overall regional and metropolitan disparities in where whites and minorities lived remained intact over the decade.

Immigration-Internal Migration Dynamics

Disparities in minority and white population distribution during the 1980s drew largely from the interplay of immigration and internal migration dynamics. States and metropolitan areas that received large inflows of immigrants also received large inflows of minorities. Black distribution patterns differ from those of Asians and Latinos, but they remain distinct from majority whites (Long 1988; McHugh 1987). Black communities in their traditional areas of residence still remain a powerful incentive for black migration streams.

White migration is more nationwide in scope and, by virtue of its magnitude, dominates internal migration patterns. The migration patterns of professional, well-educated whites respond sharply to the economic "pushes and pulls" of the national labor market (Long 1988; Lansing and Mueller 1967). Push factors are those that encourage residents to move away from an area, such as the closing of factories, while pull factors are those that attract migrants, such as burgeoning employment opportunities. Whites with lesser incomes or more locally oriented blue- and pink-collar jobs are less likely to make long-distance moves but are, nonetheless, responsive to strong economic "pushes" from declining areas. In addition, the growing segment of retired elderly whites also contributes significantly to national internal migration streams. (Serow 1987; Longino 1990). States and metropolitan areas with growing employment or high amenities soon become destinations for white-dominated internal migration streams. Likewise, areas with sharp or prolonged economic downturns and Snowbelt areas with large cohorts of soon-to-be-retired elderly will be the source of white-dominated outmigration streams to other parts of the country.

Impact on states. This distinction between minority-dominated immigration streams and white-dominated internal migration streams is particularly relevant to the 1980s, when a disparity emerged between areas that grew predominantly from the former and areas that grew predominantly from the latter. The states that grew primarily from immigration include California, New York, Texas, New Jersey, Illinois, and Massachusetts. These states contain traditional port-of-entry cities and metropolitan areas, and therefore benefited from the large surge of national immigrant growth. The importance of the immigration component for these states' population growth cannot be overstated. In all except one (California), migration from abroad was the total source of gains during the 1985–1990 period.[4] Each of the other states lost internal migrants in their exchanges with the rest of the country. Even in California, the large immigration from abroad overwhelmed the relatively small internal migration gain for this period (1.5 million versus fewer than 200,000). Clearly, these states had less appeal for internal migrants than did other parts of the country.

States that grew primarily from internal migration over the 1985–1990 period are clustered in the economically booming South Atlantic region as well as in the West. The largest gains accrued to Florida, Georgia, North Carolina, Virginia, Washington, and Arizona—states that benefited from the largely coastal restructuring and amenity-related economic gains discussed earlier. While immigration also contributes to these states' gains, only Florida might be considered one of the country's major immigration magnets. But its substantial immigration from abroad (almost 400,000 over the 1985–1990 period) is dwarfed by net internal migration gains from other parts of the country (totaling over one million for the late 1980s).

The relative impact of the minority-dominated immigration for the former states can be contrasted with that of white-dominated internal migration for the latter by examining Figure 6.6. Both California's and New York's minority compositions are increased as a result of these dynamics. California's large minority-dominated immigration stream overwhelms the effect of internal migration. In New York, a minority-dominant immigrant flow displaces a white-dominant outmigration. This general pattern also characterizes migration dynamics for Texas, New Jersey, Illinois, and Massachusetts. For each of these states, there is a net gain of minorities and net loss of whites as a result of these immigration-internal migration streams.

Contrasting patterns of white gain are shown for Florida and Georgia as a result of the white-dominant internal migration to these states in the late 1980s.

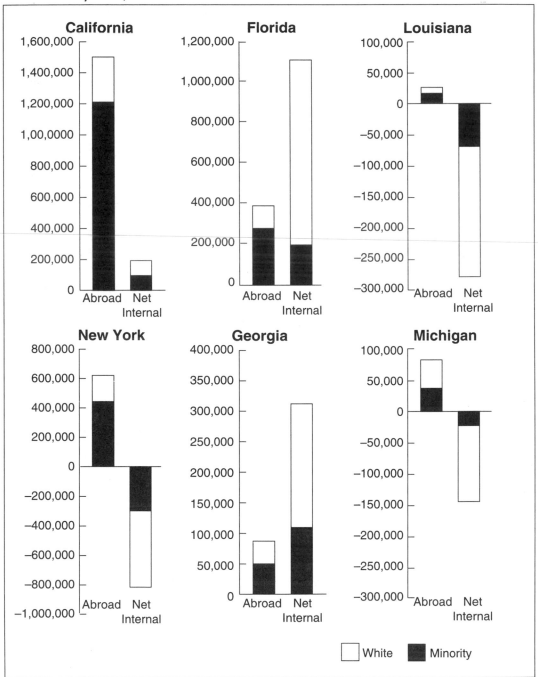

FIGURE 6.6 Migration from abroad and net internal migration, by race, selected states: 1985–1990.

SOURCE: Tabulations of "residence 5 years ago" question from 1990 U.S. Census of Population.

Similar white gains are shown for other states where internal migration is the major contributor of recent growth. (In several southern states, including Georgia and Virginia, blacks make a significant contribution to new inmigration as well.) A broad swath of states in the nation's Rustbelt, Farmbelt, and Oil Patch regions lost whites due to internal migration to other parts of the country, as a result of their stagnant or declining economies. The patterns of two such states, Louisiana and Michigan, are depicted in Figure 6.6. Unlike the large port-of-entry states, these states did not recoup their net internal migration losses with large numbers of immigrants from abroad.

The above dynamics, if continued, suggest a scenario where a few immigrant port-of-entry states will continue to gain bigger minority populations while losing whites to other prosperous areas. This could eventually lead to a racial and ethnic balkanization pattern. This prediction assumes that the late 1980s flight from high immigration states will continue, and that it is precipitated by aspects of the immigration itself—competition for jobs and housing or the avoidance of social and financial costs associated with the assimilation of large numbers of immigrants into the area.

Two aspects of the outmigration from these states give credence to the view that international immigration is now pushing natives out. First, the outmigration is led by whites with lower incomes and less-than-college educations. This low-income outmigration pattern is also evident for California. This differs from conventional long-distance migration which typically is selective of the most educated. This suggests that outmigration is a response to job competition from low-skilled immigrants. Second, this outmigration involves a spreading to adjacent states (to Oregon, Nevada, and Arizona from California, to Wisconsin from Illinois, to Pennsylvania from New Jersey, to Arkansas from Texas) and to other diffuse destinations, suggesting a response to a "push" factor at the former place of residence rather than to destination "pulls" (Frey 1994b).

Impacts on metro areas. The impacts of minority-dominated immigration and white-dominated internal migration streams can be even sharper for individual metro areas. Distinct immigration and internal migration impacts are clearly shown for the different categories of metro areas listed in Table 6.2.

The ten highest immigration metropolitan areas are shown in the top panel, led by Los Angeles and New York. These constitute dominant port-of-entry areas for immigrants during the late 1980s. Most are old, long-established metropolitan areas. It is noteworthy that seven of these register losses via internal migration outflows to the rest of the country, and for two others (Miami and Washington, D.C.) internal inmigration is small. Only San Diego registers internal gains that are comparable in scope to immigration. In this respect, it is unique among major metropolitan areas since its growth is not dominated by one type of migration or the other.

TABLE 6.2   Metropolitan areas classed by dominant immigration and internal migration contributions to population change: 1985–1990.

Rank	State	Contribution to 1985–1990 Change (1,000s)		1990 Percent White
		Migration from Abroad	Net Interstate Migration*	
High Immigration Metros[a]				
1	Los Angeles	899	−175	50%
2	New York	756	−1,066	63
3	San Francisco	293	−103	61
4	Miami	211	45	48
5	Washington DC	191	34	63
6	Chicago	180	−293	67
7	Boston	120	−117	87
8	San Diego	116	127	65
9	Houston	97	−142	58
10	Philadelphia	80	−28	76
High Internal Migration Metros[b]				
1	Atlanta	43	192	70%
2	Tampa-St. Petersburg	35	159	83
3	Seattle	64	146	85
4	Phoenix	44	140	77
5	Orlando	35	132	77
6	Las Vegas	21	129	75
7	Sacramento	36	118	73
8	West Palm Beach	21	108	79
9	Charlotte	9	67	78
10	Raleigh-Durham	12	66	72
High Outmigration Metros[c]				
1	Detroit	45	−136	75%
2	Pittsburgh	11	−90	91
3	New Orleans	10	−88	59
4	Cleveland	21	−80	81
5	Denver	28	−61	80
6	Oklahoma City	12	−41	80
7	St. Louis	19	−37	81
8	Milwaukee	13	−35	81
9	Honolulu	41	−33	30
10	Buffalo	11	−31	86

SOURCES: Compiled from 1990 census files at the Population Studies Center, The University of Michigan.

*1985–1990 Inmigrants from other states minus 1985–1990 outmigrants to other states.

[a]Metro with largest 1985–1990 migration from abroad that exceeds net internal migration.
[b]Metro with largest 1985–1990 net internal migration and exceeds migration from abroad.
[c]Metro with largest negative internal migration and not recipients of large migration from abroad.

The ten highest internal migration metros are, by and large, newer metropolitan areas located primarily in the nation's late 1980s high growth regions. In contrast to the high immigration metros, each of these is dominated strongly by internal migration from the rest of the country. (San Diego, which could also be included in this list, is the singular exception.) It is noteworthy that three Florida metros—Tampa-St. Petersburg, Orlando, and West Palm Beach—are among those most influenced by internal migration, while Miami is more greatly impacted by immigration from abroad. The young and elderly white migrants who move to Florida from other states are directed to different intrastate destinations than are the immigrants from abroad.

Metropolitan areas affected by immigrant-dominated population change have substantially larger minority population profiles than those whose gains stem from internal migration. Eight of the ten highest immigration metropolitan areas have white percentages well below the white national percentage—including two where whites are now the minority—Los Angeles and Miami. Among the highest internal migration metros, all but two show white shares that are close to or greater than the national average. The major exceptions are Atlanta and Raleigh-Durham, which also attract blacks through internal migration.

Finally, most of the ten metros that lost population via internal migration have large white shares (see bottom panel, Table 6.2). These areas tend to be located in heavily white parts of the Midwest where immigration has hardly made a dent. While they are losing many people through outmigration, places like Pittsburgh, Cleveland, St. Louis, Milwaukee, and Buffalo still remain predominantly white.

Majority-Minority Metro Area Gainers

The separate immigration-internal migration dynamics, just reviewed, explain why the greatest minority population gains occurred in different metros than the greatest white population gains. This minority-majority disparity will persist and intensify as a result of the concentrated nature of minority growth—leaving many parts of the country virtually untouched or slightly sprinkled with minorities. Metro patterns of population growth and decline (resulting from both migration and natural increase) point up these differences.

Whites.   Because the national white growth level was not high or infused with a significant immigration component, the redistribution of whites within the country is a zero-sum game, since white population gains for some metropolitan areas resulted in white population losses for others. During the 1980s, 89 of 280 metro areas lost white population, led by New York, where the decade-wide loss exceeded 800,000 whites. Additionally, Chicago, Pittsburgh, Detroit, and Cleveland lost more than 100,000 whites. Thirty-one other metros (including Miami, Milwaukee, and Boston) lost more than 10,000 whites. These losses were influenced by a variety of factors, including deindustrialization of the Rustbelt, declines in smaller Rustbelt and Oil Patch towns, as well as the immigration-induced flight discussed earlier.

While the remaining 191 metro areas gained whites through both migration and natural increase, the largest gains (over 100,000) were located primarily in the coastal South, Texas, and selected western states. Led by Dallas, Atlanta, and Phoenix (with gains exceeding 400,000 whites), these areas included large diversified regional centers (such as Seattle and Minneapolis-St. Paul), booming South Atlantic centers (such as Charlotte, Norfolk, and Raleigh-Durham), resort and retirement recreation centers in Florida (such as Tampa-St. Petersburg, Fort Myers-Cape Coral) and other Sunbelt states, and a smattering of high-tech centers (such as Austin, Texas). Many of these large white gainers have only small minority populations, and only a few gained more minorities than majorities over the 1980s. This profile of white losers and gainers indicates that white internal migration responded closely to the economic restructuring and period influences of the 1980s.

Hispanics.   The nation's Hispanic population has grown since the late 1960s as a consequence of immigration reform, refugee movements, and illegal immigration from Mexico and other Latin American nations.[5] The Hispanic population grew by more than 50 percent during the 1980s as compared with 13 percent for blacks and less than 5 percent for whites. However, because it is a diverse population, Hispanics from different origins are attracted to different parts of the country. Although Mexican-Americans can be found in all regions, they reside predominantly in the West and Southwest. Puerto Ricans are more concentrated in the Northeast, and Cubans are most prevalent in Florida.

The Hispanic population is highly concentrated in a few metro areas, and recent immigration has consolidated that concentration. Large Hispanic populations continue to reside in Los Angeles (4.8 million), New York (2.8 million), and Miami (1.1 million). These three areas register the greatest 1980–1990 increases in their Hispanic populations. Los Angeles, alone, contains 21 percent of the nation's Hispanic population and gained over 2 million Hispanics over the decade.

This consolidation of Hispanic population gains into traditional port-of-entry metro areas is a product of immigration. While immigrants tend to locate in these traditional areas, internal Hispanic migrants tend to spread outward as they assimilate (McHugh 1989; Bartel 1989). This is indicated by a comparison of the destinations for Hispanic immigrants from abroad with areas that gained most from Hispanic internal migration over the 1985–1990 period (see Table 6.3). While Miami attracts internal migrants as well as migrants from abroad, neither Los Angeles nor New York is on the list of top internal migration mag-

TABLE 6.3 List of metropolitan areas with greatest net internal migration gains and greatest immigration from abroad for Hispanics, Asians, and blacks: 1985–1990.

Greatest Gains Due to Net Internal Migration: 1985–1990*

Rank	Hispanics Area	Size	Asians Area	Size	Blacks Area	Size
1	Miami	48,270	Los Angeles	31,804	Atlanta	74,949
2	Orlando	23,701	Sacramento	11,203	Norfolk	28,909
3	San Diego	19,711	San Francisco	10,345	Washington	20,205
4	Las Vegas	16,216	San Diego	6,355	Raleigh-Durham	17,428
5	Tampa-St. Petersburg	13,763	Boston	5,364	Dallas	16,075
6	Dallas	12,271	Atlanta	4,760	Orlando	13,836
7	Phoenix	11,127	Seattle	3,990	Richmond	12,508
8	Sacramento	11,053	Washington	3,854	San Diego	12,482
9	Modesto	10,072	Orlando	3,842	Minn-St. Paul	11,506
10	Washington	9,912	Las Vegas	3,326	Sacramento	10,848

Greatest Gains due to Immigration from Abroad: 1985–1990†

Rank	Hispanics Area	Size	Asians Area	Size	Blacks Area	Size
1	Los Angeles	467,003	Los Angeles	219,652	New York	140,270
2	New York	121,153	New York	190,512	Miami	36,228
3	Miami	152,962	San Francisco	137,006	Washington	29,526
4	San Francisco	61,917	Chicago	44,823	Los Angeles	16,925
5	Chicago	55,550	Washington	43,481	Boston	13,437
6	San Diego	74,415	San Diego	31,274	Philadelphia	9,446
7	Washington	61,633	Boston	27,219	San Francisco	7,656
8	Houston	43,140	Honolulu	26,869	Atlanta	7,464
9	Boston	33,770	Seattle	26,817	Chicago	6,777
10	Dallas	46,933	Philadelphia	22,347	Norfolk	6,537

SOURCE: Tabulations of "Residence 5 Years Ago" question from 1990 U.S. Census of Population.

* 1985–1990 inmigrants from elsewhere in the United States, minus 1985–1990 outmigrants to elsewhere in the United States.
† 1985–1990 immigrants from abroad.

nets. (In fact, both register a significant outmigration of Hispanic internal migrants.) Instead, Hispanic internal migrants gravitate to metros, such as Orlando and Tampa in Florida, Las Vegas, Nevada, or Sacramento and Modesto in California—places that are in close proximity to major immigrant destinations. These internal migration patterns contribute to a greater spread of the Hispanic population, such that 29 metro areas had at least 100,000 Hispanics in 1990, compared with only 22 in 1980. Still, the relative magnitude of these areas' net internal migration gains are small compared with those of Hispanic immigration from abroad. It is these latter streams that serve to concentrate the Hispanic population into selected metro areas.

Asians.   Although Asians have settled into American cities for generations, the Asian population more than doubled during the 1980s. As a consequence, a larger share of Asians are foreign-born (66 percent) than are Hispanics (41 percent) (Barringer, Gardner, and Levin 1993). Originally, Asians came mostly from China and Japan, but since the immigration statutes changed in the 1960s, significant numbers have come from the Philippines, Korea, and India. More recently, immigrants and refugees arrived from Vietnam, Cambodia, and Laos. The growth and diversity of Asian immigration has led to greater mixes of Asian groups in metropolitan areas. For example, in 1990 metropolitan Washington, D.C.'s population included more than 35,000 each of Koreans, Chinese, and Indians; over 20,000 Filipinos and Vietnamese; and almost 10,000 Japanese. Also, some of the newer, smaller Asian groups follow unique settlement patterns, such as the Hmongs, who were resettled by local sponsors in communities in Minnesota and Wisconsin.

Yet, despite this diversity, a large immigrant component of recent Asian growth continues to concentrate the Asian population in or near traditional ports of entry. In 1990, over half the U.S. Asian population resided in Los Angeles, San Francisco, and New York. These areas also accounted for the greatest 1980–1990 gains of Asians. Yet, as with the Hispanic population, the internal migration of Asians does not take them to the same destinations as immigrants (see Table 6.3). Los Angeles leads in gains for both types of migrants, but many internal Asian migrants go to Sacramento, Atlanta, Orlando, or Las Vegas—areas that are not in the top ten list of destinations for Asian immigrants. Moreover, during the late 1980s, there was a net outmigration of Asian internal migrants from traditional immigrant metros: New York, Chicago, and Honolulu (data not shown).

Because Asians come from more diverse origins and are more likely to be college-educated than Hispanics are, they tend to disperse from the traditional immigrant metros as they assimilate. Already in 1990, the number of metropolitan areas with more than 100,000 Asians rose to 12, as compared with just 5 in 1980. Nonetheless, the strong immigration component of Asian growth during the 1980s served to reinforce their concentration in a few select metropolitan areas. Although Asians constitute 2.8 percent of the total U.S. population, only 36 of the nation's 284 metro areas have Asian proportions as high as that.

Blacks The black population differs from the previous two in that its redistribution occurs largely through internal migration. Yet the black population has shown a history of regional and metropolitan distribution that differs from that of whites (Long 1988; McHugh 1987; Johnson 1990). For most of the present century, the greatest black migrations occurred between the rural South and large industrial cities in the North, Northeast, and Midwest, and later, San Francisco and Los Angeles on the West Coast. Since 1970, blacks began to move away from the North to locate in large and small metropolitan areas in the South, as well as in other parts of the country. Until the 1980s, black migration patterns had tended to lag behind those of whites in the movement to the suburbs as well as into the more growing regions of the country. The 1980s decade is significant for black redistribution in two ways. First, black growth is now occurring in many of the same states and metro areas as that of whites. Second, black redistribution patterns are becoming more polarized, such that college graduate blacks are apt to follow mainstream migration patterns.

The evolution of black migration over the 1965–1990 period can be followed from the maps in Figure 6.7, which display black net internal migration patterns for states over the intervals 1965–1970, 1975–1980, and 1985–1990. During the late 1960s, blacks were still leaving most southern states for North and West locations. California was the largest gainer, with Michigan, Maryland, New Jersey, and Ohio following close behind. The greatest origins were the Deep South states of Mississippi, Alabama, and Louisiana, with Arkansas and the Carolinas following close behind. By the late 1970s, the South-to-North pattern had reversed, as black migration responded to the deindustrialization process, which eliminated many of the semiskilled blue collar jobs in manufacturing. New York, Illinois, and Pennsylvania shifted to strong black outmigration states. While most of the South gained black migrants, California in the late 1970s still remained the greatest black destination.

The northern exodus continued through the late 1980s. But California is no longer the top black migrant destination. Its black gains of the 1970s were reduced by one-third, and Georgia moved up to be the top black gainer. It was during this period that black internal movement, like that of whites, shifted to the growing South Atlantic region. Maryland, Florida, Virginia, and North Carolina followed Georgia as the top black migrant-receiving states. Each of these (except Maryland) more than doubled their black migration gains of the 1975–1980 period. Texas is no longer among the top ten black magnet states, falling behind Nevada and Arizona in the West, Tennessee in the Southeast, and Minnesota, the greatest northern black-gaining state in the late 1980s.

Even greater similarities to recent white migration patterns are seen with black metropolitan area net migration gains. Again, for 1985–1990, blacks

FIGURE 6.7   Net internal migration of black population for 3 periods.

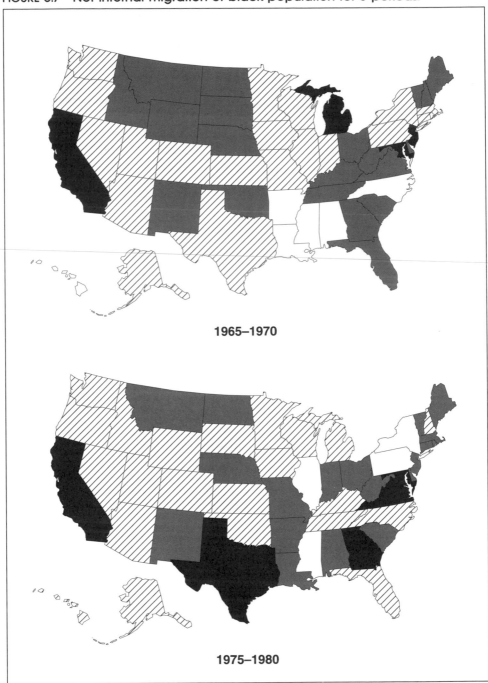

1965–1970

1975–1980

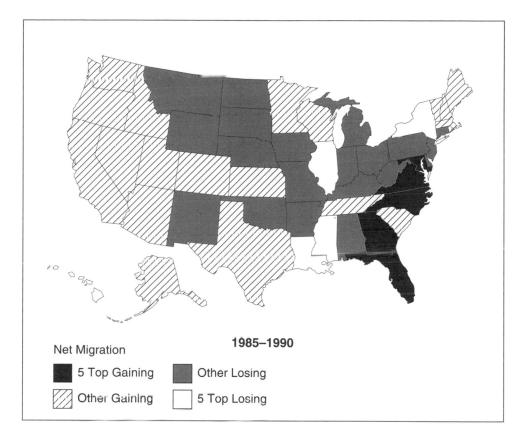

Net Migration

1985–1990

■ 5 Top Gaining   ▨ Other Losing

▨ Other Gaining   □ 5 Top Losing

drawn to the South Atlantic regions selected Atlanta, Washington, D.C., Norfolk, and Raleigh-Durham, as well as many smaller areas and nonmetropolitan communities (see Table 6.3). Among 21 metropolitan areas of all sizes that gained more than 5,000 black net migrants, 15 are located in the South Atlantic region. Blacks, like whites, were attracted to the dynamic economies of this region's larger metropolitan areas as well as to its growing manufacturing communities, university towns, and coastal retirement areas. Also important is the continued lure of friends and family kinship networks for black return migrants from the North. While South Atlantic metro areas dominated as black migrant destinations, Dallas and San Diego also received large numbers. Increased black migration also occurred to Sacramento, Las Vegas, and Phoenix in the West and Minneapolis-St. Paul in the North—again, consistent with 1980s white patterns.

The two metropolitan areas which still house the largest black populations in the country—New York and Chicago—together accounted for a quarter-million net migration loss of blacks over the 1985–1990 period. New to the 1980s were migration losses for the two historic West Coast black metro destinations—Los Angeles and San Francisco. These 1980s trends, more consistent with white shifts, do not reinforce earlier black distribution trends. Still, more so than whites, blacks were prone to select southern metro destinations and those with significant existing black communities.

GEOGRAPHIC SHIFTS BY POVERTY AND SKILL LEVEL

The previous section showed how post–1980 redistribution across regions and metro areas became segmented by race and ethnicity. The present section addresses the question: Has redistribution also become segmented on measures of socioeconomic status? Two such measures, education attainment and poverty status, will be evaluated. Both are related to migration decision making (Long 1988; Lansing and Mueller 1967). As a proxy for skill level, education distinguishes between college graduates—who are more likely to move long distances in response to a nationwide labor market—and those with lesser educations. Persons in poverty are often less mobile than other population segments, and their destinations are often influenced by the availability of friends and family.

Redistribution became segmented across the status dimensions of education attainment and poverty status. The widening disparities in earnings potential available to college-degreed persons as compared with lesser-educated persons occurred while regional industrial restructuring trends created greater spatial separation between the locations of "knowledge-based" employment opportunities and those that required lesser skills (Noyelle and Stanback 1984). Poverty populations became more entrenched in certain rural parts of the country and in select metropolitan areas. Moreover, the higher poverty levels of some race and ethnic groups, which remain concentrated in specific regions, heighten the poverty levels of those regions.

The discussion that follows addresses three broad questions: Just how segmented are post–1980 redistribution patterns on the dimensions of education attainment and poverty status? To what extent do race and ethnic distributions account for these patterns? And what roles do selective immigration and internal migration play in the process?

Metro Areas

Metro areas that show large gains or declines in the total population might be expected to show these same patterns for different population subgroups—particularly if they are large, diverse metropolises. However, this is not the case. Distinct distribution patterns for different economic and educational groups show that different individual metro areas gain or lose population for these groups—in some cases, as a consequence of their racial compositions.

The upper portion of Table 6.4 contrasts the largest individual metro areas

TABLE 6.4   Metropolian areas with greatest 1980–1990 population increases, by poverty and education attainment status.

Growth Rank	1980–1990 Increase (1,000s)	Metros Areas	Growth Rank	1980–1990 Increase (1,000s)	Metro Areas
		Poverty Population			Nonpoverty Population
1	529	Los Angeles	1	2419	Los Angeles
2	233	Houston	2	810	San Francisco-Oakland
3	162	Dallas-Fort Worth	3	778	Dallas-Fort Worth
4	134	Miami	4	664	Atlanta
5	116	Detroit	5	659	Washington, D.C.
6	101	Phoenix	6	623	New York
7	73	San Diego	7	561	San Diego
8	67	Fresno	8	500	Phoenix
9	60	McAllen-TX	9	420	Seattle
10	60	San Antonio	10	396	Miami
11	57	Milwaukee	11	394	Tampa-St. Petersburg
12	54	Minneapolis-St. Paul	12	362	Houston
13	54	El Paso-TX	13	340	Orlando
14	52	Pittsburgh	14	318	Sacramento
15	51	Sacramento	15	273	Minneapolis-St. Paul
		College Graduates			Less than College Graduate
1	996	New York	1	1482	Los Angeles
2	727	Los Angeles	2	457	Dallas-Fort Worth
3	460	San Francisco-Oakland	3	392	San Francisco-Oakland
4	385	Chicago	4	358	Houston
5	370	Washington, D.C.	5	328	Atlanta
6	301	Boston	6	327	Phoenix
7	298	Philadelphia	7	315	San Diego
8	282	Dallas-Fort Worth	8	302	Miami
9	232	Atlanta	9	279	Tampa-St. Petersburg
10	178	Seattle	10	259	Washington, D.C.
11	174	Houston	11	243	Seattle
12	170	San Diego	12	204	New York
13	158	Minneapolis-St. Paul	13	196	Sacramento
14	153	Detroit	14	195	Orlando
15	140	Baltimore	15	182	Las Vegas

gaining in poverty with those gaining in nonpoverty populations over the 1980–1990 decade. (Note that poverty refers to the pretax cash income of the migrant in 1989.) This table shows the net change in poverty population in metropolises. Some of the increase is due to the inmigration of people who were poor in 1990, but some is attributable to increasing poverty among long-term residents. It is noteworthy that only eight metro areas appear on *both* top 15 lists and that only two—Los Angeles and Dallas—appear among the top six on each. Metros gaining large numbers of people who fell below the poverty line tend to be those with a large Hispanic presence, as well as port-of-entry areas for recent immigrants. They include smaller-sized border areas (McAllen and El Paso, Texas) as well as northern manufacturing areas with large numbers of impoverished blacks (Detroit, Milwaukee). The metros gaining the most nonpoverty persons represent a broader geographic spread, including national and regional financial centers (San Francisco, Atlanta), government centers (Washington, D.C.), as well as resort and retirement areas (Tampa-St. Petersburg, Orlando). Presumably, low-skill migrants avoid moving to these metros.

Turning to educational attainment, the lower portion of Table 6.4 contrasts metro areas with greatest 1980–1990 gains in college graduates with metro areas that gained the largest numbers of people with less than a college education. Again, these data refer to net changes in the 1980s, due to both selective migration and changes in the attainment of long-term residents. Although there is an overlap of areas on both lists (9 of 15 areas), this overlap occurs primarily with South and West region metro areas (New York is the lone northern region exception). A good part of the attraction for college graduates is attributable to the industrial structures of the particular metro areas listed in Table 6.4. These include large corporate and "advanced service" centers at both the national and regional levels, with occupation structures heavily weighted toward professionals and managers. Alternatively, several of the Sunbelt areas attracting many migrants with a less-than-college education are retirement centers, consumer service centers, and areas that have attracted large numbers of immigrants.

Poverty, Education, and Minority Shifts

Are the 1980s distribution disparities by poverty and skill level related to these areas' racial compositions? Several race-specific analyses (not shown) indicate that the answer is generally "no"—at least for whites and blacks (Frey 1993b). When focusing on poverty status, significant geographic growth disparities exist between the poverty and nonpoverty populations *within* the white and black racial groups. In contrast, the geographic differences between the Hispanic poverty and nonpoverty growth patterns are not substantial. Hence, more so than for whites or blacks, Hispanic gains tend to be associated with poverty gains. Asian poverty levels are much lower than Hispanic levels, so Asian population gains are not linked to large poverty increases.

Poverty, immigration, and "flight." Poverty populations have grown sharply in several large immigrant port-of-entry states and metro areas, and internal migrants who are below the poverty line are being pushed to other parts of the country. Many of these areas are attracting college-educated internal migrants at the same time that they are losing poverty migrants via internal migration. These migration dynamics suggest that the minority gains and white population losses observed for high immigration metropolitan areas will be most pronounced at the lower end of the socioeconomic status spectrum. The impact of immigration on poverty population change was most evident in the Los Angeles metropolitan area. Over the 1985–1990 period, Los Angeles attracted 207,000 poverty migrants who were classified as impoverished by the census of 1990.[6] This represents the sum of 282,000 poverty immigrants from abroad and the net outmigration of 75,000 poverty internal migrants to other parts of the United States. Among the poverty immigrants from abroad, the majority were Hispanics.

California is the state with the largest poverty gains from all migration sources; Florida (with 180,000) is second; and New York and Texas (65,000 and 62,000) come next. An additional eight states gained between 30,000 and 62,000 poverty migrants from all sources. But California, New York, and Texas received *all* of their poverty migration gains through immigration because they registered net losses of internal poverty migrants in their exchanges with other states. In contrast, Florida's poverty gains were more equally divided between immigrants from abroad and internal inmigrants from other states. This is also the case for Washington and Arizona, which rank fifth and sixth, respectively, in total poverty migration gains from all sources in the late 1980s.

The late 1980s migration data show a consistent pattern in which states and metro areas that receive large flows of poverty immigrants from abroad lose their existing poverty migrants through internal migration to other states. Of the ten largest immigration metro areas over the 1985–1990 period (shown in Table 6.2), seven had net losses of internal poverty migrants to other parts of the country. In fact, led by the New York metro area with a net loss of 166,000 internal migrants impoverished in 1990, five of these areas had the greatest outflows of poverty persons through internal migration among all metro areas. These patterns suggest that the impact of immigration in these port-of-entry areas exerts the greatest strains on economic prospects for the less well-off segments of the native-born population. Immigrants are competing with less-skilled native workers for jobs, leading some of the natives to move away.

At the same time, many of these metro areas continue to attract college graduate migrants through internal migration from other states. For example, the Los Angeles metropolitan area had a net gain of 59,000 college graduates over the same period that it lost poverty migrants through internal migration. Seven of the ten highest immigrant-attracting metros also gained college graduates that were internal migrants. These high immigration metro areas, which pull college graduates and push poverty migrants in their exchanges with other states, have diversified economies that continue to create employment opportunities in professional and high-skilled jobs, but the low-skilled jobs in such places are increasingly filled by immigrants from abroad. (Mollenkopf and Castells 1991; Waldinger 1989).

"Segmented" migration by poverty, skill level, and race.   Aside from patterns for high immigration areas, the pushes and pulls of internal migration streams differ across status dimensions. This is indicated on the maps in Figure 6.8 which contrast late 1980s internal migration patterns for college graduates with those of the poverty population. States are classified by the net numbers of college graduates or poverty population they gained or lost in their exchange of internal migrants with other states between 1985 and 1990. College graduate destinations are much more focused toward the growing South Atlantic and West Coast states, which have economically revived in the late 1980s. Poverty migration patterns are much more diffuse, spreading over a broader swath of states. Also, poverty internal migrants are moving away from the high immigration states—particularly New York, Illinois, Texas, New Jersey, and California. The latter outmigration reflects the push of competition with immigrants to these states for low-pay jobs, rather than the more focused pulls for college graduate migrants (Abowd and Freeman 1991). The internal migration data for individual metropolitan areas (not shown) reveal similar disparities. Several metropolitan areas, such as Los Angeles, Washington, D.C., and San Francisco, which registered highest college graduate gains via internal migration, were among the top senders of poverty migrants to other parts of the country.

Migration differences by socioeconomic status are evident within both the white and black populations. White internal migration patterns by educational attainment and poverty status are similar to those for the total population (see Figure 6.8). While black patterns do not exactly follow those of whites, the states and metro areas that attract black poverty migrants are largely different from those that attract black college graduates. During the late 1980s, black poverty net migration was most strongly directed to smaller nonmetropolitan communities in the South Atlantic states and to selected areas of the Midwest. Internal migration to familiar locations of family and friends accounted for much of this movement. In contrast, major destinations for black college graduate migrants included large cosmopolitan areas, both inside the South (Atlanta, Washington, D.C., Dallas, Miami) and out (Los Angeles, San Francisco), as well as the growing recreation center of Orlando. Of the ten top metro magnets for black poverty and college graduate internal migrants, only Atlanta and Raleigh-Durham appear on both lists. There is, in fact, a greater overlap in the destinations of black and white college graduates. The states of Georgia, California, Florida, and Virginia are among the top six destination states for both white and black college graduates during the 1980s (Frey 1994a).

Within high immigration areas, it is the minority-dominant poverty immigrant

FIGURE 6.8   1985–1990 net internal migration for college graduates and
poverty populations.

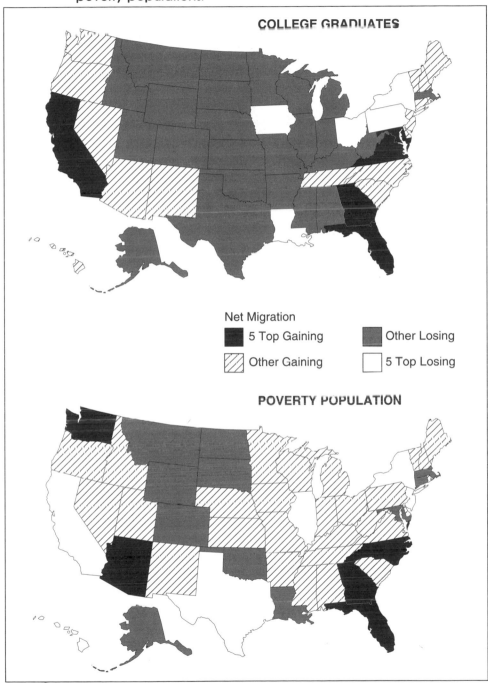

NOTE: States are classified by the net numbers of college graduates or poverty population they gained or lost
in their exchange of internal migrants with other states between 1985 and 1990. Poverty status is defined on
the basis of cash income received in 1989.

stream that exerts an economic push on low- and middle-income native-born, leading to their outmigration. Because the latter migrants are largely white, these dynamics will lead to a new socioeconomic status structure in these areas where lower-income, less-educated segments of the population are most likely to be minorities. This impact has already been felt in California, where the 1990 census shows a minority of whites in the following population segments: under age 25; less than high school educations; incomes below twice the poverty income; and male workers in service, farming, operator, and laborer occupations. These categories were strongly impacted by the 1985–1990 minority-dominated immigration from abroad and white-dominated internal outmigration from the state (Frey 1994d).

SPATIAL GENERATION GAPS: ADULT BOOMERS AND THE ELDERLY

Just as population shifts across the nation have become segmented by race, ethnicity, and social status, they are also becoming segmented by age. Historically, migration has been more frequent among young adults in their early labor force years, and they tend to be directed to areas with growing employment opportunities. Middle-aged workers do not move nearly as frequently. While the economics of the labor market play a large role in their migration patterns, personal preferences, amenities, and family ties are also considered. Finally, the retired population migrates at low rates, but to selected destinations. For them, employment opportunities are less important than quality of life, climate, amenities, and proximity to relatives. Yet elderly distribution shifts are not only affected by selective migration, but also by the aging-in-place of newly retired cohorts who remain where they live as they get older (Rogers and Woodward 1988).

Because of their different motivations, the geographic redistribution patterns of these three age groups differ from each other. During the 1980s, the young adult population (aged 25–34 in 1990) was synonymous with the late baby boom cohorts—born 1956–1965. Although well-educated, these large cohorts encountered strained entry-level job opportunities during the 1980s, and their migration patterns were strongly driven by the decade's bicoastal growth patterns. During the same decade, the early baby boom cohorts, born before 1955, entered into middle age. Although more settled, some of these older boomers were pushed by the economic downturns in the interior parts of the country, and drawn to fast-growing regions as well as to some high-amenity areas. Lastly, the elderly population continued to swell during the 1980s due to the retirement of large cohorts born just after World War I. Their movement patterns were directed southward, even more sharply than those of the two baby boomer groups.

Migration of Younger Boomers

Did later baby boomers direct themselves to destinations like Washington, D.C., San Francisco, and Atlanta—celebrated for attracting early baby boom "gentrifiers" and "yuppies" back in the 1970s? While these generally well educated, late baby boomers shared some of the career aspirations and wanderlust that characterized the older boomers when they were young adults a decade earlier, these late boomers were also more practical (Jones 1980). Having lived through and observed the effects of the mid-1970s economy on many older boomers' employment prospects—relegating many to reside in small Southwest towns rather than Nob Hill, Georgetown, or Greenwich Village—and adjusting to the higher 1980s housing costs, the late baby boomers were less attracted to the bright lights of glamour cities than to growing areas with more moderate living costs. This is evident from the list of metro areas that attracted most late baby boom internal migrants in the late 1980s (see Table 6.5).

Although Washington, D.C., still appears among the top gainers for late boomers, most of the areas attracting these young adults are in the growing South Atlantic and Pacific or Mountain regions. Not long-time centers of culture or the arts, many are upstart growth centers, such as Orlando, Las Vegas, and Charlotte, or metros like Sacramento and Portland, Oregon, which have not, historically, dominated their regions. "Interior" metros, Minneapolis-St. Paul and Dallas, are also on the list. Their strong, diversified economic bases set them apart from their immediate regional contexts. The traditional California young adult "magnets"—San Francisco and Los Angeles—still gained these young migrants in the 1980s. However, San Francisco now ranks fourteenth, behind Phoenix and Baltimore, and Los Angeles ranks eighteenth, behind West Palm Beach, Nashville, and Kansas City. Declining employment prospects and increased living costs in these areas made them far less attractive destinations.

The areas that lost most young boomers due to internal migration do not closely overlap with those for the general population (compare Table 6.5 with Table 6.2). Large numbers of boomers, like the general population, migrated away from New York and such areas as New Orleans, Pittsburgh, and Houston, which experienced economic downturns during the 1980s. However, many boomers also left Honolulu and places with large college populations, such as Boston, Austin, Oklahoma City, Provo, Utah, and Bryan College Station, Texas. These places typically lose many young adult migrants, since those enrolled in college at one date usually live elsewhere five years later. Young boomers were also moving away from nonmetropolitan communities in the same parts of the country that attracted large numbers of young adults in the recession-ridden 1970s. Between 1985–1990, nonmetropolitan areas in the South and West regions of the country experienced a net outmigration of young-adult baby boomers.

TABLE 6.5 List of metropolitan areas with greatest internal migration gains and losses for baby boomers and the elderly: 1985–1990.

Greatest Gains due to Internal Migration, 1985–1990*

	Late Baby Boomers†		Early Baby Boomers‡		Elderly§	
Rank	Area	Size	Area	Size	Area	Size
1	Atlanta	84,340	Atlanta	36,151	Tampa-St. Petersburg	33,580
2	Seattle	57,971	Seattle	27,202	West Palm Beach	27,569
3	Washington, D.C.	52,476	Tampa-St. Petersburg	23,166	Phoenix	20,966
4	Orlando	34,558	Orlando	22,816	Las Vegas	14,180
5	Minneapolis-St. Paul	33,742	Sacramento	21,286	Fort Pierce, Fl.	11,362
6	Sacramento	29,446	Las Vegas	20,528	Fort Myers, Fl.	11,348
7	Las Vegas	28,518	Phoenix	19,684	Miami	11,070
8	Dallas	26,491	West Palm Beach	14,770	Lakeland, Fl.	10,569
9	Charlotte	25,799	Portland, Or.	13,515	San Diego	10,171
10	Portland, Or.	25,700	San Diego	11,782	Daytona Beach	9,731

Greatest Losses due to Internal Migration, 1985–1990

	Late Baby Boomers		Early Baby Boomers		Elderly	
Rank	Area	Size	Area	Size	Area	Size
1	New York	−156,407	New York	−155,157	New York	−156,360
2	Boston	−25,319	Chicago	−37,524	Los Angeles	−51,949
3	New Orleans	−22,401	Houston	−33,123	Chicago	−42,981
4	Oklahoma City	−19,455	Los Angeles	−31,108	Detroit	−22,759
5	Austin	−19,002	Boston	−28,100	San Francisco	−21,883
6	Pittsburgh	−18,491	San Francisco	−24,605	Boston	−17,132
7	Honolulu	−17,069	Denver	−17,650	Washington, D.C.	−12,977
8	Houston	−16,903	New Orleans	−17,056	Philadelphia	−12,327
9	Provo, Ut.	−14,162	Detroit	−12,533	Cleveland	−9,097
10	Bryan College Station	−14,064	Pittsburgh	−10,951	Pittsburgh	−8,103

SOURCE: Tabulations of "Residence 5 Years Ago" question from 1990 U.S. Census of Population.

* 1985–1990 inmigrants from elsewhere in the United States, minus 1985–1990 outmigrants to elsewhere in the United States.
† Born between 1956–1965 (ages 25–34 in 1990).
‡ Born between 1946–1955 (ages 35–44 in 1990).
§ Ages 65 and older in 1990.

Migration of Older Boomers

The early baby boomers, born between 1946 and 1955, entered their late thirties and forties over the 1980–1990 decade. In the 1970s, as young adults, their redistribution patterns were heavily shaped by employment declines in the industrialized Northeast and Midwest. Aside from the growth in large urban yuppie meccas, the northern job shake-out served to direct their migration to the South and West, as well as to smaller and nonmetropolitan communities.[7] During the 1980s, the continued downsizing in manufacturing and, later, in service employment exerted further "pushes" from selected northern areas. At the same time, energy and resource-based declines in interior areas, and immigration-related competition in port-of-entry areas broadened the geography of places that lost older baby boomers in the late 1980s.

The bottom panel of Table 6.5 shows that the metropolises with greatest net outmigration included northern places (New York, Chicago, Boston, Detroit, Pittsburgh), southern locations (Houston, and New Orleans), and western port-of-entry metros (Los Angeles and San Francisco). Several of these large metros (especially Los Angeles, San Francisco, and Denver) constituted popular magnets for baby boomers in the 1970s, so it is clear that the geography of opportunities has changed sharply as these cohorts entered middle age.

The major gaining metros for early baby boomers show some overlap with those that attracted late baby boomers. Atlanta, Seattle, Orlando, Sacramento, and Las Vegas—all in growing regions—were among the top magnets for both groups of boomers. Older boomers, however, were more prone than younger boomers to locate in warmer metros, which also attract large numbers of retirees. Some of this movement may reflect preferences as well as economics among the more affluent middle-aged population. Among the 50 states, Florida represents the overwhelming destination for 35–44-year-old migrants. It attracted over 150,000 early baby boomers in the late 1980s—placing well ahead of Georgia, which attracted about 50,000, and the state of Washington, which attracted 42,000.

The Mobile Elderly

Because elderly migrants are more strongly attracted to warm weather, amenities, and social services, it is not surprising that metro areas in Florida dominated the list of elderly migration magnets during the late 1980s. Tampa-St. Petersburg and West Palm Beach, together, gained more than the 60,000 elderly migrants that they lost over the 1985–1990 period.[8] In fact, the state of Florida gained over 200,000 elderly net migrants during the late 1980s—5 times the gain to Arizona, the second ranking state (at 40,000), and more than 9 times that of North Carolina, which ranked third (at 17,000). Still, elderly net migration gains are spread along a broad swath of Sunbelt and high-amenity states in

FIGURE 6.9 1985–1990 net internal migration for late baby boomers, early baby boomers, and elderly populations.

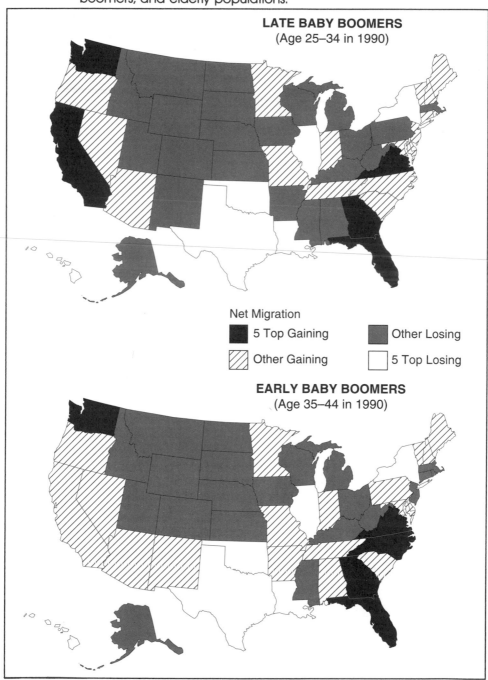

NOTE: States are classified by the net number of migrants in designated age groups gained or lost in the exchange of internal migrants with other states.

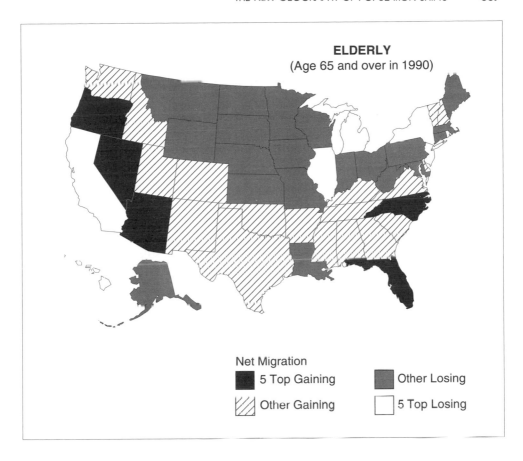

ELDERLY
(Age 65 and over in 1990)

Net Migration
- 5 Top Gaining
- Other Gaining
- Other Losing
- 5 Top Losing

the Pacific and Mountain West (see Figure 6.9). Phoenix and Las Vegas are two large elderly magnets in this region.

Just as the Sunbelt represents a strong attraction for elderly migrants, the Snowbelt lends a strong push. Net outmigration of the elderly population during the late 1980s was heavily concentrated among the states and metropolitan areas in the Midwest, Northeast, and Eastern Seaboard. The motivation here has less to do with employment decline than with the severe winters and the high costs of living in these regions. New York, Chicago, and Detroit are major northern contributors to the elderly migration south.

What is most surprising among areas losing elderly population through internal migration is the high magnitude of losses for Los Angeles and San Francisco metro areas, which contribute to a significant elderly net outmigration for the state of California as a whole. The strong 1980s push from this once magnet state for the elderly, has less to do with its temperature or climate than with high housing costs and crowding. Elderly residents who owned homes are able to trade in their equity for more tranquil environments at much lower costs, in other amenity-laden states. In fact, the high elderly outmigration from California is largely responsible for recent gains in the neighboring states of Oregon, Nevada, and Arizona. California excepted, elderly migration is a Snowbelt to Sunbelt phenomenon and stands in contrast to the interior-bicoastal migration shifts followed by the two working-aged baby boomer groups.

Elderly Growth and "Aging" Areas

Aging-in-place and migration.   An area's elderly population can also grow from aging-in-place, which refers to people under age 65 growing older without moving. Areas with relatively large 60–64-year-old populations will increase their elderly populations via this component, assuming that this group does not migrate out of the area as they reach their retirement years. Aging-in-place was a particularly important component of elderly growth during the 1980s because the large birth cohorts of the years 1916–1925 increased the elderly population in most parts of the country. As a result, the nation's elderly population grew by 22 percent over the decade, even though the total population (of all ages) grew by just under 10 percent. Most states, metropolitan areas, and counties in the United States increased their elderly population during the decade even if they lost some of their elderly population through net outmigration.

The amenity-laden Florida retirement center metros increased their populations primarily through inmigration. But for a larger number of metropolitan areas, the aging-in-place component was most important. These areas were located in parts of the country that have prospered economically in recent decades and, as a result, have built up sizable working-aged populations who are now beginning to enter their elderly years. Such areas tend to be located in the coastal South and West. Even California, which experienced late-1980s losses in their elderly populations via migration, increased its elderly population overall as a result of aging-in-place and some immigration of older persons from abroad. (The state's − 35,000 net migration loss of elderly during the 1985–1990 period is well overshadowed by an estimated 864,000 gain attributable to aging-in-place.)[9]

Areas that increased their elderly populations rapidly, due to selective inmigration, select the most affluent, younger retired elderly. This segment of the elderly population is typically in good health, is comprised of largely husband-wife households, and possesses sufficient disposable income to benefit the local economies.

The older, less mobile segment of the elderly population is more often beset by health problems and is disproportionately made up of widows who survive their male spouses. It is more common in areas that the younger elderly have moved away from. If these households move, it is typically to be near relatives or other long-term friends who can supply social and financial support.[10]

Areas with slow-growing or declining elderly populations are neither attracting large numbers of younger elderly migrants nor benefiting from aging-in-place growth. These areas typically have histories of economic decline and have not attracted large numbers of working-aged populations. As a consequence, social support services for their elderly populations are not plentiful, which adds further push to the outmigration of their young elderly populations. Such areas are concentrated in the nation's interior—in states of the Rustbelt, the Farmbelt, and Oil Patch regions. This situation also characterizes a large number of economically depressed nonmetropolitan counties, which contrast sharply with those rural and exurban retirement counties that continued to attract elderly migrants during the 1980s (Crispell and Frey 1993; Johnson 1993).

Elderly concentration.   Apart from the growth or decline of the elderly population, an area's elderly concentration (percentage of the total population that is aged 65 and above) is an index of the elderly population's impact on the area's social service requirements, tax base, and even political orientation. While 13 percent of the country's population is elderly, elderly concentration varies across individual metropolitan areas, ranging from 4 percent in Anchorage, Alaska, to 32 percent in Sarasota, Florida.

It is important to distinguish between the two primary ways that a high elderly concentration can come about. The first occurs in largely retirement communities where the elderly population grows faster than the nonelderly population, as a consequence of selective elderly inmigration. In other areas, elderly concentration arises not because of higher elderly growth levels but because of the slow growth of the nonelderly population who outmigrate. If young people consistently move away from an area, eventually a large fraction of its population will be elderly.

The first type of elderly concentration is seen in a much more positive light than the second. Because of the migration selectivity associated with young retirees, retirement communities tend to attract younger elderly with positive sociodemographic characteristics who contribute to economic growth in their destination areas, including job creation in the service and health care sectors. Furthermore, their income stream is stable and, to some degree, adjusted for inflation since it is based on Social Security and pension benefits. The second type of elderly concentration occurs in economically depressed areas, where the younger population moves out, leaving behind a nonmobile aging elderly population with less favorable sociodemographic characteristics. At the extreme, such areas are saddled with large dependent elderly populations that become reliant on declining economies and tax bases for their social and medical services (Longino 1990).

Metropolitan areas that rank on the very top of the list of elderly concentration tend to be the resort and retirement areas located, mostly, in Florida. Sarasota, Bradenton, and Ft. Myers—Florida metropolitan areas each house 1990 populations that are more than one-quarter elderly; and an additional six Florida metros have elderly concentrations that are greater than 20 percent. These places attracted large numbers of rather prosperous retirees. Yet the next highest echelon of elderly-concentrated areas include such metros as Pittsburgh, Johnstown, and Altoona, Pennsylvania; Wheeling, West Virginia; and Duluth, Minnesota—places losing their younger populations for decades. In fact, the upper third of all metropolitan areas, when ranked on elderly concentration, are more often located in the slow-growing northern and interior parts of the country than in the retirement centers of Florida, Arizona, and the Mountain West (Glasgow 1988).

In contrast to the 1970s, elderly and nonelderly growth patterns tended to diverge in the 1980s (Frey 1992b). Overall, nonelderly 1980s population gains accrued to metro areas in the coastal South and parts of the West—driven by economic "pulls" affecting labor force-aged migration. In contrast, elderly population shifts were slower-paced, less driven by migration (compared to aging-in-place), and they continued to filter to smaller metro and nonmetro communities in selected parts of the Sunbelt, such as Naples, Florida, and Yuma, Arizona. As a consequence, northern areas continued to lose their labor force-aged populations at a greater rate than their elderly populations—and within the Sunbelt, nonelderly growth focused on larger areas, while elderly growth was directed to smaller ones. This latter pattern, in particular, contrasted with the 1970s when both elderly and nonelderly components of the population helped to fuel the so-called rural renaissance.

Especially during the 1980s, the rise in elderly concentration was shaped by the selective outmigration of the nonelderly population, rather than the growth of the elderly population. Areas that encountered the most dramatic elderly concentration increases included northern interior areas of all sizes, such as Cleveland, Peoria, and Dubuque, and smaller-sized Sunbelt areas, such as Beaumont in Texas and Great Falls in Montana. This is primarily a consequence of their loss of young population. On the other hand, the urban-directed migration of the younger population served to *reduce* the elderly concentration in many large Sunbelt magnets (Frey 1992b). This was the case for Orlando, Dallas, Atlanta, and Tampa. While many of these areas also gained elderly migrants, their even stronger draw for working-aged migrants and immigrants from abroad reduced their level of elderly concentration.

WITHIN METRO AREAS, THE SUBURBS DOMINATE

The focus now turns to population shifts within the metropolitan areas, with particular emphasis on central city–suburb contrasts.[11] The population dynamics between central cities and their suburbs changed considerably since the 1950s, when the suburbs were primarily bedroom communities, and most of the metropolitan area's business, shopping, and entertainment took place within the confines of the central cities. During the 1950s and 1960s, suburbanization exploded to such an extent that, for the first time, the 1970 suburban population exceeded the central city population for the nation. During the 1980s, as in the 1970s, the country's suburban population grew at a slower pace than during the immediate postwar years. However, most metro residents already lived there.

The conventional definition of suburbia—the entire territory of the metropolitan area beyond the statistically designated central city—includes land uses and housing and population characteristics that would not have been previously designated as suburban. The broad territory surrounding major central cities has become a patchwork that includes inner suburbs, large suburban cities, office parks, retail centers, a few manufacturing communities dating from World War I, and even low-density, rural territory—in addition to the stereotypic bedroom communities. Although most of the city-suburb analysis that follows will conform to the conventional "central city versus rest-of-metro" definition, it will also discuss the growing heterogeneity of today's suburbs.

Modest City Rebounds

Just as metropolitan area growth dynamics vary widely across a country, so do growth and decline patterns of central cities and their surrounding suburbs. Because of their longer histories and greater opportunities for suburban spread, older central cities tend to comprise a smaller portion of the metropolitan populations.[12] They are at later stages of suburbanization and are more prone to show population declines or smaller growth than younger cities. Since central city declines are exacerbated when the entire metropolitan area is undergoing an economic downturn, it is not surprising that all large central cities in the older Northeast and Midwest regions lost population back in the 1970s (see Table 6.6). Most large cities in these regions lost at least 10 percent of their population, and three hard-hit areas—Detroit, Cleveland, and St. Louis—lost roughly one-fifth of their population during this period.

With this backdrop, the 1980s brought a rebound of population growth for many of these larger central cities. In some cases, entire metropolitan areas also rebounded economically. Still, industrial structures in certain kinds of metropolitan areas tend to favor the central city, typically in advanced service cities that are home to corporate headquarters, financial institutions, medical centers, and the like. Therefore, the 1980s rebound for these kinds of activities favored cities like New York, Boston, Los Angeles, San Francisco, Atlanta, and Dallas.

Yet even these central cities, which hold niches as corporate, finance, or information centers, do not dominate their metropolitan areas—either economi-

TABLE 6.6 Percent change in central city(s) and suburbs of 25 large metropolitan areas and for region, metropolitan categories: 1960–1990.

Region and Metropolitan Area*	1990 Metro Size (1,000's)	1990 Percent in City	Central City Percent 10 Year Change			Suburbs Percent 10 Year Change		
			1960–1970	1970–1980	1980–1990	1960–1970	1970–1980	1980–1990
Northeast								
New York	8747	84%	1%	-10%	4%	22%	2%	2%
Philadelphia	4857	35	-3	-14	-6	25	6	8
Boston	3784	33	2	-7	3	16	2	4
Pittsburgh	2057	19	-14	-18	-13	4	-1	-6
Midwest								
Chicago	6070	48	-5	-11	-7	40	13	7
Detroit	4382	28	-8	-19	-13	31	10	2
Cleveland	1831	28	-14	-24	-12	27	1	0
Minneapolis-St. Paul	2464	30	-2	-12	1	51	22	23
St. Louis	2444	25	-11	-22	-9	31	9	7
Cincinnati	1453	25	-10	-15	-6	22	9	7
Milwaukee	1432	48	-2	-9	0	27	10	5
Kansas City	1566	44	20	-7	1	8	17	17
South								
Washington, D.C.	3924	21	1	-14	0	65	17	28
Dallas	2553	48	31	8	16	56	56	48
Houston	3302	51	34	27	3	53	83	48
Miami	1937	33	24	12	9	45	40	25
Atlanta	2834	15	2	-13	-4	58	45	42
Baltimore	2382	32	-3	-12	-6	35	20	17
Tampa-St. Petersburg	2068	30	12	9	4	69	82	43

West								
Los Angeles	8863	48	12	5	18	22	8	19
San Francisco	1604	45	-3	-5	7	30	6	9
Seattle	1973	31	-1	-5	8	64	26	31
San Diego	2498	49	28	28	30	36	48	39
Phoenix	2122	73	67	44	36	-5	104	56
Denver	1623	29	4	-4	-5	62	58	23
Region Totals								
Northeast	45886	37	10	-1	3	21	6	5
Midwest	42421	41	13	3	3	23	14	6
South	60342	41	22	22	17	21	38	25
West	44658	42	28	23	24	30	29	25
U.S. Totals								
Large metropolitan	111187	40	18	8	12	31	18	17
Medium metropolitan	59605	39	16	14	12	16	23	14
Small metropolitan	22515	47	13	15	8	6	24	8
Total	193307	40%	17%	11%	12%	23%	20%	15%

NOTES: Large metropolitan areas have 1990 populations exceeding one million; medium metropolitan areas have 1990 populations exceeding 250,000. Data are for geographically constant metropolises.

*Metropolitan areas, central cities, and suburbs are based on MSA, PMSA, and NECMA definitions as designated on June 30, 1990. Names are abbreviated.

cally or demographically—in the way they once had. For example, Philadelphia's central city population accounted for 56 percent of the metro population in 1950, as compared with only 35 percent in 1990.[13] In many younger South and West metro areas, some city population gains (e.g., Dallas, San Diego, Phoenix) can be attributed to their "overboundedness"—linked to a past, generous annexation of suburban territory.[14]

Another important, often dominant source of growth for some central cities during this decade was immigration. As in the past, immigrant minorities were drawn to central city locations that house existing enclaves of same country-of-origin residents. Immigration played a dominant role in the 1980s population growth in New York City, Los Angeles, San Francisco, and Miami.

For a variety of reasons, central cities of the nation's largest metropolitan areas showed a 1980s rebound in population growth. The only large central cities that sustained significant population declines over the 1980s were clustered around the Great Lakes Rustbelt—Detroit, Pittsburgh, Cleveland, St. Louis, and Chicago. Even these declines were moderated at the decade's end as their metropolitan area economies adapted to the jolts inflicted by earlier manufacturing downsizing. Still, none of these central city rebounds should be misinterpreted as city revival. City population gains that draw from particular economic niches or immigrant waves displacing long-gone suburbanites will not bring back the grander, more dominant central city that shaped urban America during most of its history. Rather than causing a revival, these trends merely buy a continued survival of central cities in what has become a suburban-dominated society.

Patchwork Suburbs

America is in the suburbs. The suburbs are America. Both of these statements are valid, statistically, when referring to the suburbs as conventionally defined. That is, if suburbia is considered to be all of the metropolitan territory that lies outside its central cities, then 60 percent of metropolitan America is suburban. The full range of population, housing, and land use characteristics that one can find in any part of America can be found somewhere in America's suburbs.

If this is true, then the term suburban—using this broad definition—loses its meaning. To say that 115 million Americans now live in the suburbs does not imply much that is distinct about their lifestyles, class backgrounds, or political leanings. It is more important to understand how differences in these attributes are emerging *within* the broad expanse of suburban territory which takes in full-fledged suburban cities, smaller communities, and unincorporated rural territory. Garreau coined the term Edge City to denote suburban centers that became transformed from residential, rural, or mixed-use territory into an area that is a center of jobs, shopping, and entertainment—whether or not the area is an actual place, as defined by political boundaries. Using empirical data as well as his journalistic skills, Garreau identified 203 such Edge Cities inside 36 large metropolitan areas. Many of these do not have names that one can find in standard census volumes. Examples are: "28 & Mass Pike" surrounding Boston; "the Galleria area" in suburban Houston; and "287 & 78" New Jersey, in suburbs of the greater New York area (Garreau 1991).

What, then, does this suburban patchwork imply for our understanding of the changed dynamics within the suburban population? One solution might be to classify suburban territory, as closely as possible, to the following kinds of areas: (1) large, diversified suburban cities; (2) primarily employment centers; (3) primarily residential suburbs; and (4) a residual set of lower density areas (Frey and Speare 1992b). Each of these could be further classed as "inner" and "outer" suburbs based on their proximity to the central city. Speare (1993) applied this classification scheme to evaluate 1980s suburban growth in eight large metro areas representing different regions of the country (Boston, Detroit, Minneapolis-St. Paul, Atlanta, Houston, Phoenix, and Los Angeles). He found that the highest rates of growth occur in the low density residual portions of these metropolitan areas, with the next-highest growth rates associated with outer residential suburbs—then outer employment suburbs. Inner residential suburbs tend to have higher growth rates than inner employment centers, which showed population declines for some metro areas. Speare's study supports this classification of suburban communities.

Suburbanization reaches an even greater level of complexity in the spread of territory that surrounds the nation's largest metropolises. The most extreme example occurs in the greater New York region. This is illustrated in Figure 6.10, which depicts all 12 metropolitan areas that comprise the broader New York region.[15] Social and demographic characteristics of these areas vary with distance from the New York metropolitan area, which lies at the center of the region. The highest population growth rates in the 1980s were in the outlying metro areas: Monmouth-Ocean, and Middlesex-Somerset-Hunterdon, in New Jersey; Orange County, New York; and Danbury, Connecticut. These areas, as well as other outlying metros (Nassau-Suffolk, New York; Stanford, Norwalk, and Bridgeport-Milford, Connecticut), exhibit highest levels of so-called suburban demographic characteristics, such as the percentages of homeownership, family households, married couples, and white populations. At the other extreme lie the inner metros: Jersey City, New Jersey, and, to a lesser extent, Newark, New Jersey. These metro areas registered population declines during the 1980s, have relatively low levels of homeownership, and possess demographic characteristics that are much more consistent with the New York City metro area, located at the center of the region. In many ways this represents the history of the area, since those places closest to New York City were the first to be populated, and their housing stock and physical structures continue to be influenced by decisions of the nineteenth century.

Clearly, important community distinctions can be made both within as well

FIGURE 6.10   Component PMSAs within the Greater New York metropolitan region.

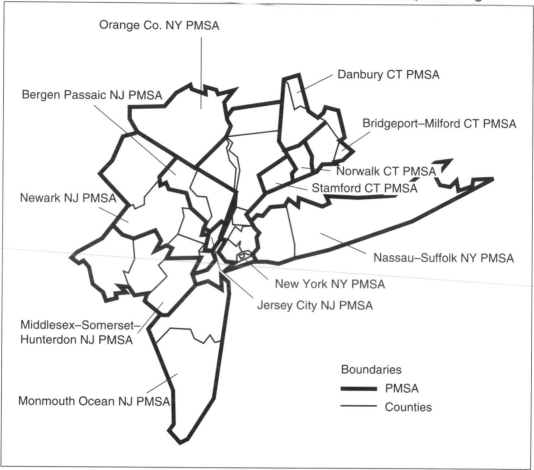

Orange Co. NY PMSA

Danbury CT PMSA

Bergen Passaic NJ PMSA

Bridgeport–Milford CT PMSA

Norwalk CT PMSA

Stamford CT PMSA

Newark NJ PMSA

Nassau–Suffolk NY PMSA

New York NY PMSA

Jersey City NJ PMSA

Middlesex–Somerset–Hunterdon NJ PMSA

Boundaries

▬▬▬ PMSA
─── Counties

Monmouth Ocean NJ PMSA

as across the metros that are associated with the greater New York region. These data illustrate that the suburbanization process in a large metropolis like New York has far-reaching impacts. To the extent that suburban race and ethnic compositions are involved, these impacts will be greatest in major metropolises that continue to receive large influxes of immigrants from abroad (such as Los Angeles and San Francisco) or serve as favored destinations for minority internal migrants (such as Atlanta for blacks).

CITY–SUBURB STATUS GAPS

When the suburbanization movement was just beginning, it was the suburbs that were the distinctive part of the metropolitan area. Suburban migration se-

lected the most affluent residents—those who were able to afford the more expensive suburban housing and lot sizes as well as the increased costs of commuting to central city jobs (Hawley 1971; Frey and Speare 1988). Central cities
still comprised a cross section of the entire urban area's population mix, and it
was the suburbs that were different. This is no longer the case in most of metropolitan America: suburbia is now much more representative of the entire area's
population mix, and it is the central cities that are different.

This section discusses how central cities differ on socioeconomic status characteristics. The city–suburb status gap emerged not only as a consequence of
several decades of selective suburbanization but also, in some areas, to recent
city-directed immigrant flows that add to the less well-off segments of the population. The city–suburb status gap varies across metropolitan areas in different
regions and different suburbanization or immigration histories.[16] It also depends
on the specific status measure that is being compared.

Education Gaps

To what degree are central city populations less well educated than those of
the remainder of the metro area? The answer to this question has implications
for several issues. At the upper end, it is important that cities have a sufficient
pool of well-educated college graduates who might provide leadership in both
government and informal community organizations. At the other end of the
spectrum, there is often a concern that large pools of unskilled, less-educated
workers will not match well with the white-collar, management employment
opportunities that are being created in many central cities. This is especially the
situation in cities that are establishing niches as corporate, financial service, or
information centers for the surrounding metropolitan area or region.[17]

The 1990 census findings indicate that, overall, central cities are less disadvantaged at the upper end of the educational spectrum than they are at the lower
end. That is, in comparison with the rest of the metro area, cities tend to have
smaller shares of college graduates and greater shares of persons with less than
high school educations when compared to their suburbs. But this city–suburb
imbalance is far more lopsided at the lower end of the educational spectrum.
Many college graduates and professionals still choose to live in central cities
because of the amenities and easy access to employment they offer. This is
especially the case for singles and childless couples. For the less-educated segments of the city population, there is often little choice of locating elsewhere,
since they cannot afford the more expensive housing located in the suburban
ring.

Data in Table 6.7 provide evidence for these two different dimensions of the
city-suburb education gap. They also show that these gaps vary across metropolitan areas. In fact, the college graduate gap is either nonexistent or reversed

TABLE 6.7   City–suburb measures of socioeconomic status: 1990,
for selected metro areas and region, metropolitan categories.

Metro Areas, Regions and Metropolitan Categories	Percent College Graduates*			Percent Less than High School*		
	City	Suburbs	Difference	City	Suburbs	Difference
Selected Metro Areas						
New York	23%	34%	11%	32%	18%	14%
Detroit	11	20	9	36	20	16
Atlanta	27	27	0	29	19	10
Los Angeles	23	22	−1	32	28	4
Region Totals						
Northeast	21	25	4	32	19	13
Midwest	20	22	2	26	18	8
South	22	21	−1	27	23	4
West	25	23	−2	23	20	3
U.S. Totals						
Large metropolitan	23	26	3	29	19	10
Medium metropolitan	21	20	−1	26	23	3
Small metropolitan	22	16	−6	23	25	−2
Total	22%	23%	1%	27%	20%	7%

*Persons aged 25 and older.

(such that central cities have the advantage) in metropolitan areas in the South and West. Many of these cities contain upscale, gentrified neighborhoods, and southern central cities have a history of attracting the more elite segments of the urban area. (Schnore 1965). Western metropolitan areas (and some in the South) tend to be "overbounded," where the outer perimeter of central city boundaries takes in neighborhoods and local communities that have more of a suburban character because of annexations after World War II. Smaller metropolitan areas in all four regions show the reverse college graduate gap. Some of this can be explained by the fact that the suburban territory also includes rural and semirural enclaves with older, less well-educated populations.

Although central cities can sometimes attract the best educated segments of the metro area's population, they are much more likely to house a disproportionately high number of the metro's unskilled population. Except for smaller metropolitan areas in the Midwest, South, and West, the status gap is pervasive. Overall gaps are particularly large in older metropolitan areas with significant minority populations, such as New York and Detroit. This is because selective suburbanization has occurred for a longer period of time in these areas. And many central cities house substantial populations with less than high school educations, leading to "mismatches" with the kinds of employment opportunities that are now being created there (see Chapter 5 in Volume 1).

Per Capita Income			Percent Poverty		
City	Suburbs	Difference	City	Suburbs	Difference
$16,334	$24,056	$7,722	19%	7%	12%
$10,056	$17,873	$7,817	30	6	24
$15,332	$17,182	$1,850	26	7	19
$16,128	$16,168	$40	18	12	6
$14,449	$18,328	$3,879	19	6	13
$12,496	$16,488	$3,992	19	6	13
$13,354	$15,066	$1,712	19	10	9
$15,172	$16,458	$1,286	15	10	5
$14,551	$17,953	$3,402	18	7	11
$13,082	$15,091	$2,009	17	9	8
$12,548	$12,692	$144	18	11	7
$13,840	$16,507	$2,667	18%	8%	10%

Income and Poverty Gaps

Measures of income and poverty show a much more consistent status gap across metropolitan areas. The per capita income for the nation's combined central city population was $13,840 in 1990, compared to $16,507 for the suburbs. This gap is higher for large and medium-sized metros in the Northeast and Midwest regions and large metro areas in the South. Smaller metropolitan areas and western metropolitan areas show smaller city-suburb differences, and only occasionally are there "reverse" gaps in these areas.

The overall patterns tend to be reinforced by each minority group and, generally, for whites. A major exception to the latter occurs for whites in some South and West metros, where there is a tendency for wealthy whites to reside in the city and considerably raise the per capita income shown for those areas. This is the case in Atlanta, where the per capita income for whites in the city is more than $9,000 greater than in the suburbs. Still, Atlanta's overall city per capita income is lower than that for the suburbs as a consequence of its large, low-income black population.

The status gap between the central city's and suburb's poverty percentage is more consistent across areas, regions, and races. The national poverty rate in 1990 for all central cities was 18 percent, compared to only 8 percent in the suburbs. However, there were wide variations in the poverty levels across cities.

At the extreme are areas like Detroit, where poverty is exacerbated by the existence of isolated, concentrated poverty ghettos. City-suburb disparities are more pronounced in such areas, which tend to be located in large metros of the Midwest and Northeast regions. These disparities are less sharp in the South and West, particularly in smaller metropolitan areas. For many of the latter, suburban poverty is relatively high due to the existence of rural concentrations of blacks and Hispanics.

Nonetheless, central city poverty rates are generally higher than those of the suburbs. The linkage between poverty and the concentration of minorities in many older, industrial northern cities symbolizes the increased isolation of the central city from the larger metropolitan unit.

MINORITY SUBURBANIZATION AND SEGREGATION

Historically, the residential distribution of minority racial and ethnic groups has been far more clustered within metro areas than has been the case for majority whites. Yet several national demographic trends of the 1980s held out the prospect for a much more widespread residential integration of minorities—both into the suburbs and across a wider range of neighborhoods. One of these trends is the increased size and diversity of immigrant flows which have helped to create demographically diverse populations in several metropolitan areas. Large inflows of new immigrant Hispanic and Asian populations can set off a chain reaction where more assimilated minorities move into integrated outer city or suburban communities. The prospects for this kind of integration should be particularly great in emerging multiethnic metropolitan areas that are located in newer parts of the country (Denton and Massey 1991). In such areas suburban communities are still being developed, and racial and ethnic "turf" has been less well established.

Another reason that the 1980s decade was expected to reduce minority segregation at the local level draws from continued economic gains made by the nation's black population. In the 1970s decade, the black population registered noticeable but undramatic increases in suburbanization and neighborhood integration.[18] Since another decade has passed when laws banning racial discrimination in housing sales were enforced and new cohorts of blacks entered the middle class, it was reasonable to look for an even greater reduction in black segregation during the 1980s. But, despite these improved contexts for minority integration, only modest changes occurred in the 1980s.

Racial and ethnic minorities are still largely concentrated in central cities while whites predominate in the suburbs. Levels of neighborhood segregation for Hispanics, Asians, and blacks have not changed appreciably, either. In some regions of the country significant changes have occurred and, happily, they are the regions that grew in population.

Minority concentration patterns are evaluated from three perspectives. The first contrasts the racial compositions of central cities with their surrounding suburbs and identifies metro areas where suburban minority gains have been greatest over the last decade. Then, minority suburbanization is evaluated from the perspective of specific minorities. Nationally, 39 percent of the minority population resided in the suburbs in 1990, compared with 67 percent for whites. How does this percentage vary for different minority groups and in different parts of the country?

The final part of this section focuses on neighborhood-level residential segregation. Variations in segregation by geography and by specific racial and ethnic groups are described. Particular attention is given to black segregation patterns in multiethnic metropolitan areas that are recipients of recent, large immigration flows. An important finding here is the considerable decline in black segregation that is registered in most of these areas.

Still Mostly White Suburbs

While the simple central city–suburb dichotomy is a crude one for most types of analysis, it is still meaningful for the analysis of minority versus white distribution. All three major minorities—Hispanics, Asians, and blacks—remain more concentrated in central cities than in suburbs in most parts of the country. Inner-city racial and ethnic enclaves are still prevalent for new and recent immigrant minorities, and the history of discrimination in metros where large numbers of blacks still live shapes the continuing concentration of blacks in central cities. Although all three minorities exhibited a higher percentage growth in the nation's suburbs than in its central cities in the 1980s (see Figure 6.11), the impact of this suburban growth for minority population change is small because these high growth rates apply to tiny initial suburban minority populations.

Nationally, minorities comprised 41 percent of the central city population and less than 18 percent of the suburban population. The minority share of both populations grew by about 5 percent over the 1980s, so the city–suburb minority disparity remained about the same. These disparities vary widely across metropolitan areas. Detroit, where blacks comprise most of the minority population, shows one of the most highly imbalanced city–suburb racial compositions. This is attributable to decades of selective "white flight" from the city accompanied by a minimal suburbanization of minorities, where institutionalized discrimination played an important role (Farley et al. 1978; Darden et al. 1987). Blacks also make up most of Atlanta's minority populations, but here the central city–suburban racial distribution is less imbalanced than in Detroit as a consequence of recent high levels of black suburbanization (see Figure 6.11). This is facilitated by Atlanta's emerging status as a migration "magnet" for middle-class blacks.

FIGURE 6.11   Race/ethnic percent compositions of central city
and suburb populations: 1980–1990.

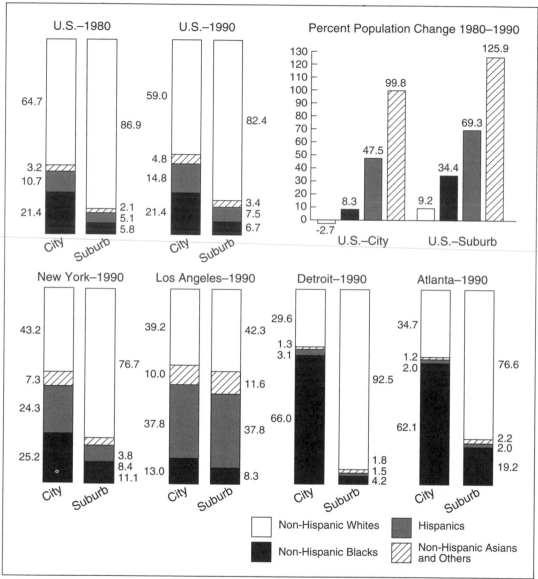

NOTE: Definitions are consistent with the metropolitan definitions cited in Note 11.

Another contrast can be made between two metropolitan areas with multiethnic populations that continue to grow via immigration—New York and Los Angeles. New York's city–suburb racial composition is much more imbalanced as a result of its longer history of white suburbanization. Los Angeles is a newer, more sprawling metropolitan area that evolved in the low density mode.

Blacks and other minorities have been spreading into the suburbs for several decades. As a consequence, in both the central city of Los Angeles and its suburbs, minorities comprise the majority of the population.

These illustrations point up the fact that a wide range of city–suburb racial and ethnic distributions exist across the nation's metropolitan areas. The most highly imbalanced distributions occur in the older Northeast and Midwest regions, particularly among larger metropolitan areas, which have undergone a longer history of whites-only suburbanization—just as decades of minority immigrants (especially blacks) were directed toward central city destinations only. A similar situation characterizes older southern metropolitan areas although, in many of these, the suburbs encircled black rural enclaves so southern suburban rings have large black populations. It is in the younger southern metros and metros in the West where central city–suburb racial distributions are less distinct. This has to do, again, with the more recent, low-density suburban development mode prevalent in this part of the country. And minorities in the West are more often Hispanics and Asians, who are more likely to locate in the suburbs.

Despite these variations, most of suburban America is predominantly white. Only one-third of all individual metro suburban areas have minority percentages that are at least as large as the national suburban minority percentage (18 percent). And in only 11 of 279 metro areas do the majority of minorities live in the suburbs, including several small Texas border towns—Los Angeles and Miami are the two largest. Nonetheless, more than three-quarters of all metros increased their suburban minority percentage over the 1980s. Large increases occurred within the suburbs of metros located in the high immigration states—especially California and Texas. Moreover, the minority compositions in many of these suburbs increased as a result of both minority gains *and* white losses. This suggests that the intrametropolitan dynamics of racial turnover and integration are playing out quite differently in high immigration multiethnic metros. Aside from these special cases, a predominantly white suburbia continues to reign in 1990. And in those suburbs that have attracted significant minority shares, the minorities still tend to be confined to a small subset of suburban communities (Speare 1993).

Suburban Exposure

In contrast to the previous discussion focusing on the suburb's race and ethnic composition, this discussion focuses on specific minority groups' exposure to the suburbs. Which minority groups are more likely to reside in the suburbs? In what kinds of areas is this likely to occur? And where has minority suburban exposure increased the most? Based on the simple measure, "proportion residing in the suburbs," national statistics show that suburban exposure is greatest for Asians, followed by Hispanics, then blacks (with respective proportions of .51,

.43, and .32). All three groups have lower suburban proportions than majority whites (at .67), yet each of the three groups increased their suburban exposure over the 1980s, if only slightly, based on nationwide statistics (Frey 1994c). However, residing in the suburbs does not necessarily mean that minorities share the same housing, neighborhood conditions, and access to services that are often associated with suburban living (Logan and Schneider 1984). But it does provide a crude indicator of progress in this direction for purposes of comparing minority groups' progress across areas and over time.

All three minorities tend to be more confined to the central cities in the Northeast and Midwest regions than in the South and West. Again, this has to do with the history of suburban development in the former areas, which made the city boundary a much more formidable barrier to cross for minorities, especially blacks. In 1990 the black suburban proportion was .22 in northern metros, in comparison with .39 in the South and .41 in the West. For Hispanics, these regional differences were not much higher than blacks' in the northern and southern metropolitan areas (with suburban proportions of .27 and .41, respectively) but increased significantly in the West (.53). Variation in suburban exposure is not as sharp for Asians. In both the North and South they are significantly more likely to reside in the suburbs than blacks or Hispanics (Asian North and South suburban proportions are .45 and .58). In the West, their suburban proportion of .51 is closer to Hispanics, leaving blacks lagging behind both groups.

The increasing suburban exposure of blacks is of particular interest in light of their long history of relegation to city-only residences. During the 1970s, the black suburban proportion increased slightly (from .23 to .27), after registering a decrease during the 1960s (Frey 1994c). The national increase in the black suburban proportion, over the 1980–1990 decade, was only slightly higher— from .27 to .32. And while black suburban proportions increased in about two-thirds of all metros during the 1980s, substantial increases occurred in only a handful. Atlanta experienced the greatest increase from .45 in 1980 to .63 in 1990; that is, almost two-thirds of Atlanta area blacks live in the suburban ring, one-third in the central city. Large gains also occurred in Washington, D.C., Dallas, and Houston in the South, as well as in Seattle, Denver, and Riverside–San Bernardino in the West. A number of northern metros also showed black suburbanization increases, yet their increases tended to be smaller in the 1980s than in the previous decade. These patterns indicate that the door to black suburbanization is not open very wide, and that future gains are most likely to be made in metro areas that house and continue to attract a growing black middle-class population. These include New South metros like Atlanta and Dallas, as well as areas in other parts of the country that have begun to attract more college-educated and professional blacks.

The link between socioeconomic status and suburban exposure has not always been a strong one for minorities, and particularly the black population (Alba and Logan 1991; Frey and Speare: Chap. 9). That is, whites at all socioeconomic levels were more likely to live in the suburbs than even the most educated, highest income blacks. For blacks, increased education or a rise in income did not necessarily imply a greater probability of suburban residence. This still applies in 1990, as illustrated in Figure 6.12.

In the United States as a whole, whites of all education levels are more suburbanized than even black college graduates. However, more so than in the past, there is a stronger link between black socioeconomic status and residence in the suburbs, which became accentuated during the 1980s. National statistics do not mirror all individual metro areas, and three distinct patterns are illustrated for Detroit, Dallas, and Los Angeles. In each of these—areas with very different black suburbanization histories—black gains in education are linked with increased suburban exposure (1980–1990 change data are not shown in Figure 6.12). This is the case even in Detroit, where overall black suburban exposure levels are much lower than other race and ethnic groups. Particularly in the 1980s, college graduate blacks were leading the move to the suburbs.

For Dallas, the education–suburban linkage is new in the 1990 data, attributable to substantial increases in suburban proportions among high school and college-educated blacks. A similar pattern is evident in Atlanta and several other New South areas that are attracting middle-class black inmigrants. Los Angeles represents a different model, where black suburbanization has occurred for several decades. The link between socioeconomic gains and suburban location was already in place, reinforced by modest black suburban exposure increases at all education levels.

Figure 6.12 provides a perspective on Asian and Hispanic suburbanization. While these groups' suburban exposure levels lie between those of whites and blacks, their socioeconomic status–suburban location linkage is far more pronounced. For these groups, increases in socioeconomic status represent a more significant steppingstone to suburban residence than is the case for blacks. This is consistent with earlier research which shows that for both Hispanics and Asians, increased socioeconomic achievement and residence in the country are related to greater spatial integration with whites (Frey and Fielding 1993).

Race and Ethnic Segregation

A final perspective on within-metro race and ethnic concentration focuses on segregation at the neighborhood level. A common index of neighborhood segregation is the Index of Dissimilarity, which was popularized in Karl and Alma Taeuber's classic, *Negroes in Cities* (1965; see also White 1986; Massey and Denton 1993). As used here, this index measures the degree to which one race or ethnic group is distributed evenly across neighborhoods (census-defined

FIGURE 6.12 1990 proportions residing in suburbs, by years of schooling and race-ethnicity for U.S. metropolitan population and selected metropolitan areas.

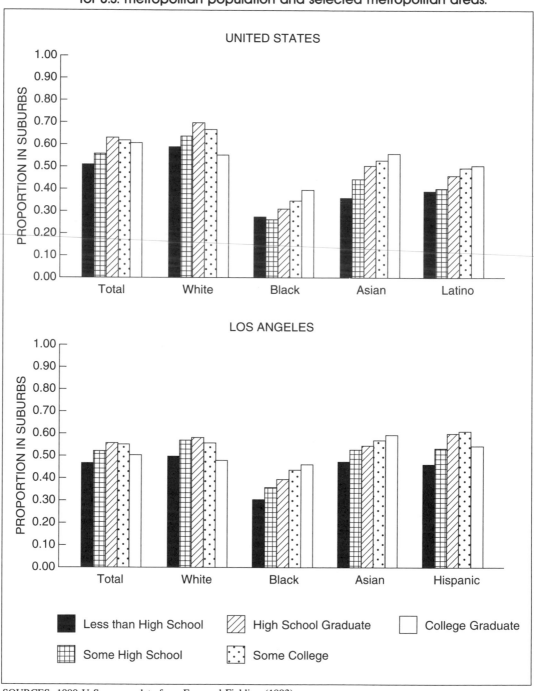

SOURCES: 1990 U.S. census data from Frey and Fielding (1993).

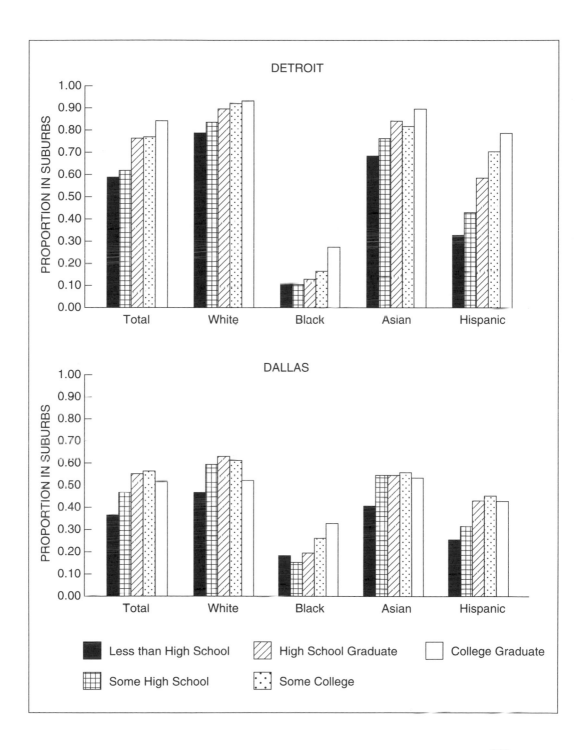

DETROIT

DALLAS

Legend:
- Less than High School
- Some High School
- High School Graduate
- Some College
- College Graduate

327

block groups) as compared with the rest of the population. For example, the index for blacks compares the distribution of all blacks across neighborhoods compared with the distribution of all nonblacks across neighborhoods. Segregation scores on this index can vary between 0 and 100, where 0 indicates complete integration (e.g., blacks are distributed exactly the same as nonblacks), and 100 indicates complete segregation (e.g., blacks are in completely different neighborhoods than nonblacks). The segregation score can also be interpreted as the percentage of the group's population that would have to move in order to be distributed like the rest of the population. Segregation scores above 60 are considered to indicate a high level of segregation, whereas those below 30 are considered to be low (Massey and Denton 1989).

When calculated for 1990, black segregation is considerably higher than Hispanic or Asian segregation, consistent with past patterns (Frey and Farley 1993). What is not consistent with the past is the pervasive *decrease* in the black segregation score among nearly nine-tenths of metropolitan areas with at least minimal black populations, while the majority of metros with minimal Hispanic and Asian populations showed segregation *increases* for those groups. The trends for blacks and Hispanics were already hinted at in the 1970s (Massey and Denton 1987). Increased Asian segregation is new and, like heightened Hispanic concentration, follows from the many recent immigrants who tend to cluster in same-group neighborhoods.

Most of these segregation changes are small in magnitude. However, the most notable ones emerging in the 1980s involve the reduced segregation of blacks in multiethnic metropolitan areas. The discussion below reviews the post–1980 segregation shifts for Hispanics, Asians, and blacks, and the unique segregation changes occurring within multiethnic metros.

Hispanics and Asians.   Both Hispanic and Asian populations showed widespread segregation increases over the 1980s. This can be related to their high immigration levels, where new immigrants "pile up" in immigrant enclaves.

The average Hispanic segregation score was 43 among the 132 metros with minimal 1990 Hispanic populations.[19] While individual metro segregation scores ranged from 15 to 71, most were in the range of 25–60. Highest Hispanic segregation scores exist in the northeast metropolitan areas, where Puerto Ricans comprise a large share of the population. Moderate-sized metro areas surrounding the New York region in Pennsylvania and New England are among the most highly segregated areas with respect to Hispanics. Many of these attracted Puerto Ricans who moved away from the New York area in the 1980s. At the other extreme are Pacific coastal areas and those in the Southwest where segregation scores hover in the 30s and 40s range. Still, traditional port-of-entry Hispanic metros—Los Angeles, New York, Miami, and Chicago—register segregation scores in the 50s, which are propped up by continued levels of concentrated Hispanic immigration. Other areas that received Hispanic migrants for the first time in the 1980s increased their segregation: over half of the metros experienced some increase in their Hispanic segregation scores.

As with Hispanics, the average 1990 Asian segregation score was also 43 (among the 66 metros with at least sufficiently large Asian populations to permit calculation of meaningful indices). These scores tend to fall within a narrower range, with most metros having 30s–40s level segregation. Yet again, the large port-of-entry areas exhibit some of the highest scores—including Honolulu (63), New York (52), Los Angeles (45), San Francisco (47), and Chicago (54). Most of these areas increased their segregation over the 1980s. Metros with low Asian segregation scores are found in the West, but not in the traditional Asian destination areas. Many are located outside of California, such as Las Vegas, Reno, or Denver. Still, in the 1980s, most metros increased their Asian segregation scores, if only slightly. The greatest increases occurred in areas that attracted the lower-status new Asian groups—Vietnamese, Cambodians, and Laotians.

Blacks. Black segregation declines were pervasive during the 1980s. Among the 232 metros with sufficient black populations to calculate indices, the average 1990 black segregation score was 64—five points lower than the 1980 average. There are several similarities in the trends for black neighborhood segregation and those for black suburbanization. First, the geographic locations of areas with highest segregation tended to be in the Northeast and Midwest—areas that also showed lowest black suburbanization. Gary, Detroit, Chicago, and Cleveland led all metros with very high segregation scores in the upper 80s. Second, areas that showed the greatest decreases in black segregation tended to be located in growing, newer parts of the country where much of the housing stock was built since the enactment of the 1968 Civil Rights Act. Large metro areas that showed the greatest segregation declines included New South areas—Dallas (from 80 to 64), Orlando (from 81 to 65), and Atlanta (from 79 to 72), as well as several western metros which also attracted many middle-class blacks during the 1980s (Farley and Frey 1994).

Black declines in multiethnic metros. The large waves of Hispanic and Asian immigration during the 1980s have had significant effects on many of the redistribution trends already discussed in this chapter. An additional impact relevant to intrametropolitan dynamics is the context that immigration and multiethnic metros provide for a *reduction* in black segregation (Frey and Farley 1993). There are several reasons why this occurs.

First, most high-immigration multiethnic areas are not located in the Black Belt of the old South, nor are they typically first destinations of the original rural-to-urban black migration streams out of the South. As a result, they do not have the long, sometimes turbulent history of racial conflict, which is the case for many southern and industrial north metros. Second, the black inmi-

TABLE 6.8 Residential segregation scores and 1980–1990 changes for race and ethnic groups in multiethnic metropolitan areas.

Metropolitan Area*	Race/Ethnic Group†	1990 Residential Segregation Scores			1980–1990 Change in Score for:		
		Latinos/ Non-Latinos	Asians/ Non-Asians	Blacks/ Nonblacks	Latinos/ Non-Latinos	Asians/ Non-Asians	Blacks/ Nonblacks
New York	Black-Latino-Asian	54	52	71	−1	0	−3
Chicago	Black-Latino-Asian	66	54	86	0	1	−4
Houston	Latino-Black-Asian	49	49	66	−1	−1	−11
Oakland	Black-Latino-Asian	35	37	64	1	1	−8
Jersey City	Latino-Black-Asian	47	49	68	−5	−4	−9
Dallas	Black-Latino	50	49	64	1	−1	−16
Miami	Latino-Black	56	40	74	−1	1	−6
Newark	Black-Latino	59	43	81	−2	0	−1
Killeen, TX	Black-Latino	22	38	43	−5	0	−7
Galveston	Black-Latino	32	47	64	−2	−5	−10
Waco, TX	Black-Latino	43	49	60	−1	−4	−11
Vineland, NJ	Black-Latino	54	48	55	−3	−4	2
Los Angeles	Latino-Asian	53	45	66	0	1	−12
Riverside	Latino-Asian	38	38	47	−1	4	−10
San Diego	Latino-Asian	43	45	54	4	3	−7
Anaheim	Latino-Asian	53	36	40	9	8	−4
San Francisco	Asian-Latino	45	47	61	4	−1	−4
San Jose	Latino-Asian	45	37	38	2	8	−5

Sacramento	Latino-Asian	34	46	54	−1	1	−3
Bergen, NJ	Latino-Asian	56	41	73	−2	−1	−6
Las Vegas	Latino-Asian	30	28	49	6	1	−14
Oxnard, CA	Latino-Asian	53	35	42	1	−1	−8
Fresno, CA	Latino-Asian	46	46	54	−1	15	−9
Bakersfield, CA	Latino-Asian	53	47	56	1	1	−8
Stockton, CA	Latino-Asian	34	52	54	−1	12	−9
Vallejo, CA	Latino-Asian	26	45	46	3	4	−5
Modesto, CA	Latino-Asian	37	40	43	−4	5	−12
Santa Barbara	Latino-Asian	46	33	44	5	3	1
Salinas, CA	Latino-Asian	58	36	60	2	2	−7
Visalia, CA	Latino-Asian	44	49	58	3	3	−3
Reno, NV	Latino-Asian	36	33	46	18	6	−1
Santa Cruz, CA	Latino-Asian	57	29	39	4	−4	−2
Merced, CA	Latino-Asian	35	48	43	−4	10	−6
Yuba City, CA	Latino-Asian	33	41	49	5	6	1
Bryan-C-T, TX	Latino-Asian	35	56	53	−6	10	−19
Washington, D.C.	Black-Asian	41	39	66	8	0	−5
Trenton	Black-Asian	51	49	74	0	1	−2

NOTES: Minority percentages of the U.S. population in 1990 were 12.1 percent blacks; 9 percent Hispanics; 2.9 percent Asians. Primary metropolitan areas rather than consolidated metropolitan areas are used in this analysis. Constant boundaries based on the 1990 definition are used.

* Abbreviated name.

† Denotes minority groups (blacks, Latinos, or Asians), which comprise a percentage of the metropolitan area's population that exceeds the group's percentage of the U.S. population. Groups are listed in order of their relative representation.

grants to these multiethnic areas tend to be urban-origin "second destination" black migrants. Third, the presence of an additional Hispanic or Asian ethnic group changes the housing market away from a simple black–white dynamic. The experience of past multiethnic areas has shown that Hispanics have served as a buffer group between blacks and whites and helped to facilitate the stability of mixed, multiethnic neighborhoods (Santiago 1991). The potential for buffering improves when the metro area's black population is outnumbered by those of other minorities.

Fourth, the continuing immigration of Hispanics and Asians into these metro areas helped to fuel an outmigrant "flight" to other neighborhoods of earlier generations for these groups, as well as for whites. To the extent that blacks are also pushed out of these areas, they are more inclined to settle in newly emerging mixed-race neighborhoods. Some of these may prove to be only transitional, but there is evidence that many will remain integrated.

These processes are possible in multiethnic metros, and serve to counter the traditional white-to-black neighborhood transition process that has been all too familiar in many northern, industrial metropolitan areas. That these different racial transition patterns occur in these multiethnic areas was hinted at in studies of neighborhood transition during the 1970s (Lee and Wood 1991). A Los Angeles investigation showed that between 1970 and 1990 the percentage of whites living in mostly white neighborhoods fell from 75 percent to 29 percent. At the same time, the percentage of blacks living in predominantly black neighborhoods fell from 55 to only 13 percent. Fueled by the outmovement from largely Hispanic immigrant enclaves, Blacks and whites were more likely to reside in mixed-race neighborhoods in 1990, and whites or blacks who stayed in their old neighborhoods in Los Angeles increasingly found that they had Hispanic or Asian neighbors (Ong and Lawrence 1992).

The effects of multiethnic metropolitan context are illustrated with the segregation scores presented in Table 6.8. Shown are segregation indices for the 37 metro areas classed as multiethnic. Each of these metro areas has greater than the national proportion of at least two of the three major minority groups—blacks, Hispanics, and Asians (Frey and Farley 1993). Recent immigration waves are strongly linked to most of these areas, and their Hispanic and Asian populations are typically growing much faster than their black populations. The impact of this context on black segregation is apparent from the last column of the table: over the 1980s, most of these areas reduced their black segregation levels, and in two-thirds of them the reduction exceeded 5 points.

In nine of these areas, black segregation was reduced by at least 10 points, and this list includes large metros—Los Angeles (-12), Dallas (-16), and Houston (-11). Two effects are working in these areas. First, there is the impact of multiethnic context, which increases the integration possibilities for reasons discussed above. Second, these areas are attracting middle-class black migrants, who are more easily assimilated into integrated, middle-class neigh-borhoods. These two kinds of areas—multiethnic metros and black middle-class magnet metros—were most strongly linked to black segregation declines during the 1980s decade.

TRENDS TOWARD BALKANIZATION

The spatial demographic shifts that characterize the 1980s and 1990s are a far cry from the 1970s days of Snowbelt urban declines, Texas oil booms, and California dreaming. Nor is there much talk of a back-to-nature rural renais-sance. The new, post–1980 urban revival is an uneven one—rewarding corpo-rate nodes, information centers, and other tie-ins to the global economy. Areas specializing in high-tech manufacturing, recreation, or retirement have also grown. And while these kinds of areas can be found in most parts of the coun-try, they are now especially prominent in newly developing regions—the South Atlantic coastal states, and states *around* California.

The population growth in these areas, driven largely by industrial restructur-ing, can be contrasted with the immigration-driven growth in the large port-of-entry metro areas located in California, Texas, the greater New York region, Miami, and Chicago, where immigration has been dominated by Hispanic and Asian minorities. The demographic makeup of these areas in terms of race, age, poverty, and skill level are becoming more distinct from the former areas, which are attracting, in some cases, native-born white and black professionals and, in other cases, amenity-seeking retirees. At the same time, a broad swath of the interior of the country is not attracting any of these groups. These are largely white, and their populations continue to grow older as a result of the outmigration of the young.

Industrial restructuring, immigration, and segmented redistribution patterns along the lines of race, status, and age have widened demographic disparities across broad regions and metropolitan areas. Such disparities also exist within metropolitan areas where the suburbs have now come to dominate. In many of the older metropolitan areas, central cities do not resemble mainstream America in the sense that they disproportionately house the poor, the unskilled, and mi-nority populations, while their suburbs represent much more of a cross section of American life. Yet, segmentation occurs within the suburbs, as well, and there is the need for a new nomenclature that goes beyond the simple city-suburb typology.

Racial segregation is one area in which simply taking a national snapshot is misleading. When this is done, one finds only modest gains in black suburbani-zation and modest increases in neighborhood integration over the 1980s decade. However, regional black migration patterns have become much more like those of whites. Those areas that are most attractive to middle-class blacks (Atlanta, Dallas, and Washington, D.C.) have shown significant increases in black suburbanization and integration. Other areas where black integration has risen noticeably are the West Coast and Southwest multiethnic immigrant port-of-entry areas, such as Los Angeles and Houston. In most parts of the country, black segregation levels are substantially greater than those for Asians or Hispanics. The trend toward convergence, displayed by the areas just described, is the exception.

The portrait that has been painted in this review of post–1980 population shifts is clearly one of divisions—divisions across areas of growth and decline, divisions brought on by the segmented redistribution pattern of immigrants, minorities, whites, and even across age groups, and divisions between cities and suburbs as well as within the suburbs. The latter divisions, those within metropolitan areas, are most familiar because they have evolved over decades. What is new in the 1980 and 1990 trends is that redistribution patterns reinforce divisions across broad regions and metropolitan areas. A demographic balkanization is a likely outcome if these trends continue. The large multiethnic port-of-entry metros will house decidedly younger, more diverse, and ethnically vibrant populations than the more staid, white older populations in declining regions, while the more educated middle-aged populations will reside in the most prosperous metropolises—those oriented to information processing and high technology manufacturing. The geographic boundaries that take shape according to these distinctions will bring profound changes to established economic and political alliances as well as to the lifestyles and attitudes of residents of these areas. Yet, this balkanization scenario may be premature. Forces that strongly influence these patterns—industrial restructuring and focused immigration—could become altered as the global marketplace changes, as minority immigrants assimilate in their migration patterns, and as technological improvements continue to reinvent the way we work, travel, and communicate. Still, the current trends toward greater regional demographic divisions are unmistakable, and they need to be watched closely in the decade ahead.

ENDNOTES

1. For a review of explanations, see Frey 1987:240–257; and 1989; Frey and Speare 1992a.

2. Analyses of redistribution across metropolitan areas in early sections of this chapter are based on Metropolitan Statistical Areas (MSAs), Consolidated Metropolitan Statistical Areas (CMSAs), and in some cases New England Country Metropolitan Area (NECMA) counterparts, as defined by the Office of Management and Budget,

June 30, 1990. (See U.S. Bureau of the Census [1991]. Appendix 1; and Forstall and Gonzalez [1984] for definitions and discussions of these concepts.) This differs, somewhat, from the definitions used in the analysis of intra-metropolitan redistribution in later sections. Unless otherwise indicated, all trend analyses employ geographically constant boundaries.

3, David L. Brown et al. 1988; Swanson and Brown 1993; Center for the New West, 1992.

4. These migration data were compiled from the 1990 census "residence 5 years ago" tabulations. Immigration from abroad pertains to a state's 1990 residents who lived abroad in 1985. Internal migrants pertain to the (net) difference between inmigrants from elsewhere in the U.S. (resident in state in 1990, resident elsewhere in the U.S., 1985) minus outmigrants from the state to other parts of the U.S. (resident in state, 1985, resident elsewhere in the U.S., 1990).

5. Bean and Tienda (1987); Bean, Edmonston, and Passel (1990); Jasso and Rosenzweig (1990).

6. These migration gains were compiled from the "residence 5 years ago" question of the 1990 census (see Note 4). Migrant's poverty status pertains to 1989, as reported in the census.

7. Plane and Rogerson 1991; Frey and Speare (1988); Fuguitt, Brown, and Beale (1989); Frey (1990).

8. Data are based on "residence 5 years ago" tabulations of the 1990 census (see Note 4).

9. Here, net migration is estimated from tabulations from the 1990 census "residence 5 years ago" question (see Note 4). Aging-in-place is estimated as the surviving 1985–1990 California nonmigrants who aged from 60–64 in 1985 to 65–69 in 1990.

10. Oldakowski and Roseman (1986); Litwak and Longino (1987); Scrow and Charity (1988); Speare and McNally (1992).

11. The analyses of city–suburb redistribution will be based on Metropolitan Statistical Areas (MSAs), Primary Metropolitan Statistical Areas (PMSAs), and, in New England, New England County Metropolitan Areas (NECMAs). These differ from the units for the analysis of across metropolitan area redistribution in the previous sections. PMSA rather than CMSA definitions are used here because they are more appropriate for a within metropolitan area city–suburb redistribution analysis (see Note 2).

12. See Frey and Speare (1988), Chapter 7; Hawley (1971); Schnore (1965).

13. Frey and Speare (1988), Appendix Table E.7A.

14. Norton (1979); Frey and Speare (1988), Chapter 7.

15. These are the 12 Primary Metropolitan Statistical Areas (PMSAs), which comprise the New York Consolidated Metropolitan Statistical Area (CMSA) as defined on June 30, 1990. As indicated in Note 11, these PMSA units are typically used for within metropolitan area city–suburb redistribution analysis.

16. Schnore (1965); Frey and Speare (1988), Chapter 9.

17. Kasarda (1988); Frey and Speare (1988), Chapter 11.

18. Frey and Speare (1988), Chapter 8; Massey and Denton (1987).

19. These include metropolitan areas where the minority population comprises at least 20,000 people or represents at least 3 percent of the total metropolitan population. See Frey and Farley (1993).

Bibliography

Abowd, John M., and Richard B. Freeman. 1991. *Immigration, Trade, and the Labor Market*. Chicago: University of Chicago Press.

Achdut, Lea, and Yossi Tamir. 1990. "Retirement and Well-being Among the Elderly." In *Poverty, Inequality and Income Distribution in Comparative Perspective*. Edited by Timothy M. Smeeding, Michael O'Higgins, and Lee Rainwater. New York: Harvester Wheatshaft.

Ahlburg, Dennis A. 1993. "The Census Bureau's New Projections of the U.S. Population." *Population and Development Review* 19:159–174.

Alba, Richard, and John Logan. 1991. "Variations on Two Themes: Racial and Ethnic Patterns in the Attainment of Suburban Residence." *Demography* 28:431–454.

Anderson, Elijah. 1991. *Streetwise: Race, Class, and Change in an Urban Community*. Chicago: University of Chicago Press.

Anderson, Margo. 1988. *The American Census: A Social History*. New Haven, CT: Yale University Press.

Bane, Mary Jo. 1986. "Household Composition and Poverty." In *Fighting Poverty: What Works and What Doesn't*. Edited by S. H. Danzinger and D. H. Weinberg. Cambridge, MA: Harvard University Press, pp. 209–231.

Barringer, Herbert R., Robert W. Gardner, and Michael J. Levin. 1993. *Asians and Pacific Islanders in the United States*. New York: Russell Sage Foundation.

Bartel, Ann P. 1989. "Where Do the New Immigrants Live?" *Journal of Labor Economics* 7 (October): 371–391.

Beale, Calvin L. 1988. "Americans Heading for the Cities, Once Again." *Rural Development Perspectives* 4:2–6.

Bean, Frank D., and Gary Swicegood. 1985. *Mexican American Fertility Patterns*. Austin: University of Texas Press.

Bean, Frank D., and Marta Tienda. 1987. *The Hispanic Population of the United States*. New York: Russell Sage Foundation.

Bean, Frank D., Harley L. Browning, and W. Parker Frisbie. 1984. "The Socio-Demographic Characteristics of Mexican Immigrant Status Groups: Implications for Studying Undocumented Mexicans." *International Migration Review* 18 (Fall): 672–691.

Bean, Frank D., Barry Edmonston, and Jeffrey S. Passel. 1990. *Undocumented Migration to the United States: IRCA and the Experience of the 1980s*. Washington, DC: Urban Institute Press.

Bean, Frank D., Allan G. King, and Jeffrey S. Passel. 1983. "The Number of Illegal Migrants of Mexican Origin in the United States: Sex-Ratio Based Estimates for 1980." *Demography* 20 (February): 99–109.

Bean, Frank D., Georges Vernez, and Charles B. Keely. 1989. *Opening and Closing the Doors: Evaluating Immigration Reform and Control*. Santa Monica, CA and Washington, DC: RAND Corporation and Urban Institute.

Becker, Gary S. 1981. *A Treatise on the Family*. Cambridge, MA: Harvard University Press.

Bellah, R., R. Adsen, A. Swindler, W. Sullivan, and S. Tipton. 1985. *Habits of the Heart: Individualism and Commitment in American Life*. Berkeley: University of California Press.

Belsky, Jay, and David Eggebeen. 1991. "Early and Extensive Maternal Employment and Young Children's Socioeconomic Development: Children of the National Longitudinal Survey of Youth." *Journal of Marriage and the Family* 53:1083–1110.

Bergmann, Barbara. 1986. *The Economic Emergence of Women*. New York: Basic Books.

Bianchi, Suzanne M. 1993. "Children of Poverty: Why Are They Poor?" In *Child Poverty and Public Policy*. Edited by Judith Chafel. Washington, DC: Urban Institute Press.

Bianchi, Suzanne M., and Edith McArthur. 1991. "Family Distribution and Economic Hardship: The Short Run Picture for Children." U.S. Bureau of the Census, *Current Population Reports,* Series P70-23. Washington, DC: U.S. Government Printing Office.

Bianchi, Suzanne M., and Daphne Spain. 1986. *American Women in Transition*. New York: Russell Sage Foundation.

Blau, Francine D. 1992. "The Fertility of Immigrant Women: Evidence from High-Fertility Source Countries." In *Immigration and the Work Force: Economic Consequences for the United States and Source Areas*. Edited by George J. Borjas and Richard B. Freeman. Chicago: University of Chicago Press, pp. 93–133.

Bonacich, Edna. 1984. "Some Basic Facts: Patterns of Asian Immigration and Exclusion." In *Labor Immigration Under Capitalism: Asian Workers in the United States before World War II*. Edited by Lucie Cheng and Edna Bonacich. Berkeley: University of California Press, pp. 60–78.

Briody, Elizabeth K. 1987. "Patterns of Household Immigration into South Texas." *International Migration Review* 21 (Spring): 27–47.

Brooks-Gunn, Jeané, Greg J. Duncan, Pamela Kato Klebanov, and Naomi Sealand. 1993. "Do Neighborhoods Influence Child and Adolescent Behavior?" *American Journal of Sociology* 99:353–95.

Brown, David L., Jane Norman Reid, Herman Bluestone, David A. McGranahan, and Sara M. Mazie, eds. 1988. *Rural Economic Development in the 1980s: Prospects for the Future Rural Development*. Research Report No. 69. Washington, DC: U.S. Department of Agriculture.

Brownstein, Ronald. 1994. "Welfare Aid to Older Immigrants Imperiled." *Los Angeles Times*, March 17, Part A, Page 3, Column 2.

Bumpass, Larry. 1984. "Children and Marital Disruption: A Replication and Update." *Demography* 21:71–82.

Bumpass, Larry, and James Sweet. 1989a. "Children's Experience in Single-Parent Families: Implications of Cohabitation and Marital Transitions." *Family Planning Perspectives* 21(6):256–260.

———. 1989b. "National Estimates of Cohabitation." *Demography* 26:615–625.

Bumpass, Larry, James Sweet, and Andrew Cherlin. 1991. "The Role of Cohabitation in Declining Rates of Marriage." *Journal of Marriage and the Family* 53(4):913–927.

Burek, Debbie, ed. 1993. *Encyclopedia of Associations, Vol. 1, Part 2: National Organizations*. Detroit, MI: Gale Research, Inc.

Burkhauser, Richard V., and Dallas L. Salisbury, eds. 1993. *Pensions in a Changing Economy*. Washington, DC: Employee Benefit Research Institute.

Cafferty, Pastora San Juan, Barry R. Chiswick, Andrew M. Greeley, and Teresa A. Sullivan. 1983. *The Dilemma of American Immigration: Beyond the Golden Door*. New Brunswick, NJ: Transaction Press.

Carpenter, Niles. 1927. *Immigrants and Their Children, 1920*. Washington, DC: U.S. Government Printing Office.

Casper, Lynne M. 1992. "Community Norms and Cohabitation: Effects of Level and Degree of Consensus." Paper presented at the American Population Association annual meeting, Denver, Colorado.

Casper, Lynne M., Sara McLanahan, and Irwin Garfinkel. 1994. "The Gender Poverty Gap: What We Can Learn from Other Countries." *American Sociological Review* 59:594–605.

Castro-Martin, Theresa, and Larry Bumpass. 1989. "Recent Trends and Differentials in Marital Disruption." *Demography* 26(1):37–51.

Center for the New West. 1992. *The Great Plains in Transition: Overview of Change in America's New Economy*. Denver, CO: Center for the New West.

Cervero, Robert. 1986. *Suburban Gridlock*. New Brunswick, NJ: Rutgers University Center for Urban Policy Research.

———. 1989. *America's Suburban Centers: The Land Use Transportation Link*. London: Unwi-Hyman.

Cherlin, Andrew. 1992. *Marriage, Divorce, Remarriage*. Cambridge, MA: Harvard University Press.

Children's Defense Fund. 1991. *The State of America's Children 1990*. Washington, DC: Children's Defense Fund.

Chiswick, Barry R. 1982. *The Employment of Immigrants in the United States*. Washington, DC: American Enterprise Institute.

———. 1986. "Is the New Immigration Less Skilled than the Old?" *Journal of Labour Economics* 4:168–192.

———. 1988. "Illegal Immigration and Immigration Control." *Journal of Economic Perspectives* 2(August):101–115.

Chiswick, Barry R., and Paul W. Miller. 1992. "Language in the Immigrant Labor Market." In *Immigration, Language and Ethnicity: Canada and the United States.* Edited by Barry R. Chiswick. Washington, DC: American Enterprise Institute, pp. 229–296.

————. 1994. "The Determinants of Post-Migration Investments in Schooling." *Economics of Education Review* 13 (June):163–177.

Chiswick, Carmel U., Barry R. Chiswick, and George Karras. 1992. "The Impact of Immigrants on the Macroeconomy." *Carnegie-Rochester Conference Series on Public Policy* 37(December):279–316.

Clark, William A. V., and Peter Morrison. 1993. "The Demographic Context of Minority Political Strength." Paper presented at the Annual Meeting of the Population Association of America, Cincinnati, Ohio.

Cooney, Teresa, and Peter M. Uhlenberg. 1990. "The Role of Divorce in Men's Relations with Their Adult Children after Mid-Life." *Journal of Marriage and the Family* 52:677–688.

Corbett, Thomas. 1993. "Child Poverty and Welfare Reform: Progress or Paralysis?" *Focus* 15(Spring): 1–17.

Crane, Jonathan. 1991. "The Epidemic Theory of Ghettos and Neighborhood Effects on Dropping Out and Teenage Childbearing." *American Journal of Sociology* 96:1226–1259.

Crimmins, Eileen. 1981. "The Changing Pattern of American Mortality Decline, 1940–1977, and Its Implications for the Future." *Population and Development Review* 7:229–254.

Crimmins, Eileen, Yasuhiko Saito, and Dominique Ignegneri. 1989. "Changes in Life Expectancy and Disability-Free Life Expectancy in the United States." *Population and Development Review* 15:235–267.

Crispell, Diane, and William H. Frey. 1993. "American Maturity." *American Demographics* 15:31–42.

Danziger, Sheldon, Gary D. Sandefur, and Daniel Weinberg, eds. 1994. *Confronting Poverty.* Cambridge, MA: Harvard University Press.

Darden, Joe T., Richard Child Hill, June Thomas, and Richard Thomas. 1987. *Detroit: Race and Uneven Development.* Philadelphia, PA: Temple University Press.

Da Vanzo, Julie, and M. Omar Rahman. 1994. "American Families: Trends and Correlates." *Population Index* 59(3):350–386.

Da Vanzo, Julie, M. Omar Rahman, and Kul T. Wadhwa. 1994. "American Families: Policy Issues." *Population Index* 59(4):547–566.

Davis, Steven J., and John Haltiwanger. 1991. "Wage Dispersion Between and Within U.S. Manufacturing Plants, 1963–86." *Brookings Papers on Economic Activity: Microeconomics.* Washington, DC: Brookings Institution, pp. 115–180.

Dawson, Deborah, Gerry Hendershot, and John Fulton. 1987. "Aging in the Eighties: Functional Limitations of Individuals Age 65 and Over." NCHS Advancedata. No. 133.

Day, Alice. 1991. *Remarkable Survivors: Insights into Successful Aging among Women.* Washington, DC: Urban Institute Press.

Day, Jennifer C. 1992. "Population Projections of the United States, by Age, Sex, Race, and Hispanic Origin: 1992 to 2050." *Current Population Reports,* 25–1104. U.S. Bureau of the Census. Washington, DC: U.S. Government Printing Office.

———. 1993. "Population Projections of the United States, by Age, Sex, Race, and Hispanic Origin: 1993 to 2050." U.S. Bureau of the Census, *Current Population Reports,* P 25-1104. Washington, DC: U.S. Government Printing Office.

De la Puente, Manuel. 1993. "Why Are People Missed or Erroneously Included by the Census: A Summary of Findings from Ethnographic Coverage Reports." Report prepared for the Advisory Committee for the Design of the Year 2000 Census. Mimeo.

Denton, Nancy A., and Douglas S. Massey. 1991. "Patterns of Neighborhood Transition in a Multi-Ethnic World: U.S. Metropolitan Areas, 1970–1980." *Demography* 28:41–63.

Dizon, Lily. 1992. "Growing Old in a New Land: Senior Center Is Cultural Anchor for Vietnamese Who Feel Adrift." *Los Angeles Times,* April 10, Part B, Page 1, Column 3.

Doty, Pamela J. 1992. "The Oldest Old and the Use of Institutional Long-Term Care from an International Perspective." In *The Oldest Old.* Edited by Richard M. Suzman, David P. Willis, and Kenneth G. Manton. New York: Oxford University Press.

Duncan, Greg J. 1991. "The Economic Environment of Childhood." In *Children in Poverty.* Edited by A. C. Huston. Cambridge, England: Cambridge University Press, pp. 23–50.

Duncan, Greg J., and Willard L. Rodgers. 1988. "Longitudinal Aspects of Childhood Poverty." *Journal of Marriage and the Family* 50:1007–1021.

———. 1991. "Has Children's Poverty Become More Persistent?" *American Sociological Review* 56:538–550.

Easterlin, Richard A. 1987. "The New Age Structure of Poverty in America: Permanent or Transient?" *Population and Development Review* 13:195–207.

Easterlin, Richard A., Christine M. Schaeffer, and Diane J. Macunovich. 1993. "Will the Baby Boomers Be Less Well Off Than Their Parents? Income, Wealth, and Family Circumstances Over the Life Cycle in the United States." *Population and Development Review* 19:497–522.

Edsall, Thomas B., and Mary D. Edsall, eds. 1992. *Chain Reaction: The Impact of Race, Rights and Taxes on American Politics.* New York: Norton.

Eggebeen, David J., and Daniel T. Lichter. 1991. "Race, Family Structure, and Changing Poverty Among American Children." *American Sociological Review* 56:801–817.

Encyclopedia of Associations, 1993, Volume 1, Part 2.

Farley, Reynolds. 1984. *Blacks and Whites: Narrowing the Gap?* Cambridge, MA: Harvard University Press.

———. 1991. "Residential Segregation of Social and Economic Groups Among Blacks, 1970–1980." In *The Urban Underclass.* Edited by Christopher Jencks and Paul E. Peterson. Washington, DC: The Brookings Institution.

Farley, Reynolds, and William H. Frey. 1994. "Changes in the Segregation of Whites from Blacks During the 1980s: Small Steps toward a More Integrated Society." *American Sociological Review* 59:23–45.

Farley, Reynolds, Howard Schuman, Suzanne Bianchi, Diane Colasanto, and Shirley Hatchett. 1978. "Chocolate City, Vanilla Suburbs: Will the Trend toward Racially Separate Communities Continue?" *Social Science Research* 7:314–344.

Featherman, David L., and Robert M. Hauser. 1975. *Opportunity and Change*. New York: Academic Press.

Filer, Randall K. 1992. "The Effect of Immigrant Arrivals on Migratory Patterns of Native Workers." In *Immigration and the Work Force: Economic Consequences for the United States and Source Areas*. Edited by George J. Borjas and Richard B. Freeman. Chicago: University of Chicago Press, pp. 245–269.

Fix, Michael, and Jeffrey S. Passel. 1991. *The Door Remains Open: Recent Immigration to the United States and a Preliminary Analysis of the Immigration Act of 1990*. Program for Research on Immigration Policy, PRIP-UI-14. Washington, DC: The Urban Institute.

Forstall, Richard L., and Elena Gonzalez. 1984. "Twenty Questions: What You Should Know About the New Metropolitan Areas." *American Demographics* (April):22–49.

Frey, William H. 1987. "Migration and Depopulation of the Metropolis: Regional Restructuring or Rural Renaissance?" *American Sociological Review* 52:240–257.

———. 1989. "United States: Counterurbanization and Metropolis Depopulation." In *Counterurbanization: The Changing Pace and Nature of Population Deconcentration*. Edited by A. G. Champion. London: Edward Arnold.

———. 1990. "Metropolitan America: Beyond the Transition." Population Reference Bureau, Inc. *Population Bulletin* 45(2):3–49.

———. 1991. "Are Two Americas Emerging?" *Population Today*. Washington, DC: Population Reference Bureau.

———. 1992a. "Boomer Magnets." *American Demographics* 14(3):34.

———. 1992b. "Metropolitan Redistribution of the U.S. Elderly: 1960–70, 1970–80, 1980–90." In *Elderly Migration and Population Redistribution: A Comparative Perspective*. Edited by Andrei Rogers. London: Belhaven Press.

———. 1992c. "Minority Suburbanization and Continued 'White Flight' in U.S. Metropolitan Areas: Assessing Findings from the 1990 Census." *Research Reports* No. 92-247. Ann Arbor: Population Studies Center, University of Michigan.

———. 1993a. "Interstate Migration and Immigration for Whites and Minorities, 1985–90: The Emergence of Multi-Ethnic States." Population Studies Center, Research Reports 93-297. Ann Arbor: University of Michigan.

———. 1993b. "Race, Class and Poverty Polarization across Metro Areas and States: Population Shifts and Migration Dynamics." Population Studies Center, Research Reports 93-293. Ann Arbor: University of Michigan.

———. 1994a. "Black College Grads, Those in Poverty Take Different Paths." *Population Today*. Washington, DC: Population Reference Bureau, February.

———. 1994b. "Immigration and Internal Migration 'Flight': A California Case Study." *Population and Environment,* Forthcoming.

———. 1994c. "Minority Suburbanization and Continued 'White Flight' in U.S. Metropolitan Areas: Assessing Findings from the 1990 Census." *Research on Community Sociology* 4:15–42.

————. 1994d. "The New White Flight." *American Demographics* (April):40–38.

Frey, William H., and Reynolds Farley. 1993. "Latino, Asian and Black Segregation in Multi-Ethnic Metro Areas: Findings from the 1990 Census." Population Studies Center, Research Reports No. 93-278. Ann Arbor: University of Michigan.

Frey, William H., and Elaine L. Fielding. 1993. "Race and Class Suburbanization in Multi-Ethnic Areas: Whites, Blacks, Latinos and Asians." Presented at the 1993 Annual Meeting of the American Sociological Association, Miami, FL.

Frey, William H., and Alden Speare, Jr. 1988. *Regional and Metropolitan Growth and Decline in the United States.* New York: Russell Sage Foundation.

————. 1992a. "The Revival of Metropolitan Population Growth in the United States: An Assessment of Findings from the 1990 Census." *Population and Development Review* 18(1):129–146.

————. 1992b. Metropolitan Areas as Functional Communities: A Proposal for a New Definition." *Research Report* No. 92-245. Ann Arbor: Population Studies Center, University of Michigan.

Fries, J. F. 1980. "Aging, Natural Death, and the Compression of Mortality." *The New England Journal of Medicine* 303:130–135.

Frisbie, W. Parker, Frank D. Bean, Robert Kaufman, and Jan E. Mutchler. 1986. "Immigration and Household Structure Among the Mexican Origin Population of the United States." In *Mexican Immigrants and Mexican Americans: An Evolving Relation.* Edited by Harley L. Browning and Rodolfo de la Garza. Austin, TX: Center for Mexican American Studies, pp. 74–99.

Fuchs, Victor, and Diane Reklis. 1992. "America's Children: Economic Perspectives and Policy Options." *Science* 255(Jan. 3):41–46.

Fuguitt, Glenn V. 1985. "The Nonmetropolitan Population Turnaround." *Annual Review of Sociology* 11:259–80.

Fuguitt, Glenn V., and David L. Brown. 1990. "Residential Preferences and Population Redistribution: 1972–1988." *Demography* 27:589–600.

Fuguitt, Glenn V., David L. Brown, and Calvin L. Beale. 1989. *Rural and Small Town America.* New York: Russell Sage Foundation.

Fullerton, Howard N., Jr. 1991. "Labor Force Projections: The Baby Boom Moves On." *Monthly Labor Review* 114:31–44.

Galston, William A. 1993. "Causes of Declining Well-Being Among U.S. Children." *Aspen Institute Quarterly* 5:52–77.

Gardner, Robert W., Bryant Robey, and Peter C. Smith. 1985. "Asian Americans: Growth, Change, and Diversity." *Population Bulletin* 40(October):1–44.

Garfinkel, Irwin. 1992. *Assuring Child Support.* New York: Russell Sage Foundation.

Garfinkel, Irwin, and Sara McLanahan. 1986. *Single Mothers and Their Children: A New American Dilemma.* Washington, DC: The Urban Institute.

————. 1994. "Single-Mother Families, Economic Insecurity and Government Policy." In *Confronting Poverty.* Edited by S. Danziger, G. Sandefur, and D. Weinberg. Cambridge, MA: Harvard University Press.

Garreau, Joel. 1991. *Edge City: Life on the New Frontier.* New York: Doubleday.

Gendell, Murray, and Jacob S. Siegel. 1992. "Trends in Retirement Age by Sex, 1950–2005." *Monthly Labor Review* 115:22–28.

Gill, Richard T. 1992. "For the Sake of the Children." *The Public Interest* 108:81–96.

Glasgow, Nina. 1988. *The Nonmetropolitan Elderly: Economic and Demographic Status*. RDRR-70. Washington, DC: Economic Research Service, U.S. Department of Agriculture.

Glazer, Nathan. 1954. "Ethnic Groups in America." In *Freedom and Control in Modern Society*. Edited by Morroe Berger, Theodore Abel, and Charles Page. New York: Van Nostrand, pp. 158–173.

Goldscheider, Frances K., and Calvin Goldscheider. 1993. *Leaving Home Before Marriage*. Madison: University of Wisconsin Press.

Goldscheider, Frances K., and Linda J. Waite. 1991. *New Families, No Families?* Berkeley: University of California Press.

Grad, Shelby. 1993. "Irvine: 70-Year-Old Couple Bike 240 Miles." *Los Angeles Times*, August 4, Part B, Page 2, Column 1.

Grad, Susan. 1990. "Income Change at Retirement." *Social Security Bulletin* 53:2–10.

Greeley, Andrew M. 1971. *Why Can't They Be Like Us? America's White Ethnic Groups*. New York: E. P. Dutton.

Gross, Edward. 1968. "Plus ça Change? The Sexual Structure of Occupations over Time." *Social Problems* 16:198–208.

Gruman, G. J. 1966. *The Evolution of Prolongevity Hypothesis to 1800*. Philadelphia, PA: American Philosophical Society.

Hagan, Jacqueline Maria, and Nestor P. Rodriguez. 1992. "Recent Economic Restructuring and Evolving Intergroup Relations in Houston." In *Structuring Diversity: Ethnographic Perspectives on the New Immigration*. Edited by Louise Lamphere. Chicago: University of Chicago Press, pp. 145–172.

Harris, Louis, and Associates. 1981. "Aging in the Eighties: America in Transition." Survey conducted for the National Council on Aging, Inc.

Harrison, Roderick J., and Daniel H. Weinberg. 1992. "How Important Were Changes in Racial and Ethnic Residential Segregation Between 1980 and 1990?" In *1992 Proceedings of the Social Statistics Section*. Alexandria, VA: The American Statistical Association, pp. 61–67.

Hartshorn, Truman A., and Peter O. Muller. 1986. *Suburban Business Centers: Employment Expectations*. Final Report for U.S. Department of Commerce, EDA. Washington, DC: U.S. Department of Commerce.

Haveman, Robert, and Barbara Wolfe. 1993. "Children's Prospects and Children's Policy." *Journal of Economic Perspectives* 7:153–174.

———. 1994. *Succeeding Generations*. New York: Russell Sage Foundation.

Hawley, Amos H. 1971. *Urban Society: An Ecological Approach*. New York: Ronald Press.

Hayghe, Howard. 1990. "Family Members in the Work Force." *Monthly Labor Review* 113(3):14–19.

Hayward, Mark, William R. Grady, and Steven D. McLaughlin. 1988. "Changes in the Retirement Process Among Older Men in the United States, 1972–1980." *Demography* 25:371–86.

Heckman, James J. 1989. "The Impact of Government on the Economic Status of Black Americans." In *The Question of Discrimination: Racial Inequality in the U.S. Labor Market*. Edited by Steven Shulman and William Darrity, Jr. Middletown, CT: Wesleyan University Press, pp. 50–80.

Hernandez, Donald J. 1993. *America's Children: Resources From Family, Government and the Economy*. New York: Russell Sage Foundation.

Herz, Diane E., and Philip L. Rones. 1989. "Institutional Barriers to Employment of Older Workers." *Monthly Labor Review* 112:14–21.

Hirschman, Charles O. 1978. "Prior U.S. Residence Among Mexican Immigrants." *Social Forces* 56(June):1179–1202.

Hogan, Dennis P. 1981. *Transitions and Social Change: The Early Lives of American Men*. New York: Academic Press.

———. 1985. "Parental Influences on the Timing of Early Life Transitions." *Current Perspectives on Aging and the Life Cycle* 1:1–59.

Hogan, Dennis P., and Nan Marie Astone. 1986. "The Transition to Adulthood." *Annual Review of Sociology* 12:109–130.

Hout, Michael. 1988. "More Universalism, Less Structural Mobility: The American Occupational Structure in the 1980s." *American Journal of Sociology* 93:1358–1400.

Huston, Aletha C., ed. 1991. *Children in Poverty: Child Development and Public Policy*. Cambridge, England. Cambridge University Press.

Hutchinson, Edward P. 1956. *Immigrants and Their Children, 1850–1950*. New York: Wiley.

Jasso, Guillermina, and Mark R. Rosenzweig. 1986. "Family Reunification and the Immigration Multiplier: U.S. Immigration Law, Origin-Country Conditions, and the Reproduction of Immigrants." *Demography* 23(August):291–311.

———. 1990. *The New Chosen People: Immigrants in the United States*. New York: Russell Sage Foundation.

Jencks, Christopher. 1987. "The Politics of Income Measurement." In *The Politics of Numbers*. Edited by W. Alonso and P. Starr. New York: Russell Sage Foundation, pp. 83–133.

Jensen, Leif. 1989. *The New Immigration: Implications for Poverty and Public Assistance Utilization*. New York: Greenwood Press.

Jensen, Leif, David J. Eggebeen, and Daniel T. Lichter. 1993. "Child Poverty and the Ameliorative Effects of Public Assistance." *Social Science Quarterly* 74:542–559.

Johnson, James H., Jr. 1990. "Recent African-American Trends in the United States." *Urban League Review* 14:39–55.

Johnson, James H., Jr., and Melvin L. Oliver. 1989. "Interethnic Minority Conflict in Urban America: The Effects of Economic and Social Dislocations." *Urban Geography* 10:449–463.

Johnson, Kenneth M. 1993. "Nonmetropolitan Demographic Change in the 1980s." Presented at Annual Meeting of the Population Association of America, April, Cincinnati, Ohio.

Jones, Landon Y. 1980. *Great Expectations: America and the Baby Boom Generation.* New York: Coward, McCann and Geoghegan.

Judkins, David, Joseph Waksberg, and James Massey. 1992. "Patterns of Residential Segregation." In *1992 Proceedings of the Social Statistics Section.* Alexandria, VA: The American Statistical Association, pp. 68–76.

Kasarda, John D. 1988. "Jobs, Migration and Emerging Urban Mismatches." In *Urban Change and Poverty.* Edited by Michael McGeary and Lawrence E. Lynn, Jr. Washington, DC: National Academy Press.

Keely, Charles B. 1971. "Effects of the Immigration Act of 1965 on Selected Population Characteristics of Immigrants to the United States." *Demography* 8 (May): 157–169.

———. 1975. "Effects of U.S. Immigration Law on Manpower Characteristics of Immigrants." *Demography* 12 (May): 179–192.

Landale, Nancy S., and Susan Huaun. 1993. "The Family Life-Course of Puerto Rican Children." *Journal of Marriage and the Family* 54:912–924.

Lansing, John B., and Evan Mueller. 1967. *The Geographic Mobility of Labor.* Ann Arbor: University of Michigan, Survey Research Center, ISR.

Lee, Barrett A., and Peter Wood. 1991. "Is Neighborhood Racial Succession Place-Specific?" *Demography* 28:21–40.

Lerman, Robert. 1989. "Employment Opportunities of Young Men and Family Formation." *American Economic Review,* AEA papers and proceedings (May):62–66.

Lestaeghe, R., and J. Surkyn. 1988. "Cultural Dynamics and Economic Theories of Fertility Change." *Population and Development Review* 14:1–45.

Lichter, Daniel, Felicia LeClere, and Diane McLaughlin. 1991. "Local Marriage Markets and the Marital Behavior of Black and White Women." *American Journal of Sociology* 96:843–867.

Lichter, Daniel T., and David J. Eggebeen. 1992. "Child Poverty and the Changing Rural Family." *Rural Sociology* 57:151–172.

———. 1993. "Rich Kids, Poor Kids: Changing Income Inequality Among American Children." *Social Forces* 71:761–780.

———. 1994. "The Effect of Parental Employment on Child Poverty." *Journal of Marriage and the Family* 55.

Lieberson, Stanley. 1980. *A Piece of the Pie: Blacks and White Immigrants since 1880.* Berkeley: University of California Press.

Lieberson, Stanley, and Mary C. Waters. 1990. *From Many Strands: Ethnic and Racial Groups in Contemporary America.* New York: Russell Sage Foundation.

Litwak, Eugene, and Charles F. Longino, Jr. 1987. "Migration Patterns Among the Elderly: A Developmental Perspective." *The Gerontologist* 27:266–272.

Logan, John R. 1993. "Locational Returns to Human Capital: Minority Access to Suburban Community Resources." *Demography* 30: 243–268.

Logan, John R., and Richard D. Alba. 1992. "Analyzing Locational Attainments: Constructing Individual-Level Regression Models Using Aggregate Data." *Sociological Methods and Research* 20:367–397.

Logan, John R., and Mark Schneider. 1984. "Racial Segregation and Racial Change in American Suburbs, 1970–80." *American Journal of Sociology* 89:874–888.

Long, Larry. 1988. *Migration and Residential Mobility in the United States*. New York: Russell Sage Foundation.

Longino, Charles F., Jr. 1990. "Geographical Distribution and Migration." In *Handbook of Aging and the Social Sciences*. Edited by Robert H. Binstock and Linda George. New York: Academic Press.

Los Angeles Times. April 10, 1992, p. B1.

————. February 12, 1993, p. B2.

————. July 30, 1993, p. B2.

————. August 4, 1993, p. B2.

————. March 17, 1994, p. A3, A20.

McHugh, Kevin E. 1987. "Black Migration Reversal in the United States." *Geographical Review* 77:171–187.

————. 1989. "Hispanic Migration and Population Redistribution in the United States." *Professional Geographer* 41:429–439.

McLanahan, Sara. 1994. "The Consequences of Single Parenthood." *American Prospect* (summer):

————. 1994. "The Consequences of Single Motherhood." *American Prospect.* (summer):

McLanahan, Sara, Lynne Casper, and Annemette Sørensen. Forthcoming. "Women's Roles and Women's Economic Poverty in Eight Industrialized Countries." In *Gender and Family Change in Industrialized Countries*. Edited by K. O. Mason and A. M. Jensen. Oxford, England: Oxford University Press.

McLanahan, Sara, and Gary D. Sandefur. 1994. *Growing Up With a Single Parent*. Cambridge, MA: Harvard University Press.

Macunovich, Diane J., and Richard A. Easterlin. 1990. "How Parents Have Coped: The Effect of Life Cycle Demographic Decisions on the Economic Status of Pre-School-Age Children, 1964–87." *Population and Development Review* 16:301–325.

Mare, Robert, and Christopher Winship. 1991. "Socioeconomic Change and Decline of Marriage." In *The Urban Underclass*. Edited by C. Jencks and P. Peterson. Washington, DC: The Brookings Institution, pp. 175–202.

Martin, Teresa Castro, and Larry L. Bumpass. 1989. "Recent Trends in Marital Disruption." *Demography* 26:37–51.

Massey, Douglas S., and Nancy A. Denton. 1987. "Trends in the Residential Segregation of Blacks, Hispanics, and Asians." *American Sociological Review* 52:802–825.

————. 1988a. "Suburbanization and Segregation in U.S. Metropolitan Areas." *American Journal of Sociology* 94:592–626.

————. 1988b. "The Dimensions of Residential Segregation." *Social Forces* 67 (2):281–309.

———. 1989. "Hypersegregation in U.S. Metropolitan Areas: Black and Hispanic Segregation among Five Dimensions." *Demography* 26:373–92.

———. 1993. *American Apartheid: Segregation and the Making of the Underclass.* Cambridge, MA: Harvard University Press.

Massey, Douglas S., Rafael Alarcon, Jorge Durand, and Humberto Gonzalez. 1987. *Return to Aztlan: The Social Process of International Migration.* Berkeley: University of California Press.

Miller, Martin. 1993. "Lake Forest: Love Lights Way to 75th Anniversary." *Los Angeles Times,* July 30, Part B, Page 2, Column 1.

Moffitt, Robert. 1992. "Incentive Effects of the U.S. Welfare System: A Review." *Journal of Economic Literature.* 30:1–61.

Mollenkopf, John F., and Manuel Castells, eds. 1991. *Dual City: Restructuring New York.* New York: Russell Sage Foundation.

Moore, David W., and Leslie McAneny. 1993. "Workers Concerned They Can't Afford to Retire." *The Gallup Poll Monthly* 332:16–25.

Moynihan, Daniel P. 1965. *The Negro Family: The Case for National Action.* U.S. Department of Labor. Washington, DC: Office of Planning and Policy Research.

Murray, Charles. 1984. *Losing Ground: American Social Policy, 1950–1980.* New York: Basic Books.

———. 1993. "The Coming White Underclass." *Wall Street Journal.* October 12, p. A13.

Myers, George C., Barbara Torrey, and Kevin G. Kinsella. 1992. "The Paradox of the Oldest Old in the United States: An International Comparison." In *The Oldest Old.* Edited by Richard M. Suzman, Kenneth G. Manton, and David P. Willis. New York: Oxford University Press.

National Center for Health Statistics. 1991. *Vital Statistics of the United States, 1987, Vol. III, Marriage and Divorce.* Washington, DC: U.S. Government Printing Office.

———. 1991. *Vital Statistics of the United States, 1989, Vol. III, Mortality, Part A.* Washington, DC: Public Health Service.

———. 1993. "Advance Report of Final Natality Statistics, Volume 1, No. 3 1991." *Monthly Vital Statistics Report.* Washington, DC: U.S. Department of Health and Human Services.

———. 1993. *Health, United States, 1992.* Hyattsville, MD: Public Health Service.

National Commission on Children. 1991. *Beyond Rhetoric: A New American Agenda for Children and Families.* Washington, DC: U.S. Government Printing Office.

Neugarten, Bernice L. 1974. "Age Groups in American Society and the Rise of the Young-Old." *Annals of the American Academy of Political and Social Sciences* 415:187–198.

Norton, Arthur J., and Louisa F. Miller. 1992. "Marriage, Divorce, and Remarriage in the 1990s." U.S. Bureau of the Census, *Current Population Reports* P23-180. Washington, DC: U.S. Government Printing Office.

Norton, Arthur J., and Jeanne E. Moorman. 1987. "Current Trends in Marriage and Divorce among American Women." *Journal of Marriage and the Family* 49:3–14.

Norton, R. D. 1979. *City Life-Cycles and American Public Policy*. New York: Academic Press.

Noyelle, Thierry J., and Thomas M. Stanback, Jr. 1984. *The Economic Transformation of American Cities*. Totowa, NJ: Rowman & Allanheld.

Oldakowski, Raymond K., and Curtis C. Roseman. 1986. "The Development of Migration Expectations: Changes Throughout the Lifecourse." *Journal of Gerontology* 41:290–295.

Ong, Paul M., and Janet R. Lawrence. 1992. "Pluralism and Residential Patterns in Los Angeles." Manuscript No. D-9202. Los Angeles, CA: Graduate School of Architecture and Urban Planning, UCLA.

Packard, Michael D., and Virginia P. Reno. 1989. "A Look at Early Retirees." *Social Security Bulletin* 52:16–29.

Parish, William L., Lingxin Hao, and Dennis P. Hogan. 1991. "Family Support Networks, Welfare, and Work Among Young Mothers." *Journal of Marriage and the Family* 53:203–215.

Passel, Jeffrey S., and Karen A. Woodrow. 1984. "Geographic Distribution of Undocumented Immigrants: Estimates of Undocumented Aliens Counted in the 1980 Census by State." *International Migration Review* 18(Fall):642–671.

———. 1987. "Change in the Undocumented Alien Population in the United States, 1979–1983." *International Migration Review* 21(Winter):1304–1323.

Pearce, Diana. 1978. "The Feminization of Poverty: Women, Work and Welfare." *Urban and Social Change Review* (February): 28–36.

Pisarski, Alan E. 1987. *Commuting in America*. Washington, DC: ENO Foundation for Transportation.

Plane, David A., and Peter A. Rogerson. 1991. "Tracking the Baby Boom, Baby Bust and Echo Generations: How Age Compositions Generate US Migration." *Professional Geographer* 43:416–430.

Pollard, Kelvin M. 1993. "Youth on the Cutting Edge of Diversity." *Population Today* 21(July/August):3.

Population Reference Bureau. 1993. *World Population Data Sheet*. Washington, DC.

Portes, Alejandro, and Robert L. Bach. 1985. *Latin Journey: Cuban and Mexican Immigrants in the United States*. Berkeley: University of California Press.

Portes, Alejandro, and Ruben Rumbaut. 1990. *Immigrant America: A Portrait*. Berkeley: University of California Press.

Presser, Harriet B. 1989. "Can We Make Time for Children? The Economy, Work Schedules, and Child Care." *Demography* 26:523–543.

Preston, Samuel H. 1976. "Family Size of Children and Family Sizes of Women." *Demography* 13:105–114.

———. 1984. "Children and the Elderly: Divergent Paths for America's Dependents." *Demography* 21:435–457.

Radner, Daniel B. 1987. "Money Income of Aged and Nonaged Family Units, 1967–84." *Social Security Bulletin* 50:9–28.

————. 1991. "Changes in the Incomes of Age Groups, 1984–1989." *Social Security Bulletin* 54:2–18.

Reynolds, Gretchen. 1992. "The Rising Significance of Race." *Chicago* 41(December):80–85.

Rindfuss, Ronald R. 1991. "The Young Adult Years: Diversity, Structural Change, and Fertility." *Demography* 28:493–512.

Rindfuss, Ronald R., and James R. Sweet. 1977. *Post-War Fertility Trends and Differentials in the United States.* New York: Academic Press.

Rindfuss, Ronald, and Audrey Vandenheuvel. 1990. "Cohabitation: Precursor to Marriage or Alternative to Being Single?" *Population and Development Review.* 16(4):103–126.

Rodriguez, Nestor P. 1987. "Undocumented Central Americans in Houston: Diverse Populations." *International Migration Review* 21(Spring):4–26.

Rogers, Andrei, and Jennifer Woodward. 1988. "The Sources of Regional Elderly Population Growth: Migration and Aging-in-Place." *The Professional Geographer* 40:450–459.

Romero, Mary. 1992. "Ethnographic Evaluation of Behavioral Causes of Census Undercount of Undocumented Immigrants and Salvadorans in the Mission District of San Francisco, California." *Ethnographic Evaluation of the 1990 Decennial Census #18.* U.S. Bureau of the Census. Washington, DC: U.S. Government Printing Office.

Rosenwaike, Ira, and Barbara Logue. 1985. *The Extreme Aged in America: A Portrait of an Expanding Population.* Westport, CT: Greenwood Press.

Rossi, Alice, and Peter M. Rossi. 1990. *Of Human Bonding: Parent-Child Relations Across the Life Course.* New York: Aldine de Gruyter.

Ruggles, Patricia. 1990. *Drawing the Line.* Washington DC: The Urban Institute.

Ryder, Norman B. 1955. "The Interpretation of Origin Statistics." *Canadian Journal of Economics and Political Science* 21(February):466–479.

Saluter, Arlene F. 1989. "Changes in American Family Life." U.S. Bureau of the Census, *Current Population Reports* P23-163. Washington, DC: U.S. Government Printing Office.

Sandefur, Gary D. 1986. "American Indian Migration and Economic Opportunities." *International Migration Review* 20:55–68.

Sandefur, Gary D., and Jiwon Jeon. 1991. "Migration, Race and Ethnicity, 1960–1980." *International Migration Review* 25(2):392–407.

Sandefur, Gary D., Sara McLanahan, and Roger A. Wojtkiewicz. 1992. "The Effects of Parental Marital Status During Adolescence on High School Graduation." *Social Forces* 71:103–121.

Santiago, Anne M. 1991. "The Spatial Dimensions of Ethnic and Racial Stratification." Population Studies Center, Research Reports No. 91-230. Ann Arbor: University of Michigan.

Schnore, Leo F. 1965. *The Urban Scene.* New York: Free Press.

Schoen, Robert, and Robin M. Weinick. 1993. "The Slowing Metabolism of Marriage: Figures from 1980 U.S. Marital Status Life Tables." *Demography* 30:737–746.

Schultz, T. Paul. 1984. "The Schooling and Health of Children of U.S. Immigrants and Natives." In *Research in Population Economics,* Vol. 5. Edited by Kenneth Wolpin and Paul Schultz. Greenwich, CT: JAI Press, pp. 251–288.

Serow, William J. 1987. "Determinants of Interstate Migration: Differences Between Elderly and Non-Elderly Movers." *Journal of Gerontology* 42:95–100.

Serow, William J., and Douglas A. Charity. 1988. "Return Migration of the Elderly in the United States: Recent Trends." *Research on Aging* 10:155–168.

Sheldon, Henry D. 1958. *The Older Population of the United States.* New York: Wiley.

Shryock, Henry S., and Jacob S. Siegel. 1976. *The Methods and Materials of Demography.* Condensed edition. New York: Academic Press.

Shulman, Steven, and William Darity, Jr. 1989. *The Question of Discrimination.* Middletown, CT: Wesleyan University Press.

Siegel, Jacob S. 1993. *A Generation of Change: A Profile of America's Older Population.* New York: Russell Sage Foundation.

Siegel, Jacob S., and Jeffrey S. Passell. 1976. "New Estimates of the Number of Centenarians in the United States." *Journal of the American Statistical Association* 71:559–566.

Smeeding, Timothy M., and Barbara Torrey. 1988. "Poor Children in Rich Countries." *Science* 242:873–877.

Smith, Herbert L., and Phillips Cutright. 1988. "Thinking About Change in Illegitimacy Ratios: United States: 1963–1983." *Demography* 25(2):235–247.

Sorrentino, Constance. 1990. "The Changing Family in International Perspective." *Monthly Labor Review* 113(3):41–58.

Speare, Alden, Jr. 1993. "Stages in Urban Growth Patterns, 1980–90." Working Paper WP-93, AS-1. Cambridge, MA: Lincoln Institute of Land Policy.

Speare, Alden, Jr., and James McNally. 1992. "The Relation of Migration and Household Change Among Elderly Persons." In *Elderly Migration and Population Redistribution: A Comparative Perspective.* Edited by Andrei Rogers. London: Belhaven Press.

Stanback, Thomas M. 1991. *The New Suburbanization: Challenge to the Central City.* Boulder, CO: Westview Press.

Sullivan, Teresa A. 1992. "The Changing Demographic Characteristics and Impact of Immigrants in Canada." In *Immigration, Language, and Ethnicity: Canada and the United States.* Edited by Barry R. Chiswick. Washington, DC: American Enterprise Institute, pp. 119–144.

Suzman, Richard M., David P. Willis, and Kenneth G. Manton, eds. 1992. *The Oldest Old.* New York: Oxford University Press.

Swanson, Linda L., and David L. Brown, eds. 1993. *Population Change and the Future of Rural America: A Conference Proceedings.* Staff Report No. AGES 9324. Washington, DC: Economic Research Service, U.S. Department of Agriculture.

Sweet, James, and Larry Bumpass. 1992. "Young Adults' Views of Marriage, Cohabitation and Family." In *The Changing American Family: Sociological and Demographic Perspectives.* Edited by Scott South and Stewart Tolnay. Boulder CO: Westview Press, pp. 143–170.

Taeuber, Cynthia. 1991. *Statistical Handbook of Women in America.* Phoenix: Oryx Press.

Taeuber, Karl E., and Alma F. Taeuber. 1965. *Negroes in Cities.* Chicago: Aldine.

Thornton, Arland. 1985. "Changing Attitudes Toward Separation and Divorce: Causes and Consequences." *American Journal of Sociology* 90:856–872.

Thorton, Russell. 1987. *American Indian Holocaust and Survival: A Population History Since 1492.* Norman: University of Oklahoma Press.

Tienda, Marta. 1980. "Familism and Structural Assimilation of Mexican Immigrants in the U.S." *International Migration Review* 14(Fall):383–408.

Tilly, Chris. 1991. "Reasons for the Continuing Growth of Part-Time Employment." *Monthly Labor Review* 114:10–18.

Treas, Judith, and Barbara Logue. 1986. "Economic Development and the Older Population." *Population and Development Review* 12:645–673.

Treas, Judith, and Ramon Torrecilha. 1994. "The Older Population: Demographic, Social, and Economic Trends." *1990 Census Monographs,* Vol. 1.

Uhlenberg, Peter, Teresa Cooney, and Robert Boyd. 1990. "Divorce for Women after Midlife." *Journal of Gerontology* 45:677–688.

Uhlenberg, Peter, and David Eggebeen. 1986. "The Declining Well-Being of American Adolescents." *The Public Interest* 82:25–38.

United Nations Statistical Office. 1991. *The World's Women 1970–1990: Trends and Statistics.* Series K, No. 8. New York: United Nations.

U.S. Department of Commerce, Bureau of the Census. 1953. *U.S. Census of Population.* Vol. II, *Characteristics of the Population.* Part 1. United States Summary. Washington, DC: U.S. Government Printing Office.

―――. 1960. *Historical Statistics of the United States: Colonial Times to 1957.* Washington, DC: U.S. Government Printing Office.

―――. 1960. "Marital Status and Family Status: March 1960." *Current Population Reports* P20-105. Washington, DC: U.S. Government Printing Office.

―――. 1970. "Marital Status and Family Status: March 1970." *Current Population Reports* P20-212. Washington, DC: U.S. Government Printing Office.

―――. 1973. *1970 Census of Population, General Population Characteristics. United States* (Chapter B.) Washington, DC: Government Printing Office.

―――. 1983. *1980 Census of Population, General Social and Economic Characteristics. United States* (PC80-1-C1). Washington, DC: U.S. Government Printing Office.

―――. 1981. "Marital Status and Living Arrangements: March 1980." *Current Population Reports.* Series P-20, No. 365. Washington, DC: U.S. Government Printing Office.

―――. 1990. "Household and Family Characteristics: March 1990 and 1989." *Current Population Reports* P20-447. Washington, DC: U.S. Government Printing Office.

―――. 1990. "Poverty in the United States: 1988 and 1989." *Current Population Reports* P60-171. Washington, DC: U.S. Government Printing Office.

————. 1990. "Trends in Income, by Selected Characteristics: 1947 to 1988." *Current Population Reports* P60-167. Washington, DC: U.S. Government Printing Office.

————. 1991. *1990 Census Profile, Race and Hispanic Origin,* Number 2. Washington, DC: U.S. Government Printing Office.

————. 1991. "Detail Race." *Commerce News Bureau of the Census, Press Release* CB91-215. Washington, DC: U.S. Government Printing Office.

————. 1991. "Marital Status and Other Living Arrangements: March 1990." *Current Population Reports* P20-450. Washington, DC: U.S. Government Printing Office.

————. 1991. "Money Income of Households, Families, and Persons in the United States: 1990." *Current Population Reports* P60-174. Washington, DC: U.S. Government Printing Office.

————. 1991. *State and Metropolitan Area Data Book, 1991.* Washington, DC: U.S. Government Printing Office.

————. 1991. *Statistical Abstract of the United States, 1991.* Washington, DC: U.S. Government Printing Office.

————. 1991. "Voting and Registration in the Election of November 1990." *Current Population Reports Series* P20-453. Washington, DC: U.S. Government Printing Office.

————. 1991. Census Bureau Releases 1990 Census Counts on Specific Racial Groups CB91-215. U.S. Department of Commerce Washington, DC. U.S. Government Printing Office.

————. 1992. *1990 Census of Population and Housing, Summary Social, Economic and Housing Characteristics.* United States CPH-5-1. Washington, DC: U.S. Government Printing Office.

————. 1992. "An Aging World II." *International Population Reports* P25-3. Washington, DC: U.S. Government Printing Office.

————. 1992. "Household and Family Characteristics 1991." *Current Population Reports* P20 458. Washington, DC: U.S. Government Printing Office.

———— . 1992. "Money Income of Households, Families, and Persons in the United States: 1991." *Current Population Reports* P60-180. Washington, DC: U.S. Government Printing Office.

————. 1992. *1990 Census of Population, General Population Characteristics,* United States CP-1-1. Washington, DC: U.S. Government Printing Office.

———— 1992. *1990 Census of Population and Housing, Public use Microdata Samples. United States.* Washington, DC: U.S. Government Printing Office.

————. 1992. *1990 Census of Population, Supplementary Reports, Detailed Occupation and Other Characteristics from the EEO File for the United States* CP-S-1-1. Washington, DC: U.S. Government Printing Office.

————. 1992. "Population Projections of the United States, by Age, Sex, Race, and Hispanic Origin: 1992–2050." *Current Population Reports* P-25-1092. Washington, DC: U.S. Government Printing Office.

————. 1992. "Population Trends in the 1980s." *Current Population Reports* P23-175. Washington, DC: U.S. Government Printing Office.

————. 1992. "Poverty in the United States: 1991." *Current Population Reports* P60-181. Washington, DC: U.S. Government Printing Office.

————. 1992. *Statistical Abstract of the United States, 1992.* Washington, DC: U.S. Government Printing Office.

————. 1993. "Poverty in the United States 1992." *Current Population Reports* P60-185. Washington, DC: U.S. Government Printing Office.

————. 1993. *Statistical Abstract of the United States 1993.* Washington, DC: U.S. Government Printing Office.

————. 1993. "U.S. Population Estimates, by Age, Sex, Race, and Hispanic Origin: 1980 to 1991." *Current Population Reports* P25-1095. Washington, DC: U.S. Government Printing Office.

U.S. Department of Education. 1992. *Youth Indicators 1991.* Washington, DC: U.S. Government Printing Office.

U.S. Department of Health and Human Services. 1992. *Child Health USA '91.* Maternal and Child Health Bureau, Publication Number HRS-M-CH91-1. Washington, DC: Maternal and Child Health Bureau.

U.S. Department of Justice, Immigration and Naturalization Service. 1991. *An Immigrant Nation: United States Regulations of Immigration, 1798 to 1991.* Washington, DC: U.S. Government Printing Office.

————. 1992. *1991 Statistical Yearbook of the Immigration and Naturalization Service.* Washington, DC: Immigration and Naturalization Services.

————. 1993. *Advance Report: Immigration Statistics, Fiscal Year 1992.* Washington, DC: Immigration and Naturalization Services.

U.S. Department of Labor, Bureau of Labor Statistics. 1991. *Employment and Earnings* 38:202.

————. 1991. *Employment and Earnings* 38:1.

U.S. General Accounting Office. 1993. *Immigration Enforcement: Problems in Controlling the Flow of Illegal Aliens.* GAO/T-GGD-93-39. Washington, DC: U.S. Government Printing Office.

U.S. House of Representatives. *U.S. Children and Their Families: Current Conditions and Recent Trends.* Report 101-356. Washington, DC: U.S. Government Printing Office.

U.S. House of Representatives Select Committee on Children, Youth, and Families. 1989. *U.S. Children and Their Families: Current Conditions and Recent Trends.* Washington, DC: U.S. Government Printing Office.

U.S. House of Representatives Ways and Means Committee. 1990. *Overview of Entitlement Programs.* Washington, DC: U.S. Government Printing Office.

————. 1991. *Overview of Entitlement Programs.* Washington, DC: U.S. Government Printing Office.

————. 1993. *Overview of Entitlement Programs.* Washington, DC: U.S. Government Printing Office.

U.S. Senate Special Committee on Aging. 1991. *Aging America: Trends and Projections: 1991.* Washington, DC: U.S. Government Printing Office.

Usdansky, Margaret L. 1992. "Suburbanites Switch Loyalty to Clinton." *USA Today* November 4, p. 6A.

Velasco, Alfredo. 1992. "Ethnographic Evaluation of the Behavioral Causes of Undercount in the Community of Sherman Heights, California." In *Ethnographic Evaluation of the 1990 Decennial Census #22*. Washington, DC: U.S. Bureau of the Census.

Waldinger, Roger. 1989. "Immigration and Urban Change." *Annual Review of Sociology* 15:211–232.

Wardwell, John M. 1980. "Toward a Theory of Urban-Rural Migration in the Developed World." In *New Directions in Urban-Rural Migration*. Edited by David L. Brown and John M. Wardwell. New York: Academic Press.

Waters, Mary. 1990. *Ethnic Options: Choosing Identities in America*. Berkeley: University of California Press.

Wetzel, James R. 1990. "American Families: 75 Years of Change." *Monthly Labor Review* 113(3):4–13.

White, Michael J. 1986. *American Neighborhoods and Residential Differentiation*. New York: Russell Sage Foundation.

Whitehead, Barbara DaFoe. 1993. "Dan Quayle Was Right." *The Atlantic Monthly* (April): 47–83.

Wiatrowski, William J. 1993. "Factors Affecting Retirement Income." *Monthly Labor Review* 116:25–35.

Wilson, William J. 1987. *The Truly Disadvantaged: The Inner City, the Underclass, and Public Policy*. Chicago: University of Chicago Press.

Wilson, William J., and Katherine Neckerman. 1986. "Poverty and Family Structure: The Widening Gap Between Evidence and Public Policy Issues." In *Fighting Poverty: What Works and What Doesn't*. Cambridge, MA: Harvard University Press.

Wojtkiewicz, Roger, Sara McLanahan, and Irwin Garfinkel. 1990. "The Growth of Female-Headed Families in the United States, 1950 to 1980." *Demography* 27(2):19–30.

Wong, Yin-Ling Irene, Irwin Garfinkel, and Sara McLanahan. 1993. "Single-Mother Families in Eight Countries: Economic Status and Social Policy." *Social Services Review* 67(2):177–197.

Zill, Nicholas. 1993. "The Changing Realities of Family Life." *The Aspen Institute Quarterly* 5:27–51.

Name Index

Abowd, John M., 300, 337
Achdut, Lea, 79, 337
Adsen, R., 338
Ahlburg, Dennis A., 50, 337
Alarcon, Rafael, 348
Alba, Richard, 209n, 325, 337
American Association of Retired Persons, 49–50
Anderson, Elijah, 233, 337
Anderson, Margo, 337
Astone, Nan Marie, 117, 125, 345

Bach, Robert L., 222, 349
Bane, Mary Jo, 106, 337
Barringer, Herbert R., 337
Bartel, Ann P., 226, 290, 337
Beale, Calvin L., 335n, 337, 343
Bean, Frank D., 209n, 220, 256, 269n, 335n, 337, 338, 343
Becker, Gary S., 4, 32, 338
Bellah, R., 4, 44n, 338
Belsky, Jay, 136n, 338
Bennett, Claudette, 141–210
Bergman, Barbara, 338
Bianchi, Suzanne M., 12, 26, 84, 101, 104, 135n, 136n, 338, 342
Blau, Francine D., 256, 338
Bluestone, Herman, 338
Bonacich, Edna, 219, 338
Boyd, Robert, 68, 352
Briody, Elizabeth K., 251, 338
Brooks-Gunn, Jean, 197, 199, 338
Brown, David L., 269n, 335n, 338, 343, 351
Browning, Harley L., 337
Brownstein, Ronald, 339

Bumpass, Larry, 8, 9, 12, 15, 28, 68, 104, 135n, 339, 347, 351
Burek, Debbie, 339
Burkhauser, Richard V., 88–89, 339

Cafferty, Pastora San Juan, 219, 339
Carpenter, Niles, 219, 269n, 339
Casper, Lynne M., 1–45, 8, 16, 43n, 44n, 93, 120, 339, 347
Castells, Manuel, 300, 348
Castro, Fidel, 224
Castro-Martin, Theresa, 9, 339
Center for the New West, 339
Cervero, Robert, 275, 339
Charity, Douglas L., 335n, 351
Cheeseman, J. D., 208n
Cherlin, Andrew, 6, 8, 44n, 68, 103, 339
Children's Defense Fund, 103, 135n, 339
Chiswick, Barry R., 211–270, 212, 220, 236, 238, 261, 270n, 339, 340
Chiswick, Carmel, 212, 340
Clark, William A. V., 233, 340
Clinton, Bill, 78, 275
Colasanto, Diane, 342
Cooney, Teresa, 68, 340, 352
Corbett, Thomas, 102, 340
Crane, Jonathan, 197, 340
Crimmins, Eileen, 63, 340
Crispell, Diane, 282, 309, 340
Cutright, Phillips, 351

Danziger, Sheldon, 340
Darden, Joe T., 321, 340
Darity, William, Jr., 174, 351
Da Vanzo, Julie, 2, 6, 340

357

Subject Index

Boldface numbers refer to figures and tables.

adolescents: mothers, **198,** 199, 201
adoption, 104
adulthood: early roles, 125–130; human capital and, 128–130
AFDC. *See* Aid to Families with Dependent Children (AFDC)
AFDC-food stamps. *See* food stamps
African Americans: adolescent mothers, 201; age 65–74, living arrangements, 70; annual earnings, 184; assimilation, 144; children, poverty, 103–105, 107–108, 112–116; disabled young adults, 121; divorce rate, 10; dual-earner families, 43n; earning power, effect on marriage rate, 39–43; educational attainment, 25, 134, 170–174, 181, 325; elderly population, 59, 81, 82; families, 109, 111–112, 187–188, 190–191; fertility rates, 148; health of elderly population, 65; hourly earnings, 174–175; household income, 21; intergroup marriage, 164, 165–167; Jim Crow segregation, 143; labor force participation, 34, 111–112, 124, 187; marital status, 13; marriage and economic status, 22–23; marriage markets, **41,** 44–45n; median family income, 106, 194; median wages, 37–38; metropolitan areas, 293–296; middle class, 334; migration, **154–155,** 284, 287, 300; mortality rate, 62; net internal migration, **291, 294–295;** net return migration to South, 149; occupations, 178, 181; percent by region, 150–151; population shifts, 283–284; poverty, 23, 33, 81, 82, 103–105, 130–131, 194, 196, 200–201, 298; regional variations in population, 153; residential segregation, 158, 161–164, 320–321, 323, 328–331, 334; return migration to South,

153; segregation, 158; single-father families, 27, 29; single-mother families, 2, 13–14, 23–26; single-parent families, 95, 115; slavery, 143, 147, 208n; suburbs, 323–325; traditional family, 19; unemployment, 185; young adults, 33, 120, 127–128, 130–131
African immigrants: fertility rate, 257; legislation, ramification of, 219; naturalization, 232; occupational attainment, 249; population pressures, 220; race of, 225
age 15–44: fertility rates, **11**
age 18–24. *See* young adults
age 25–34: educational attainment, 172; hourly earnings, 174; median income, 84
age 25–44: population, 51
age 25–64: immigrants, 216, **218, 241, 245, 246, 247–248, 250, 260**
age 30–34: never-married persons, 6
age 35–64: educational attainment, 172
age 60–64: divorce, 67; insights into aging, 48; marital status, 67; widows and widowers, 67
age 65–69: health problems, 64; widows and widowers, 66. *See also* age 65 and over
age 65–74: economic status of, 80–81; living arrangements, 70; "wellderly," as, 48; youth of, 48. *See also* age 65 and over
age 55 and over: labor force participation, 73
age 65 and over: comfortable, economically, 78, **81,** 82; divorce rate, 68; 1870, 49; foreign-born, **87;** growth of population, 47–48, 50; householder units, 69; immigrants, 254; income groups of, **79;** labor force participation, 73–77; living alone, 70; living arrangements, **69,** 70; marital status, 65–68; median income, **85;** nursing homes, in, 71–